Ambient Urbanities as the Intersection Between the IoT and the IoP in Smart Cities

H. Patricia McKenna
AmbientEase, Canada

A volume in the Advances in Civil and Industrial Engineering (ACIE) Book Series

Published in the United States of America by
   IGI Global
   Engineering Science Reference (an imprint of IGI Global)
   701 E. Chocolate Avenue
   Hershey PA, USA 17033
   Tel: 717-533-8845
   Fax: 717-533-8661
   E-mail: cust@igi-global.com
   Web site: http://www.igi-global.com

Library of Congress Cataloging-in-Publication Data

Names: McKenna, H. Patricia, 1954- author.
Title: Ambient urbanities as the intersection between the IoT and the IoP in
   smart cities / by H. Patricia McKenna.
Description: Hershey, PA : Engineering Science Reference, an imprint of IGI
   Global, [2019] | Includes bilbiographical references and index.
Identifiers: LCCN 2018037300| ISBN 9781522578826 (hardcover) | ISBN
   9781522578833 (ebook)
Subjects: LCSH: Ubiquitous computing. | Internet of things--Social aspects. |
   City and town life. | Information behavior.
Classification: LCC QA76.5915 .M38 2019 | DDC 004--dc23 LC record available at https://lccn.
loc.gov/2018037300

This book is published in the IGI Global book series Advances in Civil and Industrial Engineering (ACIE) (ISSN: 2326-6139; eISSN: 2326-6155)

British Cataloguing in Publication Data
A Cataloguing in Publication record for this book is available from the British Library.

All work contributed to this book is new, previously-unpublished material.
The views expressed in this book are those of the authors, but not necessarily of the publisher.

For electronic access to this publication, please contact: eresources@igi-global.com.

Advances in Civil and Industrial Engineering (ACIE) Book Series

ISSN:2326-6139
EISSN:2326-6155

Editor-in-Chief: Ioan Constantin Dima, University Valahia of Târgoviște, Romania

MISSION

Private and public sector infrastructures begin to age, or require change in the face of developing technologies, the fields of civil and industrial engineering have become increasingly important as a method to mitigate and manage these changes. As governments and the public at large begin to grapple with climate change and growing populations, civil engineering has become more interdisciplinary and the need for publications that discuss the rapid changes and advancements in the field have become more in-demand. Additionally, private corporations and companies are facing similar changes and challenges, with the pressure for new and innovative methods being placed on those involved in industrial engineering.

The **Advances in Civil and Industrial Engineering (ACIE) Book Series** aims to present research and methodology that will provide solutions and discussions to meet such needs. The latest methodologies, applications, tools, and analysis will be published through the books included in **ACIE** in order to keep the available research in civil and industrial engineering as current and timely as possible.

COVERAGE

- Optimization Techniques
- Productivity
- Transportation Engineering
- Coastal Engineering
- Operations research
- Earthquake engineering
- Quality Engineering
- Hydraulic Engineering
- Engineering Economics
- Materials Management

IGI Global is currently accepting manuscripts for publication within this series. To submit a proposal for a volume in this series, please contact our Acquisition Editors at Acquisitions@igi-global.com or visit: http://www.igi-global.com/publish/.

Titles in this Series

For a list of additional titles in this series, please visit:
https://www.igi-global.com/book-series/advances-civil-industrial-engineering/73673

Optimizing Current Strategies and Applications in Industrial Engineering
Prasanta Sahoo (Jadavpur University, India)
Engineering Science Reference • ©2019 • 382pp • H/C (ISBN: 9781522582236) • US $245.00

Big Data Analytics in Traffic and Transportation Engineering Emerging Research and ...
Sara Moridpour (RMIT University, Australia)
Engineering Science Reference • ©2019 • 188pp • H/C (ISBN: 9781522579434) • US $165.00

Optimization of Design for Better Structural Capacity
Mourad Belgasmia (Setif 1 University, Algeria)
Engineering Science Reference • ©2019 • 283pp • H/C (ISBN: 9781522570592) • US $215.00

Reusable and Sustainable Building Materials in Modern Architecture
Gülşah Koç (Yildiz Technical University, Turkey) and Bryan Christiansen (Global Research Society, LLC, USA)
Engineering Science Reference • ©2019 • 302pp • H/C (ISBN: 9781522569954) • US $195.00

Measuring Maturity in Complex Engineering Projects
João Carlos Araújo da Silva Neto (Magnesita SA, Brazil) Ítalo Coutinho (Saletto Engenharia de Serviços, Brazil) Gustavo Teixeira (PM BASIS, Brazil) and Alexandro Avila de Moura (Paranapanema SA, Brazil)
Engineering Science Reference • ©2019 • 277pp • H/C (ISBN: 9781522558644) • US $245.00

Big Data Analytics for Smart and Connected Cities
Nilanjan Dey (Techno India College of Technology, India) and Sharvari Tamane (Jawaharlal Nehru Engineering College, India)
Engineering Science Reference • ©2019 • 348pp • H/C (ISBN: 9781522562078) • US $225.00

Contemporary Strategies and Approaches in 3-D Information Modeling
Bimal Kumar (Glasgow Caledonian University, UK)
Engineering Science Reference • ©2018 • 313pp • H/C (ISBN: 9781522556251) • US $205.00

For an entire list of titles in this series, please visit:
https://www.igi-global.com/book-series/advances-civil-industrial-engineering/73673

701 East Chocolate Avenue, Hershey, PA 17033, USA
Tel: 717-533-8845 x100 • Fax: 717-533-8661
E-Mail: cust@igi-global.com • www.igi-global.com

Table of Contents

Section 3
Theories, Methods, Openness, and Metrics

Section 4
A Synthesis and Future Directions

Foreword

When I go to conferences, I typically come back inspired – rejuvenated even. At a minimum, I come back with a strong sense that I acquired new lifelong knowledge. Occasionally, however, I take home something more precious: a human connection and the joy that comes when you meet a passionate intellectual fellow traveler. This is why, after a conversation at the Future Technologies Conference in November 2018, I knew that the invisible thread Patricia and I created over lunch would likely continue beyond that brief encounter.

During our conversation, we shared insights and perspectives on seemingly disparate topics, including to name a few: ambient technology, participatory design, urban landscapes, Michel de Certeau, notions of place and space, the beauty of imperfections, ethnographic practice, multi-sensoriality, ethics, aesthetics, artificial intelligence, experimental and art-informed research, and a shared antipathy for technology that does not advance humanity. When I suggest a connection among so many *seemingly unrelated yet intertwined* themes in the space of one conversation, newly met humans often opt for one (or more) of three approaches to deal with the complexity overload: the puzzled look, the topic shift, or the escape. Patricia instead nodded, smiled and had even richer dimensions to offer. In retrospect, that shared meal and conversation is my highlight of the conference.

Besides feeling honored and humbled by it, the reasons behind the request to write this foreword were clear as soon as I started reading the manuscript. With *Ambient Urbanities*, Patricia McKenna has woven an ambitious tapestry, which aims at bringing together *seemingly unrelated yet fully intertwined* fields, with the ultimate purpose of pointing us toward a future where cities can account for – and support – its many visible and invisible actors. This tapestry puts of course a responsibility on all those that are involved in imagining and developing future cities: architects, designers, planners, administrators, and technologists.

Since the beginning of my career, *seemingly unrelated yet intertwined* fields have defined my practice and passions – interestingly enough, many of such fields and passions are an integral part of *Ambient Urbanities'* foundations. These include architecture, environmental design, information technology, distributed sensors, sociology, philosophy, social and spatial practices, and participatory design.

In the 80s, I was undecided on whether I wanted to design spaces or study people, mostly due to a strong attraction toward existing and designed relationships between the two. My fascination lasted well beyond my architectural studies, and culminated with a thesis dissertation on kinesthesia and crude experimentations to translate body movements and visual representations into audio artefacts (and vice versa). These first steps, and those that followed throughout and beyond my doctoral studies, were all directed in similar directions, although in *seemingly unrelated yet intertwined* ways.

During my PhD, for instance, I developed the notion of Playful Triggers: design tools to generate collaborative practices in organizational contexts. The design of these tools arose from the realization (based on longitudinal observations in collaborative spaces) that designers have reduced agency when dealing with human-rich spaces: they can support or scaffold, but ultimately such spaces are complex beasts, impossible to control or shape with mere architectural or interior design techniques. In other words, if people do not wish to collaborate, a perfectly designed collaborative space will not magically transform them into collaborators. My development of Playful Triggers was fundamentally a reaction to the realization that design and designers alone are important yet not enough, and that *seemingly unrelated yet intertwined* techniques and sets of expertize are needed when dealing with such complex and human-rich spaces. The key role of humans and that of Participatory Design became central tenets of that work, radically transforming the shape of the thesis, submitted as a 15Kg suitcase for readers to experience and enrich, through multi-sensory use.

One may be tempted to believe that my current role at Intel Corporation has little to do with those early research endeavors – after all, I now focus on Artificial Intelligence and the use of distributed sensors in home or workspaces. However, at the heart of my current work there are the same traits and curiosities that underline my earlier work: a fascination for space, senses, human agency, beauty and the potential for designed tools to scaffold meaningful conversations.

This is precisely why *Ambient Urbanities* is such a fascinating book. By threading together an incredible set of theories and practices, it aims at benefiting and addressing diverse audiences by explaining the complexities and subtleties that govern – and should govern – the design of ambient-based urbanities. McKenna's rich literature review of issues, controversies, and problems associated with smart cities not only points out the complexities and intricacies of this field: it shows how any framework focused on it will require more than traditional design tools and techniques. More crucially, McKenna asks us to reflect on <u>who</u> should actively contribute to the design of ambient-based urbanities, <u>how</u> that should take place, and <u>what</u> the impact may be. She asks us to remember that at the core of that ambient urbanities' complexity there are people, the ways in which they experience space, and their wished experiences.

McKenna rightly advocates for frameworks to scaffold "more aware and informed people" and does so by asking crucial questions around awareness, engagement, participation, learning, smartness and best approaches. These are critical, not negotiable questions – only by addressing them, we will be in a position to create solid foundations for our future urban spaces and places.

The framework offered in this book is a modular, flexible, adaptive compass to help us understand, navigate, and be inspired by the richness and the *seemingly unrelated yet intertwined* complexities that define *Ambient Urbanities*. With it, McKenna helps us envision novel opportunities and appreciate how meaningful ambient urbanities may only emerge from a deep appreciation for the power of transformation. A transformation of space, people and technology.

Daria Loi
Intel Corporation, USA
February 2019

Daria Loi *(PhD; BArch) is a senior technical leader, with 20+ years' experience in and passion for mixing design strategy with agile UX research & innovation to enrich people's everyday life. In her current Principal Engineer role at Intel Corporation, she focuses on distributed sensing and AI, with an emphasis on smart home, aging in place and collaborative environments. As a Participatory Design and User Experience researcher and strategist, Daria throughout her career has focused on diverse domains, including: ambient and affective computing, smart spaces, multimodal experiences, PC and TV products, and tangible user interfaces. Dr. Loi has a long track record in exploring novel territories and leading the way through design innovation. Her seminal work on people's use of touch* *screens, for instance, played a crucial role in enabling today's touch-enabled laptops, convertibles and 2in1 devices. Her PhD thesis-in-a-suitcase, often referenced as pioneering because of its unique arts-based approach, has been showcased in diverse venues, including the Museum of Modern and Contemporary Art of Trento and Rovereto (MART). Before joining Intel Corporation in 2006, she worked as an architect in Italy and Senior Research Fellow at the Royal Melbourne Institute of Technology in Australia. Daria has conducted research and presented her work in most continents, published 60+ papers, filed several IP, and serves as chair or committee member on a number of international journals, institutes and conferences. In 2018 she was recognized as one of Italy's 50 most inspiring women in tech as part of the InspiringFifty initiative. More details at http://www.darialoi.com.*

Preface

This work explores urbanity in terms of what happens in contemporary urban environments at the human level when technologies become embedded, pervasive, and increasingly aware, as in, ambient. In response to the emerging, evolving, and continuous transformation occurring with the digitalization of everything, this work focuses on the ambient and the adaptive and dynamic nature of information, enabled by what is referred to in this volume as *aware technologies* that are influencing and being influenced by people's everyday interactions and activities. As such, this work is concerned with the combination of elements that contribute to the digital transformation of information – the Internet, information and communication technologies (ICT), information infrastructures, sensors, and now the Internet of Things (IoT), the Internet of People (IoP), the Internet of Experiences (IoE), and the Internet of Data (IoD) – as aware technologies in combination with the potential for more *aware people* in the context of contemporary understandings of urbanity.

This work came about from a need to lend coherence to an emerging body of research literature, thinking, discussion, debate, and theorizing about the ambient in 21st century smart cities, learning cities, responsive cities, and future cities. Crucial to this body of work is the importance of people as critical to the urban fabric of cities and more particularly, to smart cities that are increasingly embedded with pervasive, and often invisible technologies. Urbanity, a concept that takes people into consideration, is explored in this work from multiple perspectives ranging from the cultural to the geographic to the economic to the cinematographic and more, across multiple cities, mostly in Canada, and extending to other cities and countries such as Tel Aviv in Israel. Methodologically, this work is based on an urban research study beginning in 2015 and continuing into 2018 using an emergent, exploratory, and explanatory case study approach. In parallel with this study, this work is further enriched through discussions with many individuals and groups in diverse community settings. As smart cities are said to be on a spectrum where efforts are underway to become smarter, so too, this work argues for a spectrum of urbanity. With multiple perspectives, dimensions, and potentialities on a spectrum, it is in this sense that urbanity is pluralized and expanded in this work to urbanities. Theoretically, this work draws on thinking and literature from earlier work developed by the author that is reconsidered and reconfigured here within the context of ambient urbanities.

This book is intended for a broad and diverse audience including students, educators, researchers, the business community, city government staff and officials and other urban practitioners, community members, and those concerned with contemporary and emerging complex urban challenges and opportunities. As such, this work will have interdisciplinary appeal across multiple domains of research, study, practice, and urban living more generally. Domains of interest include, but are not limited to, architecture, environmental design, human geography, information technology, sociology, and urban planning and design, to name a few. Those interested in creativity, innovation, imagination, and practical issues associated with taking people into consideration in smart cities will also be drawn to this work. Uses for this work are many and varied. Educators and students will find this work helpful as an introduction to the people dimension of smart cities. City managers and officials, urban practitioners, and community members will find this book useful as a guide to creating smarter cities, new learning modalities and spaces, and improving livability. Researchers and practitioners will find many new directions, potentials, and provocations pertaining to smart cities, urbanities, urban studies, creativity, innovation and more. Urban researchers will be challenged to explore existing theoretical spaces and methodologies in new ways, adapt theory and methods in navigating new approaches to urban complexities, or undertake formulation of new theoretical spaces and methodologies in addressing intractable issues in uncertain and unstable contexts.

A CHAPTER BY CHAPTER GLIMPSE

This book is organized into eleven chapters designed to provide an overview of the urbanities literature and the emerging ambient urbanities concept. Chapter 1 begins with an introduction to urbanity, urbanities, and ambient urbanities. A framework for ambient urbanities is developed identifying the key dimensions for ambient urbanities in smart cities. Included in the framework are constructs for exploring each of the dimensions that are then used in formulation of the key research questions in this work that will be explored as propositions in the chapters that follow. For example, each chapter addresses the main aspects of a particular dimension of urbanities and provides a literature review identifying key issues, controversies, and problems, followed by solutions and recommendations. Chapter 2 provides an exploration of technologies and people focusing on urban sensing, awareness, the Internet of Things (IoT), the Internet of People (IoP), and the Internet of Experiences (IoE). Chapter 3 develops understandings of new urban layers and spaces in the city in relation to digital infrastructures and those that are forming around human experiences and interactions in relation to technology. Chapter 4 sheds light on culture and economies as ambient, extending to many other aspects of urban life-giving rise to what is advanced as the *ambient turn*. Chapter 5 draws attention to the importance of learning, play, and inclusion as ambient and the need for a range of novel literacies to accompany and support these dimensions of ambient urbanities. Chapter 6 addresses the data dimension of ambient urbanities, the Internet of Data (IoD), and the need for smart information architectures and in turn, the need for smarter governance. Chapter 7 focuses on the importance of new methodologies and theoretical spaces to support understandings of ambient urbanities in smart cities focusing on the subtle and not so subtle interweaving of the visible and invisible aspects. Chapter 8 responds to concerns with sharing, collaboration, and openness in awareness-based urban spaces and the need for innovating privacy to accommodate ambient urbanities. Chapter 9 takes a look at approaches to measuring ambient urbanities building upon emerging and evolving metrics, standards, indices, and indicators for smart cities. Chapter 10 provides a synthesis and summary of the book and revisits and revises the ambient urbanities framework developed in Chapter 1. Chapter 11 concludes by offering some perspectives on what the future may hold, delving into parallel and complementary approaches including microgrids, wise cities, and the quantum city.

Additionally, the findings in each chapter point to variables that will be relevant to researchers, practitioners, and city managers who are interested in an ambient urbanities approach to smart cities. And, each chapter concludes with the identification of added value and novelty contributed, along with key insights, ideas, and lessons for the reader.

In summary, the key dimensions of ambient urbanities are formulated and advanced, chapter-by-chapter in this work, enabling the reader to develop an understanding of the complexities, debates, directions, challenges, opportunities, and potentials. While an overview of the chapter-by-chapter coverage of ambient urbanities provided in this preface enables a glimpse of the broad coverage of this work, each chapter focuses more specifically on several elements as follows:

- Sensing in relation to pulse, vibrancy, space, and spatialities (actors)
- Engagement in relation to connected, contextual, and continuous
- Participation in relation to privacy, reliability, and social acceptance (personalized)
- Learning and literacies in relation to awareness, involvement, and collaboration
- Smartness in relation to information architectures, data, and governance
- Theoretical spaces and methodologies in relation to ambiances, atmospheres, and augmentations
- Openness in relation to amplifications and being informed
- Metrics in relation to adaptive, dynamic, contextual, and responsive
- Ambient and other elements in relation to contextuality, in/visibilities, and trust (complementarity, overlap, uncertainty)

With insights and findings being gathered iteratively over a three-year period and going forward, it is expected that this work will serve as a handbook for ambient urbanities and continue to be updated, refined, and extended. As such, your feedback is very much welcomed and encouraged.

H. Patricia McKenna
AmbientEase, Canada

Acknowledgment

First and foremost, I would like to acknowledge the important contributions from the many individuals who participated in the urban research study forming the basis for this work as well as the many individuals and groups who shared their time, thinking, concerns, and insights in discussions about smart cities.

A special thanks is extended to IGI Global for the invitation and opportunity to contribute to the Research Insights Series. Evaluations received through the blind peer review process managed by IGI Global provided important and valuable feedback for the editing and revising of this manuscript. Additionally, the guidance and timely support received from the IGI Global Team throughout this project are very much appreciated.

A very special note of appreciation goes out to Daria Loi for preparing a thoughtful, moving, and insightful Foreword for this work. Thank you Michelle for planting the idea of a book on the ambient in my mind during one of our discussions several years ago. To friends and colleagues always ready to provide supportive and encouraging words, and to those of you who tracked my progress, a huge thank you. And I am infinitely grateful to Jeanine for her unwavering support in untold ways from the beginning to the end of this book project.

Section 1
Urbanities, Sensing, and Infrastructures

Chapter 1

Urbanities and Smart Cities:
An Introduction

ABSTRACT

The purpose of this chapter is to provide an introduction to the urbanity concept from a variety of perspectives and in the context of smart cities. A key element characterizing smart cities is the introduction of information and communication technologies and other pervasive and aware technologies providing a space for the exploration of new understandings of urbanity. Aware technologies in combination with aware people enable formulation of an ambient urbanities framework. The chapters that follow provide an exploration of the challenges and opportunities for elements of the ambient urbanities framework, with Chapter 2 focusing on sensing; Chapter 3 on infrastructures; Chapter 4 on culture, economies, and everything as ambient; Chapter 5 on digital literacies; Chapter 6 on smart information architectures; Chapter 7 on the need for new methodologies and theoretical spaces; Chapter 8 on innovating privacy; Chapter 9 on measuring ambient urbanities; Chapter 10, a synthesis; and Chapter 11 on ambient urbanities and beyond.

DOI: 10.4018/978-1-5225-7882-6.ch001

1. INTRODUCTION

The purpose of this chapter is to provide an introduction to the urbanity concept from a variety of perspectives and in the context of smart cities. A key element characterizing the emergence of smart cities (Hernández-Muñoz et al., 2011; Schaffers et al., 2011; Batty et al., 2012; Chourabi et al., 2012) is the introduction of information and communication technologies (ICTs) (Nam and Pardo, 2011a; Nam and Pardo, 2011b; Caragliu, Del Bo, and Nijkamp, 2011; Naphade et al., 2011) and other pervasive and aware technologies, including the Internet of Things (IoT) (Zanella et al., 2014) providing a space for the exploration of new understandings of urbanity (Lévy, 2011; 2013; 2015). The increasing presence of aware technologies in combination with more aware people enables the conceptualization and formulation in this work of an ambient urbanities framework for smart cities. Guided by this framework, the chapters that follow provide an exploration of the challenges and opportunities for each dimension of the ambient urbanities framework with Chapter 2 focusing on sensing; Chapter 3 on infrastructures; Chapter 4 on culture, economies and everything as ambient; Chapter 5 on digital literacies; Chapter 6 on smart information architectures, data, and governance; Chapter 7 on the need for new methodologies and theoretical spaces; Chapter 8 on innovating privacy; Chapter 9 on measuring ambient urbanities; Chapter 10 providing a synthesis of perspectives on ambient urbanities; and Chapter 11 concluding with a look beyond for ambient urbanities going forward.

Objectives: The key objectives of this chapter are to: a) provide evolving perspectives on urbanity; b) contribute insight into emergent understandings of urbanities in the context of smart cities; and c) articulate an ambient urbanities framework for 21st century urban environments.

2. BACKGROUND AND CONTEXT

The interweaving of several key forces in 21st century urban environments provides the background and rationale for this chapter. Namely, the rapid growth of cities (Chourabi et al., 2012); the swift uptake and evolving nature of information and communication technologies (ICTs) (Nam and Pardo, 2011a) and other aware technologies including the Internet of Things (IoT) (Hashem et al. 2016); interest in smart cities as a strategy for cities to innovate (Komninos, 2015; Nam and Pardo, 2011b); and the emergence of smart cities as a new urban agenda to handle complex and unprecedented challenges (Gil-Garcia, Pardo, and Nam, 2016). This interweaving of forces represents the coming together of people, technologies, and cities in ways unique to the needs and requirements of healthy and sustainable 21st century urban environments for living, working, and learning (Garau and Pavan, 2018; McKenna, 2017). This work argues that the synergistic people, technologies, and cities dynamic gives rise to the opportunity for rethinking, reimaging, and coming to new understandings of urbanity (Lévy, 2015; Lévy, 2013) in the context of smart cities. While Neirotti et al. (2014) found there to be "no unique global definition" of the smart city (SC) concept, they argue that, "current trends and evolution patterns of any individual SC depend to a great extent on the local context factors." However, Lara et al. (2016) argue that although "widely used", the smart cities concept is "highly fuzzy" such that "the fuzziness hinders our understanding" of "the benefits of its adoption" while serving to "explain" some of the "fragmented or distorted views" of smart cities.

This chapter provides an overview of perspectives and theory on the urbanity concept; a review of the research literature for urbanities and smart cities; and the emergence of thinking around the ambient concept. Development of the people, technologies, and cities dynamic in the context of urbanities and smart cities enables conceptualization of an ambient urbanities framework for understanding the nature of aware people and aware technologies in contemporary urban environments. Exploring and developing the ambient urbanities construct provides a way of highlighting the people dimension as critical to smart cities. Based on an exploration of urban experiences using a case study approach, the socio-techno-cultural-affective nature of people's interactions and relationships with technology and with each other in the city emerges. This exploration is intended to surface a wide range of insights pertaining to the Internet of Things (IoT), the Internet of People (IoP), and the Internet of Experiences. As such, this work is also intended to generate a range of evolving discourse spaces in further developing Dourish and Bell's (2007) notion of the experience of infrastructure and an infrastructure of experience in the context of smart environments (Dourish and Bell, 2011) and urban spaces (Mattern, 2013).

2.1 Definitions

For the purposes of this work, definitions for key terms used in this chapter are presented here based on the research literature. A more comprehensive listing of terms with definitions, as articulated by this work, are located in the *key terms and definitions* section at the end of this chapter.

- **Ambient:** Described by McCullough (2013), ambient is, "that which surrounds but does not distract"; "a continuum of awareness and an awareness of continuum"; and "a new sensibility."
- **Smart City:** According to Nam and Pardo (2011a), smart city "integrates technologies, systems, infrastructures, services, capabilities into an organic network that is sufficiently complex for unexpected emergent properties to develop" with an "emphasis on human infrastructure" highlighting "social learning and education."
- **Urbanity:** Lévy (2015:xix) claims that urbanity "is what makes an urban space urban."

2.2 Overview

As an introduction to this book, the current chapter provides a range of perspectives on urbanity and an overview of urbanities and smart cities in Section 3along with the identification of issues, controversies, and problems. An emerging conceptual framework for ambient urbanities in contemporary urban environments is provided in Section 4 (Figure 4). In the form of solutions and recommendations, Section 5 provides an operationalization of the ambient urbanities framework for smart cities, describing approaches fostering more aware and informed people that are employed and the case study research design and methodology. A research question is identified for each dimension of the ambient urbanities framework along with a construct to guide the exploration for each of the nine questions. Each research question is reformulated into a proposition to be explored in the chapters that follow. Section 6 identifies practice and research explorations with an overview of how each chapter in this book contributes to ambient urbanities in relation to the conceptual framework in Figure 4. Section 7 consists of the conclusion, highlighting the objectives of this chapter in relation to the surfacing of insights, ideas, added value, and lessons for the reader.

The primary audiences for this work include students, educators, researchers, community builders and organizers, community members, city managers, urban practitioners, and anyone concerned with urbanity, smarter and more responsive cities, urban innovation, and collaborative approaches to complex urban challenges. As an interdisciplinary work, this chapter will appeal to multiple domains of study and practice, including but not limited to, architecture, environmental design, data science, human geography, information technology, sociology, and urban planning, design, governance, and engagement.

3. PERSPECTIVES ON URBANITY AND URBANITIES AND SMART CITIES

The theoretical perspective for this work is developed through a review of the research literature for urbanity focusing on the many dimensions that emerge – cultural, economic, sociological, and technological, among others. A review of the literature on urbanities and smart cities is then provided identifying the multiple dimensions of urbanity in the context of rapidly emerging pervasive and aware technologies.

3.1 Urbanity

This review of the research literature for urbanity is organized into a number of categories, intended not to be comprehensive, but rather, to highlight the range of perspectives in terms of spatial practices; social practices; history, culture, and economics; and digital practices.

Spatial Practices

De Certeau (1984) pointed to trajectories of movements and interactions in the city based on daily habits and spatial practices before the advent of pervasive technologies. From a human geography perspective, Lévy (2015:xix) claims that urbanity consists of "an association of density and diversity." Density for Lévy encompasses "people in their homes, at work, in hotels, in shops, in the street or in buildings" and also includes "material as well as immaterial objects." Diversity according to Lévy (2015:xix) refers to "people ('social mix'), activities (industry, commerce, school), and functions (housing, transport)" including "historical complexity." It is worth noting that Lévy (2015:xix) goes on to claim that cities are a "type of urban space" arguing that "urbanity can be found elsewhere" but that "a city is a space where the intensity of urbanity is maximal." Lévy (2015:xix) adds that, "urbanity, urbaneness, urbanness, and Wirth's 'urbanism' are roughly synonymous." Indeed, Perrone, Paba, and Rossi (2018) look to the dynamic nature of cities as "cities in motion" where they explore the global periphery concept "with reference to marginal urban areas, remote zones, peripheral territories, in-between cities and abandoned European urban landscapes" in search of "a new urbanity." Tursic (2017:15) claims a space for urbanity that "belongs to the type of unplanned and unintended phenomena that emerge from people's intensions and actions." Drawing on the work of Lévy (2013), Tursic refers to "urban types (or models of urbanity)" consisting of "the center, the suburb, the peri-urban, the infra-urban, the para-urban, the meta-urban."

Social Practices

Referring to the work of Tonkiss (2014), Tursic notes that 'designing for diversity' refers not simply to "prescribing 'mixed uses'," but also and importantly "leaving undefined grounds for improvisation." From this perspective, Tursic observes that, "urbanity unleashes its full strength because it allows the emergence of a variety of unpredicted social practices" as potential "important elements of social change." Similarly, Tursic notes that Lévy (2011) "stresses the role of serendipity as a particularly creative force of urban public spaces." It is worth noting that Tursic refers to the "cityness" described by Sassen (2005) as "the strength of intersections of difference that occur frequently in unobtrusive and incidental ways" as a kind of "'high' or 'strong' urbanity." According to Tursic (2017:83), "the level of urbanity always comes with certain tensions that appear to be an element behind both vibrancy and liveliness" on the one hand and "conflict, in big dense cities" on the other hand.

History, Culture, and Economics

In the late 1990s, Zijderveld (1998) explored the history of urbanity in formulation of a theory of urbanity in terms of "the economic and civic culture of cities" arguing that, "Simmel, Wirth, Mumford, and Jacobs pioneered in the identification of urbanity as a legitimate object of scientific analysis and research." Zijderveld (1998) articulates "the idea of the city as a distinct phenomenon" as "outdated in view of a world increasingly fragmented and borderless, if not limitless, and highly flexible due to the seminal impact of electronic technologies." Zijderveld (1998) highlights the "many ambiguities" of urbanity while employing the urbanity concept as a "synonym for urban culture" that is "tied to the concept of civic culture" maintaining that the urbanity concept was "indispensable" to "a need for a more or less systematic and comprehensive theory of urban culture." According to Zijderveld (1998), "urban economists, urban sociologists and specialists of urban design and urban planning are predominantly occupied by the spatial morphology, the political power structures, and the quantitative economic and social parameters of cities" such that "many useful data and insights may be gained from their studies, but urbanity is clearly not at the center of their interests." Melnyk (2007) describes urbanity from a cinematographic perspective as "a wholistic term that refers to the totality of urban culture" in that " urban ways of life are primarily human ways of being." For Melnyk (2007), urbanity encompasses nine dimensions emanating from multiple domains "dealing with human life" and these include – "physicality or architecture of urban space; biology or urban environment; emotive personality or psychology; philosophy or meaning of the city; economics or work life of a city; technology embodied in urban life and how it affects humans; ethnic diversity and sociological dramas; history; and a speculative vision for a city's future."

Digital Practices

Graham and Marvin (2002) articulate the notion of *splintering urbanism* in explorations of the 21st century urban condition in the context of "new technologies and increasingly privatised systems of infrastructure provision." Beaude (2016) identifies the key part of urbanity as "its complexity" observing that "urban representations" are now extending beyond those "limited to buildings and transport infrastructures" to include those "built from digital footprints" contributing to "the potential of urbanity" since such footprints "greatly contribute to the actualization of the city." According to Baude (2016), "digital footprints are not a mere reflection of urbanity: they are liable to change it." Bharne (2013) addresses the notion of "vertical urbanism" noting that, "east Asia's rising towers have cast long shadows over neighbourhoods, streets, and wind-swept public spaces" extending to "professional discourse and practices." Bharne (2013) employs the concept of "horizontal urbanity" in arguing "for a more multifaceted and inclusive view of urbanity" embodying "the full complexity and possibilities of its cities" and "the full array of urbanity." Pointing to the importance of both vertical urbanism and horizontal urbanity as "formal and physical dimensions of city building," Bharne (2013) also includes "the social and economic networks that depend on the intricacy and efficacy of interconnected urban fabrics." For Bharne (2013), it is such "dense activity networks and spaces" that provide insight into "how cities truly function and 'metabolize' and how urban life is practiced and supported."

In summary, multiple perspectives on urbanity are presented as depicted in Figure 1, from a range of domains spanning human geography to economics, to cinematography, to architecture, to technology, to philosophy, to urbanism, to social and spatial practices.

Figure 1. Urbanity: Perspectives from a range of domains

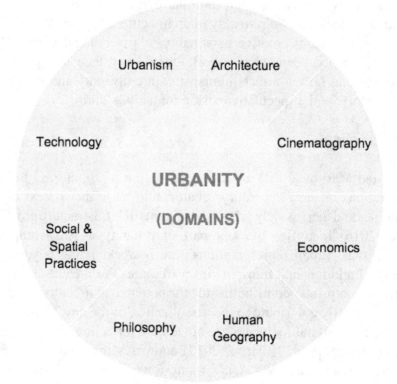

3.2 Urbanities and Smart Cities

This review of the research literature for urbanities and smart cities is organized into key categories that are intended, not to be comprehensive, but rather, to highlight the range of perspectives on: urban life and experiences; urban theory; and urban data, information, and technologies.

Urban Life and Experience

Bharne (2013) describes urbanities as "the myriad phenomenological traits of urban life and experience" and, used in conjunction with the term urbanisms, is "intended to describe diverse physical characteristics" of a city. Lara et al. (2016) argue for a type of smartness in cities that is "comprehensive and human-centered" in moving beyond smart cities definitions "in the academic literature" that "have limited scope, and are overly focused on strategic drivers and specific actions." Lara et al. (2016) encourage "the direct participation of local actors and stakeholders in the process of thinking, defining, planning, and executing social, technological and urban transformations in cities" while Streitz (2018) argues for keeping humans in the loop and a change in the 'smart-everything' paradigm.

Urban Theory

As the city grows and extends itself through the use of new technologies, the potential for new dimensionalities emerges, calling for new theorizing. Brenner and Schmid (2015) argue that the concept of city extends more broadly to encompass other cities, oceans, and even the planet. New geographies of theory in support of "imagination and epistemology for urban theory" are advanced by Roy (2009) in the form of "new conceptual vectors for understanding the worlding of cities, the production of space, and dynamics of exurbanity." Worlding of cities shifts the focus from "concepts of world cities and world systems to that of worlding practices" where Roy and Ong (2011) present the worlding city space "as a milieu of intervention, a source of ambitious visions, and of speculative experiments that have different possibilities of success and failure." As such, worlding practices, according to Roy and Ong (2011), provide an interpretation of the urban "as a milieu that is in constant formation" is "shaped by multitudinous ongoing activities" is "inherently unstable" and "inevitably subject to intense contestation" and is "always incomplete."

Urban Data, Information, and Technologies

Bohlen and Frei (2010), citing Mitchell (1995), note that, "urbanity today is as much a function of transmitted data as it is of built houses, streets and monuments." According to Bohlen and Frei (2010), "sociality, spatialization and temporality refer to the readings between the lines of urban culture" that was "formalized by de Certeau" giving rise to questions such as, is there more activity occurring in a physical space than meets the eye? For Zijderveld (1998), "the notion of a specifically urban culture has become superfluous" in the context of an "age of cyberspace and virtual reality." According to Zijderveld (1998), "the informational city of today" is "characterized by incessant flows, mobilities, decentered fragmentations" and the "evolution of suburbia" toward "in particular" what is described as "the rapid emergence of so-called *edge cities*." It is in this sense that Zijderveld (1998) speaks of "cities-without-urbanity." Contributing further to the human geography perspective advanced by Batty (2013), Lévy (2015) places a focus on space and people interacting in contemporary urban environments and regions, extending through digital reach to new understandings where the Internet is described as an innovation of space (Baude, 2016). Campbell (2012) highlights the learning dimension of cities and the importance of cities networking with each other. The work of Williams, Robles, and Dourish (2009) on 'urbane-ing' contributes to broader perspectives on urban informatics incorporating insights from networked, global, and infrastructural examples. Brenner articulates the changing role of the city in relation to urbanization (2017).

As depicted in Table 1, perspectives on urbanity, urbanities, and smart cities highlighted in this review of the literature introduce a range of issues from data to the spatial to temporality from a variety of domains spanning human geography to economics to politics to psychology to philosophy to urbanism. And the interdisciplinary nature of this space is particularly evident in the work of researchers such as Graham and Marvin and Lévy, encompassing several domains.

3.3 Issues, Controversies, Problems

Issues, controversies, and problems that emerged in this chapter through the review of the research literature for urbanity and urbanities and smart cities, although not exhaustive or comprehensive, is intended to shed light on the rich nature, variety, and range. For example, a brief overview reveals the following:

Table 1. Perspectives on urbanities and smart cities

Domains and Issues	Researchers								
	Baude	Bharne	Bohlen & Frei	De Certeau	Graham & Marvin	Lévy	Melnyk	Tursic	Zijderveld
Data			✓		✓	✓			✓
Economic					✓		✓		✓
Emotive							✓		
Environment							✓		
Geography	✓	✓			✓	✓			✓
History		✓		✓	✓		✓		
Philosophical				✓		✓	✓	✓	
Political		✓			✓				✓
Psychological				✓			✓		
Social			✓	✓	✓	✓			
Socio-cultural					✓			✓	✓
Socio-technical					✓				
Spatial	✓		✓	✓	✓	✓			✓
Temporality			✓		✓	✓			

Issues

Beaude (2016) identified the issue of "urban representations built from digital footprints" in terms of the potential to change urbanity. Komninos (2015) describes intelligent cities as "an attractive prospect, strategy and a vision" noting the "long way to go before this planning vision is turned into reality" as in, "an agglomeration of communities fully connected and instrumented" where "knowledge flows of learning, collective intelligence, and creativity enable all members to address their individual or communal problems and fulfill their aspirations." Komninos (2015) presents five interrelated models to guide the transition process focusing on structure, spatial intelligence, function, strategic planning, and governance.

Controversies

Controversies emerge in terms of tensions identified by Tursic (2017) where the "vibrancy and liveliness" associated with a certain "level of urbanity" gives way to "conflict, in big dense cities." Roy and Ong (2011) conceptualize "worlding practices" in terms of interventions, visions, and speculative experiments in support of dynamic and adaptive spaces with "multitudinous ongoing activities" while acknowledging the inherent instabilities, contestations, and incompleteness of urban environments that are "in constant formation."

Problems

Chourabi et al. (2012) described "social and organizational problems" as being "associated with multiple and diverse stakeholders, high levels of interdependence, competing objectives and values, and social and political complexity" contributing to the notion of "city problems" as "wicked and tangled."

This work however, argues that the depth and breadth of urbanity depicted in Figure 1, as spanning a wide range of domains, as well as the characteristics of urbanity presented in Figures 2 and the characteristics of smart cities presented in Figure 3, are intricately interwoven with the issues, controversies, and problems identified. For example, the nature of urbanity emerges through a rich array of characteristics as depicted in Figure 2. At a glance, the characteristics of urbanity include the *ambiguities* of human life and culture; *complexity* associated with digital, vertical, and horizontal infrastructures, whether physical, social, economic, or technological; *density and diversity* related to people, activities, and functions; the *serendipity* of the unplanned and unintentional; and *practices* pertaining to social interactions, spatial movement, tensions (e.g., data transmissions/footprints or other elements), and habits.

Figure 2. Urbanity: Characteristics at a glance

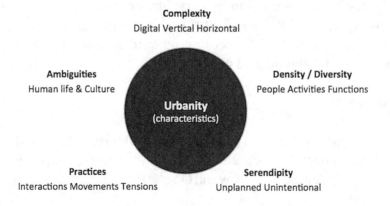

Key characteristics of smart cities emerging from the research literature are depicted in Figure 3 with *complexities* in terms of the intractable and wicked issues associated with the rapid growth of urban areas calling for cities to innovate themselves and become smarter in response, aided by technologies such as ICTs, the IoT, and the like.

The problem of multiple, fuzzy, and emergent *definitions* for smart cities emerges along with the *interdisciplinary* nature of smart cities that touch upon every aspect of urban life, systems, and services requiring approaches that cross multiple boundaries and domains of research and practice. The *adaptive and dynamic* nature of requirements for smart cities is highlighted calling for highly responsive infrastructures and services in support of everyday interactions in-the-moment. The *unexpected and unpredictable* nature of interactions, movements, and tensions at once contribute to and give rise to the need for adaptive and dynamic responses. The emerging shifts in thinking and approaches necessitated by new technologies point to an *under-theorizing* of smart cities and the need for new and evolving theory to accommodate new dimensionalities, spaces, practices, and understandings.

As such, this work develops an approach for exploring the intricate interweaving of urbanity and smart city issues, controversies, and problems associated with technology-infused urban environments. This approach offers an avenue to solutions and recommendations, through the development of ambient urbanities in Section 4. Issues, controversies, and problems are then addressed as challenges and opportunities through operationalization of the ambient urbanities framework in Section 5.

Figure 3. Smart Cities: Characteristics at a glance

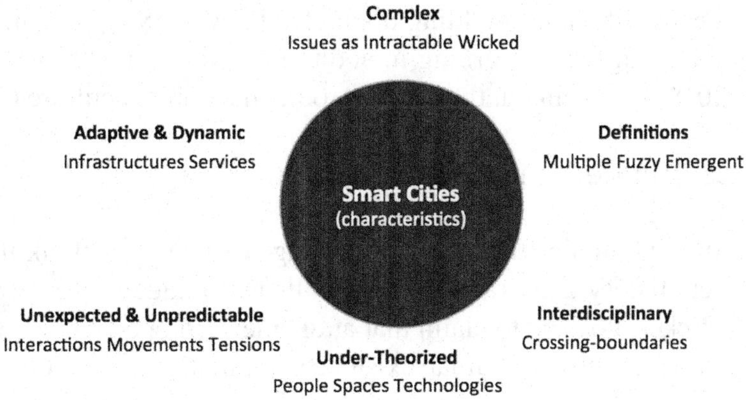

Complex
Issues as Intractable Wicked

Adaptive & Dynamic
Infrastructures Services

Definitions
Multiple Fuzzy Emergent

Smart Cities
(characteristics)

Unexpected & Unpredictable
Interactions Movements Tensions

Interdisciplinary
Crossing-boundaries

Under-Theorized
People Spaces Technologies

4. CONCEPTUALIZING AMBIENT URBANITIES FOR SMART CITIES

This review of the research literature for ambient urbanities in relation to smart cities is organized into several categories intended, not to be comprehensive, but rather, to highlight the range of perspectives for selected concepts.

4.1 Perspectives on Ambient Urbanities and Smart Cities

Perspectives on ambient urbanities and smart cities are provided here in relation to the concepts of: ambient; ambience, attunement, and movement; ambient technologies; and urban informatics.

Ambient

Building upon McCullough's (2013) conceptualization of ambient as "how this new technology, these new surroundings, and this new outlook for attention have begun to interrelate" this work develops an exploratory space for ambient urbanities. McCullough (2013) describes the sensing of an ambient commons as a momentary kind of thing. Going further, this work conceptualizes ambient urbanities as a space that may be momentary or more prolonged; more extended temporally and geographically for the duration of a physical and/or virtual event; no longer just technology-mediated, but with the layers suggested by Dourish and Bell (2011) of infrastructure, experience and interaction, contributing to the complexity also noted by Nam and Pardo (2011b) and by Rickert (2013); and moving toward a more dynamic and interactive understanding of the city, featuring more aware people. In developing emerging understandings of the ambient, this work delves further into the research literature building upon efforts by McKenna et al. (2013) on ambient and emergent learning in addition to work on relationships for learning (2016a); learning in the city (2016c); and ambient culture (2016b).

Ambience, Attunement, and Movement

Rickert (2013) maintains that, "an ambient age calls us to rethink much of our rhetorical theory and practice" and "calls us to understand rhetoric as ambient." Rickert goes on to claim that attunement, in opening "us onto the ambience of all and not just human existence, implicitly changes our view of human being." To accommodate ambience and attunement, Rickert (2013) undertakes to "consider how networks and complexity can augment a theory of ambient rhetoric" where "ambience captures the 'software' play of being and doing from the network and create its conditions of possibility." In the context of timeliness, Rickert introduces the worlding concept discussed by Roy (2009), stating that, "every decision, every action, is immersed in a situation or world" and as such "is in a sense 'worlded'."

Ambient Technologies

Acknowledging pervasive technologies such as ambient intelligence, Rickert (2013) advances the notion of "achieving new forms of fittingness in everyday life" where "fittingness brings with it increased awareness of the importance of world in our being in the world." Rickert encourages an understanding of the ambient in terms of "seeing that which surrounds and encompasses as also gifting and guiding us." In other words, the ambient for Rickert offers, "promise, challenge, and ultimately hope" as articulated perhaps in conceptualizing the concept of smartness in government by Gil-Carcia, Zhang, and Puron-Cid (2016) with respect to pervasive and aware technologies. Servières, L'Her, and Siret (2017) explore urban ambiances in the context of mobile devices, particularly "connected, wearable tools" that "change the ways we perceive and design public spaces." Servières et al. (2017) claim that, "mobile tools change urbanity and also collective practices" while contributing "to various performative cartography cultures emerging in and around the urban." The concept of "digital ambient urbanity" as described by Servières et al. (2017) is "a change in everyday life" giving rise to the notion of "an augmented urban experience."

Urban Informatics

Foth, Forlano, Satchell, and Gibbs (2011) address the areas of urban informatics, social media, ubiquitous computing, and mobile technologies in engaging people in the city. According to Foth et al. (2011), urban informatics differentiates itself from scientific and economic models of sustainability through "a nuanced focus on cultural practices and people and on how these practices are enhanced or constrained by technologies." Hjorth (2015) articulates the ambient play concept through camera phone practices and the lens of urban cartographies, highlighting – "water, emotional, social, playful, psychological, historical, geographic" while enabling a rethinking of urban space as a digital-material environment and the entanglements and complexities of electronic privacy and electronic publics.

Where Townsend (2013) highlights a world of big data, civic hackers, and a utopian quest in the smart cities proposition, this work offers instead a space that transcends the dystopian and utopian views, with potentials for practical opportunities for engagement and participation, in moving toward understandings of ambient urbanities. Temporary interventions have been demonstrated by Placemaking Networks (PPS, 2016) in the form of a pop-up street closure in support of the organizing of events and spaces for pedestrians on a Sunday afternoon or other do-able projects using tactical approaches. However, in an interview with Jenkins (2016), Pendleton-Jullian describes the tactical in terms of viable and possible short-term solutions that are appropriate for "simple or complicated problems," as distinct from complex problems characterizing smart cities. For these more wicked problems, Pendleton-Jullian calls for "thinking forward" and use of the pragmatic imagination, as in, cognitive activity (on the spectrum of perception, reasoning, speculation, experimentation, and free play) generating "possibilities around civic action and then carrying them out" through the pragmatic work of "instrumentalizing the products of the imagination" which this current work interprets to be a complementing of the technical instrumentation of the smart city (SMC, 2017). It is worth noting that Goldsmith and Crawford (2014) address metrics for smart cities in the *Responsive City* in relation to civic engagement. This current work navigates additional approaches and perspectives for metrics in the smart cities context, proposing the notion of ambient metrics in support of more adaptive and dynamic indicators for more meaningful engagement and participation.

In summary, as depicted in Figure 4, a conceptualization of ambient urbanities for 21st century smart cities consists of the interweaving of people, technologies, and cities enabled and augmented by the Internet of Things (IoT), the Internet of People (IoP), and the Internet of Experiences (IoE) in terms of multiple emerging dimensions as ambient, in relation to a series of constructs contributing to an evolving framework. The constructs employed in this work are drawn from the research literature and include: awareness, engagement, in/visibilities, learning, metrics, openness, participation, and smartness. Each construct is used in the exploration of a particular dimension. Dimensions are based on emerging understandings of the ambient and include:

ambient data and smart information architectures for smarter interactions and governance; evolving understandings of cultures, economies, and everything as ambient; ambient inclusion, ambient play, and other forms of ambient learning as emergent digital literacies; mechanisms for measuring ambient urbanities; innovating privacy through sharing, collaboration, and other forms of openness; sensing cities through more aware people in combination with aware technologies; new theory and methods driven by urban visibilities and invisibilities, referred to as in/visibiities; and new urban layers and spaces for infrastructures, experiences, and interactions.

This conceptual framework is designed to guide the operationalization of an ambient urbanities exploration for people, technologies, and cities where research questions pertaining to each of the dimensions are addressed, chapter-by-chapter, in relation to a particular construct for each. Evidence for components of the ambient urbanities conceptual framework in Figure 4 is further developed in Section 5 and in the chapters that follow.

Figure 4. Ambient urbanities: An emerging conceptual framework for 21st century smart cities

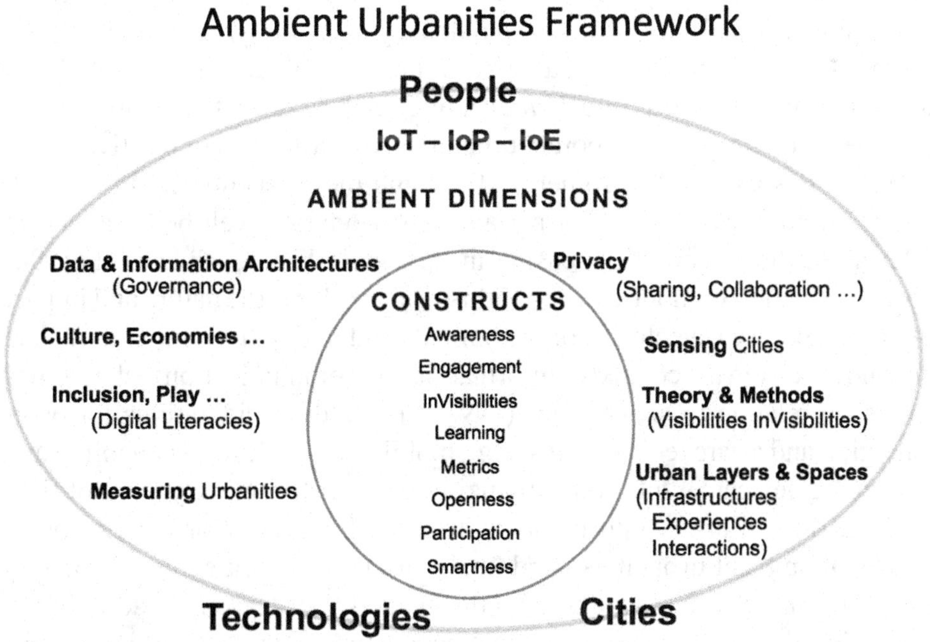

5. OPERATIONALIZING AMBIENT URBANITIES: SOLUTIONS AND RECOMMENDATIONS

This work operationalizes the ambient urbanities framework to bring about solutions and recommendations to issues, controversies, and problems associated with smart cities through use of approaches that support more aware and informed people, articulation of a series of research questions, description of a research design, and reformulation of the research questions into propositions to be explored chapter-by-chapter in the remainder of this book.

5.1 Approaches Fostering More Aware and Informed People

Employing approaches that foster and support more aware and informed people, this work provides an inquiry into the sensibilities of people; people and their interactions with sensing technologies; and new types of relationships and collaborations within fluid timeframes and spaces. As such, this work focuses on the new sensibilities as identified by McCullough such as, "when you feel renewed sensibility to your surroundings" and by Rickert (2013) as "ambient sensibility" further enabled by technology. Concerned with design, this work accommodates in the interdisciplinary space of ambient urbanities, works such as *Eco-Urbanity* by Radović (2009) that contributes to an understanding of contemporary urbanities from a design perspective. Work on urban design by Montgomery (2014) and more recently by Loi (2019) brings in the affective dimension pertaining to people and well-being, an aspect relevant to the construct of sensing in this work. Where Zijderveld (1998) speaks of "cities-without-urbanity," this work explores the nature and impact of contemporary trajectories of movements and interactions in, around, and beyond the city in the context of information and communication technologies (ICTs) in relation to smart cities (UN, 2015) and considerations for other emerging and aware technologies (e.g., mobile, wearable, other enabling and enhancing devices) while contextualizing the interdisciplinary work of Foth et al. (2011) on urban informatics within the framework of the expansive spaces of ambient urbanities. And importantly, this work explores ambient urbanities in smart cities, taking up the challenge of Rickert in adhering to the notion that the ambient is about 'movement', as in, "something always ongoing and transforming in accordance with the play of being-in-the-world" with "an ensemble of interacting human and nonhuman actants" articulated here as aware people and aware technologies.

Guided by the ambient urbanities framework in Figure 4, exploration of the dimensions identified gives rise to a series of research question to be explored, chapter-by-chapter, where each question employs one of the constructs (awareness, engagement, participation, learning, smartness, in/visibilities, openness, and metrics), beginning in Chapter 2 through to Chapter 9, a synthesis in Chapter 10, with a final inquiry in Chapter 11.

Research Question (Q1): How does *awareness* inform urbanity in smart cities?

Research Question (Q2): How do new urban layers of urbanity enable spaces for *engagement* in smart cities?

Research Question (Q3): How do evolving understandings of the urban and urbanity influence *participation* in smart cities?

Research Question (Q4): Why does *learning* matter for urbanity in relation to emergent digital literacies in smart cities?

Research Question (Q5): How does *smartness* contribute to urbanity in contemporary urban environments?

Research Question (Q6): Why are new theoretical and methodological approaches important for explorations of urbanity in relation to smart cities?

Research Question (Q7): Why is *openness* important for innovating privacy for urbanities in smart cities?

Research Question (Q8): How and why are *metrics* important for ambient urbanities in smart cities?

Research Question (Q9): How and why are *ambient and other elements (e.g., quantum)* important for ambient urbanities in smart cities and beyond?

5.2 Research Design

Methodologically, this work uses an emergent, exploratory single case study approach, said to be particularly appropriate for the study of contemporary and dynamic information technology (IT) phenomena (Yin, 2018).

The research design involved the use of a website to: describe the study; invite and enable sign up; basic demographic data gathering; and the opportunity for people to self-identify in one or more categories (e.g., student, educator, business, city official, community member, visitor, etc.).

Upon sign up, participants were invited to complete an online survey along with the opportunity to discuss in-depth (online or in person) the experience of their community, city, or urban region as a smart city. The invitation to participate in the research study was posted online in webspaces that attract researchers, practitioners, and anyone interested in evolving urban spaces and smart cities. Sampling procedures consisted of heterogeneity sampling, a type of purposive sampling in support of a broad range of perspectives (Trochim, 2006). Over a multi-year time period (2015-2018) this study attracted interest from around the world and participation from people in small to medium to large sized cities, mostly in Canada (e.g., Greater Victoria, Ottawa, St. John's) and extending also to cities in other countries (e.g., Europe, Israel).

Data Collection

The interview protocol consisted of twelve questions providing an opportunity for people to think about and comment on their urban experiences and understandings of smart cities. The protocol was pre-tested prior to use in this study. Three questions contained in the interview protocol are:

1. If we developed a web/social media space, in your opinion what would this space look like if designed to be helpful, enabling people to be more involved in making the city and community smarter?
2. Is there some way to get people more involved in the city and in the community?
3. What do you think an achievable goal should be for cities for 2025?

Survey instrument design, although aligned closely with the interview protocol, consisted of twenty questions (closed and open-end), and pre-testing occurred prior to use in this study. Three questions contained in the survey instrument are:

1. What do you like about being in the city?
2. In your opinion what contributes to the making of a smart city?
3. In your opinion, what do cities need to do to become smarter?

In addition to quantitative data collected through surveys and qualitative data gathered through interviews and open-ended survey questions, data were also collected systematically in parallel with this study. Guided by the case study interview protocol, this third source of evidence emerged through group and individual meetings enabling diverse voices across many sectors (e.g., information technology, business, higher education, city councilors, architects, etc.) in various cities (e.g., Greater Victoria, Toronto, Vancouver) to speak about smart cities.

Data Analysis

Analysis for quantitative data consisted of descriptive statistics and exploratory use of Anderson's (2011) body insight scale (BIS) was employed in relation to the construct of awareness in urban environments. Content analysis, pattern matching, and explanation building were used in the analysis of qualitative data. Content analysis consisted of deductive analysis of terms emerging from the research literature and inductive analysis of terms emerging from the collected data. Working iteratively with the three data sources enabled simultaneous analysis, comparison, and triangulation. In sum, an analysis was conducted in this work based on n=73 with 41% females and 59% males for people ranging in age from their 20s to their 70s. Overall, the experiences of a diverse range of people at the urban level in multiple cities in a number of countries, constitutes the case study for this work. As such, insights from this case are designed to shed light on the situation of urbanities in the underlying sampling areas.

The nine research questions are restated here as propositions to be explored in Chapter 2 through Chapter 11 of this work. Depicted visually, Figure 5 forms a framework for the exploration of the nine propositions, focusing on a construct (e.g., awareness, engagement, participation, learning, smartness, in/visible (theory/methods), openness, metrics, and ambient) for each while providing an overview and a chapter-by-chapter guide to this work.

The propositions under exploration in this work are stated as follows:

Proposition (P1) – Chapter 2: *Awareness* informs urbanity in smart cities through sensing and getting smarter, aided by the Internet of Things (IoT), the Internet of People (IoP), and the Internet of Experiences (IoE) influencing designs, spaces, interactions, and smartness.

Proposition (P2) – Chapter 3: New urban layers of urbanity enable spaces for *engagement* in smart cities through emergent infrastructures, experiences, and interactions.

Proposition (P3) – Chapter 4: Evolving understandings of the urban and urbanity influence *participation* in smart cities when culture, economies, and everything are considered through the lens of the ambient.

Figure 5. Framework for the exploration of ambient urbanities in 21ˢᵗ century smart cities

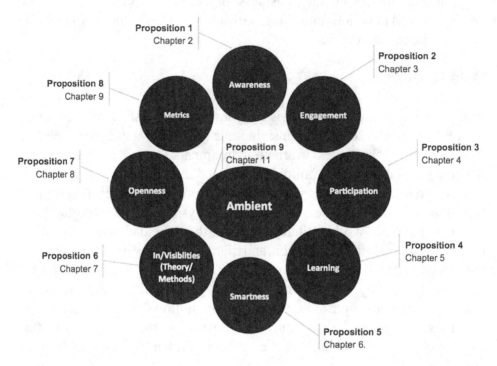

Proposition (P4) – Chapter 5: *Learning* matters for urbanity in relation to emergent digital literacies in smart cities because of the highly dynamic and ever-changing ecologies and requirements.

Proposition (P5) – Chapter 6: *Smartness* contributes to urbanity in contemporary urban environments through evolving information architectures in support of more adaptive approaches to data and governance.

Proposition (P6) – Chapter 7: New theoretical and methodological approaches are important for explorations of urbanity in smart cities in relation to emergent and evolving spaces for the *invisible*, *visible*, augmented, and other extensibilities.

Proposition (P7) – Chapter 8: *Openness* is important for innovating privacy for urbanities in smart cities because it enables innovations in other related spaces associated with sharing, collaboration, and other creative interactions.

Proposition (P8) – Chapter 9: *Metrics* are important for ambient urbanities in smart cities through more adaptive standards, indices, and other dynamic indicators because of the emergent, continuous, and evolving nature of the people-technologies-cities ecosystem.

Proposition (P9) – Chapter 11: *Ambient and other elements (e.g., quantum)* are important for ambient urbanities in smart cities and beyond because of the emergent, continuous, and evolving nature of the people-technologies-cities ecosystem looking to future cities.

Figure 5 also provides a roadmap to the practice and research explorations to be undertaken in the reminder of this work as described in Section 6.

6. PRACTICE AND RESEARCH EXPLORATIONS

Guided by the propositions under exploration in this work, in response to the research questions, a description of the focus for each of the chapters that follow is presented.

Chapter two explores awareness and the experience of sensing and smartness in the city; where intelligence resides; and what constitutes and contributes to the notion of making cities smarter, as in, "augmenting urbanity" (Böhlen and Frei, 2010). Chapter three develops the dynamic of infrastructures, experiences, and interactions in relation to new urban layers and spaces for engagement to complement and extend the physical and the emerging interweaving of the material and the digital. Chapter four explores visible and invisible flows of information as a new and emerging landscape in technology-infused experiences of the city, shedding additional light on the concept of the ambient in terms of participation in relation to culture, economies, and everything. Culture as a dimension of smart cities and ambient culture as a reconceptualization of culture is advanced to complement and extend existing understandings of culture. Chapter five explores digital literacies in terms of what it means to experience the notion of ambient learning in relation to the wicked challenges facing education, educators, and learners while re-imagining play and inclusion as social, urban, and ambient enabled by more dynamic, adaptive, and interactive infrastructures for innovating and urbanizing in the city. Chapter six explores smartness in relation to smart information architectures and advances a more aware and informed approach for people to understand big data (Batty, 2013) and small data (Estrin, 2013) in support of the purposeful leveraging of real-time analytics for interactions in the city and for smarter governance. Potential for the SmartCityCube is advanced as, an adaptive data management framework and information architecture for smart cities. Chapter seven explores urban visibilities and invisibilities in terms of the physical and digital as challenges and opportunities for methodologies and theoretical spaces for ambient urbanities. Chapter eight looks at privacy in relation to smart cities in response to the state of the privacy construct that was said to be in disarray (Solove, 2006). A rethinking and innovating of the privacy construct in formulation of an ambient privacy framework in support of sharing, collaboration, and openness is described as a critical dimension of ambient urbanities. Chapter nine develops and advances the ambient metrics concept as a way of shedding light on the evolving nature of standards and indices in dynamic and aware environments in relation to the potential for more informed city experiences and increased engagement and participation. Chapter ten provides a summary and synthesis of the book; an overview of the key themes, constructs, and dimensions contributing to and constituting ambient urbanities; and the conceptual framework for ambient urbanities is revisited in providing guidance on future directions for both practitioners and researchers. Chapter eleven looks beyond and into the future of ambient urbanities.

7. CONCLUSION

In meeting the key objectives of this chapter, an introduction to the urbanity concept is provided through a review of the research literature from multiple perspectives across a range of disciplines. The urbanities concept is then explored in the context of smart cities based on a review of the emerging and evolving research literature for information and communication technologies (ICT), other emerging and aware technologies, and the ambient concept. Key issues, controversies, and problems are surfaced through a review of the research literature. The primary argument of this chapter is that 21st century technology-rich environments require a reconceptualization of urbanity as ambient urbanities, complementing and extending existing understandings and interpretations. As such, a conceptualization for ambient urbanities is developed in this chapter along with a framework to guide and advance understandings of the importance of aware people in combination with aware technologies.

This background supports the formulation of propositions to be explored in the remainder of the work, from chapters two to eleven, guided by the ambient urbanities framework for smart cities. Additionally, the ambient urbanities framework is intended to foster spaces for thinking, acting, and interacting in novel, agile, adaptive, interdisciplinary, and solutions-oriented ways. As such, this chapter provides added value to the reader through: a) development of the ambient urbanities concept; b) the novelty of the conceptualization and operationalization of the framework for 21st century smart cities; and c) utilization of the framework as a guide to involving people more meaningfully, knowingly, and directly – from city managers to community members – in understanding and responding to urban issues, controversies, and problems.

This chapter provides definitions for key terms as an introduction to the book; identifies the focus for each chapter based on the particular research question in the form of the proposition under exploration using one or more constructs; highlights the range of elements contributing to ambient urbanities addressed by this work; and provides a focus for potential practice and research spaces going forward. In summary, this chapter sets the stage for the exploring, theorizing, and operationalizing of the ambient urbanities conceptual framework for 21st century smart cities.

Insights of particular interest to the reader include the following:

1. The rich history of research and practice associated with urbanity
2. The need for extending understandings of urbanity to accommodate technology-rich environments
3. The importance of ambient urbanities as an approach/framework to foster more aware/informed people

Ideas highlighted in this chapter pertain to the following:

1. The importance of more aware people as a fundamental element of ambient urbanities
2. The value potential of people interacting with each other, with and through aware technologies
3. The potential of the ambient concept for aiding understandings of smart spaces and interactions.

Lessons for the reader in this chapter are associated with the following:

1.   The transformative potential of the ambient urbanities conceptualization of smart cities;
2.   Constructs to guide, explore, and understand the multiple dimensions of ambient urbanities
3.   The importance of adaptive and cross-domain mindsets for people acting in smart environments.

All chapters in this work seek to contribute to current theory underlying emerging 21st century cities, said to be an underdeveloped area (Batty, 2013; Roy, 2009). The analysis of findings in each chapter points to variables relevant to the study, practice, and management of ambient urbanities in smart cities.

This work will be of interest to a diverse audience as described in Section 2.2 of this chapter. In particular, this work will attract readers concerned with emerging understandings of urbanities, smart cities, and interdisciplinary approaches to addressing complex urban challenges and the opportunities for responding with novel and adaptive solutions.

REFERENCES

Anderson, R. (2011). *Body Insight Scale*. Retrieved 29 December 2017 from http://www.mindgarden.com/73-body-insight-scale#horizontalTab3

Batty, M. (2013). Big data, smart cities and city planning. *Dialogues in Human Geography, 3*(3), 274–279. doi:10.1177/2043820613513390 PMID:29472982

Batty, M., Axhausen, K. W., Giannotti, F., Pozdnoukhov, A., Bazzani, A., Wachowicz, M., ... Portugali, Y. (2012). Smart cities of the future. *The European Physical Journal. Special Topics, 214*(1), 481–518. doi:10.1140/epjst/e2012-01703-3

Baude, B. (2016). From digital footprints to urbanity: Lost in transduction. In J. Lévy (Ed.), *A cartographic turn* (pp. 273–297). Lausanne, Switzerland: Routledge.

Bharne, V. (2013). *The emerging Asian city: Concomitant urbanities and urbanisms*. Routledge.

Böhlen, M., & Frei, H. (2010). Ambient intelligence in the city: Overview and new perspectives. In H. Nakashima, H. Aghajan, & J. C. Augusto (Eds.), *Handbook of ambient intelligence and smart environments* (pp. 911–938). New York, NY: Springer. doi:10.1007/978-0-387-93808-0_34

Brenner, N. (2017). *Critique of urbanization: Selected essays.* Basel, Switzerland: Birkhauser.

Brenner, N., & Schmid, C. (2015). Towards a new epistemology of the urban? *City, 19*(2-3), 151–182. doi:10.1080/13604813.2015.1014712

Campbell, T. (2012). *Beyond smart cities: How cities network, learn, and innovate.* Earthscan.

Caragliu, A., Del Bo, C., & Nijkamp, P. (2011). Smart Cities in Europe. *Journal of Urban Technology, 18*(2), 65–82. doi:10.1080/10630732.2011.601117

Chourabi, H., Nam, T., Walker, S., Gil-Garcia, J. R., Mellouli, S., Nahon, K., ... Scholl, H. J. (2012). Understanding smart cities: An integrative framework. In *Proceedings of the 45th Hawaii International Conference on System Sciences* (pp. 2289-2297). Washington, DC: IEEE Computer Society.

De Certeau, M. (1984). *The practice of everyday life.* Berkeley, CA: University of California Press.

Dourish, P., & Bell, G. (2007). The infrastructure of experience and the experience of infrastructure: Meaning and structure in everyday encounters with space. *Environment and Planning. B, Planning & Design, 34*(3), 414–443. doi:10.1068/b32035t

Dourish, P., & Bell, G. (2011). *Divining our digital future: Mess and mythology in ubiquitous computing.* Cambridge, MA: MIT Press. doi:10.7551/mitpress/9780262015554.001.0001

Estrin, D. (2013). small data, where n = me. *Communications of the ACM, 57*(4), 32–34. doi:10.1145/2580944

Foth, M., Forlano, L., Satchell, C., & Gibbs, M. (2011). *From social butterfly to engaged citizen: Urban informatics, social media, ubiquitous computing, and mobile technology to support citizen engagement.* Cambridge, MA: MIT Press. doi:10.7551/mitpress/8744.001.0001

Garau, C., & Pavan, V. M. (2018). Evaluating urban quality: Indicators and assessment tools for smart sustainable cities. *Sustainability, 10*(3), 575. doi:10.3390u10030575

Gil-Garcia, J. R., Pardo, T. A., & Nam, T. (2016). A comprehensive view of the 21st century city: Smartness as technologies and innovation in urban contexts. In J. R. Gil-Garcia, T. A. Pardo, & T. Nam (Eds.), *Smarter as the new urban agenda: A comprehensive view of the 21st century city* (Vol. 11, pp. 1–19). Springer. doi:10.1007/978-3-319-17620-8_1

Gil-Garcia, J. R., Zhang, J., & Puron-Cid, G. (2016). Conceptualizing smartness in government: An integrative and multi-dimensional view. *Government Information Quarterly*.

Goldsmith, S., & Crawford, S. (2014). *The responsive city: Engaging communities through data-smart governance*. San Francisco, CA: John Wiley & Sons Inc.

Graham, S., & Marvin, S. (2002). *Splintering Urbanism: Networked Infrastructures, Technological Mobilities and the Urban Condition*. Routledge. doi:10.4324/9780203452202

Hashem, I. A. T., Chang, V., Anuar, N. B., Adewole, K., Yaqoob, I., Gani, A., ... Chiroma, H. (2016). The role of big data in smart city. *International Journal of Information Management, 36*(5), 748–758. doi:10.1016/j.ijinfomgt.2016.05.002

Hernández-Muñoz, J. M., Vercher, J. B., Muñoz, L., Galache, J. A., Presser, M., Hernández Gómez, L. A., & Pettersson, J. (2011). Smart cities at the forefront of the future Internet. In J. Domingue & ... (Eds.), *Future Internet Assembly, LNCS 6656* (pp. 447–462). Springer. doi:10.1007/978-3-642-20898-0_32

Hjorth, L. (2015). Narratives of ambient play: Camera phone practices in urban cartographies. In *Citizen's Right to the Digital City*. Singapore: Springer. doi:10.1007/978-981-287-919-6_2

Jenkins, H. (2016). *Mapping the pragmatic imagination: An interview with Ann M. Pendleton-Jullian*. Retrieved 16 December 2016 from http://henryjenkins. org/2016/11/mapping-the-pragmatic-imagination-an-interview-with-ann-m-pendleton-jullian-part-3.html

Komninos, N. (2015). *The age of intelligent cities: Smart environments and innovation-for-all strategies.* New York: Routledge.

Lara, A. P., Da Costa, E. M., Furlani, T. Z., & Yigitcanlar, T. (2016). Smartness that matters: Towards a comprehensive and human-centered characterisation of smart cities. *Journal of Open Innovation: Technology, Market, and Complexity*, 2(1), 8. doi:10.118640852-016-0034-z

Lévy, J. (2011). La sérendipité comme interaction environnementale. *La Sérendipité: Le Hasard Heureux*, 279–85.

Lévy, J. (2013). Inhabiting. In *The Sage Handbook of Human Geography* (Vol. 1, pp. 45–68). Newcastle: Sage.

Lévy, J. (2015). Urbanisation and urbanism. In EPFLx: SpaceX Exploring Humans' Space: An Introduction to Geographicity. Massive Open Online Course (MOOC), edX.

Loi, D. (2019) Ten guidelines for intelligent systems futures. In *Proceedings of the Future Technologies Conference (FTC) 2018* (pp. 788-805). Springer. 10.1007/978-3-030-02686-8_59

Mattern, S. (2013). Infrastructural tourism. *Places Journal.* Retrieved 16 August 2016 from https://placesjournal.org/article/infrastructural-tourism/

McCullough, M. (2013). *Ambient commons: Attention in the age of embodied information.* Cambridge, MA: The MIT Press. doi:10.7551/mitpress/8947.001.0001

McKenna, H. P. (2016a). Innovating relationships for learning in 21st century smart cities. *Proceedings of the 9th Annual International Conference of Education, Research and Innovation (iCERi2016)*, 4695-4704. 10.21125/iceri.2016.2115

McKenna, H. P. (2016b). Emergent ambient culture in smart cities: Exploring the Internet of Cultural Things (IoCTs) and applications in 21st century urban spaces. *3rd International Workshop on Visions on Internet of Cultural Things & Applications (VICTA2016), Proceedings of the 12th International Conference on Signal-Image Technology and Internet-Based Systems (SITIS 2016)*, 420-427. 10.1109/SITIS.2016.72

McKenna, H. P. (2016c). Learning in the city: Leveraging urban spaces as real world environments for interactive solution-making. *Proceedings of the 10th International Technology, Education & Development Conference (INTED2016)*, 4367-4375. 10.21125/inted.2016.2081

McKenna, H. P. (2017). Urbanizing the ambient: Why people matter so much in smart cities. In S. Konomi & G. Roussos (Eds.), *Enriching urban spaces with ambient computing, the Internet of Things, and smart city design* (pp. 209–231). Hershey, PA: IGI Global. doi:10.4018/978-1-5225-0827-4.ch011

McKenna, H. P., Arnone, M. P., Kaarst-Brown, M. L., McKnight, L. W., & Chauncey, S. A. (2013). Ambient and emergent learning with wireless grid technologies. *Proceedings of the 5th International Conference on Education and New Learning Technologies (EduLearn13), IATED*, 4046-4053.

Melnyk, G. (2007). The imagined city: Toward a theory of urbanity in Canadian cinema. *CineAction, 73/74*, 20–27.

Mitchell, W. J. (1995). *City of bits: Space, place, and the infobahn*. Cambridge, MA: The MIT Press.

Montgomery, C. (2014). *Happy city: Transforming our lives through urban design*. Farrar, Straus and Giroux.

Nam, T., & Pardo, T. A. (2011a). Conceptualizing smart city with dimensions of technology, people, and institutions. In *Proceedings of the 12th Annual International Conference on Digital Government Research*, (pp. 282-291). ACM. 10.1145/2037556.2037602

Nam, T., & Pardo, T. A. (2011b). Smart city as urban innovation: Focusing on management, policy, and context. In E. Estevez, & M. Janssen (Eds.), *Proceedings of the 5th International Conference on Theory and Practice of Electronic Governance (ICEGOV2011)*, (pp. 185-194). ACM. 10.1145/2072069.2072100

Naphade, M., Banavar, G., Harrison, C., Paraszczak, J., & Morris, R. (2011). Smarter cities and their innovation challenges. *Computer, 44*(6), 32–39. doi:10.1109/MC.2011.187

Neirotti, P., De Marco, A., Cagliano, A. C., Mangano, G., & Scorrano, F. (2014). Current trends in Smart City initiatives: Some stylised facts. *Cities (London, England), 38*, 25–36. doi:10.1016/j.cities.2013.12.010

Perrone, C., Paba, G., & Rossi, M. (2018). Cities in motion: Looking for a new urbanity at the global periphery. *Proceedings of the Annual Meeting of the American Association of Geogra*phers. Retrieved 30 November 2017 from https://aag.secure-abstracts.com/AAG%20Annual%20Meeting%20 2018/abstracts-gallery/15761

PPS. (2016). *The lighter, quicker, cheaper transformation of public spaces.* Retrieved 24 December 2016 from http://www.pps.org/reference/lighter-quicker-cheaper/

Radović, D. (2009). *Eco-urbanity: Towards well-mannered built environments.* Routledge.

Rickert, T. (2013). *Ambient rhetoric: The attunements of rhetorical being.* Pittsburgh, PA: University of Pittsburgh Press. doi:10.2307/j.ctt5hjqwx

Roy, A. (2009). The 21st Century metropolis: New geographies of theory. *Regional Studies, 43*(6), 819–830. doi:10.1080/00343400701809665

Roy, A., & Ong, A. (2011). *Worlding cities: Asian experiments and the art of being global.* Blackwell. doi:10.1002/9781444346800

Sassen, S. (2005). Cityness in the urban age. *Urban Age Bulletin, 2,* 1–3.

Schaffers, H., Komninos, N., Pallot, M., Trousse, B., Nilsson, M., & Oliveira, A. (2011). Smart Cities and the Future Internet: Towards Cooperation Frameworks for Open Innovation. In The Future Internet. Berlin: Springer Berlin Heidelberg.

Servières, M., L'Her, G., & Siret, D. (2017). Mobile devices and urban ambiances: How connected wearable tools change the ways we perceive and design public spaces. In B. E. A. Piga & R. Salerno (Eds.), *Urban design and representation: A multidisciplinary and multisensory approach.* Cham, Switzerland: Springer. doi:10.1007/978-3-319-51804-6_16

SMC. (2017). *Instrumentation and control.* Reston, VA: Smart Cities Council. Retrieved 13 December 2017 from https://smartcitiescouncil.com/smart-cities-information-center/instrumentation-and-control

Solove, D. J. (2006). A taxonomy of privacy. *University of Pennsylvania Law Review, 154*(3), 477–560. doi:10.2307/40041279

Streitz, N. (2018). Beyond 'smart-only' cities: Redefining the 'smart-everything' paradigm. *Journal of Ambient Intelligence and Humanized Computing*. doi:10.100712652-018-0824-1

Tonkiss, F. (2014). *Cities by design: The social life of urban form*. Hoboken, NJ: John Wiley & Sons.

Townsend, A. M. (2013). *Smart cities: Big data, civic hackers and the quest for a new utopia*. W. W. Norton & Company.

Trochim, W. M. K. (2006). *Research methods knowledge base*. Retrieved 15 December 2011 from http://www.socialresearchmethods.net/kb

Tursic, M. (2017). *Aesthetic space: The visible and the invisible in urban agency* (Thèse No. 6445). Lausanne, Switzerland: EPFL.

UN. (2015). *Smart cities – Habitat III Issue Papers, No. 21*. New York: United Nations. Retrieved 13 December 2017 from http://habitat3.org/wp-content/uploads/Habitat-III-Issue-Paper-21_Smart-Cities-2.0.pdf

Williams, A., Robles, E., & Dourish, P. (2009). Urbane-ing the city: Examining and refining the assumptions behind urban informatics. In M. Foth (Ed.), *Handbook of research on urban informatics: The practice and promise of the real-time city*. Hershey, PA: IGI Global. doi:10.4018/978-1-60566-152-0.ch001

Yin, R. (2018). *Case study research and applications: Design and methods*. Thousand Oaks, CA: Sage.

Zanella, A., Bui, N., Castellani, A., Vangelista, L., & Zorzi, M. (2014). Internet of Things for Smart Cities. *IEEE Internet of Things Journal*, *1*(1), 22–32. doi:10.1109/JIOT.2014.2306328

Zijderveld, A. C. (1998). *A theory of urbanity: The economic and civic culture of cities*. Taylor and Francis.

ADDITIONAL READING

Jacobs, J. (1961). *The death and life of great American cities*. New York: Random House.

Mumford, L. (1961). *The city in history: Its origins, its transformations, and its prospects*. Orlando, FL: Harcourt.

Sassen, S. (2013). Does the city have speech? (Urban challenges: Essay.). *Public Culture*, 25(2), 209–221. doi:10.1215/08992363-2020557

Sassen, S. (2016). How Jane Jacobs changed the way we look at cities. *The Guardian*, 4 May. Retrieved 13 December 2017 from https://www.theguardian.com/cities/2016/may/04/jane-jacobs-100th-birthday-saskia-sassen

Schmitt, G. (2017). *Future Cities*. MOOC (Massive Open Online Course). Zurich, Switzerland: ETHzurich. Retrieved 11 December 2017 from https://www.edx.org/course/future-cities-ethx-fc-01x

Simmel, G. (1971). The metropolis and mental life. In D. N. Levine (Ed.), *On individuality and social form* (pp. 324–339). Chicago, IL: University of Chicago Press.

Wirth, L. (1964). *Louis Wirth on cities and social life: Selected papers*. Chicago, IL: University of Chicago Press.

KEY TERMS AND DEFINITIONS

Ambient: The increasing presence of aware technologies in and around human activity affecting the nature and experience of awareness, information, economies, literacies, and everything.

Ambient Urbanities: Urban life infused, augmented, and extended with aware technologies in combination with more aware people.

Digital Literacies: Continually emerging adaptations required by emergent and evolving technologies supported by ongoing learning.

Information and Communication Technologies (ICT): Technologies designed for communication and information sharing.

Internet of People (IoP): Human connections and interactions enabled and augmented through the Internet.

Internet of Things (IoT): Computing connections and interactions enabling the networking of things through the Internet.

Smart Cities: Smart cities are urban areas, regions, territories, and beyond that are characterized by more aware and engaged people, in combination with and aided by, the use of awareness enhancing technologies for mobility, livability, and sustainability. For example, using a smartphone with location and other awareness features to quickly and effectively navigate in the city while using the device to share with others what you are noticing, discovering, or reimagining in the moment in urban spaces.

Urbanities: Awareness of urbanity in multiple, diverse, and ever-emergent forms.

Urbanity: Urban spaces infused with the vibrancy of people.

Chapter 2
Sensing Cities and Getting Smarter:
Awareness and the Internet of Things and People

ABSTRACT

This chapter explores awareness in relation to sensing and smartness in the city enabled through aware people and aware technologies, including the internet of things (IoT), the internet of people (IoP), and the internet of experiences (IoE). The main aim of this chapter is to shed light on where intelligence resides in the city and what constitutes and contributes to sensing and making cities smarter in relation to evolving notions of urbanity. The research literature for awareness, sensing, sensors, the IoT, the IoP, and the IoE is explored in this chapter in the context of urbanity and smart cities, enabling identification of issues, controversies, and problems. Using an exploratory case study approach, solutions and recommendations are advanced. This chapter makes a contribution to 1) research and practice across multiple domains including the IoT, the IoP, and IoE and 2) emerging thinking on human sensing and associated behaviors in smart cities.

DOI: 10.4018/978-1-5225-7882-6.ch002

1. INTRODUCTION

This chapter focuses on the construct of awareness in relation to sensing and smartness in the context of 21st century cities as an approach to exploring aware technologies and aware people. Gil-Garcia, Zhang, and Puron-Cid (2016) provide a conceptualization of smartness in government involving an integrative and multi-dimensional view along 14 dimensions, one of which is citizen engagement while Loi (2019) speaks in terms of "acceptable smartness" in everyday contexts such as "home, car, and workspace." Others dimensions of smartness identified by Gil-Garcia et al. (2016) include: creativity, effectiveness, efficiency, equality, entrepreneurialism, openness, resiliency, technology services, integration, innovation, evidence-based, citizen centricity, and sustainability. Citing Nam and Pardo (2011) and Torres, Pina, and Acerete (2006), citizen engagement is said to have "the potential to develop citizen's sense of ownership of their city, enhance the local authority's awareness of their needs, and ultimately reshape the citizen government relationship" (Gil-Garcia et al., 2016). In coming to an understanding of smartness involving the digital, Böhlen and Frei (2010) addressed conceptual and design deficits for ambient intelligence in the context of urban environments, calling for pervasive sensing issues to be included in urban planning in terms of a negotiating of interests across public and private spaces. To this end and in response to critical voices, Böhlen and Frei (2010) argued for a "re-making of urbanity with pervasive technologies as a means to invigorate urban life" for improved livability while "recalibrating all of the ambient intelligence research" in order for cities to "scale to urban satisfaction." In arguing for everyone to work together, despite the many challenges, in building "ambient cities," Böhlen and Frei (2010) were perhaps opening the way for ambient urbanities and the notion of smartness as conceptualized by Gil-Garcia et al. (2016).

Objectives: The key objectives of this chapter are to explore: a) awareness as it manifests in the city through people and their experience of sensing and smartness in the city; b) where intelligence resides; and c) what constitutes and contributes to the notion of making cities smarter and Böhlen and Frei's (2010) notion of "augmenting urbanity." As such, this exploration gives rise to the key question to be explored in this chapter – How does awareness inform urbanity in smart cities?

2. BACKGROUND AND OVERVIEW

Deakin and Al Waer (2011) identify a transition from intelligent to smart cities focusing on social intelligence to highlight the "information-rich and highly communicative qualities." According to Deakin and Al Waer (2011), "networks of innovation and creative partnerships" play a "critically insightful role" in the embedding of intelligence in support of the "learning, knowledge transfer and capacity building exercises servicing" the "community led transition." Hinting at the smart part of our being, Judge and Powles (2015) argue that, "our default way of interacting with the world isn't by peering at screens" suggesting instead that "we respond to the environment, to what it offers us, in an automatic and intuitive way" such that "in most everyday scenarios, we don't see our things as *things*, we just use them." This exploration of awareness is operationalized through an inquiry into the movements, interactions, and practices of people in the technology-rich environment of cities and communities. Drawing on the work of Rickert (2013) and of Lévy (2015; 2013) on space and spatialities (actors in urban spaces), in relation to the construct of awareness, the vibrancy and pulse of urban areas is probed. Using an abbreviated set of questions from Anderson's (2006; 2011) body insight scale (BIS), adapted here as a mechanism for sensing in urban environments, an early stage attempt is made to highlight the importance of human capabilities and potentials used in conjunction with Anderson's (2004) exploratory method of intuitive inquiry.

2.1 Definitions

For the purposes of this work, definitions for key terms used in this chapter are presented here based on the research literature.

- **Awareness:** Guo, Riboni, and Hu (2014) describe awareness in terms of context awareness through pervasive computing encompassing the three areas of personal awareness, social awareness, and urban awareness.
- **Internet of Things (IoT):** Atzori, Iera, and Morabito (2017) define the IoT as "a conceptual framework that leverages the availability of heterogeneous devices and interconnection solutions, as well as augmented physical objects providing a shared information based on [a] global scale, to support the design of applications involving at the same virtual level both people and representations of objects."

- **Sensing:** Ruiz-Correa et al. (2017) engage people in relation to technology to "sense, feel, and share" in order to "define, document, and reflect on their city's problems."
- **Sensor:** The ITU (2012) defines a sensor as "an electronic device that senses a physical condition or chemical compound and delivers an electronic signal proportional to the observed characteristic."
- **Smartness:** Gil-Garcia, Zhang, and Puron-Cid (2016) claim that "smartness has recently emerged as a desirable characteristic of governments, cities, communities, infrastructures and devices."

2.2 Overview

This chapter provides a range of perspectives from the research literature on awareness in smart cities in relation to the Internet of Things (IoT); the Internet of People (IoP); and the Internet of Experiences (IoE) in Section 3, followed by an overview of issues, controversies, and problems. Section 4 provides a discussion of sensing the city in relation to people and technologies in smart cities and a conceptual framework for sensing cities and getting smarter is developed to guide the exploration under investigation in this chapter. Based on findings, a framework for ambient sensing in smart city urbanities is advanced in support of the potential for solutions and recommendations. Section 5 identifies future directions for research and practice and Section 6 concludes with chapter coverage highlights, the major contributions, and the key insights, ideas, and lessons.

The primary audiences for this chapter include students, educators, researchers, community members, and urban practitioners concerned with awareness, sensing, smart cities, and smarter governance involving aware people and aware technologies in addressing complex urban challenges.

3. PERSPECTIVES ON AWARENESS IN SMART CITIES

This section provides a review of the research literature for awareness in relation to the Internet of Things (IoT), the Internet of People (IoP), and the Internet of Experiences (IoE) in the context of smart cities.

3.1 Awareness and the Internet of Things (IoT)

Awareness and the IoT is explored in this section in relation to the technical, the cartographic, sensors and sensing, the cyber-physical, and infrastructural elements for the IoT and the IoP.

Technically Speaking

The International Telecommunications Union (ITU) (2016) cites a definition for the IoT, based on Recommendation ITU-T Y.2060 (06/2012), as "a global infrastructure for the information society, enabling advanced services by interconnecting (physical and virtual) things based on existing and evolving interoperable information and communication technologies." Lea and Blackstock (2014) identify challenges of the IoT associated with interoperability as in, "how do devices/sensors/things work together" and "how are they found" or "represented on the Internet, accessed and controlled" proposing a hub, IoT-centric approach. Based on a "comprehensive survey of the enabling technologies, protocols, and architecture for an urban IoT," Zanella et al. (2014) identify interoperability issues associated with "heterogeneous technologies currently used in city and urban development" claiming that, "the IoT vision can become the building block to realize a unified urban scale ICT platform." Sicari et al. (2015) identify key challenges for IoT security, privacy, and trust associated with "data confidentiality and authentication, access control within the IoT network, privacy and trust among users and things, and the enforcement of security and privacy policies." Additionally, Sicari et al. (2015) point to open issues, scalability issues, and the need for "flexible infrastructure able to deal with security threats in such a dynamic environment." More recently, the ITU (2016) includes two notes with the 2012 definition for the IoT where note 1 states that "through the exploitation of identification, data capture, processing and communication capabilities, the IoT makes full use of things to offer services to all kinds of applications, whilst ensuring that security and privacy requirements are fulfilled." Note 2 (ITU, 2016) states that "in a broad perspective, the IoT can be perceived as a vision with technological and societal implications." Among "IoT actors" is the "IoT user" that "uses all possible services related with things, such as monitoring, location tracking, and service discovery" (ITU, 2016). Ahlgren, Hidell, and Ngai (2016) focus on the interoperability issue for the IoT and smart cities in relation to open data along with a discussion of "the advantages of open data and standards within the IoT, current limitations, and future trends."

Herzberg (2017) describes the Internet of Things (IoT) as "a network that enables physical objects to collect and exchange data" and looking to the future, the Internet of Everything (IoE) is said to encompass "devices, appliances, people and process." Thiele (2017) highlights the importance of trust, claiming that, "society will increasingly depend on the Internet of Things" but that "trustworthy behavior is key for societal acceptance." According to Thiele (2017) interference in many forms (e.g., environmental, energy, and the like) must be addressed both extrinsically and intrinsically. As such, "IoT infrastructure should be dependable and trustworthy" giving rise to the need for "appropriate models, design, testing, and verification methods." Park, del Pobil, and Kwon (2018) describe the importance of the role of the IoT in smart cities in terms of technology roadmap-oriented approaches encompassing five sectors and industries (e.g., energy and electricity, architecture and building, automation and transportation, security, and healthcare and monitoring). Six broad areas of smartness are also identified by Park et al. (2018) in support of open data and the use of "IoT technologies in smart cities to allow citizens to solve current urban problems" as – smart home platform; wind and wireless home network interworking technology; intelligent information home applications; home sensor technology; security technology for homes; and smart building automation and systems. Alavi et al. (2018) provide a review of the research literature focusing on "key features and applications of the IoT paradigm to support sustainable development of smart cities" highlighting the need for research to address challenges associated with "privacy, participatory sensing, energy efficiency, visualization, cloud computing, and edge computing." According to Alavi et al. (2018) such challenges require "continuing collaboration between public authorities, private companies, and academia" while focusing on "developing smart city infrastructures to support the IoT" that involve the issue of "economic cost." Looking to the future, Alavi et al. (2018) claim that in the near term, "IoT will profoundly change" the area of "human habits and physical well-being" giving rise to the need "to consider the social impacts of IoT-based technologies on individuals and communities as part of planning, design, and deployment."

Cartographically Speaking

From a cartographic perspective, Mattern (2017) argues that, "we need multiple ears, eyes, hands, sensors, and brains – automated and manual, digital and analog, machinic and human." Using the example of a bear tracking project (Bear 71 website – https://bear71vr.nfb.ca/), Mattern (2017) chooses to highlight from the project "the intersection between humans, animals, and technology" where the bear is "tracked and logged as data" as in, "qualifying and quantifying everything" in contrast to "experiencing and interacting." Mattern (2017) observes that while "we can now map everything" it will be important to "do so critically and intentionally" being mindful "that those subjects and agents have their own geographies and spatial sensibilities" as "do the instruments we use to map them." Pointing to the growing use of "artificially intelligent sensing machines – with their purportedly more objective, efficient, exhaustive, and reliable means of observation and orientation – to shape the protocols and politics of interaction among the various being who share our cartographic terrain" Mattern (2017) cautions that "computational instruments operationalize space differently" and "differently from one another and from other 'species' of intelligent agents, including us." As such, Mattern (2017) argues that, "we need to recognize the myriad intelligent agents not only *on* our maps, but also in our cartographic methods." In "experiencing and representing place" Mattern (2017) calls for "a prismatic collection of mappings, that invites comparison and appreciation of the ways in which our world is both known and unknown."

Speaking of Sensors and Sensing

Perera et al. (2014) explore the notion of sensing as a service in relation to the Internet of Things as a service model from technological, economical, and social perspectives along with identifying "the major open challenges and opportunities." Referring to the work of Guillemin and Friess (2009), Perera et al. (2014) note that, "IoT allows people and things to be connected anytime, anyplace, with anything and anyone, ideally using any path/ network and any service." Perera et al. (2014) claim that the "sensing as a service model resides in between" smart cities and the IoT "with many other technological and business models." Among the many benefits identified by Perera et al. (2014) for sensing as a service, "sharing, participatory, and reuse" are emphasized, as in "sense once and use by many." The sensing as a service model is also said to enable "real-time data for decision making and policy making" (Perera et al., 2014). Konomi and Sasao (2018) explore human-in-the-loop sensing in an effort to move "beyond the limitations to conventional urban sensing" identifying five challenges as: in-situ sampling; estimating social activities and emotion; improving data quality in context; meta-sensing; and context-aware privacy and data modeling.

Cyber-Physically Speaking

Petrolo, Loscri, and Mitton (2016) address cyber-physical systems (CPSs) and their Cyber-Physical Objects (CPOs) where the latter are described as the "integration of computation and physical processes" and are said to be critical to smart-cyber cities. Petrolo et al. (2016) define a smart-cyber city as "a city where the urban environment is an integration between people, processes, places, and technologies." Additionally, Petrolo et al. (2016) claim that "this ecosystem is able to self-organize and to react in order to adapt itself to the surrounding situations" where CPS can play a key role as enabler of a "synergy between the different actors" in terms of applications that "communicate and interact." CloutT is identified by Petrolo et al. (2016) as one of several European Commission initiatives for smart cities that "uses cloud computing as an enabler to bridge the Internet of Things with the Internet of People via the Internet of Services." As such, CloutT "is designed to establish an efficient communication and collaboration platform" drawing upon "all possible information sources to make the cities smarter" in the provision of "infrastructures, services, tools, and applications" for reuse by many urban groups including "municipalities, citizens, service developers, and application integrators" in order to "create, deploy, and manage user-centric applications" (Petrolo et al., 2016). Naunes, Sá Silva, and Boavida (2018) describe the evolution of IoT and CPSs where "a focus on 'things' has evolved to the monitoring of entire environments and, more recently, of human users." Lindley, Coulton, & Cooper (2019) point to challenges posed by the IoT associated with "two of the guiding design paradigms of our times" Privacy by Design (PbD) and Human Centered Design (HCD), claiming that to describe "systems as private, or designs as human centered – is irrational." According to Lindley et al. (2019), simply ticking all the boxes does not ensure adequate privacy protection, arguing that for IoT contexts "complexities of non-functional requirements" need to "be approached heuristically" where "users, and every other actor in the given constellation, be given the agency to understand any given situation for themselves." As such, Lindley et al. (2019) speak in terms of "informed design" calling for "subtly shifting our design paradigms" in order to accommodate "constellations of meaning" that "inform all participants in a constellation of their roles within it."

IoT and IoP

Infrastructure was proposed by Miranda et al. (2015) in support of "moving from the Internet of Things to the Internet of People" where "smartphones play a central role" serving "as the main interface connecting people to the Internet." Khatoun and Zeadally (2016) advance a smart city model comprised of the Internet of Things (IoT), the Internet of Services (IoS), the Internet of Data (IoD), and the Internet of People (IoP) highlighting smart living and smart people for the IoP, smart governance for the IoD, smart environments for the IoT, and smart mobility and smart economy for the IoS. Vilarinho et al. (2013) note that "social networks connect people while Internet of things platforms connect things" based on platforms that "use various communication tools in efficient ways." Atzori, Iera, and Morabito (2017) seek to provide an understanding of the IoT in terms of the "evolutionary stages" as "generations" in the development of the phenomenon beginning with "tagged things", as in RFID, to "interconnection of Things and the (social) Web of Things" to the "age of social objects, cloud computing, and future internet." It is worth noting that Naunes et al. (2018) point to the likelihood "that human-machine collaboration will play an important role in future technologies."

In summary, key issues, controversies, and challenges for the IoT in smart cites are highlighted in Figure 1. The economic costs associated with the development of infrastructure to support IoT testing, prototyping, and implementation are highlighted (Alavi et al., 2018) along with IoT interoperability challenges related to open data, heterogeneous devices, and technologies more generally (Lea and Blackstock, 2014; Zanella et al., 2014; Ahlgren et al., 2016). Geographies and spatial sensibilities (Mattern, 2017) emerge as well as the social impacts anticipated for communities and individuals (Alavi et al., 2018) in terms of IoT planning, design, and deployment influencing people and their habits and well-being. Sensing is highlighted as it pertains to meta-sensing, participatory sensing, and sensing services with people-in-the-loop, along with sensing technologies extending beyond conventional urban limitations (Konomi and Sasao, 2018).

Figure 1. Overview of key IoT issues, controversies, and challenges for smart cities

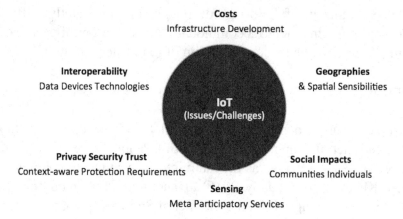

A range of privacy, security, and trust issues are identified by Sicari et al. (2015) pertaining to data confidentiality, access control, users and things, and the enforcement of policies, along with issues of openness and scalability.

3.2 Awareness and the Internet of People (IoP)

Awareness and the IoP is explored in this section in terms of emerging understandings of the IoP, the multidisciplinary and multisensory, and the Internet of All (IoA).

The IoP Speaks

Cuff, Hansen, and Kang (2008) describe the notion of "urban sensing" pointing to "a fundamental shift" that is occurring in pervasive computing, moving "from the lab to the environment" and "into the realms of politics, aesthetics, interpretation, and motivation" involving "a more contentious move to the city." Cuff et al. (2008) refer to "embedded networked sensing" and the likelihood that "citizens will be the target of data collection." In the context of smart cities and the future Internet, Hernández-Muñoz et al. (2011) describe the IoP as "people becoming part of ubiquitous intelligent networks having the potential to seamlessly connect, interact and exchange information about themselves and their social context and environment." According to Miranda et al. (2015) key principles of the IoP include: social, personalized, proactive, and predictable. Estrin (2011) described a range of participatory urban sensing research projects involving people and their use of mobile phone technologies. Judge and Powles (2015) identify the need to "forget about the things" and "stop obsessing over 'smart' objects" and begin "thinking smart about people." As such, Judge and Powles (2015) maintain that, "we maneuver things with our bodies unthinkingly" in "performing immensely complicated calculations without even being aware of it" reminding us that "the world is full of information that we access instinctively." Judge and Powles (2015) pose the question – "what if, like the Pompidou Centre, the pipes of each thing were worn on the outside?" Judge and Powles (2015) point to the enormous "potential of the internet of things" in that "it could put our vast stores of tacit, embodied knowledge to work online" serving to "unite the physical and digital worlds." For Judge and Powles (2015), the IoT "could put us in control of our own information and contextual integrity" so as to "become an internet, not of smart things, but of smart, empowered people." Judge and Powles (2015) admit that "it's hard to see what this would look like, exactly" adding that "imagining it shouldn't just be delegated to tech companies and opportunists riding the hype cycle" but should extend to "artists, designers, philosophers, lawyers, psychologists, and social workers" to be "just as involved as engineers and internet users in shaping our collective digital future." Conti, Passarella, and Das (2017) advance the notion of "a radically new Internet paradigm" in the form of "the Internet of People (IoP)" designed as space for people to "become active elements of the Internet" as in, cyber-physical convergence, moving beyond earlier thinking "where humans and their personal devices are seen merely as end users of applications." Judge and Powles (2015) observe that "the internet has become such an ubiquitous part of our lives that we tend to forget that it is in its infancy" and that "it's still a crude prototype of what it could be" so that "the internet of the future doesn't have to be like the internet of today: flat, monopolized and dangerously opaque" because "its form, contours and feel are still, quite literally, up for grabs" giving way to more imaginative possibilities and creative opportunities.

Speaking of the Multidisciplinary and Multisensory

The introduction of the *Ambiances Review* by Thibaud (2013) highlighted the importance of the sensory world in urban spaces. From a human geography perspective, Lévy et al. (2015) indicate that people are: multi-sensorial; able to interact with the world in multiple ways; and capable of interacting "through immaterial vectors" including telecommunications and the Internet as space.

Lévy et al. (2015) described the concept of spaces as environments and the notion of spatialities as actors in an urban context. According to Lévy et al. (2015) people are space and "we are constantly changed by space" and "we constantly change it through our acts." For Baude (2015) the space of the Internet is an innovation of space contributing to a new kind of space that is being evolved and remade by our emerging uses. Indeed, Peterson (2016) claims that the "IoP is not just more sensor data, but it is a learning process or a study of how people interact with sensor data." Piga and Salerno (2017) provide a multidisciplinary and multisensory approach to urban design and representation.

Speaking of the Internet of All (IoA)

Enabled by advances in "miniaturization, computational power, sensing, information linkage, and machine learning" along with mobile devices, smartphones and social networking, Naunes, Sá Silva, and Boavida (2018) point to the "range, limits, and possibilities of these new 'human-aware' paradigms." As such, a general reference model is defined for the Internet of All (IoA) "where human actions become a fundamental part of the control loop of CPSs" (Cyber-Physical Systems) according to Naunes et al. (2018). In this model what emerges is a theory for *humans in the loop cyber-physical systems* (HiTLCPS) focusing on the role of humans in three basic processes– data acquisition, state inference, and actuation. Described by Naunes et al. (2018), data acquisition refers to "data related to the human individual" that "is gathered from the available sensors" and "is then processed in the 'state inference' stage with the objective of inferring the human's physical and/ or psychological state." Naunes et al. (2018) note that, "some approaches may attempt to predict future states based on historical data and the current state." The final process is that of actuation where "the system may or may not perform certain actions based on the observed state." Systems are described as: a) "open loop" such that they "do not affect the system while their results are merely informative, without direct actuation" or, b) as "closed loop" and "actuate directly on the environment or the human." Naunes et al. (2018) refer to this model as the Internet of all (IoA) "meaning that it includes not only (traditional) IoT but all humans as fundamental elements" so as to "emphasize that this Internet is made by humans, for humans, and with humans." Naunes et al. (2018) explain that "IoA is built from spatially distributed devices" from "standard IoT like laptops, mobile phones, sensors, actuators, network elements, RFID tags, cars, intelligent clothes, wearable devices, home appliances" to "robotics and its interaction with intelligent devices and sensors" and "on top of these man-made devices" are "human beings themselves as part of the system" in terms of "their actions, drives, desires, and emotions." Three types of HiTL control are identified including applications: 1) enabling direct human control of the system (*human control*); 2) enabling passive monitoring of humans by the system and the taking of "appropriate actions (*human monitoring*)"; and 3) hybrids of the two (Naunes et al., 2018). McKenna (2018b) explored the IoP in relation to responsive cities and developed an ambient urbanizing framework for the IoT-IoP in smart cities using the constructs of awareness, creativity, and serendipity in support of designs, spaces, things, and interactions in fostering potentials for ambient creativity.

Figure 2 highlights in summary form key issues, controversies, and challenges for the IoP in smart cities.

Cuff et al. (2008) flagged the potential for people to become data collection targets in urban sensing projects while Estrin (2011) describes participatory urban sensing projects involving people and their mobile phone use. Hernández-Muñoz et al. (2011) describe seamless networks where people are able to connect, interact, and exchange personal, social, and contextual information. Judge and Powles (2015) argue for an IoP in support of smart empowered people in control of their own contextual integrity and cognizant of people and their instinctual and tacit capabilities. Lévy et al. (2015) identify the importance of people as space and actors in urban spaces while Peterson (2016) points to the importance of sensor data in terms of learning about how

Figure 2. Overview of key IoP issues, controversies, and challenges for smart cities

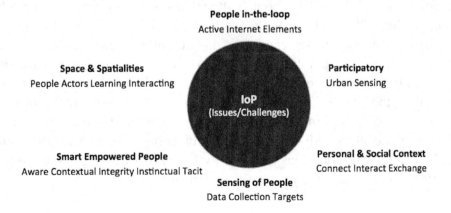

people interact with this type of data. While people are included in humans in-the-loop (HiTL) as active Internet elements in the Internet of All (IoA) articulated by Naunes et al. (2018) where humans have direct control in one mode, perhaps more controversial is the mode where people are monitored by the system, which takes "appropriate actions." It is worth noting that in work pertaining to the IoT and the IoP (McKenna, 2018b) an area identified for further research is that of the Internet of Experiences (IoE) "as a complement to the Internet of People" while also serving to expand the ambient urbanizing framework for the IoT-IoP in smart cities.

3.3 Awareness and the Internet of Experiences

Although Herzberg (2017) refers to the IoE as the Internet of Everything, for the purposes of this work the Internet of Experiences is referred to as the IoE.

From a knowledge management perspective, Wellsandt et al. (2013) advance "an experience-centered approach for innovation enabled by the Internet of Experience" based on "experience from intelligent objects and human users." Wilber (2016) claims that "at its most basic level, the IoT offers an affordable means to understand and manage real-world things from a distance" such that "a thermostat, for example" is provided with "the data and capabilities" needed for devices "to manage themselves." For Wilber (2016), "once the things in the IoT are connected and given a voice, they become more than just 'things'" in that "they become contributors to what beckons just beyond the IoT" giving way to the Internet of Experiences (IoE). Wilber (2016) describes the IoE in terms of "personal, evolving experiences" whereby "conventional physical products are mere 'delivery vehicles,' or conduits, for ever-evolving experiences." According to Wilber (2016) "this transformation is already evident" taking the form of product upgrades that "arrive in consumers' homes virtually" through "ongoing software updates to devices they already own." Wilber (2016) draws on the work of Pine, known for developing the concept of 'the experience economy' and co-author James Gilmore (Pine and Gilmore, 2011), pointing to the importance of personalization and the potential for the IoE to highlight the individual as the focus for engagement. Describing the Virtual Singapore Project, Moore (2017) speaks of the Internet of Things and the Internet of Experience "to augment the interface and its diverse applications." Moore (2017) cites Ingeborg Rocker, Vice President of the Project who identifies the need to "adapt to what is going to be the best way for the user to have a tactile experience."

As depicted in Figure 3, key issues, controversies and challenges associated with the IoE in smart cities pertain to the personal nature of experiences, the dynamic and trackable nature of people's interactions and interests, and the evolving and updatable aspects of people's experiences.

3.4 Issues, Controversies, Problems

Issues, controversies, and problems associated with the IoT, the IoP, and the IoE in smart cities begin to emerge in the review of the research literature explored in this chapter, with a few examples provided below. While coverage of issues, controversies, and problems is not intended to be exhaustive or comprehensive this work seeks to highlight the nature, variety, and range.

Issues

Cuff et al. (2008) call for "careful, transdiscipinary study" of this "transition" to "urban sensing" enabled through technologies such as the IoT, the IoP, and the IoE since it will "touch on issues that go far beyond the scientific realm." Acknowledging the value of social networks and IoT platforms, Vilarinho et al. (2013) argue that a key issue is that "platforms for things often don't communicate and interoperate with social networks." Perera et al. (2014) identify "open challenges and issues" with the sensing as a service model in the

Figure 3. Overview of key IoE issues, controversies, and challenges for smart cities

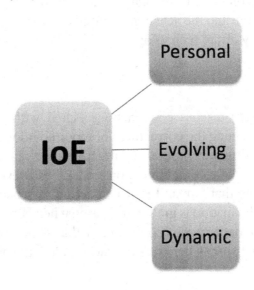

context of the IoT and smart cities in terms of the "technological, economical, and social" or a combination of categories. While understandings of the IoE as advanced by Wilber (2016) emerge from economics and marketing, this work points to the potential for other value associated with well-being, quality of life, learning, creativity and the like. Similarly, where Wilber (2016) describes the updatable nature of devices such as a thermostat, this work looks to the potential for learning more about people's experiences in urban contexts.

Controversies

Using the examples of big data in an environmental context, Gabrys (2016) discusses types of data practices, materializations, and contestations along with "how data is sensed, felt, placed, or accounted for" and how this data "comes into form, is constructed and also stabilized" pointing to the interplay of people and technologies. Where human sensing capabilities may be challenged, Mone (2018) describes "sensory substitution technologies" as coming of age and possibly less hotly contested in the form of "apps and devices that collect visual, auditory, and in some cases haptic stimuli, and feed the information to the user through another sensory channel." The "informed designs" advanced by Lindley et al. (2019) as an alternative to their claim that privacy by design (PbD) and human-centered designs (HCD) paradigms for privacy are not "rational" would seem to support this work in terms of the emphasis here on the importance of fostering more aware people in relation to aware technologies. In this chapter, the notion of more aware people takes the form of recognizing and fostering the multi-sensorial capabilities of people and the sensing potentials of people that may enhance and be enhanced by aware technologies.

Problems

Naunes et al. (2018) discuss concerns associated with "unreliable data" noting that, "ascertaining the correctness of reported information is referred to as the 'truth estimation problem'" affecting "the ability of humans to act as both sensors and communication nodes." However, Naunes et al. (2018) acknowledge that "much like when acting as sensors, the ability of communicating information is greatly increased when humans and machines work together." Naunes et al. (2018) claim that, "humans are no longer external entities that simply benefit from the system" in that "their presence, actions, and emotional states strongly affect how IoT things react" adding that, "human information should not be undervalued." For Naunes et al. (2018), in humans in-the-loop cyber physical systems (HiTLCPSs), human and machine actuation go hand-in-hand and can often complement each other" such that "IoA systems are not 'devoid of human soul' but make human actuation an integral part of their functioning."

However, this work argues that 'human-aware' paradigms described by Naunes et al. (2018) will benefit from being complemented by understandings in this chapter of *aware human paradigms* given form through ambient urbanities. As such, the combination of aware people and aware technologies contributes to understandings of ambient environments, situations, events, and dynamics that are emergent, adaptive, unplanned, and unexpected.

In tabulated form, by year and author, an overview is provided in Table 1 of perspectives on issues, controversies, and problems emerging from the research literature for the IoT, IoP, and IoE. Perspectives range from costs associated with IoT development to geographies and spatial sensibilities, to interoperability, to privacy/security/trust, to sensing, and to social impacts. For the IoP, perspectives range from the cyber-physical and humans in-the-loop to space and spatialities, to empowering people, to the predictive and proactive, to learning about people interacting with sensor data, to the multi-sensorial capabilities of people, to participatory and other forms of sensing, to the sensing of people as data targets, and to the social and personal.

For the IoE perspectives focus mostly on the personal with the potential for personalization. Spatially and geographically, the concern by Mattern (2017) with "experiencing and representing place" points to the importance of multi-sensory, multi-dimensional, and multi-domain awareness in relation to the design and use of technologies for enhancing, augmenting, and learning in and beyond urban environments. From sensing as a service (Perera et al. 2014) to human in the loop (Konomi and Sasao, 2018) privacy challenges figure strongly, among other issues, and efforts to demonstrate potential benefits for awareness and more informed decision making are advanced.

Figure 4 provides an overview of emerging characteristics of the IoT, the IoP, and the IoE at a glance as a way of illustrating the evolving elements of the developing relationships and interactions between aware technologies and aware people in smart environments, with implications more broadly for understandings of ambient urbanities.

Table 1. Perspectives on issues, controversies, and problems for the IoT, IoP, and IoE in smart cities

Author(s)	Year	IoT	IoP	IoE
Lindley et al.	2019	PrivacyByDesign/HCD as irrational		
Alavi et al.	2018	Cost; Social Impacts		
Konomi & Sasao	2018	Sensing (participatory, meta, etc.)		
Naunes et al.	2018		Cyber-Physical/HiTL	
Conti et al.	2017		Cyber-Physical	
Mattern	2017	Geographies & Spatial Sensibilities		
Piga & Salerno	2017		Multi-sensorial	
Wilber	2017			Personal
Lévy et al.	2015		Space & Spatialities	
Ahlgren et al.	2016	Interoperability		
Peterson	2016		Learning & sensors	
Judge & Powles	2015		Potential to Empower	
Lévy et al.	2015		Multi-sensorial	
Miranda et al.	2015		Predictive, Proactive Social, Personal	
Sicari et al.	2015	Privacy/Security/Trust (data, access, control, etc.)		
Lea & Blackstock; Zanella et al.	2014	Interoperability		
Estrin	2011		Sensing/Participatory	
Hernández-Muñoz et al.	2011		Seamless sharing	
Cuff et al.	2008		Sensing (people as data targets)	

Figure 4. Characteristics of the IoT – IoP – IoE at a glance

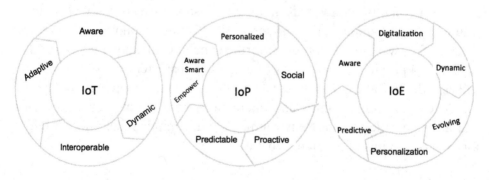

It is worth noting that the IoT, the IoP, and the IoE are characterized by the elements of being aware and dynamic. The adaptive and interoperable elements of the IoT support the potential for the predictable, proactive, social, and personalized elements of the IoP and in turn, for the predictive and personalization elements of the IoE. The aware and smart elements of the IoP have the potential for people to empower themselves in any number of ways through innovation and other creative opportunities. Similarly, the digitalization of experience in the IoE and the evolving nature of this space point to considerable potential.

By way of solutions and recommendations, the issues, controversies, and problems highlighted in this Section are re-conceptualized as challenges and opportunities to be addressed through operationalization of selected elements of the ambient urbanities framework in Section 4.

4. SENSING THE CITY: AWARE PEOPLE AND TECHNOLOGIES IN SMART CITIES

In response to the range of perspectives presented in Section 3 from a review of the research literature on awareness and smart cities in relation to the IoT, IoP, and IoE, formulation of a framework for sensing cities and getting smarter, centered on the notion of aware people in combination with aware technologies, is described in Section 4.1.

4.1 Conceptual Framework for Sensing Cities and Getting Smarter

Sensing in cities is often approached from a technological perspective involving the use of sensor and embedded technologies and increasingly, the leveraging of the IoT (SMC, 2017). This work seeks to extend the technological approach to sensing to include the multi-sensorial capabilities of people in moving toward further realizations of the IoP. Additionally, this work seeks to act upon Pendleton-Julian's notion of "instrumentalizing the products of the imagination" (Jenkins, 2016) to complement and extend the instrumentation of the smart city (SMC, 2017) in moving toward further realizations of the potential of the IoE. As such, this work explores with people their multi-sensorial capabilities for sensing in the city, using an adaptation of Anderson's intuitive inquiry method (2004) along with an adaptation of Anderson's (2011) body insight scale (BIS), as a mechanism for operationalizing the framework for sensing cities and getting smarter. The intuitive inquiry method and the BIS are described in more detail in Section 4.2.1 focusing on a range of elements in the city in relation to designs – spaces – interactions – smartness, in advancing solutions and recommendations to the issues, controversies, and problems identified in Section 3.4.

A conceptual framework for awareness and smart cities was advanced by McKenna (2016) in relation to the physical/material, aware technologies, and social/media where awareness is said to be "enabled through noticing, sensing, sharing" in smartness-enabled urban spaces. In exploring spaces for action based on awareness, McKenna (2017) proposed the ambient urbanizing framework for enriching spaces, things, and designs in smart cities involving city-focused social media. These two frameworks were extended (McKenna, 2018b) to form the ambient urbanizing framework for the IoT-IoP in smart cities focusing on the construct of awareness in relation to creativity and serendipity. As illustrated in Figure 5, this chapter proposes further extending of earlier frameworks in the form of a framework for sensing cities and getting smarter using the construct of awareness in relation to sensors and sensing in emerging contexts of the IoT, the IoP, and the IoE where potentials are explored for fostering evolving designs, spaces, interactions, and smartness.

In Section 4.2 this framework is operationalized for use in this chapter to explore solutions and recommendations for the issues, controversies, and challenges posed by the IoT, IoP, and IoE in smart cities as presented in Section 3.

Figure 5. Framework for sensing cities and getting smarter with the IoT, IoP, and IoE

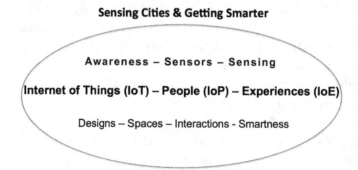

4.2 Sensing in the City and Getting Smarter: Solutions and Recommendations

Highlighting the people component of smart cities, the key question posed in this chapter is:

Q: How does *awareness* inform urbanity in smart cities?

This question is restated as a proposition under exploration in this chapter, as follows:

P: *Awareness* informs urbanity in smart cities through sensing and getting smarter, aided by the Internet of Things (IoT), the Internet of People (IoP), and the Internet of Experiences (IoE) influencing designs, spaces, interactions, and smartness.

How awareness informs urbanity is explored first through an online survey followed by interview discussions using Anderson's (2006) measures for a body insight scale (BIS) as described in Section 4.2.1. How awareness informs urbanity is then explored through in-depth interviews enabling discussion of sensing in the city in relation to aware technologies as described in Section 4.2.2. A discussion of findings in relation to sensing, awareness, and urbanities is provided in Section 4.2.3.

4.2.1 Awareness, Urbanity, and Subtle Human Qualities

Intuitive inquiry incorporates the body insight scale (BIS) (Anderson, 2006), consisting of the three sub-scales, as follows:

- **Energy Body:** "Measures awareness of energy inside and surrounding your physical body"
- **Comfort Body:** "Measures feelings of ease and satisfaction with your body in everyday life"
- **Inner Body:** "Measures awareness of minor changes inside the body and the relationship of these sensations to immediate and changing circumstances"

Intuitive inquiry is referred to as 'innovative' and 'crossing boundaries' (Anderson, 2004) and contains characteristics relevant to sensibilities. The BIS scale was designed for "assessing subtle human qualities" and this body insight scale (Anderson, 2011), formerly the body intelligence scale (Anderson, 2006), consists of the three subscales – energy body awareness (E-BAS); comfort body awareness (C-BAS); and inner body awareness (I-BAS). Anderson encourages use of the scale in other domains and it is expected that all three subscales – E-BAS, C-BAS, and I- BAS may enable exploring and learning about 'subtle human qualities' pertaining to movements, interactions, and practices in urban environments in this work. Where use of the scale in urban contexts was explored in relation to awareness and smart city implementation (McKenna, 2018a) and also as an approach for exploring people-aware quantified experience (McKenna, 2019), in this current chapter, the BIS may contribute to an understanding of ambient urbanities on the one hand and on the other, to the potential for shedding light on human sensing and associated behaviors in the context of smart cities. It is worth noting that work by the ITU (2015) provides a comparison of indicators for smart sustainable cities (SSC) where 22 indicators are identified, some of which are associated with quality of life including comfort, security, and safety. Societal performance indicators (ITU, 2015) from the viewpoint of residents of a city include convenient, comfortable, secure, and safe.

Three questions from the BIS were adapted for use in this work as follows:

1. Regarding your body awareness in your city, would you agree that your body lets you know when your environment is safe (On a scale of 1 to 7 on a continuum of disagree to agree)?
2. Regarding your comfort body awareness in your city, would you agree that you feel comfortable in your city most of the time (On a scale of 1 to 7)?
3. Regarding your inner body awareness in your city, would you agree that you can feel your body tighten up when you are angry (On a scale of 1 to 7)?

Exploratory use of the BIS was well received in that people tended to engage with the questions without reservation, responding with readiness and awareness. Initially a 5-point scale was used but then extended to a 7-point scale, based on suggestions from people during interviews. Extending the scale from 5 to 7 points allows for greater range in response, described by Pearse (2011) as granularity, believed to achieve more precision, validity and reliability, and usefulness of data. It is worth noting that after extending the scale from 5 to 7 points, people still tended to respond emphatically at the higher end (67%) in the case of question 1 related to body awareness and feeling safe. However, responses also emerged toward the lower end of the scale (33%) for question 1 where people were visitors to a city. Regarding question 2 related to feelings of comfort in the city, while responses emerged at the upper end of the scale (33%), a higher percentage emerged toward the lower end at position 3 (67%), signaling issues requiring further probing. For example, responses would drop to the lower range when respondents identified a design or other urban issue affecting one's sense of comfort. Regarding question 3 related to inner body awareness and feelings of tension and anger, responses were evenly spread (33%) across positions 4, 5, and 6. It is worth noting that responses toward the upper end tended to emerge for smaller cities but shifted to the mid-range as respondents considered their experiences in larger cities.

4.2.2 Awareness, Urbanity, and Aware Technologies

How awareness informs urbanity was also explored through protocol-guided interviews and open-ended survey questions focusing discussions on sensing in the city in relation to aware technologies. This mixing of methods provided an opportunity for exploration of the human multi-sensorial awareness capability, along with spontaneous, interwoven interactions with aware technologies (e.g. smartphones, etc.) and emergent renderings of the Internet of Things (IoT), the Internet of People (IoP), and the Internet of Experiences (IoE). Focus for this exploration centered on the elements of pulse, vibrancy, space, and spatialities (actors).

An overview and summary of sensing the city through aware people and aware technologies including the IoT, the IoP, and the IoE focusing on the elements of pulse, vibrancy, space, and spatialities (actors in space) is provided through an exploration of awareness in relation to sensing and smartness as depicted in Figure 6.

Pulse

Awareness of the pulse of the city highlighted a range of elements that figure strongly in relation to buildings; businesses; gatherings; mobility and movement; nightlife; the people; and the students. For example, a city councilor referred to technology "as a tool that will allow people to connect

Figure 6. Sensing the city through the pulse, vibrancy, space, and spatialities

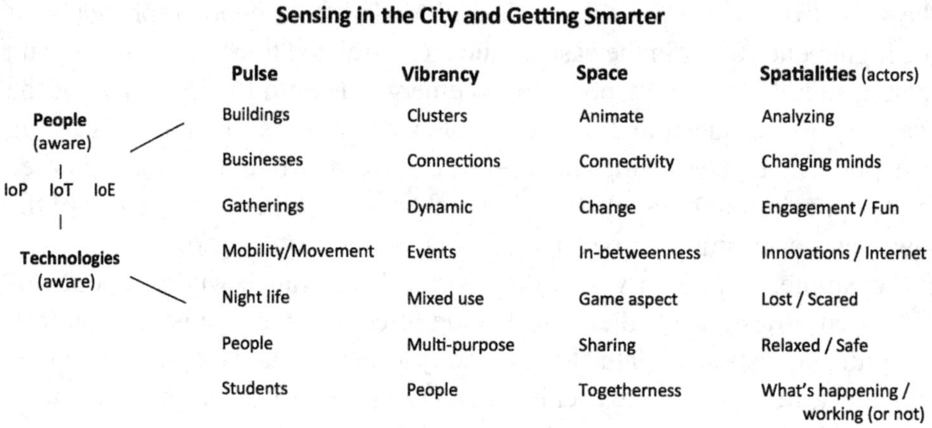

Sensing in the City and Getting Smarter

	Pulse	Vibrancy	Space	Spatialities (actors)
People (aware)	Buildings	Clusters	Animate	Analyzing
	Businesses	Connections	Connectivity	Changing minds
IoP IoT IoE	Gatherings	Dynamic	Change	Engagement / Fun
	Mobility/Movement	Events	In-betweenness	Innovations / Internet
Technologies (aware)	Night life	Mixed use	Game aspect	Lost / Scared
	People	Multi-purpose	Sharing	Relaxed / Safe
	Students	People	Togetherness	What's happening / working (or not)

to each other and to their surroundings" while city information technology (IT) staff described the IoT as "more about the instrumentation of things, with everything connected and communicated."

Vibrancy

Awareness of the vibrancy of the city was identified in relation to the elements of clusters of people; connections; dynamic aspects; events; mixed-use; multi-purpose; and again, very simply, the people. For example, a city councilor commented that "vibrancy is created by people and connections between people," adding that, "the way that comes to life" is by "creating activity."

Space

Awareness of the space of the city was highlighted in terms of the potentials for animating a space; connectivity; change; in-betweenness; the game aspect; sharing; and togetherness. For example, an educator referred to a locally developed mobile app with the potential for anyone in the city "to transform contributions both in terms of unique ideas and patterns into the design of some urban space or buildings."

Spatialities

Awareness of spatialities, as in, actors in urban spaces, was highlighted in terms of analyzing; changing minds; engagement linked with fun; innovation generally and in relation to the Internet; the sense of feeling lost or feeling scared in the city; feeling relaxed in the city and safe; and the importance of knowing what is happening in the city and being able to participate in identifying what is working and what is not working. For example, the phenomenon of "accidental data collection" and "data that I don't think anybody saw a need for" was highlighted by city IT staff. Additionally, it was noted that open, diverse datasets enable "data analysis that you've not thought of" with the potential for uses that are "serendipitous or accidental" or "unintended" and not "even in our mindset" contributing to the potential for unforeseen value.

Patterns, flows, relationships, and possibilities begin to emerge enabling a glimpse of the overlapping, challenging, and complex nature of sensing in the city. Awareness emerged in discussions with people in terms of the pulse, vibrancy, space, and spatialities (actors in urban spaces) of the city, spanning a wide variety of elements. As such, this exploration would seem to support the claims by Tursic (2017) that "urbanity belongs to the type of unplanned and unintended phenomena that emerge from people's intensions and actions."

4.2.3 Discussion of Sensing, Awareness, and Urbanities

Findings in this chapter, summarized in Figure 6, highlight the interweaving of people and technologies in urban spaces; the increasing seamlessness of the physical and digital; and the overlapping and intermingling of many elements of the experience of city life in support of interaction, connection, and connectivity. In response to issues, controversies, and problems associated with sensing identified in this chapter, along with findings from urban explorations, Figure 7 advances a framework for ambient sensing in smart city urbanities. Through sensing by aware people drawing on their multi-sensorial capabilities, a more personalized approach is enabled to complement and extend sensing by aware technologies. Elements of urbanity in terms of pulse, space, spatialities (actors), and vibrancy guide explorations while awareness is investigated using an adapted and minimal version of the body insight scale (BIS) in urban environments in terms of more aware people sensing through internal/external affective capabilities based on body energy, feelings of comfort, and feelings of safety.

Aided by assessment tools such as Anderson's Body Insight Scale (BIS) and subscales, the evolving of such tools for use with the IoT and other emerging and aware technologies, the potential for new pathways to be created for linkages between more aware people and the IoT, the IoP, and the IoE begin to

Figure 7. Framework for ambient sensing in smart city urbanities

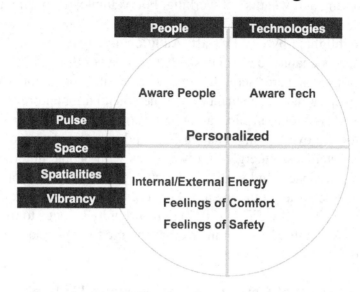

emerge. Further, development and use of the BIS and subscales may provide important intersections with other smart city indices (ITU, 2015) contributing to improved comfort, safety, security, and livability. Indeed, evolving of the BIS and subscales for use in contemporary urban environments could begin to contribute insight into the notion of "smart, empowered people" advanced by Judge and Powles (2015) and to the ambient awareness and ambient urbanities constructs. As such, awareness is integrally interwoven into the urban fabric in the form of aware people interacting through and with aware technologies and with each other, influencing designs, spaces, interactions, and smartness.

This chapter points to the potential for multi-sensorial awareness by people in urban spaces to inform safety, comfort, and affective states as variables relevant to the study and practice of ambient urbanities in smart cities.

Dependent Variable (DV)

The dependent variable (DV) emerging from this chapter is *awareness and affect.* Associated independent variables include: feelings of comfort and urban elements; feelings of safety and sense of the city; and feelings of tension and urban experience. Such variables may also benefit city officials, community members, and others involved in governance practices and with urban planning, design, and engagement.

5. FUTURE DIRECTIONS

Going forward, this chapter points to the potential for further explorations in the spaces of both practice and research, as described in Sections 5.1 and 5.2, respectively.

5.1 Practice

In practical terms, potential exists for application of the body insight scale (BIS) in urban spaces as well as for the variables emerging from this chapter to enhance or extend selected ITU (2015) indicators.

Body Insight Scale (BIS)

Based on early stage guidance provided in this chapter, potential exists for application of the BIS to inquiry informed by people and their everyday awareness in urban spaces on the one hand, and their uses of aware technologies and other sensing technologies on the other hand.

Variables and Indicators

Value may emerge from practical considerations of selected SSC (smart sustainable cities) indicators (ITU, 2015) in relation to the *awareness and affect* dependent variable and the independent variables of feelings of comfort and urban elements; feelings of safety and sense of the city; and feelings of tension and urban experience.

5.2 Research

This chapter opens the way for further exploration, debate, and theorizing related to intuitive inquiry, the body insight scale (BIS), and ambient sensing in the context of ambient urbanities.

Ambient Sensing

The ambient sensing concept advanced in this chapter opens the way for further explorations pertaining to the questions:

1. How are multi-sensorial capabilities affected, augmented, or extended by the use of say, smartphones, other smart devices, and sensing applications in urban spaces?
2. How are experiences of sensing the pulse, vibrancy, space, and spatialities of the city affected (positively or adversely) by the use of smartphones, sensing apps, and other sensing technologies?

Body Insight Scale (BIS)

This chapter contributes further support for application of the BIS to explorations of urban issues, controversies, and problems.

Intuitive Inquiry

This chapter serves to open discourse spaces for intuitive inquiry as a method for the exploration of awareness and smartness in urban contexts and in the smart cities domain more generally.

6. CONCLUSION

This chapter provides an overview of awareness in cities from the perspective of sensing in relation to aware people and aware technologies. A review of the research literature reveals a range of disciplinary perspectives on the Internet of Things (IoT), the Internet of People (IoP), and the Internet of Experiences (IoE), highlighting issues, controversies, and problems. The importance of interrelated and evolving characteristics associated with the IoT, the IoP, and IoE are also identified. In meeting the objectives of this chapter, awareness is explored and described as it manifests in the city through people and their experiences of sensing and smartness aided by exploratory use of the body insight scale (BIS). Through adaptation of the BIS for use in urban environments, people become more aware of their multi-sensorial capabilities, contributing to additional insights pertaining to where intelligence resides. As such, more aware people becoming more aware of, and interacting with aware technologies, sheds light on what constitutes and contributes to making cities smarter, and the notion by Böhlen and Frei (2010) of "re-making" and "augmenting urbanity." This work makes several contributions in that it: a) articulates and operationalizes a conceptual framework for sensing cities and getting smarter with the IoT, IoP, and IoE to explore and learn more about how awareness informs urbanity; b) offers insight into emergent understandings of sensing the city through pulse, vibrancy, space, and spatialities (actors) in the context of smart cities; and c) formulates a framework for ambient sensing in smart city urbanities to guide future directions for research and practice.

This chapter begins to give shape and details to the broader Ambient Urbanites Framework presented in Chapter 1 (Figure 4) through utilization of the awareness construct in articulating the sensing cities dimension. Use of the body insight scale enabled data collection and comparisons for experiences of the city by people in multiple cities in relation to feelings of comfort, safety, and tension serving as emerging evidence of the added value that sensing by more aware people affords. The analysis of findings in this chapter points to variables associated with *awareness and affect* relevant to the study, practice, and management of sensing in smart cities. As such, this chapter contributes to theorizing for 21st century cities, and to sensing associated with the urban, urbanities, and the ambient.

Insights of particular interest to the reader include the following:

1. Potential of multi-sensorial capabilities to inform designs, experiences, and smartness of urban spaces
2. The interconnectedness and interrelationships of the IoT, the IoP, and the IoE for ambient urbanities
3. The emergence of variables associated with *awareness and affect* for sensing in smart cities

Ideas highlighted in this chapter pertain to the following:

1. The importance of people becoming more aware of their multi-sensorial capabilities in urban spaces
2. The potential for urban environments infused with aware technologies to benefit from aware people
3. Ambient sensing as an integrating element for aware people and technologies in ambient urbanities

Lessons for the reader in this chapter are associated with the following:

1. The potential for the sensing by people in urban environments to augment aware systems
2. The potential for aware systems to enhance the multi-sensorial capabilities of people
3. The vast array of issues, controversies, and problems for the IoT, IoP, and IoE in urban environments

This work will be of interest to a diverse audience including, but not limited to, students; educators; urban planners, developers, innovators; businesses; community members; researchers; and practitioners concerned with emerging understandings of awareness for fostering more aware people in relation to smart city urbanities, aware technologies, and interdisciplinary approaches to addressing complex urban challenges and opportunities.

REFERENCES

Ahlgren, B., Hidell, M., & Ngai, E. C.-H. (2016). Internet of Things for smart cities: Interoperability and open data. *IEEE Internet Computing*, *20*(6), 52–56. doi:10.1109/MIC.2016.124

Alavi, A. H., Jiao, P., Buttlar, W. G., & Lajnef, N. (2018). Internet of Things-enabled smart cities: State-of-the-art and future trends. *Measurement*, *129*, 589–606. doi:10.1016/j.measurement.2018.07.067

Anderson, R. (2004). Intuitive inquiry: An epistemology of the heart for scientific inquiry. *The Humanistic Psychologist*, *32*(4), 307–341. doi:10.10 80/08873267.2004.9961758

Anderson, R. (2006). Body Intelligence Scale: Defining and measuring the intelligence of the body. *The Humanistic Psychologist*, *34*(4), 357–367. doi:10.120715473333thp3404_5

Anderson, R. (2011). *Body Insight Scale*. Retrieved 29 December 2017 from http://www.mindgarden.com/73-body-insight-scale#horizontalTab3

Atzori, Z., Iera, A., & Morabito, G. (2017). Understanding the Internet of Things: Definition, potentials, and societal role of a fast evolving paradigm. *Ad Hoc Networks*, *56*, 122–140. doi:10.1016/j.adhoc.2016.12.004

Beaude, B. (2015). Internet: A unique space of coexistence. In *EPFLx: SpaceX Exploring Humans' Space: An Introduction to Geographicity Massive. Open Online Course (MOOC), edX, Fall.* Lausanne, Switzerland: EPFL.

Böhlen, M., & Frei, H. (2010). Ambient intelligence in the city: Overview and new perspectives. In H. Nakashima, H. Aghajan, & J. C. Augusto (Eds.), *Handbook of ambient intelligence and smart environments* (pp. 911–938). New York, NY: Springer. doi:10.1007/978-0-387-93808-0_34

Conti, M., Passarella, A., & Das, S. K. (2017). The Internet of People (IoP): A new wave in pervasive mobile computing. *Pervasive and Mobile Computing, 41*, 1–27. doi:10.1016/j.pmcj.2017.07.009

Cuff, D., Hansen, M., & Kang, J. (2008). Urban sensing: Out of the woods. *Communications of the ACM, 51*(3), 24–33. doi:10.1145/1325555.1325562

Deakin, M., & Al Waer, H. (2011). From intelligent to smart cities. *Intelligent Buildings International, 3*(3), 140–152. doi:10.1080/17508975.2011.586671

Estrin, D. (2011). Participatory urban sensing. *Scientific American.* Retrieved 26 December 2016 from https://www.scientificamerican.com/citizen-science/participatory-urban-sensing-ucla/

Gabrys, J. (2016). Practicing, materialising, and contesting environmental data. *Big Data & Society.* Retrieved 26 December 2016 from http://journals.sagepub.com/doi/full/10.1177/2053951716673391

Gil-Garcia, J. R., Zhang, J., & Puron-Cid, G. (2016). Conceptualizing smartness in government: An integrative and multi-dimensional view. *Government Information Quarterly, 33*(3), 524–534. doi:10.1016/j.giq.2016.03.002

Guillemin, P., & Friess, P. (2009). *Internet of things strategic research roadmap. The Cluster of European Research Projects.* Tech. Rep., September 2009. Retrieved 24 December 2017 from http://www.internet-of-things-research.eu/pdf/IoT_Cluster_Strategic_Research_Agenda_2009.pdf

Guo, B., Riboni, D., & Hu, P. (Eds.). (2014). *Creating personal, social, and urban awareness through pervasive computing.* Hershey, PA: IGI Global. doi:10.4018/978-1-4666-4695-7

Hernández-Muñoz, J. M., Vercher, J. B., Muñoz, L., Galache, J. A., Presser, M., Hernández Gómez, L. A., & Pettersson, J. (2011). Smart cities at the forefront of the future Internet. In *Future Internet Assembly, LNCS 6656* (pp. 447–462). Springer. doi:10.1007/978-3-642-20898-0_32

Herzberg, C. (2017). *Smart cities, digital nations: How digital urban infrastructure can deliver a better life in tomorrow's crowded world.* Petaluma, CA: Roundtree Press.

ITU. (2012). *Terms and definitions for the Internet of Things. Series Y: Global information infrastructure, Internet protocol aspects and next-generation networks – Frameworks and functional architecture models. Recommendation ITU-T Y.2069.* Geneva, Switzerland: International Telecommunications Union.

ITU. (2015). *Key performance indicators definitions for smart sustainable cities. ITU-T Focus Group on Smart Sustainable Cities.* Geneva, Switzerland: International Telecommunications Union.

ITU. (2016). *Unleashing the potential of the Internet of Things.* Geneva, Switzerland: International Telecommunications Union. Retrieved 19 December 2017 from https://www.itu.int/en/publications/Documents/tsb/2016-InternetOfThings/mobile/index.html#p=90

Jenkins, H. (2016). *Mapping the pragmatic imagination: An interview with Ann M. Pendleton-Jullian. (Part 3).* Retrieved 16 December 2016 from http://henryjenkins.org/2016/11/mapping-the-pragmatic-imagination-an-interview-with-ann-m-pendleton-jullian-part-3.html

Judge, J., & Powles, J. (2015). Forget the internet of things – we need an internet of people. *The Guardian.* Retrieved 21 December 2017 from https://www.theguardian.com/technology/2015/may/25/forget-internet-of-things-people

Khatoun, R., & Zeadally, S. (2016). Smart cities: Concepts, architectures, research opportunities. *Communications of the ACM*, *59*(8), 46–57. doi:10.1145/2858789

Konomi, S., & Sasao, T. (2018). Designing a mobile behavior sampling tool for spatial analytics. In N. Streitz & S. Konomi (Eds.), *DAPI 2018, LNCS 10922* (pp. 92–100). doi:10.1007/978-3-319-91131-1_7

Lea, R., & Blackstock, M. (2014). Smart cities: An IoT-centric approach. IWWIS'14. In *Proceedings of the 2014 International Workshop on Web Intelligence and Smart Sensing.* New York, NY: ACM.

Lévy, J. (2013). Inhabiting. In *The Sage Handbook of Human Geography* (Vol. 1, pp. 45–68). Newcastle: Sage.

Lévy, J. (2015). Urbanisation and urbanism. In *EPFLx: SpaceX Exploring Humans' Space: An Introduction to Geographicity. Massive Open Online Course (MOOC), edX, Fall*. Lausanne, Switzerland: EPFL.

Lévy, J., Beaude, B., Poncet, P., Noizet, H., Laurent-Lucchetti, B., Bahrani, F., ... Rommany, T. (2015). *EPFLx: SpaceX Exploring Humans' Space: An Introduction to Geographicity. Massive Open Online Course (MOOC), edX, Fall*. Lausanne, Switzerland: EPFL.

Lindley, J., Coulton, P., & Cooper, R. (2019). The IoT and unpacking the Heffalump's Trunk. In *Proceedings of the Future Technologies Conference (FTC) 2018* (pp. 134-151). Springer. 10.1007/978-3-030-02686-8_11

Loi, D. (2019). Ten guidelines for intelligent systems futures. In *Proceedings of the Future Technologies Conference (FTC) 2018* (pp. 788-805). Springer. 10.1007/978-3-030-02686-8_59

Mattern, S. (2017). Mapping's intelligent agents. *Places Journal*. Retrieved 19 December 2017 from https://placesjournal.org/article/mappings-intelligent-agents/

McKenna, H. P. (2016). Is it all about awareness? People, smart cities 3.0, and evolving spaces for IT. *ACM SIGMIS-CPR, 16*, 47–56.

McKenna, H. P. (2017). Urbanizing the ambient: Why people matter so much in smart cities. In S. Konomi & G. Roussos (Eds.), *Enriching urban spaces with ambient computing, the Internet of Things, and smart city design* (pp. 209–231). Hershey, PA: IGI Global. doi:10.4018/978-1-5225-0827-4.ch011

McKenna, H. P. (2018b). Creativity and ambient urbanizing at the intersection of the Internet of Things and People in smart cities. In M. Antona & C. Stephanidis (Eds.), *UAHCI 2018, LNCS 10908* (pp. 295–307). Springer. doi:10.1007/978-3-319-92052-8_23

McKenna, H. P. (2019). Exploring the quantified experience: Finding spaces for people and their voices in smarter more responsive cities. In *Proceedings of the Future Technologies Conference (FTC) 2018* (pp. 269-282). Springer. 10.1007/978-3-030-02686-8_22

McKenna, H. P. (In Press). Awareness and smart city implementations: Sensing, sensors, and the IoT in the public sector. In J. R. Gil-Garcia, T. A. Pardo, & M. Gascó (Eds.), *Beyond smart and connected governments: Sensors and the Internet of Things in the public sector*. Springer.

Miranda, J., Mäkitalo, N., Garcia-Alonso, J., Berrocal, J., Mikkonen, T., Canal, C., & Murillo, J. M. (2015). From the Internet of Things to the Internet of People. *IEEE Internet Computing, 19*(2), 40–47. doi:10.1109/MIC.2015.24

Mone, G. (2018). Feeling sounds, hearing sights. *Communications of the ACM, 61*(1), 15–17. doi:10.1145/3157075

Moore, C. (2017). The virtual Singapore project aims to digitize an entire city. *Digital Trends*. Retrieved 8 January 2018 from https://www.digitaltrends.com/home/virtual-singapore-project-mapping-out-entire-city-in-3d/

Nam, T., & Pardo, T. A. (2011). Smart city as urban innovation: Focusing on management, policy, and context. *Proceedings of the 5th International Conference on Theory and Practice of Electronic Governance*, 185–194. 10.1145/2072069.2072100

Naunes, D., Sá Silva, J., & Boavida, F. (2018). *A practical guide to human-in-the-loop cyber-physical systems*. Hoboken, NJ: Wiley.

Park, E., del Pobil, A. P., & Kwon, S. J. (2018). The role of the Internet of Things (IoT) in smart cities: Technology roadmap-oriented approaches. *Sustainability, 10*(1388), 1–13. PMID:30607262

Pearse, N. (2011). Deciding on the scale granularity of response categories of Likert type scales: The case of a 21-point scale. *Electronic Journal of Business Research Methods, 9*(2), 159–171.

Perera, C., Zaslavsky, A., Christen, P., & Georgakopoulos, D. (2014). *Sensing as a service model for smart cities supported by Internet of Things*. Trans. Emerging Tel. Tech; doi:10.1002/ett.2704

Peterson, D. (2016). Internet of People (IoP): The next frontier for IoT. *TechTarget blog: IoT Agenda*. Retrieved 21 December 2017 from http://internetofthingsagenda.techtarget.com/blog/IoT-Agenda/Internet-of-People-IoP-The-next-frontier-for-IoT

Petrolo, R., Loscri, V., & Mitton, N. (2016). Cyber-physical objects as key elements for a smart cyber-city. In *Management of cyber-physical objects in the future Internet of Things*. Springer. doi:10.1007/978-3-319-26869-9_2

Piga, B. E. A., & Salerno, R. (Eds.). (2017). *Urban design and representation: A multidisciplinary and multisensory approach*. Cham, Switzerland: Springer. doi:10.1007/978-3-319-51804-6

Pine, B. J., & Gilmore, J. H. (2011). The Experience Economy. Boston, MA: Harvard Business School Publishing.

Rickert, T. (2013). *Ambient rhetoric: The attunements of rhetorical being.* Pittsburgh, PA: University of Pittsburgh Press. doi:10.2307/j.ctt5hjqwx

Ruiz-Correa, S., Santani, D., Ramírez-Salazar, B., Ruiz-Correa, I., Rendón-Huerta, F. A., Olmos-Carrillo, C., ... Gatica-Perez, D. (2017). SenseCityVity: Mobile crowdsourcing, urban awareness, and collective action in Mexico. *IEEE Pervasive Computing*, *16*(2), 44–53. doi:10.1109/MPRV.2017.32

Sicari, S., Rizzardi, A., Grieco, L. A., & Coen-Porisini, A. (2015). Security, privacy and trust in Internet of Things: The road ahead. *Computer Networks*, *76*, 146–164. doi:10.1016/j.comnet.2014.11.008

SMC. (2017). *Instrumentation and control.* Reston, VA: Smart Cities Council. Retrieved 13 December 2017 from https://smartcitiescouncil.com/smart-cities-information-center/instrumentation-and-control

Thibaud, J-P. (2013). Into the sensory world. *Ambiances: International Journal of Sensory Environment, Architecture and Space*, 188.

Thiele, L. (2017). Internet of Things: The quest for trust. *IEEE Design & Test*, *34*(6), 102–108. doi:10.1109/MDAT.2017.2757146

Torres, L., Pina, V., & Acerete, B. (2006). E-governance developments in EU cities: Reshaping government's relationship with citizens. *Governance: An International Journal of Policy, Administration and Institutions*, *19*(2), 272–302. doi:10.1111/j.1468-0491.2006.00315.x

Tursic, M. (2017). *Aesthetic space: The visible and the invisible in urban agency* (Thèse No. 6445). Lausanne, Switzerland: EPFL.

Vilarinho, T., Farshchian, B. A., Floch, J., & Mathisen, B. M. (2013). A communication framework for the Internet of People and Things based on the concept of activity feeds in social computing. *Proceedings of the 9th International Conference on Intelligent Environments*, 1-8. 10.1109/IE.2013.24

Wellsandt, S., Wuest, T., Durugbo, C., & Thoben, K. D. (2013). The Internet of Experiences – Towards an experience-centred innovation approach. In C. Emmanouilidis, M. Taisch, & D. Kiritsis (Eds.), *Advances in Production Management Systems. Competitive Manufacturing for Innovative Products and Services. APMS 2012. IFIP Advances in Information and Communication Technology* (Vol. 397, pp. 669–676). Berlin: Springer. doi:10.1007/978-3-642-40352-1_84

Wilber, L. (2016). Beyond the IoT: The Internet of Experiences will change the way the world operates. *Compass: The 3D Experience Magazine*. Retrieved 9 January 2018 from https://compassmag.3ds.com/#/8/Cover-Story/BEYOND-THE-IOT

Zanella, A., Bui, N., Castellani, A., Vangelista, L., & Zorzi, M. (2014). Internet of Things for Smart Cities. *IEEE Internet of Things Journal*, *1*(1), 22–32. doi:10.1109/JIOT.2014.2306328

ADDITIONAL READING

Anderson, R. (2011). Intuitive inquiry: Exploring the mirroring discourse of disease. In F. J. Wertz, K. Charmaz, L. M. McMullen, R. Josselson, R. Anderson, & E. McSpadden (Eds.), *Five ways of doing qualitative analysis: Phenomenological psychology, grounded theory, discourse analysis, narrative research, and intuitive inquiry*. New York, NY: The Guilford Press.

Batty, M. (2013). Big data, smart cities and city planning. *Dialogues in Human Geography*, *3*(3), 274–279. doi:10.1177/2043820613513390 PMID:29472982

Miller, B. (2018). Cities are rapidly taking on Internet of Things technology. *GovTech*. Retrieved 20 November 2018 from http://www.govtech.com/biz/data/Cities-Are-Rapidly-Taking-on-Internet-of-Things-Technology.html

Mitchell, W. J. (1995). *City of bits: Space, place, and the infobahn*. Cambridge, MA: The MIT Press.

Montgomery, C. (2014). *Happy city: Transforming our lives through urban design*. NY: Farrar, Straus and Giroux.

Mulder, I. (2015). Opening up: Towards a sociable smart city. In M. Foth & ... (Eds.), *Citizen's right to the digital city* (pp. 161–173). Singapore: Springer. doi:10.1007/978-981-287-919-6_9

Tonkiss, F. (2014). *Cities by design: The social life of urban form*. Hoboken, NJ: John Wiley & Sons.

Townsend, A. M. (2013). *Smart cities: Big data, civic hackers and the quest for a new utopia*. NY: W. W. Norton & Company.

KEY TERMS AND DEFINITIONS

Awareness: Awareness refers to the concept or quality of being aware as it applies to people on the one hand, to technologies on the other, and to a combination of aware people and aware technologies.

Internet of Experiences (IoE): Internet of experiences refers to the experiences of people enabled by the Internet and other aware technologies.

Internet of People (IoP): IoP refers to the connection and communication capabilities between people enabled by the internet and other aware technologies.

Internet of Things (IoT): IoT refers to the connection and communication capabilities between things enabled by the internet and other aware technologies.

Sensibilities: Sensibilities refer to subtle human multi-sensorial capabilities ranging from the emotional to the aesthetic.

Sensing: Sensing refers to human detection capabilities enabled by one or more senses, as in multi-sensorial.

Smart Cities: Smart cities are urban areas, regions, territories, and beyond that are characterized by aware and engaged people, in combination with and aided by, the use of awareness enhancing technologies for mobility, livability, and sustainability.

Smartness: Smartness pertains to the awareness of people, technologies, and any combination of people interacting with each other and/or technologies, or technologies interacting with each other and/or with people.

Spatialities: Spatialities refer to people as actors engaging, interacting, and participating in activities in urban spaces and beyond.

Chapter 3

New Urban Layers and Spaces:
Infrastructures, Experiences, and Interactions

ABSTRACT

This chapter explores infrastructures, experiences, and interactions in relation to emerging urban layers and spaces for engagement in the city. The purpose of this chapter is to shed light on the digital layers enabled by information and communication technologies, the internet of things, the internet of people, and other emerging technologies to complement and extend existing urban infrastructural layers. The research literature for infrastructures, experiences, and interactions is explored in this chapter in the context of smart cities, enabling identification of issues, controversies, and problems. Using an exploratory case study approach, solutions and recommendations are advanced. This chapter makes a contribution to 1) the research literature across multiple domains, 2) the identification of challenges and opportunities for research and practice relating to emerging urban layers and spaces going forward, and 3) the extending of existing understandings of urbanity to incorporate digital layers and spaces enabling connected, contextual, and continuous engagement.

DOI: 10.4018/978-1-5225-7882-6.ch003

1. INTRODUCTION

This chapter explores infrastructures (Finger, 2016), experiences (Dourish and Bell, 2011), and interactions (Vertesi, 2014) in relation to emerging urban layers and spaces for engagement in the city. The purpose of this chapter is to shed light on the digital layers enabled by information and communication technologies, the Internet of Things (IoT), the Internet of People (IoP), the Internet of Experiences (IoE), and other emerging technologies to complement and extend existing urban infrastructural layers. The research literature for infrastructures, experiences, and interactions is explored in this chapter in the context of smart cities, enabling identification of issues, controversies, and problems. Using an exploratory case study approach, solutions and recommendations are advanced. As such, this chapter presents an overview of emerging understandings of infrastructures in contemporary urban environments in terms of new digital layers and spaces in relation to existing physical and services layers and their complex intermingling (Finger, 2016).

Objectives: A key objective of this chapter is to explore emerging infrastructures, experiences, and interactions from the perspectives of diverse individuals across urban environments in terms of the potential for more connected, contextual, and continuous engagement. As such, the key question to be explored in this chapter is – How do new urban layers of urbanity enable spaces for engagement in smart cities?

2. BACKGROUND AND OVERVIEW

Highlighting the importance of urban experience in informatics research, Williams, Robles, and Dourish (2009) employ the concept of urbane-ing pointing to the importance of the social and technological aspects of infrastructures for material, spatial, and institutional interactions. Further motivating this work is the call by Luskin (2010), from a media psychology perspective, for discussions about the "human experience" of the "gadgets and gizmos" that constitute "important devices that we use in daily life." Information infrastructures as data infrastructures (Mattern, 2014) are highlighted along with materialized understandings of urban infrastructure (Smith, 2016) and the notion of inverse infrastructure (Egyedi and Mehos, 2012) in the form of emergent bottom-up initiatives. Described as ambient informatics, Payne and Burke (2015) combine aesthetics, technology, and innovative design in the creation of public experiences. Using the example of bus information, the project leverages pervasive computing to "communicate information in everyday environments" so that with a smartphone and an application such as Bus Next, people are able to access travel information (Payne and Burke, 2015). However, in the absence of a smartphone and app, an illuminated bench, glowing brighter as the bus approaches, communicates arrival information drawing on real-time data in support of more viable city, sidewalk, and wait-time experience (Payne and Burke, 2015). Smith (2016) distinguishes between physical urban infrastructure as roads and railways and the human infrastructure of materialized dialogue where talk and turn-taking occur between community members and planners, designers, and city managers. This materialized dialogue is said to be recursive, dynamic, unfinished, and characterized by fluid engagement, involving ongoing accommodation in the absence of perfect agreement (Gabrys, 2016).

Employing an emergent, exploratory case study approach and a framework developed from a review of the research literature, this exploration of engagement is operationalized through an inquiry into new urban layers and spaces in relation to infrastructures, experiences, and interactions placing an emphasis on the digital. This chapter makes a contribution to: a) the research literature across multiple domains; b) the identification of challenges and opportunities for research and practice relating to emerging urban layers and spaces going forward; and c) the extending of existing understandings of urbanity to incorporate digital layers and spaces enabling the potential for more meaningful engagement.

2.1 Definitions

For the purposes of this work, definitions for key terms used in this chapter are presented here based on the research literature.

- **Digitalization:** In the context of the digital or data layer, Finger (2016) describes digitalization as "the combination of the storage, the transmission, the networks and the analytics."
- **Infrastructure and Experience:** Dourish and Bell (2011) argue that linking infrastructure and experience reveals that, "infrastructures condition our encounters with the world in the course of our use of them."

- **Interactions:** Vertesi (2014) notes that, "when accomplished well, actors interweave the digital, optical, computational, and physical context of interaction so tightly that they are treated as copresent in practice."

2.2 Overview

This chapter provides a range of perspectives in Section 3 on urban layers and spaces focusing on infrastructures and smart cities; experiences, interactions, and smart cities; followed by an overview of issues, controversies, and problems. In identifying the potential for solutions and recommendations, Section 4 provides a conceptual framework for emerging layers and spaces in smart cities, using the construct of engagement as a mechanism for operationalization of the exploration under investigation in this chapter. Findings enable formulation of a framework for ambient engagement in smart city urbanities. Section 5 identifies future directions for research and practice and Section 6 concludes with chapter coverage highlights, the major contributions, along with the primary insights, ideas, and lessons.

The primary audiences for this chapter include students, educators, researchers, policy makers, community members, and urban practitioners concerned with leveraging new urban layers and spaces in smart cities as infrastructures, experiences, and interactions in addressing complex urban challenges and opportunities.

3. PERSPECTIVES ON URBAN LAYERS AND SPACES

This section provides a review of the research literature for infrastructures and smart cities; experiences, interactions, and smart cities; followed by a summary of the literature review with the identification and discussion of issues, controversies, and problems.

3.1 Infrastructures and Smart Cities

A review of the research literature for infrastructures and smart cities is provided in this section in relation to the physical, services, and digital layers; the experience of infrastructure; and inverse infrastructure.

Physical, Services, and Digital Infrastructures

Anthopoulos and Vakali (2012) explore the interrelations and reciprocities of urban planning and smart cities focusing on the user layer, service layer, infrastructure layer, and the data layer. Zygiaris (2013) identified six layers of a smart city, as: *city layer* (context); *the green city layer* (environmental sustainability); the *interconnection layer* (diffusion of green economies); the *instrumentation layer* (real-time smart meters and infrastructure sensors); the *open integration layer* (apps to communicate and share data, content, services, and information); the *application layer* (real-time responsive operation); and the *innovation layer* (foster new business opportunities). Mulder (2015) explores and advances the notion of opening up public sector information (PSI) for data release and data reuse as part of the co-creation of a sustainable information infrastructure. To this end, Mulder (2015) employs a "research-through-design approach" claiming that "connecting crucial partners can create sustainable infrastructures to opening up data" because experience with co-creatively releasing PSI, "fosters further social innovation" for "a more sociable smart city." Komninos (2015) refers to "a new spatiality of cities" encompassed by "multiple concepts" including *cyber cities*, *digital cities*, *intelligent cities*, and *smart cities*. This new spatiality for smart cities (Komninos, 2015) is described as ranging from "smart phones, mobile devices, smart meters, sensors and sensor networks, smart systems, embedded systems, smart environments" to "instrumentation sustaining the intelligence of cities." Weignen and Heuvelhof (2016) speak in terms of the next generation of physical urban infrastructures. According to Finger (2016), from a socio-technical perspective, there are three main layers of infrastructure in the smart city (physical, services, and data/digital) and underlying these are the technical, economic, social, environmental, and jurisdictional in support of efficiency, sustainability, and resilience. Finger (2016) claims that, "what is new is really this digital layer that comes in between" the physical and services infrastructure layers (PIL/SIL), adding that, "this changes everything." It is worth noting that many of the layers identified by Zygiaris (2013) pertain to the digital/data layer discussed by Finger (2016). Finger (2016) notes that ultimately what matters "is the quality of life in the city, the attractiveness of the city for firms and for the inhabitants, and the competitiveness of the city in international comparison." Finger speaks of "the role of information and communication technologies that are actually substantially changing, if not revolutionizing, the provision of urban infrastructure services" where

ICTs enable the data layer. Finger (2016) claims that the combination of the components of digitalization have a "disruptive effect on absolutely everything" including cities. For example, Finger (2016) argues that "the information contained in the data layer can be used to produce new services, new business models" while attracting "new customers." Alvarez (2017) addresses the relevance of informational infrastructures for future cities speaking in terms of "the creation of digital or 'smart' infrastructures" from the perspective of an "informational lens." Alvarez (2017) identifies the issues of "a silent privatization of the informational value of public spaces" along with "the under-development of the potential of 21st century digital infrastructures" associated with "a mono functional non-inclusive process of design." For Alvarez (2017), there is a need for cities "to adapt their design mentality and institutional models" in conjunction with fostering "social participation and open technology standards" in support of "our interactions with cities" enabling "new services and experiences." According to Alvarez (2017) "digital infrastructures grow in value by working with others" where "the value captured from the value they generate can expand dramatically when combined with more data." Further, Alvarez (2017) asserts that "the intangibility of the digital aspects of their new infrastructure systems makes it hard for cities to quantify or even comprehend their true value" making it "easy for companies to claim ownerships of the data generated using proprietary technologies." It is "in this sense" argues Alvarez (2017) that "public infrastructure systems can become privatized both in terms of functional and informational control, even when formal 'ownership' resides in city hall." For Alvarez (2017), engagement could take the form of "design exercises" and "technological demonstrations." Urssi (2018) describes the "urban informational ecosystem" where design, data and e urbanity contribute to the notion of "metacity" as "what we imagine for our cities in the near future" in terms of "an urban space, continuous and interlaced with information, new materials and projected forms" in support of "an enlarged and responsive daily life for our personal needs."

Experience of Infrastructure

Developing the concept of the "experience of infrastructure" in relation to ubiquitous computing (ubicomp), Dourish and Bell (2007) "point to ways in which infrastructure, rather than being hidden from view, becomes visible through our increasing dependence on it for the practices of everyday life."

Cuff, Hansen and Kang (2008) describe "urban sensing" as "fertile ground for participatory, collaborative efforts between citizens and scientists, artists, urbanists, and business people" contributing to "a form of public infrastructure" referred to as a "data commons." Dourish and Bell (2011) claim that "the experiential reading of infrastructure sees infrastructure and daily life as coextensive" and as such, "encompasses not just technological but also the social and cultural structures of experience in ubicomp settings." Revisiting this concept in the context of the pervasive, ambient, or the Internet of Things (IoT), Dourish and Bell (2011) provide additional insight through a discussion of "infrastructure and failure" from the "dramatic and spectacular" to the "mundane and unremarkable." For example, Dourish and Bell (2011) point to "the fragility of infrastructure" in terms of "the variety of ways that problems and failures develop" and how this highlights "the complex processes of holding it together and how active that process is" so that "stabilizing infrastructure is an ongoing effort." Dourish and Bell (2011) describe a particular feature or "property" of infrastructures as "messyness" noting that "the real world of ubicomp will always be assembling heterogeneous technologies to achieve individual and collective effects, and they will almost always be messy." Dourish and Bell (2011) draw on the work of Susan Leigh Star as "an advocate of the use of infrastructure as an analytic lens through which to consider the relationship between human action and technology." From this perspective, infrastructure is viewed not as "quiescent and stable" but rather, in need of being "actively maintained" where "relationships to them must be constantly negotiated." As such, Dourish and Bell (2011) refer to infrastructures as "inherently uneven in their operation and availability." Dourish and Bell (2011) articulate the concept of the "infrastructure of experience" to "draw attention to the ways in which the embedding of a range of infrastructures into everyday space shapes our experience of that space even as it provides a framework through which our encounters with space take on meaning." Cmar (2017) suggests that, "we still exist in the pre-smart city era" or possibly "at the very early stages of its development." This is because, according to Cmar (2017), "connectivity seems far from ubiquitous" and "data is sequestered among private companies and separate government agencies" and although "smart pieces of infrastructure link to the Internet" this linkage is "often not to each other."

Inverse Infrastructure

According to Egyedi and Mehos (2012) inverse infrastructure, as distinct from large technical systems (LTSs), is characterized as "bottom-up, user-driven, self-organizing networks" and found in initiatives such as Wikipedia. The human experience of urban spaces, services, and infrastructures (Mattern, 2014; Egyedi and Mehos, 2012) figure strongly in inverse infrastructures, with a disruptive shift said to be occurring in scale and form, along with many tensions in relation to LTSs (Egyedi and Mehos, 2012). Carroll et al. (2017) explore the Internet of Places concept in support of awareness, engagement, and interaction in relation to "human experiences, meaning making, activity, intentions, and values" through the use of data leveraged about people and places.

Figure 1 provides an overview of key issues, controversies, and challenges for infrastructures in smart cities.

Dourish and Bell (2011) identify the underlying fragility, messiness, unevenness, and instability of physical infrastructures while Finger (2016) emphasizes the effect of the digital layer of infrastructure on the services layer in terms of the potential for emerging designs and experiences. In addition to the need for a change by cities in their "design mentality," Alvarez (2017) points to the problem of the intangibility of digital infrastructures and in turn the difficulties associated with understanding and realizing the value potentials. Indeed, Alvarez (2017) claims there is a silent privatizing

Figure 1. Overview of key issues, controversies, and challenges for infrastructures in smart cities

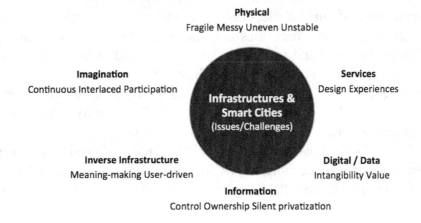

of public spaces in terms of their informational value, along with ownership and control. Egyedi and Mehos (2012) describe the disruptive influence of inverse infrastructures where bottom-up initiatives enable new forms of meaning-making and engagement that are adaptive, innovative, and user-driven building on and evolving existing infrastructures. Urssi (2018) describes the importance of the imagination in relation to information and materials for future cities as continuous and interlaced while Alvarez (2017) speaks of the social dimension, in support of the fostering of participation.

3.2 Experiences, Interactions, and Smart Cities

Experiences in Smart Environments

Dourish and Bell (2011) frame infrastructure in relation to space and in turn "the experience of space" noting that, "it is this experience that is disrupted and transformed when new technological opportunities enter those spaces." Dourish and Bell (2011) argue that "the experience of space is that of multiple infrastructures" as in, naming, movement, and interaction, adding that, "these infrastructures emerge from and are sustained by the embodied practices of the people who inhabit the spaces." Further, Dourish and Bell (2011) claim that "spaces are not neutral, and their complex interpretive structure will frame the encounter with ubicomp" and "the opportunities afforded by new technologies allow for a reinterpretation and reencounter with the meaning of space for its inhabitants." For Dourish and Bell (2011), "the transformation of space through the introduction and diffusion of pervasive computing technologies must be seen in the context" of "the experience of space." Boswijk and Peelen (2012) describe the experience economy in relation to the creation of meaningful experiences and new forms of value creation, noting the importance of "media, electronics, Internet, and convergence." Vander Veen (2015) describes smart cities as "places where ideas, infrastructure, and technology intersect" and as such, this creates the conditions for experiences and interactions. Ribet (2016) points to the need for the Internet of Things to "take an 'experience thinking' approach." As such, Ribet (2016) describes the move from "the age of experience" to what Dassault Systèmes refer to as "delivering compelling and connected experiences" as "High Tech 3C Experiences" encompassing – "connected, contextual, and continuous." On the spectrum of "machine-centric to human-centric computing," Sheth, Anantharam, and Henson (2016) describe their work on "computing for human experience" as they seek to "show how semantic, cognitive, and perceptual computing paradigms work together to produce actionable information" based on personalized and contextualized data.

People Interactions in Smart Environments

Williams, Robles, and Dourish (2009) place an emphasis on urban experience and the global networks of interactions and flows with people as users, embedded as actors. From a sociotechnical systems perspective, Vertesi (2014) articulated the notion of infrastructure as "multiple, coexisting, and nonconforming" and uses the concept of "seams" to explore "how actors work creatively with and across their seams" in "locally accountable ways to produce either *seamless* or *seamful* multi-infrastructural action and interaction." Through the notion of "living labs" with "people as innovators," Mulder (2015) extends public private partnerships (PPP) discussed by Finger (2016) to public private people partnerships (PPPP) pointing to a network of people and their rich experiences providing "a way to deal with community-driven innovation" in support of the "open(ed) mindset" and "the value of opening up data for reuse." Finger (2016) speaks of the feedback loops in cities where "social dimensions interact with technical dimensions" and "technical dimensions interact with the economic dimensions" and "different actors interact with each other" noting that "how the technology is laid out effects the social life" and "the way people work." Finger (2016) seeks to provide insight into the emerging element of "digitalization as a new layer" or the "data layer" in terms of "what it does to the management and the governance of urban infrastructure systems." From a human-centered design perspective, Shin (2017) argues that, "the exponential development of the Internet of Things (IoT) makes it essential to cater to the quality expectations of end users." As such, Shin (2017) focuses on quality of experience (QoE) and advances "a conceptual model for QoE in personal informatics" as a "guiding paradigm for managing quality provisions and applications designs in the IoT." Shin (2017) establishes "the groundwork for developing future IoT services with QoE requirements and for dimensioning the underlying network provisioning infrastructures" pertaining especially to wearable technologies. Dourish (2017) takes a representational approach arguing that "the material arrangements of information" as in, "how it is represented and how that shapes how it can be put to work – matters significantly for our experience of information and information systems." Dourish (2017) maintains that, "materials and their properties play a pivotal role in the production of new objects and experiences" and as such, is concerned with "specific ways in which the digital is already material." Sengers, Späth, and Raven (2018) advance a socio-technical perspective where "smart city experiments" as part of urban living labs "be interpreted" simultaneously as "discursive, institutional, and material construction" with cities "as sites in which actors experiment in various ways with each of these 'constructions in action'."

Technology-Driven Interactions in Smart Environments

Black (2017) claims that, "cities are sensing up" in support of "collecting vast troves of data that they're running through predictive models" and then "using the insights to solve problems that, in some cases, city managers didn't even know existed." In order to enable real-time information processing it is argued that high performance computing (HPC) is required at the edge, as in, "programmable sensors" running in "a small, parallel supercomputer" adapting to current situations at crosswalks, flood zones, and the like. An important component of the Virtual Singapore Project described by Moore (2017) is visualization "so the aggregated and integrated data from various sources can be 'seen' in a way that produces actionable intelligence." Moore (2017) notes that Rocker, Vice President of the Project, highlights "home topics and issues" and a "social turn" with "projects where the everyday person is integrated into the system" in relation to "how we make urban space and how we enable ourselves to live together." Moore (2017) provides an overview of Virtual Singapore as an initiative to "take all the data available in a living, breathing, thriving metropolitan city and use it to make a 'digital twin' that can be researched, analyzed, and manipulated in real time by multiple stakeholders" through a "dynamic 3D model." According to Moore (2017), "the idea is to collaborate on a data platform that will allow scientists, policy makers, and even regular citizens to test concepts, conduct virtual brainstorming, and enable entities to solve emerging challenges." It is worth noting that where Moore (2017) uses the term "digital twin" to describe the Virtual Singapore initiative, Finger (2016) argues that, "with digitalization you are able to mirror" the physical layer of the city "in a data layer." The "mirroring of this information" according to Finger (2016), "empowers the customer who now can become a prosumer, delivering information into the digital layer which can again be used for new services" enabling "meaningful and personalized experiences." Parmiggiani, Monteiro, and Østerlie (2016) highlight the notion of *synthetic situations* that are "characterized by physical inaccessibility and virtualization," in relation to the Internet of Things (IoT) involving algorithmic data and other IoT elements. Parmiggiani et al. (2016) consider such situations as innovative spaces for interactions whether involving Knorr Cetina's (2009) notion of synthetic situations where people are together without being "co-located" or that of Parmiggiani et al. (2016) featuring "people not co-located with the physical phenomena" in the IoT. Dourish (2017) draws attention to "the representational properties associated with digital media" and how they "affect aspects of the interactional experience" as well as "how we encounter the world through the computer."

Figure 2 provides an overview of key issues, controversies, and challenges for urban experiences and interactions in smart cities. Ribet (2016) points to the importance of an "experience thinking approach" for emerging technologies such as the Internet of Things (IoT) in support of engaging experiences that are connected, contextual, and continuous. Boswijk and Peelen (2012) highlight meaningful experiences that are social and personalized in relation to technologies and the experience economy. Dourish and Bell (2011) speak in terms of the experience of space in relation to technologies and their potential to disrupt experiences enabling reinterpretations. Boswijk and Peelen (2012) argue that meaningful experiences contribute in turn to value creation, while Finger (2016) argues for the importance of "open(ed) mindsets" engaging multiple partnerships and the opening up of data for reuse.

Vertesi (2014) articulates the challenges posed by multi-infrastructures and the creative ways in which people overcome seamful elements in support of seamless experiences and interactions while Parmiggiani et al. (2016) describe

Figure 2. Overview of key issues, controversies, and challenges for urban experiences and interactions

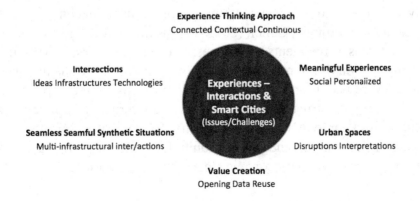

the interaction challenges associated with accessibility posed by synthetic situations. Vander Veen (2015) highlights the importance of the intersections of ideas, infrastructure, and technology for experiences and interactions.

3.3 Issues, Controversies, Problems

Key issues, controversies, and problems are surfaced in this chapter through the review of the research literature from varying perspectives on infrastructures, experiences, and interactions in relation to smart cities while exploring elements of engagement. As such, coverage of issues, controversies, and problems is not exhaustive or comprehensive, seeking instead to illustrate the nature, variety, and range.

Issues

Finger (2016) points to the issue of financing the digital infrastructures required in smart cities and the particular competencies required by everyone involved – city officials, community members, business, and educational institutions. To the public private partnerships (PPP) advanced by Finger (2016), Mulder (2015) had already called more broadly for public private people partnerships (PPPP). As such, the notion of partnerships and broad involvement is in keeping with the objectives of this chapter in exploring perspectives across diverse sectors and spaces.

Controversies

Evolving the notion of smart cities beyond a technology-driven understanding, Cohen (2015) speaks in terms of three waves or generations of smart cities with 1.0 focused on technology, 2.0 as city-driven, and 3.0 as the current wave involving people and indeed a combination of all three – technology, cities, and people. Accordingly, Cohen (2015) claims that "cities must move from treating citizens as recipients of services, or even customers, to participants in the co-creation of improved quality of life" giving rise to the importance of more aware people in urban layers and spaces as in, the experience of infrastructure, infrastructures of experience, the Internet of Experience, and the Internet of People. Alvarez (2017) pushes further calling for support and fostering of imagination and more meaningful forms of participation. The focus on the importance of people in smart cities in relation to infrastructure, experience, and interactions supports the objectives of this chapter in terms of engagement.

Problems

Dourish and Bell (2011) point to the messiness and complexities of infrastructures arguing that because infrastructure "describes a relationship between technology, people, and practice," in such an environment, "thinking of infrastructure as stable, uniform, seamless, and universally available is clearly problematic." Dourish and Bell (2011) argue that "the failures, niggles, problems, and breakdowns of contemporary ubicomp are not things to be written out of the picture, on the assumption that they are temporary problems to be overcome in the next generation of ubicomp (the 'real' ubicomp of which our current implementation is merely an approximation)." However, Dourish and Bell (2011) maintain that "while the details of the technology change, the notion of everyday practice as needing to work around infrastructure as much as through it seems likely to remain salient." Vertesi (2014) points to the creativity and adaptability of people in working with seamful, multiple, and heterogeneous infrastructures. Such approaches to infrastructures, experiences, and interactions would seem to support emerging understandings of ambient urbanities as developed in the remainder of this chapter.

Summarized in Figure 3, a glimpse of patterns, flows, relationships, and possibilities begins to emerge for new urban layers and spaces through explorations of infrastructures, experiences, interactions, and engagement enabled in relation to aware people and aware technologies including the Internet of People, Things, and Experiences. Infrastructures are characterized in terms of the digital and associated complexities, and the particular competencies required as well as the need for sources of financing. The experience of infrastructures emerges and the importance of being people-friendly while acknowledging the messiness of infrastructures and seamfulness as distinct from the seamless. Connected, contextual, and continuous speak to the experiences of new urban layers as well as the experience economy along with the quality of experience. The importance of relationships figures strongly for partnerships while acknowledging that the unstable nature of infrastructures influences experiences. Interactions are characterized by adaptability; being supportive of creativity, change, novel interrelationships enabling seamlessness and sharing on a spectrum of awareness.

Figure 3. New urban layers and spaces through infrastructures, experiences, interactions for engagement

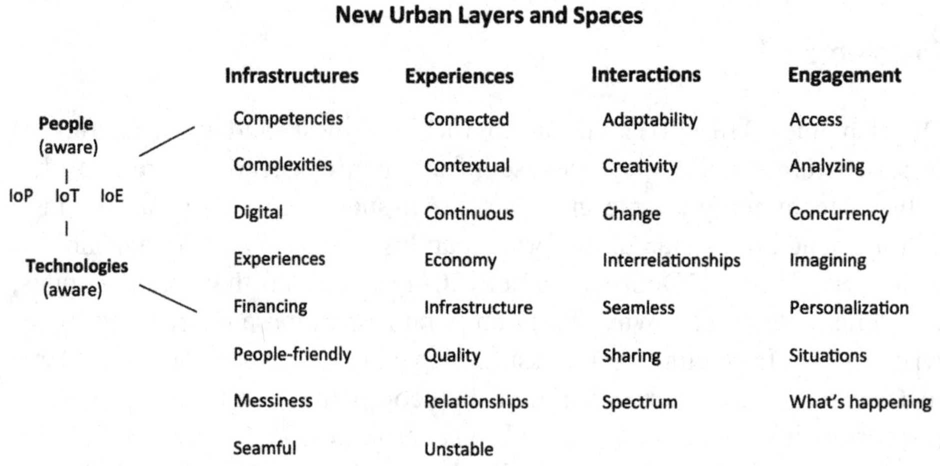

New Urban Layers and Spaces

	Infrastructures	Experiences	Interactions	Engagement
People (aware)	Competencies	Connected	Adaptability	Access
	Complexities	Contextual	Creativity	Analyzing
IoP IoT IoE	Digital	Continuous	Change	Concurrency
	Experiences	Economy	Interrelationships	Imagining
Technologies (aware)	Financing	Infrastructure	Seamless	Personalization
	People-friendly	Quality	Sharing	Situations
	Messiness	Relationships	Spectrum	What's happening
	Seamful	Unstable		

Engagement emerges in relation to the provision of access to, and capabilities for, analyzing information. Concurrency is highlighted in terms of multiple concurrent usage and usages of information supportive of increased engagement, personalization, and imaginings for any number of situations generating greater awareness of what's happening.

In summary, Table 1 provides an overview of issues, controversies, and problems for emerging layers and spaces, by author and year, focusing on infrastructures, experiences, and interactions in the context of smart cities.

Cohen (2015) highlights co-creative interactions, Finger (2016) argues for the development of competencies associated with emerging and evolving infrastructures that are, according to Dourish and Bell (2011) underpinned with complexities and messiness affecting interactions. Cmar (2017) describes infrastructure connectivity issues associated with the sequestering of data and Ribet (2017) speaks of connected and continuous experiences. Boswijk and Peelen (2012) contribute an experience economy dimension. Finger (2016) reminds us of the challenges associated with the financing of infrastructure development and Alvarez (2017) of the investments in research and development. Vertesi (2014) describes the heterogeneous nature of infrastructures and the opportunities and challenges for creativity and adaptability. Carroll et al. (2017) explore the Internet of Places in support of infrastructures for engagement based on data about people and their

Table 1. Perspectives on issues, controversies, and problems for urban layers and spaces in smart cities

Emerging Urban Layers and Spaces and Smart Cities				
Author(s)	**Year**	**Infrastructures**	**Experiences**	**Interactions**
Sengers et al.	2018			Smart city experiments
Urssi	2018	Responsive	Personal	Continuous; Interlaced
Alvarez	2017	Financing; Value		
Carroll et al.	2017	Internet of Places	Engagement	
Cmar	2017	Connectivity		
Shin	2017		Quality of experiences	
Finger	2016	Competencies; Financing	Meaningful; Personalized; Quality of life	
Parmiggiani et al.	2016			Synthetic situations
Ribet	2016		Connected; Continuous	
Cohen	2015		Quality of life	Co-creation
Komninos	2015	Spatialities		
Mulder	2015	Sustainability	Co-creation	Opening up
Vertesi	2014	Heterogeneous; Multiple; Seamful		Creativity/Adaptability
Mattern	2013		Of Infrastructure	
Zygiaris	2013	Layers		
Egyedi & Mehos	2012	Inverse		
Boswijk & Peelen	2012		Economy	
Dourish & Bell	2011	Complexity	Of Infrastructure	Messiness

experiences. Other perspectives range from that of inverse infrastructure (Egyedi & Mehos, 2012) to that of the experience of infrastructure (Mattern, 2014; Dourish and Bell, 2011) to the multiple layers of infrastructure (Zygiaris, 2013) to experiences as meaningful and personalized (Finger, 2016) to models for quality of experiences (Shin, 2017) to quality of life (Finger 2016; Cohen, 2015).

The responsive requirements of infrastructure are raised by Urssi (2018) as are personal experience and interactions as continuous and interlaced. Seners et al. (2018) highlight the importance of experiments for engagement and interaction while Komninos (2015) articulates the new spatialities enabled by emerging technologies. Mulder (2015) emphasizes the importance of the sustainability of infrastructures, the co-creation of experiences and the opening up of interactions. Parmiggiani et al. (2016) describe new forms of interactions enabled through virtualization as synthetic situations and Alvarez (2017) highlights the potentials associated with uncovering new forms of value in emerging infrastructures.

From this rich array of perspectives emerging through the review of the literature for infrastructures, experiences, and interactions, Figure 4 provides a summarized view focusing on engagement and the emerging layers and spaces related to infrastructures, experiences, and interactions in smart cities.

The upper left quadrant features the Internet and infrastructures of experience, the upper right the experience economy associated with the digital layer, the lower left features the experience of infrastructures, and the lower right the quality of experience. All four quadrants interact with each other in support of infrastructures, experiences, and interactions that engage with the cities – technologies – people dynamic. As such, these four quadrants become key factors influencing engagement with emerging layers and spaces in smart cities.

In responding to the issues, controversies, and problems in this chapter, a framework for emerging layers and spaces in smart cities is formulated in the section that follows.

Figure 4. Overview of emerging layers and spaces for engagement in smart cities

Engagement: Infrastructures – Experiences – Interactions

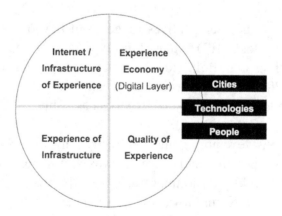

4. EMERGING URBAN LAYERS: NEW SPACES FOR SMARTER CITIES

Based on the perspectives provided in this chapter from a review of the research literature, formulation of a framework for emerging layers and spaces in smart cities is developed in this section in support of solutions and recommendations.

4.1 Framework for Urban Layers and Spaces: Solutions and Recommendations

This section builds upon and adapts a conceptual framework advanced for awareness, choice, and action in smart cities where the elements of awareness, infrastructures, and experience were present in relation to information and communication technologies (ICTs) and urban edges, surfaces, spaces, and the in-between (McKenna, 2016). As depicted in Figure 5, this work probes further into the ICTs component and employs the elements of infrastructures, experiences, and interactions in relation to physical structures and services as layers in the city, and the additional layer of the digital (encompassing technologies and data) explored as spaces for engagement in terms of connected, contextual, and continuous.

Taking up the challenge of exploring more "meaningful engagement" (McKenna, 2016), this chapter features the construct of engagement through which to explore emerging layers and spaces in smart cities in seeking to offer solutions and recommendations to issues, controversies, and problems.

Figure 5. Framework for emerging urban layers and spaces in smart cities

New Urban Layers and Spaces

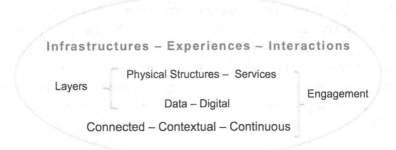

As such, the key question posed in this chapter, restated as a proposition under exploration in this chapter, is as follows:

P: New urban layers of urbanity enable spaces for *engagement* in smart cities through emergent infrastructures, experiences, and interactions.

4.2 New Urban Layers for Engagement: An Exploration

How engagement informs urbanity is explored in this chapter using a survey instrument and protocol-guided interviews with a diverse range of individuals in addition to discussions with a broad range of groups and individuals. The focus of all three methods centered on the digital layer of urban infrastructures, experiences, and interactions in order to gain insight into connected, contextual, and continuous everyday activities in real-time, as in, in the moment. The interweaving of physical, digital, and human infrastructures is explored and discussed, in terms of increasingly complex data, decision-making, and other associated challenges and opportunities.

4.2.1 Engagement Through Emergent Infrastructures, Experiences, and Interactions

Engagement through emergent infrastructures, experiences, and interactions in urban spaces in this chapter focuses on people and finds voice here through discussions with a broad spectrum of individuals across small to medium to large-sized cities.

Infrastructures

With sensor infrastructures, as if in confirmation of Black's (2017) claim about the value of data in affording the use of "insights to solve problems that, in some cases, city managers didn't even know existed," city IT (information technology) staff in Greater Victoria referred to new technologies enabling "accidental data collection" and data that "I don't think anybody saw a need for" enabling "data analysis that you've not thought of." In keeping with the notion and potential of high performance computing (HPC) at the edges, a community member in St. John's commented that "we're not smart about how we use the technology" giving rise to challenges and opportunities possibly for contributing to new layers and spaces.

Experience

A community member engaged in imagining the use of technologies "to experience the city in a different way" taking into account the environment to "create different games or opportunities for people" to interact with in the city. Mention of urban experiences contributed to a discussion of the 'experience economy' in terms of coffee shops where the cost of the coffee encompasses the broader coffee experience, as in, "you're paying for the whole experience."

Interactions

An individual in the technology industry spoke of the importance of "interactive instead of reactive" spaces in urban environments, referring to the "smart city thought process" as a "wonderful thing that connects all the pieces."

4.2.2 Engagement as Connected, Contextual, and Continuous

Engagement as meaningful in urban spaces is articulated here through the voices of a broad spectrum of individuals across the city in terms of connected, contextual, and continuous infrastructures, experiences, and interactions.

Connected

An urban designer in Greater Victoria commented that, "I'm learning" the importance of "using data from technologies to improve aspects of the city" and "the human component" of this "to enable all those connections to happen." From a city IT perspective, a staff member observed that "inside the processes of city hall we're slowly getting those connections" in order for "engineering and planning" to work together. An educator noted that "if we forget about the technology for a moment its almost" as if "there is this wireless connectivity between us happening." A community member in St. John's suggested that "much more collaboration is necessary" in how the technology is used. A community member in Greater Victoria spoke of the advantages of smartphone data, serving "to enhance the urban experience" and allowing for people to be "able to get from point a to b faster." A city councilor referred to technology "as a tool that will allow people to connect to each other and to their surroundings" noting that "vibrancy is created by people and connections between people." An individual in the technology industry observed that, "it is not necessarily about making people more connected" but "about connecting people, because we have all kinds of ways to be connected."

Contextual

An educator highlighted the importance of a mobile app for civic engagement purposes "that people could use to capture ideas, evidence of problems on the move" and "evidence of potential solutions and impact." Focusing on engagement, a community leader referred to platforms such as PlaceSpeak to "encourage people to do some observations of space and people" for sharing in a space "that's interactive" as an activity to "look at any given space and analyze what's working and what isn't and what could improve it." In the words of an educator "let's spend less time *finding* the connection" and give more time to "actually *making* it." An IT leader in higher education noted that for youth, "their legacy is change, their life's work is not materials, its social, social capital" aided by emerging technologies.

Continuous

A community member in St. John's identified the need to "provide user friendly information" as in, "not too dense" about "what's happening at a particular point" in the city, enabling people to "access information and know what's going on in real time almost." A student described the continuous sharing of "very traditional things" and events in daily life where people are "videoing them, sharing them constantly in social media" contributing to "this seamless interrelationships of local and global" forming "concurrent awareness." An educator described "a mobile cloud-based app to capture and share insights, feedback, and knowledge" as a simple, "cost efficient" mechanism for "instant awareness" intended for "business, design, infrastructure, learning, safety, sport, and tourism." City IT staff provided the example of an eTownHall meeting enabled by technology, noting that, "bringing questions in and sharing answers through Twitter" in real time generated "a dataset of documented engagement."

4.2.3 Discussion of Urbanity in New Urban Layers and Spaces

How engagement informs urbanity, enabled by aware people and aware technologies, was explored through protocol-guided interviews, open-ended survey questions, and discussions with groups and individuals across the city.

The constant sharing described by one student as contributing to "seamless interrelationships" and "concurrent awareness" also assists in navigating toward the notion of *ambient engagement*. Where the machine-centric to human-centric computing conceptualization outlined by Sheth et al. (2016) featured a spectrum from *artificial intelligence* at the extreme left as machine-centric, moving toward the right with *ambient intelligence*, then to *augmenting of human intellect* in the center position of the two extremes, and on to *human-computer symbiosis*, and then to *computing for human experience* at the far right as human centric, this work interprets the spectrum in an integrative way as aware people and aware technologies. As such, this chapter focuses on finding spaces and mechanisms for enabling more balance between people and technologies for infrastructures, experiences, and interactions. Findings in this chapter contribute to the advancing of a framework for ambient engagement in smart city urbanities as depicted in Figure 6.

The framework is organized around people and technologies characterized as aware in support of personalized infrastructures, experiences, and interactions for connected, contextual, and continuous situations and meaningful engagement.

Figure 6. Framework for ambient engagement in smart city urbanities

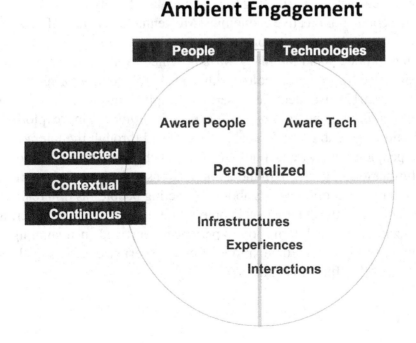

Discussion of the 'ambient spectrum' generally in smart cities and more specifically for ambient urbanities, contributes to the notion of ambient engagement and the development of a case for this concept here and going forward. The combination of more aware people with more aware technologies in support of everyday, real-time continuous information streams, fosters new spaces for engagement and for keeping people more informed in urban environments. It is worth noting that, although placed in the continuous section of 4.2.2, the "dataset of documented engagement" as described by city IT, spans all three areas of connected, contextual, and continuous in Figure 6. Such immediacy and awareness on the part of people and technologies also serves to support potentials for personalization in relation to infrastructures, experiences, and interactions thus contributing in turn to more meaningful engagement.

Dependent Variable (DV)

The dependent variable (DV) surfaced in this chapter is *engagement and personalization* in relation to infrastructures, experiences, and interactions that are found to be personally relevant or in other words, that matter. Associated independent variables include: connecting all the pieces, implying the presence of spaces for making; spaces for the generation of social capital, implying the potential for value creation; and spaces for continuous informed awareness, implying spaces for contributing to greater data integrity.

In the context of creative economies, McKenna (2017) identified a series of implications for practice, one of which is *augmenting experience* as in, "coming to understand the many ways in which everyday experiences can be augmented by aware technologies in contributing to new forms of value." McKenna (2017) also identified a series of implications for research, one of which is *imagining aware people + aware technologies* as in, "exploring the possibilities, potentials, and capabilities enabled through the interacting of aware people with aware technologies." As such, this chapter develops the case further for explorations of these implications in research and practice. As observed by one individual "its about connecting people" as if in realization of the notion of the Internet of People while a community member, as if in realization of the Internet of Experiences, engaged in imagining how technologies might be used to explore different experiences of the city through games and other fun mechanisms.

5. FUTURE RESEARCH DIRECTIONS

Future and emerging trends are identified in this chapter for both practice and research pertaining to infrastructure, experience, and interactions in sections 5.1 and 5.2 respectively.

5.1 Practice

On a practical level, the opening up of opportunities related to new understandings of engagement and the ambient engagement concept emerge from this exploration along with engagement-associated variables.

Ambient Engagement

This chapter provides evolving understandings of engagement in urban environments with aware people interacting with each other through and with aware technologies. Exposure to the ambient engagement concept and to the framework for ambient engagement in smart city urbanities may stimulate ideas for civic engagement initiatives involving games, mobile applications, or other creative undertaking that enable people to learn more about the city while also having a fun experience.

Variables and Indicators

Engagement is said to be a key indicator for the success of smart cities (SmartCitiesWorld, 2018) and this chapter advances the potential for value to emerge on a practical level for the *engagement and personalization* dependent variable and the independent variables associated with making, value creation, and contributing to greater data integrity.

5.2 Research

From the perspective of new urban layers and spaces enabled through digital technologies, this chapter opens the way to future research opportunities, challenges, debates, and theorizing related to the proposed concept of ambient engagement and the framework for emerging urban layers and spaces in smart cities.

Ambient Engagement

The concept of ambient engagement is advanced in this chapter as an example of a more adaptive, dynamic, connected, and continuous understanding of engagement in urban spaces.

Framework for Emerging Urban Layers and Spaces in Smart Cities

The viability of the framework for emerging layers and spaces in smart cities, operationalized for use in this chapter, demonstrates early-stage potentials with opportunities for further testing and validation going forward. Potential areas for exploration include:

1. *Engagement infrastructures* that involve games, mobile apps, and other creative initiatives associated with learning in urban spaces
2. *Engagement experiences* that may shed light on the use of aware technologies in combination with aware people in urban spaces
3. *Engagement interactions* involving aware technologies in combination with aware people in urban spaces

6. CONCLUSION

This chapter provides an exploration of engagement in smart cities from the perspective of evolving understandings of infrastructures, experiences, and interactions in keeping with the objectives of this chapter. The elements of connected, contextual, and continuous are highlighted as key aspects contributing to emerging understandings of ambient engagement. As such, ambient engagement is advanced as a possibly more integrative approach, providing a rethinking of the machine-centric, human-centric spectrum (Sheth et al., 2016) to one of an aware technologies, aware people spectrum for more ambient urbanities. Through the imagining of new layers and spaces for more meaningful engagement, opportunities emerge for more informed awareness of new types of data generation, reuse of data, new literacies and competencies along with the recognition of new forms of value associated with infrastructures, experiences, and interactions. The primary contributions of this chapter include: a) provision of an overview of emerging layers and spaces for engagement in smart cities based on a review of the literature for infrastructure, experiences, interactions and smart cities; b) formulation and operationalization of a framework for emerging layers and spaces in smart cities; and c) based on study findings, development of a framework for ambient engagement in smart city urbanities. This chapter also contributes to the research literature on urban theory as well as opening up discourse, debate, and practice spaces for emerging understandings of engagement as ambient.

This chapter continues to give form, detail, and definition to the broader Ambient Urbanities Framework presented in Chapter 1 (Figure 4) through exploration of the engagement construct in relation to infrastructures, experiences, and interactions. The analysis of findings in this chapter identifies variables associated with *engagement and personalization* relevant to the study, practice, and management of emerging layers and spaces in smart cities.

Insights of particular interest to the reader include the following:

1. The potential for meaningful engagement opportunities to inform emerging urban layers and spaces
2. The interconnectedness of infrastructures, experiences, and interactions informing ambient urbanities
3. The surfacing of variables associated with *engagement and personalization* for urban layers and spaces

Ideas highlighted in this chapter pertain to the following:

1. The importance of people becoming more aware of infrastructural elements in urban layers and spaces
2. The potential for people to benefit from the value of their experiences and interactions in digital spaces
3. Ambient engagement as an integrative approach contributing to a spectrum for ambient urbanities

Lessons for the reader in this chapter are associated with the following:

1. The potential for meaningful engagement experiences to influence and augment aware technologies
2. The potential for aware technologies to enhance engagement possibilities for people in urban spaces
3. The myriad issues, controversies, and problems for urban infrastructures, experiences, and interactions

This work will be of interest to a broad audience including, but not limited to, students, educators, researchers, urban practitioners, community members, urban planners and designers, urban developers, and urban innovators, civic engagement specialists, businesses, and anyone concerned with aware people and aware technologies in relation to new urban layers and spaces for smarter urbanities and smarter cities in addressing complex urban engagement challenges and opportunities.

REFERENCES

Alvarez, R. (2017). The relevance of informational infrastructures in future cities, *Field Actions Science Reports*, *17*. Retrieved from http://journals. openedition.org/factsreports/4389

Anthopoulos, L. G., & Vakali, A. (2012). *Urban planning and smart cities: Interrelations and reciprocities. In The Future Internet Assembly*. Berlin: Springer.

Black, D. (2017). How cities use HPC at the edge to get smarter. *HPCwire*. Retrieved 4 January 2018 from https://www.hpcwire.com/2017/11/17/cities-use-hpc-edge-get-smarter/

Boswijk, A., & Peelen, E. (2012). *Economy of experiences: How to create meaningful experiences*. European Centre for the Experience Economy.

Carroll, J. M., Shih, P. C., Kropczynski, J., Cai, G., Rosson, M. B., & Han, K. (2017). The Internet of Places at community-scale: Design scenarios for hyperlocal neighborhood. In S. Konomi & G. Roussos (Eds.), *Enriching urban spaces with ambient computing, the Internet of Things, and smart city design* (pp. 1–24). Hershey, PA: IGI Global. doi:10.4018/978-1-5225-0827-4.ch001

Cmar, W. (2017). What smart cities might look like, and why they're important. *FutureStructure*. Retrieved 7 January 2018 from http://www.govtech.com/fs/infrastructure/Editorial-What-Smart-Cities-Might-Look-Like-and-Why-Theyre-Important.html

Cohen, B. (2015). The 3 generations of smart cities: Inside the development of the technology driven city. *FastCompany Exist*. Retrieved 15 January 2018 from http://www.fastcoexist.com/3047795/the-3-generations-of-smart-cities

Cuff, D., Hansen, M., & Kang, J. (2008). Urban sensing: Out of the woods. *Communications of the ACM, 51*(3), 24–33. doi:10.1145/1325555.1325562

Dourish, P. (2017). *The stuff of bits: An essay on the materialities of information.* Cambridge, MA: MIT Press. doi:10.7551/mitpress/10999.001.0001

Dourish, P., & Bell, G. (2007). The infrastructure of experience and the experience of infrastructure: Meaning and structure in everyday encounters with space. *Environment and Planning. B, Planning & Design, 34*(3), 414–443. doi:10.1068/b32035t

Dourish, P., & Bell, G. (2011). *Divining our digital future: Mess and mythology in ubiquitous computing.* Cambridge, MA: MIT Press. doi:10.7551/mitpress/9780262015554.001.0001

Egyedi, T. M., & Mehos, D. C. (Eds.). (2012). *Inverse infrastructures: Disrupting networks from below.* Cheltenham, UK: Edward Elgar Pub. doi:10.4337/9781781952290

Finger, M. (2016). Managing urban infrastructures. Lausanne, Switzerland: MOOC, Fall.

Gabrys, J. (2016). Practicing, materialising, and contesting environmental data. *Big Data & Society.* Retrieved 26 December 2016 from http://journals.sagepub.com/doi/full/10.1177/2053951716673391

Knorr Cetina, K. (2009). The synthetic situation: Interactionism for a global world. *Symbolic Interaction, 32*(1), 61–87. doi:10.1525i.2009.32.1.61

Komninos, N. (2015). *The age of intelligent cities: Smart environments and innovation-for-all strategies.* New York: Routledge.

Luskin, B. (2010). Think "exciting": E-learning and the big "E". *Educause Review: Why IT Matters to Higher Ed.* Retrieved 29 July 2016 from http://bit.ly/2aDucQ1

Mattern, S. (2014). Library as infrastructure. *Places Journal.* Retrieved 16 August 2016 from https://placesjournal.org/article/library-as-infrastructure/

McKenna, H. P. (2016). Edges, surfaces, and spaces of action in 21st century urban environments – Connectivities and awareness in the city. In D. Kreps, G. Fletcher, & M. Griffiths, (Eds.), Technology and Intimacy: Choice or Coercion (pp. 328-343). Springer.

McKenna, H. P. (2017). Re-conceptualizing jobs, work, and labour: Transforming learning for more creative economies in 21st century smart cities. *Proceedings of the 10th Annual International Conference of Education, Research and Innovation (iCERi2017)*, 8367-8376. 10.21125/iceri.2017.2251

Moore, C. (2017). The virtual Singapore project aims to digitize an entire city. *Digital Trends*. Retrieved 8 January 2018 from https://www.digitaltrends.com/home/virtual-singapore-project-mapping-out-entire-city-in-3d/

Mulder, I. (2015). Opening up: Towards a sociable smart city. In M. Foth, M. Brynskov, & T. Ojala (Eds.), *Citizen's right to the digital city* (pp. 161–173). Singapore: Springer. doi:10.1007/978-981-287-919-6_9

Parmiggiani, E., Monteiro, E., & Østerlie, T. (2016). Synthetic situations in the Internet of Things. In L. Introna, D. Kavanagh, S. Kelly, W. Orlikowski, & S. Scott (Eds.), *Beyond Interpretivism? New Encounters with Technology and Organization. IS&O 2016. IFIP Advances in Information and Communication Technology* (Vol. 489, pp. 215–228). Cham: Springer. doi:10.1007/978-3-319-49733-4_13

Payne, J., & Burke, J. (2015). *Ambient informatics. UCLA: cityLab projects*. Retrieved 26 December 2016 from http://www.citylab.aud.ucla.edu/projects/ambient-informatics-/

Ribet, O. (2016). The Internet of Experience. *3D Perspectives Blog*. Retrieved 9 January 2018 from http://blogs.3ds.com/perspectives/the-internet-of-experience/

Sengers, F., Späth, P., & Raven, R. (2018). Smart city construction: Towards an analytical framework for smart urban living labs. In *Urban Living Labs* (pp. 88–102). Routledge. doi:10.4324/9781315230641-5

Sheth, A., Anantharam, P., & Henson, C. (2016). Semantic, cognitive, and perceptual computing: Paradigms that shape human experience. *Computer*, *49*(3), 64-72.

Shin, D.-H. (2017). Conceptualizing and measuring quality of experience of the internet of things: Exploring how quality is perceived by users. *Information & Management*, *54*(8), 998–1011. doi:10.1016/j.im.2017.02.006

SmartCitiesWorld. (2018). Citizen engagement is key to smart city success. *SmartCitiesWorld*. Retrieved 18 December 2018 from https://www. smartcitiesworld.net/news/news/citizen-engagement-is-key-to-smart-city-success-2685

Smith, M. L. (2016). Urban infrastructure as materialized consensus. *World Archaeology*, *48*(1), 164–178. doi:10.1080/00438243.2015.1124804

Urssi, N. J. (2018). Metacity: Design, data e urbanity. In DUXU 2018, LNCS 10919 (pp. 365-378). Springer.

Vander Veen, C. (2015). Without smart, connected people there are no smart cities. *GovTech, FutureStructure*. Retrieved 6 January 2018 from http://bit.ly/1B9FbWO

Vertesi, J. (2014). Seamful spaces: Heterogeneous infrastructures in interactions. *Science, Technology & Human Values*, *39*(2), 264–284. doi:10.1177/0162243913516012

Weignen, M., & Heuvelhof, E. (2016). *The next generation of infrastructures*. TU Delft: Massive Open Online Course (MOOC). Retrieved from https://www.edx.org/course/next-generation-infrastructure-delftx-ngix-0

Williams, A., Robles, E., & Dourish, P. (2009). Urbane-ing the city: Examining and refining the assumptions behind urban informatics. In M. Foth (Ed.), *Handbook of research on urban informatics: The practice and promise of the real-time city*. Hershey, PA: IGI Global. doi:10.4018/978-1-60566-152-0.ch001

Zygiaris, S. (2013). Smart city reference model: Assisting planners to conceptualize the building of smart city innovation ecosystems. *J. Knowl. Econ.*, *4*(2), 217–231. doi:10.100713132-012-0089-4

ADDITIONAL READING

ITU. (2015). *Key performance indicators definitions for smart sustainable cities. ITU-T Focus Group on Smart Sustainable Cities*. Geneva, Switzerland: International Telecommunications Union.

Lévy, J. (Ed.). (2008). *The city: Critical essays in human geography. Contemporary Foundations of Space and Place series*. Newcastle: Routledge.

Lévy, J., Beaude, B., Poncet, P., Noizet, H., Laurent-Lucchetti, B., Bahrani, F., ... Rommany, T. (2015). *EPFLx: SpaceX Exploring Humans' Space: An Introduction to Geographicity. Massive Open Online Course (MOOC), edX, Fall.* Lausanne, Switzerland: EPFL.

McKenna, H. P. (2016). Learning in the city: Leveraging urban spaces as real world environments for interactive solution-making. *Proceedings of the 10th International Technology, Education & Development Conference (INTED2016)*, Valencia, Spain, 7-9 March, pp. 4367-4375. 10.21125/inted.2016.2081

Meadows, M., & Kouw, M. (2017, February). Future-making: Inclusive design and smart cities. *Interaction, 24*(2), 52–56. doi:10.1145/3046429

Pak, B. (2017). Design and development of sentient collective urban spaces. In S. Konomi & G. Roussos (Eds.), *Enriching urban spaces with ambient computing, the Internet of Things, and smart city design* (pp. 167–183). Hershey, PA: IGI Global. doi:10.4018/978-1-5225-0827-4.ch009

Pine, B. J. II, & Gilmore, J. H. (2011). *The experience economy, updated edition*. Boston, MA: Harvard Business School Publishing.

van Warat, P., & Mulder, I. (2014). Meaningful interactions in a smart city. In N. Streitz & P. Markopoulos (Eds.), Lecture Notes in Computer Science: Vol. 8530. *Distributed, Ambient, and Pervasive Interactions. DAPI 2014* (pp. 617–628). Cham: Springer. doi:10.1007/978-3-319-07788-8_57

KEY TERMS AND DEFINITIONS

Awareness: Awareness refers to the concept or quality of being aware as it applies to people on the one hand, to technologies on the other, and to a combination of aware people and aware technologies.

Engagement (Meaningful): Engagement of a meaningful nature refers to informed involvement in an activity, enabling thoughtful contribution(s) and interactions.

Experience: Experience refers to an encounter, interaction, or skill developed through direct contact with an infrastructure, space, place, person, event, or situation.

Infrastructure: Structural and functional elements that contribute to the day-to-day working of a city, including human and digital components and dimensions.

Interactions: Actions involving the intersecting activities of objects, infrastructures, or people, or in any combination.

Smart Cities: Smart cities are urban areas, regions, territories, and beyond that are characterized by aware and engaged people, in combination with and aided by, the use of awareness enhancing technologies for mobility, livability, and sustainability.

Spatialities: Spatialities refer to people as actors engaging, interacting, and participating in activities in urban spaces and beyond.

Urban Layers: The perspective of layers offers a way of understanding the complexities of urban spaces consisting of a physical layer at the street level, a data layer at the digital level, and a services layer that may also be at the street layer for people moving through the city and at the governance level involving city staff, management, and officials.

Section 2
Interactions, Literacies, Architectures, and Data

Chapter 4
Evolving Urban Understandings:
Cultures, Economies, and Everything as Ambient

ABSTRACT

The purpose of this chapter is to explore visible and invisible flows of information as an emerging and evolving landscape in technology-infused experiences of the city. As such, this work aims to shed additional light on the concept of the ambient in terms of participation in relation to culture, economies, and everything. The research literature for culture, economies, and other urban elements as ambient is explored in this chapter in the context of smart cities, enabling identification of issues, controversies, and problems. Using an exploratory case study approach, solutions and recommendations are advanced. This chapter makes a contribution to 1) the research literature for ambient culture and economies and the ambient turn for smart and responsive cities, 2) the evolving of urban theory, and 3) research and practice through formulation and operationalization of a conceptual framework for ambient cultures and economies in smart cities.

DOI: 10.4018/978-1-5225-7882-6.ch004

1. INTRODUCTION

The purpose of this chapter is to explore visible and invisible flows of information (Schmitt, 2017) as an emerging and evolving landscape in technology-infused experiences of the city. As such, this work aims to shed additional light on information flows through the concept of the ambient, or the ambient turn, in relation to culture, economies, and everything – highlighting participation. The research literature for culture (McKenna, 2016a), economies (Bohn, Coroamă, Langheinrich, Mattern, and Rohs, 2005), and other urban elements and things as ambient (McKenna, 2017a) is explored in this chapter in the context of smart cities, enabling identification of issues, controversies, and problems. Using an exploratory case study approach and multiple methods of data collection and analysis, solutions and recommendations are advanced. This chapter makes a contribution to: a) the research literature for ambient culture and economies while advancing the ambient turn for smart and responsive cities; b) the evolving of urban theory for 21ˢᵗ century cities and regions; and c) research and practice through formulation and operationalization of a conceptual framework for ambient cultures and economies in smart cities.

Objectives: The main objectives of this chapter are to explore a) visible and invisible information flows pertaining to technology-related experiences of the city; the research literature for understandings of culture, economies and everything as ambient; and contemporary experiences of the city employing the construct of participation. As such, this exploration gives rise to the key question in this chapter – How do evolving understandings of the urban and urbanity influence *participation* in smart cities?

2. BACKGROUND AND CONTEXT

Culture as evolving, dynamic, adaptive, and emergent was explored and advanced as ambient by McKenna (2015) in the context of 21st century urban educational environments in relation to awareness, learning, openness, and engagement. The study of emergent ambient culture was extended to smart cities through an exploration of the Internet of Cultural Things (IoCTs) and applications in 21st century urban spaces (McKenna, 2016a). Edges, surfaces, and spaces of action are explored (McKenna, 2016b) in extending digital connectivities and awareness more broadly throughout urban environments. More recently, urban ambient culture explorations were extended to the adaptive reuse of cultural heritage elements and fragments in public spaces in advancing the Internet of Cultural Things (IoCTs) and applications as infrastructures for learning in smart cities (McKenna, 2017a). In the context of re-conceptualizing jobs, work, and labour, McKenna (2017b) advances the potential for more creative economies, opening pathways to explorations of the ambient economies concept. Schmitt (2017) articulated the notion of visible and invisible flows of information in urban areas as information cities.

Building on the prior work cited above, this chapter explores culture, economies, and potentially everything in urban spaces as ambient in smart cities in further developing the notion of urbanity as ambient and in advancing the notion of an ambient turn. As such, this chapter argues that the re-conceptualizing of culture as ambient, economies as ambient, and everything as having an ambient thread running though it – enabled by emergent, adaptive, and dynamic infrastructures, technologies, and interactions – is critical for understanding, participating in, and making cities smarter. Culture and creative economies as dimensions of urbanities in smart cities are re-conceptualized here as ambient to advance, complement, and extend existing understandings of 21st century urban environments.

2.1 Definitions

For the purposes of this work, definitions for key terms used in this chapter are presented here based on the research literature.

- **Ambient:** Ambient is described by Rickert (2013) as being about 'movement', as in, "something always ongoing and transforming" with "an ensemble of interacting human and nonhuman actants."
- **Ambient Culture:** McKenna (2016a) argues that ambient culture "extends existing understandings of culture and captures the 'now', the in-the-moment, of everyday life."
- **Ambient Economies:** McKenna (2017b) advances the potential for more creative and adaptive economies to encourage explorations of the ambient economies concept.

2.2 Overview

This chapter provides a range of perspectives on evolving urban understandings of smart cities in terms of urban culture and creative economies as ambient in Section 3, followed by a selection of associated issues, controversies, and problems. Section 4 provides an overview of the 'ambient turn' and smart cities; a conceptual framework for the ambient turn; and operationalization of the framework for exploration of the proposition under investigation in this chapter in identifying the potential for solutions and recommendations in the form of a framework for ambient participation in smart city urbanities. Section 5 identifies future directions for research and practice and Section 6 concludes with chapter coverage highlights, the major contributions, and key insights, ideas, and lessons.

The primary audiences for this chapter include students, educators, researchers, community members, business, and city practitioners concerned with evolving and innovating urban understandings pertaining to culture, economies, and everything as ambient along with associated challenges and opportunities for cities and regions.

3. EVOLVING URBAN UNDERSTANDINGS FOR SMART CITIES

In coming to evolving urban understandings in the context of smart cities, this chapter provides a review of the research literature for urban culture in smart cities; ambient and creative economies in smart cities, and ambient perspectives for smart cities. A series of associated issues, controversies, and problems are highlighted and presented in tabular form in Section 3.4.

3.1 Urban Culture in Smart Cities

Hollands (2008) questions the labelling of cities as smart in relation to what is rendered visible and invisible, explored "as a high-tech variation of the 'entrepreneurial city'." As part of the human dimension of smart cities, Nam and Pardo (2011) point to the importance of culture and the creative city in the form of human infrastructure. Khatoun and Zeadally (2016) proposed a smart city model consisting of the Internet of Things (IoT), the Internet of Services (IoS), the Internet of Data (IoD), and the Internet of People (IoP) in support of a range of elements and services including smart living and smart people. The Internet of Cultural Things and Applications is an emergent research domain that has been under exploration for several years as evidenced by the presence of venues such as the *International Workshop on Visions on Internet of Cultural Things and Applications (VICTA)*, as part of the *International Conference on Signal-Image Technology and Internet-Based Systems (SITIS)*. For example, Chianese, Bendedusi, Marulli, and Piccialli (2015) go beyond static cultural spaces to more dynamic venues including "on-site ad-hoc (e.g., exhibitions, museums, cultural events), territorial (historical downtown, touristic areas including relevant CH [cultural heritage] resources), and virtual" such as the Internet. Chianese and Piccialli (2015) describe an Internet of Things (IoT) architecture for representing and managing "the smartness inside cultural spaces" that plays "the role of connector between the physical world" and that of information, "to amplify the knowledge" as well as "the enjoyment." Seaver (2017) articulates algorithms as culture in relation to "broad patterns of meaning and practice" to be enacted ethnographically "as heterogeneous and diffuse sociotechnical systems."

Figure 1 provides a glimpse of key issues, controversies, and challenges for urban culture in smart cities.

Key issues, controversies, and challenges for urban culture in smart cities pertain to visible and invisible technologies, human infrastructure and the creative city, IoCT and applications, algorithms as culture, and elements highlighted in the smart city model.

Figure 1. Overview of key issues, controversies, and challenges for urban culture in smart cities

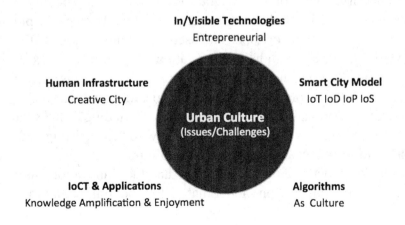

3.2 Ambient and Creative Economies in Smart Cities

Highlighting a series of issues including the invisible, Bohn et al. (2005) described the ambient economy in terms of invisible technologies embedded in products contributing to the notion of smart products and their tracking; anything, anywhere business models; and real time shopping incorporating information asymmetries. Bohn et al. (2005) hint at an awareness gap in terms of technological developments for a "smart world" that have been "pushed through largely unnoticed by the general public extending quite rapidly into our everyday lives." Risks associated with the ambient economy are said to include that of an economy on autopilot with "the exclusion of humans as decision makers" (Bohn et al., 2005) in addition to the potential for privacy-invading technologies, as a "threat to personal privacy." Bohn et al., (2005) point to the importance of ambient economies being *reliable* and *socially acceptable*. Shapiro (2006) explores smart cities in relation to quality of life, productivity, and the growth effects of human capital." Building on Florida's (2002) notion of creative capital and quality of life in urban areas, Wojan and McGranahan (2007) develop a rural variant for local manufacturing competitiveness, as *ambient returns*. Again, as part of the human dimension of smart cities, Nam and Pardo (2011) point to the importance of creative occupations and a creative workforce, among other elements.

Naphade, Banavar, Harrison, Paraszczak, and Morris (2011) highlight the innovation challenges facing smart cities pertaining to "planning, management, and operations" surmounting hurdles of interoperability, security and privacy, and the problem of organizational silos in moving toward "a new closed-loop human-computer interaction paradigm." Bătăgan (2011) argues for the importance of sustainability as a key element of smart cities. Concerned with complex challenges pertaining to socio-economic development and quality of life, Schaffers et al. (2011) undertake an exploration of 'smart cities' as spaces for "open and user-driven innovation" with a view to experimentation and validation in relation to "future Internet-enabled services" extending beyond the urban to include regions, highlighting the importance of "sustainable partnerships and cooperation strategies". Cosgrave, Arbuthnot, and Tryfonas (2013) provide an understanding of the smart city as an "information marketplace" to explore how to "use existing and tested concepts of fostering technology innovation to support city leaders" through systems thinking focusing on 'Living Labs' and the 'Innovation District' in arriving at an implementation model that is both bottom up and top down.

Anttiroiko, Pekka, and Bailey (2014) describe a conceptual framework for the new services economy within the European context for smart cities as creative, innovative, platform-based and social, and sustainable. Gray (2015) refers to the concept of an ambient workforce as in "a distributed, always-on, at-the-ready, expansive labor market, dependent on a mix of intense bursts of activity," as in 'bursty' and 'idle' workflows characterized by 24/7 shiftwork. Mulder (2015) points to the importance of co-creative partnerships and the open(ed) mindset for more creative approaches to data, sharing, and change for a more transparent and social city. Thiel (2017) builds on Florida's notion of the creative class and provides a review of the polarizing nature of the debate associated with the creative city, characterized as having great potential or as highly uncertain and divisive. Thiel employs three empirical vignettes to illustrate the interactivity of culture, the economy, and the city in arguing for the adaptability of cultural production as a reflexive economic activity, highlighting the uncertainty and need for constant change. Caragliu, Del Bo, and Nijkamp (2018) provide an exploration of policies at the smart city level, focusing on smart city initiatives and at the regional level, focusing on smart specialization strategies, finding a positive impact on regional economic performance for both types of policies.

Figure 2 provides an overview of key issues, controversies, and challenges for urban economies in smart cities and regions.

Key issues, controversies, and challenges for urban economies in smart cities pertain to invisible technologies, information asymmetries, ambient economy, sustainability, and human factors.

Figure 2. Overview of key issues, controversies, and challenges for urban economies in smart cities

3.3 Ambient Perspectives for Smart Cities

Drawing on the work of Marzano (2006), ambient culture was articulated by Rauterberg (2007) in relation to entertainment computing and in the context of ambient intelligence, to be "focused on the development of open systems that understand and support the rituals of our living" so as to "adapt themselves to people through time and space." Regarding the ambient, McCullough (2013) articulated the concept of an ambient commons while Rickert (2013) develops the space of ambient rhetoric. Goodspeed (2014) highlights the wicked nature of urban problems and the need for "municipal innovation and IT-enabled collaborative planning." McKenna (2015) theorized the concept of ambient culture for urban educational environments; then in relation to the Internet of Cultural Things and applications (IoCT) in smart cities (McKenna, 2016a); then in relation to adaptive reuse and cultural heritage (McKenna, 2017a); and in terms of creativity and ambient urbanizing in relation to the IoT and the Internet of People (IoP) (2018) involving awareness and serendipity. Denis (2016) describes the digitization of culture in relation to a joint IoCT project involving the British Library, "to shed light on the prominent role of cultural institutions in fostering access to knowledge." Related to the problem of reliability (Bohn et al., 2005), in a technology-rich world, Pink, Ruckenstein, Willim, and Duque (2018) develop the notion of data as broken in the context of "processes of decay, making, repair, re-making and growth" that are interwoven in everyday life and that can be overcome with "ongoing forms of creativity that stem from everyday contingencies and improvisatory human activity."

In summary, while a range of issues, controversies, and problems emerge from the research literature for culture, economies and the ambient in smart cities as indicated through Figures 1 and 2, what also emerges, as depicted in Figure 3, is an overview of underlying key elements as drivers in urban environments. For culture, key elements include adaptive, co-creative partnerships, digitization, improvisatory activities by people, and the rituals of everyday life. For economies, key elements include ambient and creative workforces; the creative city concept; and innovation contributing to smart products involving invisible technologies that can achieve reliability and social acceptance. For the ambient, key elements include adaptive; awareness; the notion of a commons, along with open(ed) mindsets and systems and implications for the personal and for privacy; and a rhetoric or language.

Figure 3. Overview of elements driving culture, economies, and the ambient in smart cities

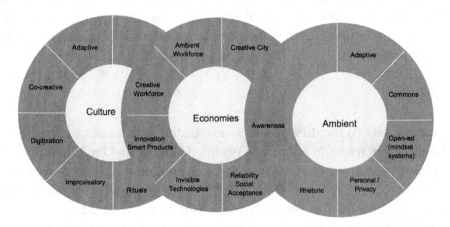

3.4 Issues, Controversies, Problems

Key issues, controversies, and problems emerging in the review of the research literature explored in this chapter are highlighted below and while coverage is not intended to be exhaustive or comprehensive it does serve to illustrate the nature, variety, and range.

Issues

Schmitt (2017) identifies the presence of information flows in cities and the idea of "information cities" to make the invisible flows of information visible. Bohn et al. (2005) suggest an awareness gap on the part of people in terms of "largely unnoticed" technological developments such as "smart products." As such, this chapter argues for more aware people in relation to aware technologies, in support of more informed and more meaningful urban participatory cultures and economies.

Controversies

Hollands (2008) challenges the very notion of the smart city concept or label in relation to what is made visible and also invisible, as in, rendered hidden from view. Thiel (2017) identifies the controversies associated with emerging understandings of the creative city while simultaneously holding great potential in the face of high uncertainty and change. This chapter argues that uncertainty, constant change, and the visible/invisible give rise to the need for dynamic, adaptive, creative, and improvisatory ambient spaces in support of new forms of participation, learning, and interactivities for cultures and economies.

Problems

Bohn et al. (2005) identify problems associated with aware and pervasive technologies in terms of a threat to personal privacy and the reliability and social acceptability of smart environments. Pink et al. (2018) point to the problem of the broken aspect of data, mitigated by creative and improvisatory activities by people. This chapter points to the potential for addressing such complex challenges through a rethinking of participation in the planning, design, and use of aware technologies in ways that more meaningfully involve informed and aware people.

In summary, Table 1 provides an overview, including author and year, of perspectives on issues, controversies, and problems associated with culture, creative economies, and the ambient in the context of smart cities.

For culture, key issues pertain to improvisatory activities, the adaptive, digitization, co-creative partnerships, the ambient, and rituals of living. For economies, key issues and controversies pertain to the creative city, invisible technologies, reliability and social acceptability of technologies, smart products, ambient workforce, services, creative workforce, and innovation. For the ambient, key issues pertain to the awareness gap, personal privacy, an open(ed) mindset, commons, rhetoric, adaptive, and open systems.

By way of solutions and recommendations, the range of issues, controversies, and problems emerging from this review of the research literature are re-conceptualized in this chapter as challenges and opportunities to be addressed through development and operationalization of the conceptual framework for the ambient turn and smart cities (Figure 4) that is formulated in Section 4.

4. THE AMBIENT TURN AND SMART CITIES

Based on the perspectives emerging in this chapter from a review of the research literature, the notion of an emerging 'ambient turn' enabled by more aware people and aware technologies in the context of smart cities is advanced.

Table 1. Perspectives on issues, controversies, and problems for culture, economies and the ambient

Culture, Economies, and Everything in Smart Cities				
Author(s)	**Year**	**Culture**	**Economies**	**Ambient**
Pink et al.	2018	Improvisatory activities		
Thiel	2017	Adaptive	Creative city	
Denis	2016	Digitization		
Bohn et al.	2015		Invisible technologies	Awareness gap
			Reliability	Personal privacy
			Smart products	
			Socially acceptable	
Gray	2015		Ambient workforce	
Mulder	2015	Co-creative partnerships		Open(ed) mindset
Anttiroiko et al.	2014		Services	
McCullough	2013			Commons
Rickert	2013			Rhetoric
Nam and Pardo	2011		Creative workforce	
Naphade et al.	2011		Innovation	
Rauterberg	2007	Ambient		
Marzano	2006	Rituals of living		Adaptive; Open systems

4.1 Conceptual Framework for the Ambient Turn or Everything as Ambient

Researchers speak of 'the turn' in relation to, for example, pedagogy (Edelglass, 2009), the socio-spatial (Banerjee, 2010), and the changing and evolving of learning and spaces for learning in smart cities (McKenna, 2016c), to name a few.

Formulation of a conceptual framework for the 'ambient turn' in smart cities is articulated in this chapter as depicted in Figure 4. Focusing on the relationship of aware people and aware technologies, a conceptual framework for the ambient turn in the context of smart cities is advanced enabling evolving understandings of culture, economies, and everything as ambient, thus constituting the ambient turn.

The construct of meaningful participation in digitally enabled urban areas and regions is used to explore visible and invisible information layers where privacy, reliability, and the social acceptability of technologies matter, amid high uncertainty and change.

Figure 4. Conceptual framework for the ambient turn and smart cities

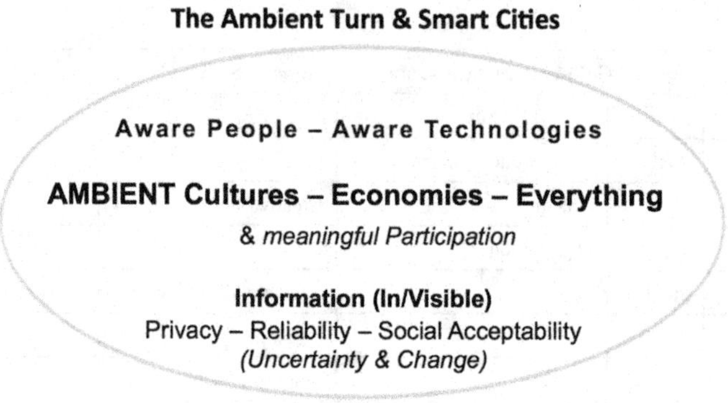

The Ambient Turn & Smart Cities

Aware People – Aware Technologies

AMBIENT Cultures – Economies – Everything
& meaningful Participation

Information (In/Visible)
Privacy – Reliability – Social Acceptability
(Uncertainty & Change)

Through emerging understandings of the 'ambient turn', this chapter focuses on aware people and aware technologies in smart cities in responding to the research question, restated as a proposition under exploration in this chapter, as follows:

P: Evolving understandings of the urban and urbanity influence *participation* in smart cities when culture, economies, and everything are considered through the lens of the ambient.

How participation informs urbanity is explored in this chapter using a survey instrument and protocol-guided in-depth interviews with a diverse range of individuals across multiple cities and countries in addition to discussions across multiple sectors with groups and individuals in several Canadian cities. The focus of the multiple data gathering methods centered on questions designed to provide insight into spaces for culture, creative economies, and the ambient in aware environments. Ambient is understood to be that which is characterized as more dynamic, in-the-moment, and adaptive in relation to reuse activities and designs pertaining to infrastructural elements, enabling new potentials for participation to occur at all stages of the urbanizing process from imagining; to definition; to design; to prototyping; to deployment for testing and use; to maintenance; to assessment; and to ongoing refinement and innovation.

As such, this work explores the ambient turn in smart cities in consideration of the potential for solutions and recommendations to issues, controversies, and problems highlighted in Table 1.

4.2 Evolving Urban Understandings:
Solutions and Recommendations

In seeking to foster evolving urban understandings in support of solutions and recommendations for challenges identified in Section 3, participation is explored in this work through a) culture, creative economies, and everything as ambient; b) in relation to the creative and the instrumented; and c) in relation to privacy, reliability, and social acceptability in a rapidly changing and uncertain world.

4.2.1. Participation Through Culture, Creative Economies, and Everything as Ambient

As if to illustrate the notion of ambient culture, an individual described their city as "almost like one giant museum." On the digital level, an educator came to the realization that the use of Twitter feeds during a conference presentation pointed to the fluidity of the online world of the Internet, expanding and extending everyday spaces into a continuum for learning and culture by those attending in person or at a distance. A student referred to the sharing of "very traditional things" and "sharing them constantly" through "social media" as generating "concurrent awareness." A community leader described an "art in public places" initiative, extending across multiple domains, supported by the city, illustrating "ways to animate a space" involving local technology, arts, culture, and cross-sector urban collaboration, characteristic of smart cities. The initiative focused on a city parkade with interactive, embedded sensor technology that "plays different sounds as you go up based on where you are in the stairwell" along with "lighting changes." A city councilor is quoted as saying that the musical railing initiative is "designed to ensure civic parkades are safe and welcoming" while highlighting the important element of culture, and other benefits (http://bit.ly/29OHwIg). From a technology business perspective, an individual wondered about the potential for the city, when building public networks in support of city infrastructure and services – to use the excess bandwidth "to drive economic value to the city?" Driven by creativity, a community leader articulated the importance of "clusters" and the need to figure out how to "move away from sector driven strategies to ones that" foster collaboration and "bring industries and sectors together rather than that sort of silo" approach while emphasizing the potential for and importance of funding for smart cities.

4.2.2. Participation as Creative and Instrumented

Responding to the survey, 67% of individuals agreed on the need to make urban participation smarter by removing the red tape and bureaucracy. An educator described a creative "mobile cloud-based app to capture and share insights, feedback, and knowledge" as a "simple, cost efficient" mechanism for "instant awareness" intended for "business, design, infrastructure, learning, safety, sport, and tourism." A technology entrepreneur highlighted the importance of the "smart city thought process" as something "that connects all the pieces," including "people, community." An Educator observed that people "choose to live somewhere" attracted in part by "smart infrastructures" and more livable lifestyles. Highlighting participation through intersections of the physical and digital, a city councilor described how "we held our first interactive e-TownHall and we were able to get feedback from people watching the live stream so we have a packed house in person and also an overflow room with hundreds tweeting, sending direct messages that we could respond to." Referring to the smartphone, a community member commented that, "there are a lot of advantages to having that to enhance the urban experience" in terms of being "able to get from point a to b faster or maybe find something out about the area." And a community leader pointed to the value of the City's ParkingApp that enables people to pay for parking on-the-go. As an example of Pendleton-Jullian's (Jenkins, 2016) notion of the instrumentalizing of the products of the imagination, the community leader suggested the idea of extending the ParkingApp to "help me find parking." City IT observed that, "almost any technology now has the ability to be more than just a single service" highlighting "more intelligent lighting" such as "lighting whenever people need it" while noting that "an intelligent fabric to communicate enables so much more." As an example, City IT pointed to the potential for "putting sensors in garbage cans so they tell you when they're full" which "reduces the number of visits or increases the number" resulting in a push for "starting to instrument more and more of those elements." For City IT, the Internet of Things (IoT) was viewed as "more about the instrumentation of things, with everything connected and communicated."

4.2.3. Participation and Privacy, Reliability, and Social Acceptance

An educator encouraged collaboration on the part of decision makers to support "societal pilots" involving "city mayors and architects" and others in order to include "the suggestions, needs, expectations and ideas of people" from project conception to implementation. Such pilots it was urged could "engage using technologies" that would be "both entertaining and meaningful" for people in the community while pointing to the importance of a willingness to fund such initiatives in "rewarding participation" in some way. As a "user of the city" services, an educator expressed appreciation that "the infrastructure is reliable." Regarding urban data, City IT staff commented that, "fundamentally there is a desire to be very, very open with the data" adding that "it is public data, we manage on behalf of the citizenry" and "where there is a purpose to utilize that data" access is important because "maybe it helps improve something." A student pointed to the "ownership and privacy" challenges of urban data in terms of "how it is housed" and the "infrastructure by which it is shared" noting that "as we work out how to sort out the data that is constantly being made, built, we will know more" about "what to do with it" influencing "notions of smart delivery." The student added that "the more that technical infrastructure can be made to constantly reciprocate the data flows that are happening between people, formal and informal, the better" in support of the "goal of smart cities." It is worth noting that 100% of individuals indicated in survey responses that, "people generally are not aware of smart cities" highlighting the awareness gap identified by Bohn et al. (2005).

City IT commented that, "we are interested in putting physical infrastructure in place" and "how we interpret using it is still open." On a regional level, cycling data is shared visually, in the moment, on a public display as cyclists use an urban multi-use trail, contributing to a dynamic tracking mechanism for the sharing of cycling data as part of the infrastructure. The value of data, the value of open data, and the value of data infrastructures were recognized by city staff and community members alike, in that, this information is said to be important in the context of the "investment in bike infrastructure." City IT commented that, "we're starting to look at the tools to help us mine the data that we already have an interest in" and "beyond that, we're very much immature in that overall data sense." For some types of data it was indicated that, "we're just starting to look at the tools that would give us the visualization of that" in lieu of any "practical application." Also identified was "that hurdle of just really starting to educate" about "what could be done" and "educating ourselves" in the absence of "any kind of funding to do these things." While cities were described in a Canadian context as necessarily conservative when it comes to data and privacy and the purpose of data collection, one participant identified the challenge of, "not knowing what to do with the data" and others shared comments on "how you might find purpose for the data." The veracity of information provided to social media and other platforms was questioned by a student, who pointed to the frequent contributing of "made up" details in an effort to maintain some degree of privacy in such spaces. A community member in St. John's observed that "we're not smart on how we use the technology" citing "improved communications about the transportation system" and "anywhere Internet" as key priorities that would be "particularly useful" suggestive of information asymmetries issues. An education innovator highlighted the importance of an "uncertain future" and an IT (information technology) leader in higher education pointed to change as the legacy of youth today with an emphasis on the social and social capital.

Summarized in Figure 5, a glimpse of patterns, flows, relationships, and potentials begins to emerge for evolving urban understandings through culture, economies, everything, and the in/visibilities of the ambient turn and smart cities. Culture is characterized as adaptive, enabling concurrent awareness in dynamic environments in support of the personalized and the visualization of culture in public spaces is highlighted. Economies as creative are articulated drawing on novel connections that are dynamic, less bureaucratic, as in smarter, in support of smart delivery mechanisms and smart products and processes while recognizing the value associated with the potential of societal pilots. Everything as ambient is enabled through collaboration, connectivity, openness to change, potentially limitless instrumenting, even products of the imagination while sharing is emphasized in the face of widespread uncertainty. And finally, in/visibilities in physical and digital urban spaces draw attention to the need for new forms of education, funding, value, and understandings of privacy, along with an emphasis on the reliability and social acceptability of digital infrastructures including the IoT (Internet of Things), the IoP (Internet of People) and the IoE (Internet of Experiences). Although neatly categorized across culture, economies, everything, and in/visibilities, it is important to note that there is considerable overlap in that personalized is associated with economies for example as well as with culture. Also, the categories are necessarily incomplete and intended only as an initial and summary overview.

Figure 5. Evolving urban understandings through culture, economies, everything and in/visibilities

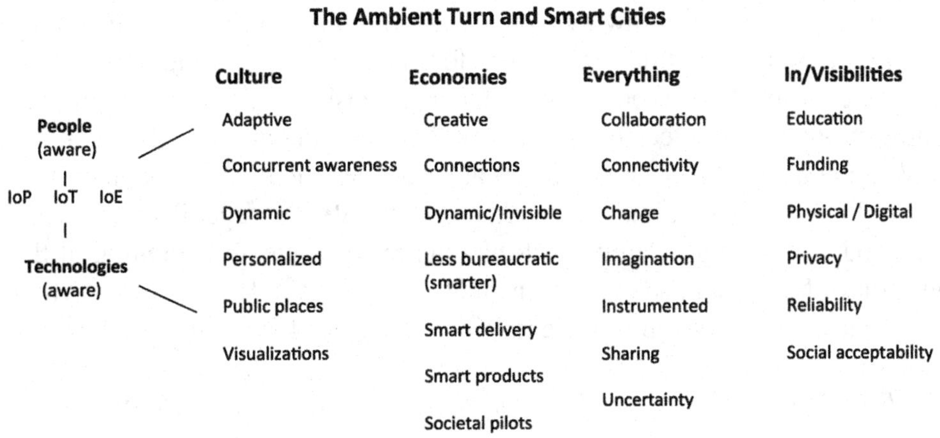

The Ambient Turn and Smart Cities

	Culture	Economies	Everything	In/Visibilities
People (aware)	Adaptive	Creative	Collaboration	Education
	Concurrent awareness	Connections	Connectivity	Funding
IoP IoT IoE	Dynamic	Dynamic/Invisible	Change	Physical / Digital
	Personalized	Less bureaucratic (smarter)	Imagination	Privacy
Technologies (aware)	Public places		Instrumented	Reliability
	Visualizations	Smart delivery	Sharing	Social acceptability
		Smart products	Uncertainty	
		Societal pilots		

4.2.4. Discussion of Participation and Evolving Urban Understandings as Ambient

How participation informs evolving urban understandings as ambient is discussed in relation to the ambient turn; the creative and instrumentalized; and privacy, reliability and social acceptance.

Participation and the Ambient Turn

Culture was depicted as very much alive and permeating a city, as in, the interpretation of an urban area in one instance as a large urban museum. The fluidity of information flows was highlighted with the interplay of the physical space of a conference with social media such as Twitter, contributing to a continuum for interaction and information sharing. The sharing of everyday moments producing a culture of "concurrent awareness" further highlights the permeability of the physical and digital. Emphasis on creative clusters for collaboration and the importance of funding for such spaces and approaches point to openings for more creative and dynamic economies and mindsets. The musical railing example of a collaboratively developed embedding of technologies in public spaces in support of participation, safety, entertainment, animation, and other benefits, supported by the city, demonstrates the cultural, economic, and ambient nature and potential of smart city initiatives.

Participation and the Creative and Instrumentalized

More creative approaches to making cities smarter emerged through less bureaucratic processes drawing on smart city thought processes. For example, the highlighting of mobile applications for instant awareness and information sharing contributes to the potential for making, decision-making, and improving connections and services more broadly. The instrumenting of things in the development of smart infrastructures and services and the instrumentalizing of products of the imagination by extending mobile app capabilities, serve to contribute to greater awareness of the interactive value and potential of the interplay of physical and digital information spaces and flows, in supporting and enhancing the urban experience, innovation, and creativity.

Participation and Privacy, Reliability, and Social Acceptance

Issues of privacy and personalized services emerged in relation to social media platforms. Also emerging is acknowledgement of the complex and wicked challenges associated with data ownership, the housing of data, and the infrastructures for the sharing of data, contributing to the potential for opportunities to provide the smart delivery of data. While the reliability of city transport infrastructures was appreciated and valued, reliability in the digital data space was recognized as a work-in-progress requiring education and improved awareness on many levels along with the need for funding to enable this to occur. Additionally, the importance of funding in the form of rewarding and valuing participation in creative economies was also highlighted. Societal pilots were emphasized as a mechanism in support of increased and meaningful participation while contributing more broadly to the potential of social acceptability for more aware technologies and more aware people.

Findings in this chapter contribute further to development of the ambient culture concept as well as to the concepts of ambient creativity and ambient economies in coming to evolving understandings of the urban in terms of the ambient turn. Indeed, findings in this chapter give rise to the potential for emerging understanding of participation as ambient, as depicted in Figure 6, organized around aware people and aware technologies encompassing the physical and digital in relation to ambient culture, ambient and creative economies, and the personalized in support of the ambient turn, fostering smarter and more responsive cities and urbanities that are attentive to privacy, reliability, and social acceptability.

Figure 6. Framework for ambient participation in smart city urbanities

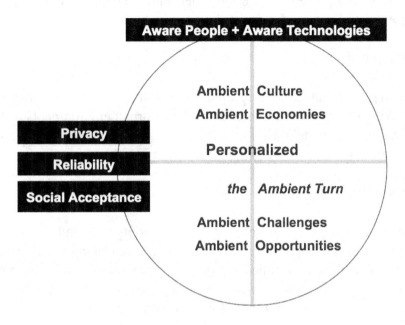

In summary, discussion of the 'ambient turn' in smart cities contributes to evolving understandings of ambient urbanities and to the notion of ambient participation. The combination of more aware people with more aware technologies in support of everyday, in-the-moment, continuous information streams, fosters new spaces for dynamic and adaptive participation and for keeping people more informed in urban environments. In the context of the ambient turn, even challenges and opportunities hold the potential to become ambient in terms of their dynamic, adaptive, and responsive nature.

Dependent Variable (DV)

The dependent variable (DV) surfaced in this chapter is *participation and personalization* in relation to culture, economies, and the 'ambient turn' with everything as ambient. Associated independent variables include: support for the creative impulse, implying the presence of spaces for making; smart city thought process, implying the potential to make urban participation smarter; rewarding participation, implying the potential for value creation; and veracity of social media data and privacy workarounds, implying spaces for contributing to greater data integrity.

5. FUTURE RESEARCH DIRECTIONS

Future and emerging trends are identified in this chapter for both practice and research in Sections 5.1 and 5.2 respectively.

5.1 Practice

For urban practitioners, this chapter offers ideas and early-stage examples for a rethinking of participation in contemporary urban environments as more adaptive, informed, and meaningful, in the moment, in the form of ambient participation, along with emerging variables and indicators.

Ambient Participation

This work opens pathways for new understandings of, and exposure to, participation as ambient, as in more adaptive, creative, and improvisatory in the moment in urban environments. As such, this work invites more meaningful participation in culture and creative economy spaces and the underlying and often invisible areas involving the flows of data and information.

Ambient Challenges and Opportunities

Challenges and opportunities for practitioners emerge in relation to real-time, dynamic, and adaptive types of participation associated with new forms of data generation, novel purposes and uses of data, and new forms of funding in support of initiatives, along with education in support of new literacies and competencies.

Variables and Indicators

This chapter advances the potential for value to emerge on a practical level for the *participation and personalization* dependent variable and the independent variables pertaining to the creative impulse, smart city thought processes, rewarding participation, and data veracity. These variables may begin to serve as indicators for some of the more intangible and invisible elements of ambient urbanities.

5.2 Research

This work opens the way to future research potentials associated with the concepts of ambient participation and the ambient turn more broadly, extending even to ambient challenges and ambient opportunities in coming to wider understandings of ambient urbanities.

Ambient Participation

The *framework for ambient participation in smart city urbanities* is intended to support improvisatory, dynamic, and adaptive spaces for participation contributing to the potential for greater reliability; social acceptability; concurrent and instant forms of awareness through mobile apps and the like; ways to animate spaces; while driving cultural, creative, and economic value to the city. As such, this chapter contributes further to the emerging research literature on ambient culture, heritage, and economies in the context of smart cities.

Ambient Turn

The viability of the *conceptual framework for the ambient turn and smart cities* operationalized for use in this chapter demonstrates early-stage potentials while offering and opening up new understandings in evolving urban spaces for testing and practice.

Ambient Challenges and Smart Cities

Research spaces are opened in this chapter for the potential to conceptualize urban challenges in smart cities as ambient, with implications for ways of seeing and theorizing issues, controversies, and problems in contemporary urban environments.

Ambient Opportunities and Smart Cities

Research spaces are opened in this chapter for the potential to conceptualize urban opportunities in smart cities as ambient, with implications for ways of approaching issues, controversies, and problems in contemporary urban environments.

6. CONCLUSION

This chapter provides an exploration of participation in smart cities from the perspective of evolving understandings of culture, economies, and the ambient turn. Issues, controversies, and problems associated with increasingly aware and invisible technologies are identified including awareness gaps; tensions associated with the creative city related to uncertainty and change; and problems pertaining to privacy, reliability, and social acceptability. As such, this chapter argues for the importance of enabling more aware people through creative initiatives, opportunities, and spaces for informed and meaningful participation. The primary contributions of this chapter are: a) provision of an overview of elements driving culture, economies, and the ambient in smart cities; b) formulation and operationalization of a conceptual framework for the ambient turn and smart cities based on a review of the literature; c) development of a framework for ambient participation in smart city urbanities; and d) extending of the existing research literature on urban theory by building out additional discourse, debate, and practice spaces to include culture, creative economies, and participation as ambient, as in the ambient turn, and extending this even to the potential for challenges and opportunities to be conceptualized as ambient.

Insights of particular interest to the reader in this chapter include the following:

1. The potential for meaningful participation opportunities to inform evolving urban understandings
2. The interconnectedness of culture, economies and everything as ambient, informing ambient urbanities
3. The surfacing of variables associated with *participation and personalization* in evolving urban spaces

Ideas highlighted in this chapter pertain to the following:

1. The importance of people becoming more aware of the ambient turn and of the smart cities phenomena
2. The potential for people to be rewarded (valued) for their participation in digital/physical urban spaces
3. Ambient participation as a novel approach contributing to smarter cities and to ambient urbanities

Lessons for the reader in this chapter are associated with the following:

1. The potential for meaningful participation to influence and be influenced by aware technologies
2. The potential for aware technologies to enhance participation possibilities and ambient creativity
3. The intractable issues, controversies, and problems for culture, economies, and the ambient turn

This work will be of interest to a broad audience including, but not limited to, students, educators, researchers, urban practitioners, community members, business, and anyone concerned with evolving urban understandings to encompass more dynamic notions of culture and economies as ambient in relation to the complex urban challenges of smart and responsive cities and urbanities.

REFERENCES

Anttiroiko, A.-V., Pekka, V., & Bailey, S. J. (2014). Smart cities in the new service economy: Building platforms for smart services. *AI & Society*, *29*(3), 323–334. doi:10.100700146-013-0464-0

Banerjee, I. (2010). Educational urbanism: The strategic alliance between educational planning, pedagogy and urban planning. In M. Schrenk, V. V. Popovich, D. Engelke, & P. Elisei (Eds.), *REAL CORP 2010: Livable, prosper, healthy cities for everyone*. Academic Press. Retrieved 13 September 2016 from http://publik.tuwien.ac.at/files/PubDat_193027.pdf

Bătăgan, L. (2011). Smart cities and sustainability models. *Informações Econômicas*, *15*(3), 80–87.

Bohn, J., Coroamă, V., Langheinrich, M., Mattern, F., & Rohs, M. (2005). Social, economic, and ethical implications of ambient intelligence and ubiquitous computing. In W. Weber, J. M. Rabaey, & E. Aarts (Eds.), *Ambient Intelligence*. Berlin: Springer. doi:10.1007/3-540-27139-2_2

Caragliu, A., Del Bo, C., & Nijkamp, P. (2018). Much ado about something? An appraisal of the relationship between smart city and smart specialisation policies. *Journal of Economic & Social Geography*, *109*(1), 129–143.

Chianese, A., Bendedusi, P., Marulli, F., & Piccialli, F. (2015). An associative engines based approach supporting collaborative analytics in the Internet of Cultural Things. *Proc. of 10ᵗʰ Intl. Conf. on P2P, Parallel, Grid, Cloud and Internet Computing (3PGCIC)*, 533-538. 10.1109/3PGCIC.2015.56

Chianese, A., & Piccialli, F. (2015). Improving user experience of cultural environment through IoT: The beauty or the truth case study. In *Intelligent interactive multimedia systems and services. Smart Innovation, Systems and Technologies, 40* (pp. 11–20). Springer. doi:10.1007/978-3-319-19830-9_2

Cosgrave, E., Arbuthnot, K., & Tryfonas, T. (2013). Living labs, innovation districts and information marketplaces: A systems approach for smart cities. *Procedia Computer Science*, *16*, 668–677. doi:10.1016/j.procs.2013.01.070

Denis, G. (2016). Living knowledge – British Library 2015 – 2023. @ *IoCT Blog*. Retrieved 15 August 2016 from https://internetofculturalthings. com/2016/03/03/blogliving-knowledge-british-library-2015-2023/

Edelglass, W. (2009). Philosophy and place-based pedagogies. In A. Kenkmann (Ed.), *Teaching philosophy* (pp. 69–80). New York, NY: Continuum.

Florida, R. (2002). *The rise of the creative class: And how it's transforming work, leisure, community, and everyday life*. New York: Basic Books.

Goodspeed, R. (2014). Smart cities: Moving beyond urban cybernetics to tackle wicked problems. *Cambridge Journal of Regions, Economy and Society*, *8*(1), 79–92. doi:10.1093/cjres/rsu013

Gray, M. L. (2015). *Re-assembling the assembly line: Digital labor economies and demands for an ambient workforce*. Berkman Klein Luncheon Series. Berkman Center for Internet & Society, Harvard University. Retrieved 1 April 2018 from https://cyber.harvard.edu/events/luncheon/2015/11/Gray

Hollands, R. G. (2008). Will the real smart city please stand up? Intelligent, progressive or entrepreneurial? *City*, *12*(3), 303–320. doi:10.1080/13604810802479126

Jenkins, H. (2016). *Mapping the pragmatic imagination: An interview with Ann M. Pendleton-Jullian. (Part 3)*. Retrieved 16 December 2016 from http://henryjenkins.org/2016/11/mapping-the-pragmatic-imagination-an-interview-with-ann-m-pendleton-jullian-part-3.html

Khatoun, R., & Zeadally, S. (2016). Smart cities: Concepts, architectures, research opportunities. *Communications of the ACM, 59*(8), 46–57. doi:10.1145/2858789

Marzano, S. (2006). Ambient culture. In E. Aarts & J. Encarnação (Eds.), *True visions: The emergence of ambient intelligence* (pp. 35–52). Springer. doi:10.1007/978-3-540-28974-6_3

McCullough, M. (2013). *Ambient commons: Attention in the age of embodied information.* Cambridge, MA: The MIT Press. doi:10.7551/mitpress/8947.001.0001

McKenna, H. P. (2015). Ambient culture in 21st century urban educational environments: An exploration of awareness, learning, openness, and engagement. *Proceedings of the 8th International Technology, Education & Development (INTED2015) Conference*, 1502-1512.

McKenna, H. P. (2016a). Emergent ambient culture in smart cities: Exploring the Internet of Cultural Things (IoCTs) and applications in 21st century urban spaces. *Proceedings of the 12th International Conference on Signal-Image Technology and Internet-Based Systems (SITIS 2016)*, 420-427. 10.1109/SITIS.2016.72

McKenna, H. P. (2016b). Edges, surfaces, and spaces of action in 21st century urban environments – Connectivities and awareness in the city. In D. Kreps, G. Fletcher, & M. Griffiths (Eds.), Technology and Intimacy: Choice or Coercion (pp. 328-343). Academic Press.

McKenna, H. P. (2016c). Innovating relationships for learning in 21st century smart cities. *Proceedings of the 9th Annual International Conference of Education, Research and Innovation (iCERi2016)*, 4695-4704. 10.21125/iceri.2016.2115

McKenna, H. P. (2017a). Adaptive reuse of cultural heritage elements and fragments in public spaces: The Internet of Cultural Things (IoCTs) and applications as infrastructures for learning in smart cities. *Proceedings of the 13th International Conference on Signal-Image Technology and Internet-Based Systems (SITIS2017)*. 10.1109/SITIS.2017.84

McKenna, H. P. (2017b). Re-conceptualizing jobs, work, and labour: Transforming learning for more creative economies in 21st century smart cities. *Proceedings of the 10th Annual International Conference of Education, Research and Innovation (iCERi2017)*, 8367-8376. 10.21125/iceri.2017.2251

McKenna, H. P. (2018). Creativity and ambient urbanizing at the intersection of the Internet of Things and People in smart cities. In M. Antona & C. Stephanidis (Eds.), *UAHCI 2018, LNCS 10908* (pp. 295–307). Springer. doi:10.1007/978-3-319-92052-8_23

Mulder, I. (2015). Opening up: Towards a sociable smart city. In *Citizen's Right to the Digital City*. Singapore: Springer. doi:10.1007/978-981-287-919-6_9

Nam, T., & Pardo, T. A. (2011). Conceptualizing smart city with dimensions of technology, people, and institutions. *Proceedings of the 12th Annual International Conference on Digital Government Research*, 282-291. 10.1145/2037556.2037602

Naphade, M., Banavar, G., Harrison, C., Paraszczak, J., & Morris, R. (2011). Smarter cities and their innovation challenges. *Computer*, *44*(6), 32–39. doi:10.1109/MC.2011.187

Pink, S., Ruckenstein, M., Willim, R., & Duque, M. (2018, January). Broken data: Conceptualising data in an emerging world. *Big Data and Society*, 1-13.

Rauterberg, M. (2007). Ambient culture: A possible future for entertainment computing. In A. Lugmayr & P. Golebiowski (Eds.), *Interactive TV: A shared experience - Adjunct Proceedings of EuroITV 2007* (pp. 37-39). Tampere, Finland: Academic Press.

Rickert, T. (2013). *Ambient rhetoric: The attunements of rhetorical being.* Pittsburgh, PA: University of Pittsburgh Press. doi:10.2307/j.ctt5hjqwx

Schaffers, H., Komninos, N., Pallot, M., Trousse, B., Nilsson, M., & Oliveira, A. (2011). Smart Cities and the Future Internet: Towards Cooperation Frameworks for Open Innovation. In *The Future Internet* (Vol. 6656, pp. 431–446). Berlin: Springer Berlin Heidelberg.

Schmitt, G. (2017). *Future Cities.* Zurich, Switzerland: ETHzurich. Retrieved 11 December 2017 from https://www.edx.org/course/future-cities-ethx-fc-01x

Seaver, N. (2017, July). Algorithms as culture: Some tactics for the ethnography of algorithmic systems. *Big Data & Society*, 1-12.

Shapiro, J. M. (2006). Smart cities: Quality of life, productivity, and the growth effects of human capital. *The Review of Economics and Statistics, 88*(2), 324–335. doi:10.1162/rest.88.2.324

Thiel, J. (2017). Creative cities and the reflexivity of the urban creative economy. *European Urban and Regional Studies, 24*(1), 21–34. doi:10.1177/0969776415595105

Wojan, T. R., & McGranahan, D. A. (2007). Ambient returns: Creative capital's contribution to local manufacturing competitiveness. *Agricultural and Resource Economics Review, 36*(1), 133–148. doi:10.1017/S1068280500009497

ADDITIONAL READING

Dourish, P. (2017). *The stuff of bits: An essay on the materialities of information.* Cambridge, MA: MIT Press. doi:10.7551/mitpress/10999.001.0001

Goldsmith, S., & Crawford, S. (2014). *The responsive city: Engaging communities through data-smart governance.* San Francisco, CA: John Wiley & Sons Inc.

Kozubaev, S. (2018). Futures as design: Explorations, images, and participations. *Interaction, XXV*(2), 46–51. doi:10.1145/3178554

Mattern, S. (2016). Instrumental city: The view from Hudson Yards, circa 2019 – The world's most ambitious "smart city" project is here. Should we worry that New York City is becoming an experimental lab? *Places Journal*, April 2017. Retrieved 5 April 2018 from https://placesjournal.org/article/instrumental-city-new-york-hudson-yards/

McKenna, H. P. (2015). Learning to iterate in the city: Interactive environments for socially responsive urban participation. In S. Carliner, C. Fulford, N. Ostashewshi (Eds.), *Proceedings of the World Conference on Educational Media and Technology (EdMedia 2015)*, (pp. 1713-1717). Association for the Advancement of Computing in Education (AACE).

Raj, J. (2016). Smart cities: A shift in technology or culture? *Desktop: The Culture of Design.* Retrieved 21 December 2016 from https://desktopmag.com.au/features/smart-cities-a-shift-in-technology-or-culture/#.WFs3-Ff6P5o

Schmitt, G. (2018). *Responsive Cities*. MOOC (Massive Open Online Course). Zurich, Switzerland: ETHzurich. Retrieved 9 April 2018 from https://www.edx.org/course/responsive-cities

Simonofski, A., Asensio, E. S., De Smedt, J., & Snoeck, M. (2017). Citizen participation in smart cities: Evaluation framework proposal. *Proceedings of the 19th Conference on Business Informatics*, IEEE. 10.1109/CBI.2017.21

KEY TERMS AND DEFINITIONS

Ambient Creativity: Ambient creativity refers to a more dynamic, adaptive, and evolving understanding of creativity, enabled by more aware people interacting with more aware technologies and with each other.

Ambient Culture: Ambient culture refers to a more dynamic, adaptive, and evolving understanding of culture, enabled by more aware people in combination with emerging, aware, and pervasive technologies.

Ambient Economies: Ambient economies refer to more dynamic, adaptive, and evolving understandings of economies enabled by more aware people in combination with more aware technologies.

Ambient Turn: The emergence of aware technologies together with more aware people creates the conditions for more adaptive, dynamic, and emergent capabilities, contexts, interactions, and situations referred to in this works as the ambient turn.

Creative Economies: Creative economies refer to economies based on more adaptive spaces for the generation of creative ideas.

Information Flows – Invisible: With the introduction of digital technologies the potential for information flows in cities to become vaster increases while becoming more embedded in objects and spaces and as such, less visible.

Information Flows – Visible: Information flows in cities are generally visible through libraries, museums and other spaces that collect, organize, and make available information artifacts.

Chapter 5
Emergent Digital Literacies:
Ambient Learning, Play, and Inclusion

ABSTRACT

The purpose of this chapter is to explore digital literacies in the context of smart cities in relation to aware people and aware technologies. This work aims to shed light on the ambient concept for learning, play, and inclusion contributing to emergent requirements for urban digital literacies. The research literature for digital literacies, ambient learning, ambient play, and ambient inclusion is explored in this chapter in the context of smart cities, enabling identification of issues, controversies, and problems. Using an exploratory case study approach, solutions and recommendations are advanced. This chapter makes a contribution to 1) the research literature for digital literacies, ambient learning, ambient play, and ambient inclusion in smart cities; 2) the evolving of urban theory for 21st century cities; and 3) ambient urbanities by formulating and operationalizing a conceptual framework for ambient learning, play, and inclusion for smart cities in support of research and practice.

1. INTRODUCTION

The purpose of this chapter is to explore digital literacies in the context of smart cities in relation to aware people and aware technologies. As such, this work aims to shed light on the ambient concept for learning, play, and inclusion contributing to emergent requirements for urban digital literacies.

DOI: 10.4018/978-1-5225-7882-6.ch005

The research literature for digital literacies (Adams Becker et al., 2017), ambient learning (McKenna, 2016b; Kölmel and Kicin, 2005), ambient play (Hjorth, 2015; McKenna et al., 2014), and ambient inclusion (McKenna, 2018b) is explored in this chapter in the context of smart cities, enabling identification of issues, controversies, and problems. Using an exploratory case study approach, solutions and recommendations are advanced. This chapter makes a contribution to: a) the research literature for digital literacies, ambient learning, ambient play, and ambient inclusion in smart cities; b) the evolving of urban theory for 21st century cities; and c) ambient urbanities by formulating and operationalizing a conceptual framework for ambient learning, play, and inclusion for smart cities in support of research and practice.

Objectives: The objective of this chapter is to explore digital literacies in terms of what it means to experience the notion of ambient learning in relation to the wicked challenges facing education, educators, and learners while re-imagining play and inclusion as social, urban, and ambient enabled by more dynamic, adaptive, and interactive infrastructures for innovating and urbanizing in the city. As such, this exploration gives rise to the key research question in this chapter – Why does *learning* matter for urbanity in relation to emergent digital literacies in smart cities?

2. BACKGROUND AND CONTEXT

The ambient learning concept is explored and developed in this chapter as part of the learning dimension of smart cities (McKenna, 2016b) while the innovating of relationships for learning (McKenna, 2016a) is addressed in bringing greater awareness to learning approaches, practices, and spaces. Aided by the work of Pendleton-Jullian (Pendleton-Jullian and Brown, 2016) on imagination and design at the intersection of culture, environment, and technology, this chapter explores creative thinking approaches to learning. A re-imagining of inclusion is developed for urban environments, as ambient inclusion, aided also by the work of Pendleton-Jullian and Brown (2016) on design and imagination. Explorations of the ambient in terms of aware people and aware technologies gives rise to the question of what it means to experience the notion of ambient learning in smart cities. The wicked challenges facing education (Adams Becker, Cummins, Davis, Freeman, Hall

Giesinger, and Ananthanarayanan, 2017), educators, and learners serve to shed light on the potentials for ambient and emergent learning (McKenna, Arnone, Kaarst-Brown, McKnight, and Chauncey, 2013) while re-imagining play (McKenna, Chauncey, Arnone, Kaarst-Brown, and McKnight, 2014) and inclusion (McKenna, 2018b; McKenna, 2016b) as social, urban, and ambient enabled by more dynamic, adaptive, and interactive infrastructures for innovating and urbanizing in the city. Shedding light on education as one of many key elements of smart cities contributes to an understanding of learning as ambient and as critical to 21st century smart urban environments and urbanities. Additionally, inclusion, social inclusion, and urban inclusion as mechanisms for addressing the digital divide (McKenna, 2018b) are explored in this chapter in the context of smart cities.

2.1 Definitions

For the purposes of this work, definitions for key terms used in this chapter are presented here based on the research literature.

- **Ambient Pedagogy:** Ravenscroft, Sagar, Baur, and Oriogun (2010) describe ambient pedagogy as "an approach to pedagogy and learning design that foregrounds the experiences that are produced through the realisation of the pedagogy, that is present but 'behind the scenes', in a learning situation."
- **Digital Literacy:** Merchant (2010) uses digital literacy to "describe written or symbolic representation that is mediated by new technology" while Adams Becker et al. (2017) extend this to "the productive and innovative use of technology" that encompasses "21st century practices that are vital for success in the workplace and beyond."
- **Emergent Learning:** Signet (2014) describes emergent learning as pragmatic, defined as learning that presents the need for "overcoming challenges, especially those that have no simple solutions, but require discipline, ongoing attention, learning through experience, and adaptation."
- **Inclusion:** In the context of public space, UNESCO (2016) defines inclusion as "an area or place that is open and accessible to all peoples, regardless of gender, race, ethnicity, age or socio-economic level."

2.2 Overview

This chapter provides a range of perspectives in Section 3 on emergent digital literacies and ambient learning, ambient play, and ambient inclusion in relation to smart cities followed by associated issues, controversies, and problems. Section 4 provides a discussion of emergent digital literacies in smart cities through development of a conceptual framework for investigating ambient learning, play, and inclusion as a mechanism for operationalization of the exploration under investigation in this chapter. Findings in this chapter assist in identifying the potential for solutions and recommendations, contributing to the formulation and advancing of a framework for ambient literacies in smart city urbanities. Section 5 identifies future directions for research and practice and Section 6 concludes with chapter coverage highlights, the major contributions, and key insights, ideas, and lessons.

The primary audiences for this chapter include students, educators, researchers, policy makers, community members, and practitioners concerned with emergent digital literacies related to learning, play, and inclusion in smart cities and learning cities for more responsive urbanities in support of improving urban experiences and livability.

3. EMERGENT DIGITAL LITERACIES

In coming to understandings of emergent digital literacies for smart cities, this chapter provides a review of the research literature, extending also to ambient learning, ambient play, and perspectives on inclusion.

3.1 Emergent Digital Literacies

Referring to the work of Li, Feng, Zhou, and Shi (2009), McKenna et al. (2013) noted the presence everywhere of learning opportunities in technology-pervasive environments. Where Signet (2014) defines emergent learning in a workplace context, McKenna and Chauncey (2014) extended this understanding to apply more generally to formal and informal educational settings in keeping with the dynamic and adaptive nature of 21st century learning environments. McKenna and Chauncey (2014) advance the notion of frictionless learning in addressing the digital divide and offering a response to digital inequalities in learning cities. Nam and Pardo (2011) articulate understandings of learning cities as a dimension of smart cities while Williamson (2015) describes the dystopian notions of "educating the smart city" and "programmable pedagogies" featuring students and citizens as "data objects" and "computational operatives" with smart cities limited to a technological interpretation through the lens of "computational urbanism." McKenna (2016b) calls for a re-thinking of learning in smart cities by introducing an exploration of potentials for "emergent behavior in relation to awareness, autonomy, creativity, and innovation." Noting the wicked challenges facing education, Adams Becker et al. (2017) point to the two solvable challenges of, improving digital literacy and integrating formal and informal learning. As part of the evolving of learning, Adams Becker et al. (2017) describe the move toward redesigning learning spaces with a focus on project-based learning where classrooms begin "to resemble real-world work and social environments that foster organic interactions and cross-disciplinary problem solving." Adams Becker et al. (2017) point to the need for improving digital literacies in "generating a deeper understanding of the digital environment, enabling intuitive adaptation to new contexts and cocreation of content with others." Looking at the pervasive presence of digital technologies in everyday life, Pink, Hjorth, Horst, Nettheim, and Bell (2018) claim that, "activities thought of as work, leisure and play become entangled in new ways" as "articulated and experienced through the use of mobile media at home." According to Pink, Lanzeni, and Horst (2018), it is important to understand the nature of "our relationships with data" that, although "riddled with anxieties", through improvisations and other familiar routines, "people are already finding ways to live comfortably with digital data" and associated uncertainties.

Figure 1. Overview of key issues, controversies, and challenges for emergent digital literacies

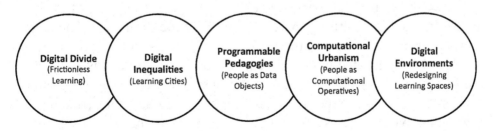

In summary, Figure 1 provides an overview of key issues, controversies, and challenges for emergent digital literacies highlighting the digital divide, digital inequalities, programmable pedagogies, computational urbanism, and the evolving of digital environments.

3.2 Ambient Learning in Smart Cities

Kölmel and Kicin (2005) explored ambient learning in terms of software applications and hardware requirements as a market validation project for networked context aware environments in terms of eLearning. Ravenscroft, Sagar, Baur, and Oriogun (2010) advance the ambient pedagogies concept as an approach to "designing learning interactions and experiences" based on "ambient learning design and experience design." According to Ravenscroft et al. (2010), this approach "reconciles relatively stable learning processes with relatively new digital practices in the context of social software and Web 2.0." The ambient pedagogy approach incorporates games for learning and is said to have "implications for future trends in designing for inclusive, highly communicative and engaging learning interactions and practices for the digital age" (Ravenscroft et al., 2010). The approach is also intended to address problems associated with interest-driven versus learning-driven motivations associated with the use of technology so as "to link learners interest-driven and typically media-centric behaviours to more learning-driven dialogue and textual practices" for meaningful learning (Ravenscroft et al., 2010). Merchant (2010) addresses learning for the future in relation to emerging technologies and social participation, highlighting the disruptive and destabilizing potentials for the "fragile ecology" of education environments. Nam and Pardo (2011) refer to smart cities as places where "continuous learning is nurtured" and where "social learning makes a city smarter." McKenna et al. (2013) note that Bick, Kummer, Pawlowski, and Veith (2007) describe ambient learning as the next generation of mobile learning where digital learning environments "provide contextualized, personalized knowledge for learners" based on anywhere, anytime learning spaces within daily life. From an urban layers perspective, it is worth noting that for Zygiaris (2013), school, as in education and learning, is located in the interconnection layer and data is situated in the instrumentation layer as well as the open integration layer for cities. McKenna et al. (2013) associated ambient learning with autonomy, finding that "awareness-based systems must be human-centered, taking into consideration the needs and requirements of people using the systems." Shafriri and Levy

(2017) explore learning experiences with mobile applications in "blended spaces" while focusing on the principles of "the device as a discovery machine" and "open playful design" in support of a "new literacy of 'mobile system thinking'." Leorke, Wyatt, and McQuire (2018) explore public libraries as part of "broader digital and 'smart city' strategies." Mersand, Gasco-Hernandez, Udoh, and Gil-Garcia (2019) provide an analysis of "innovative practices in public libraries" arguing for their potential as "anchor institutions in smart community initiatives" based on the importance of the roles they play from "bridging the digital divide" to enabling "digital inclusion" to serving as "techno-hubs" in support of "digital literacy" and their potential to become "a key actor in the governance of the smart community." Among the obstacles to be overcome for public libraries to realize their smart potentials are those associated with funding and infrastructure changes.

In summary, Figure 2 provides an overview of key issues, controversies, and challenges for ambient learning, highlighting mobile learning and the contextual and personalized; ambient pedagogies and learning interactions and experiences; meaningful learning and interest driven versus learning driven motivations; continuous learning as a smart city element; and social learning for making cities smarter.

3.3 Ambient Play in Smart Cities

McKenna et al. (2014) found that "playful interactions, serious game conceptualization and development, and emergent learning appear less as discrete and separate activities and more as an intricately interwoven and complex dynamic." Additionally, those participating in the study "were clear about the need to be involved in the design and development of such systems to accommodate human-centered considerations and autonomies" (McKenna et al., 2014). Hjorth (2015) argues that "play is integral to being human and has multiple cultural, social, historical and emotional entanglements."

Figure 2. Overview of key issues, controversies, and challenges for ambient learning

Mobile Learning (Contextual/ Personalized)   **Ambient Pedagogies** (Learning Interactions/ Experiences)   **Meaningful Learning** (Interest versus Learning)   **Continuous Learning** (Smart City Element)   **Social Learning** (Making Cities Smarter)

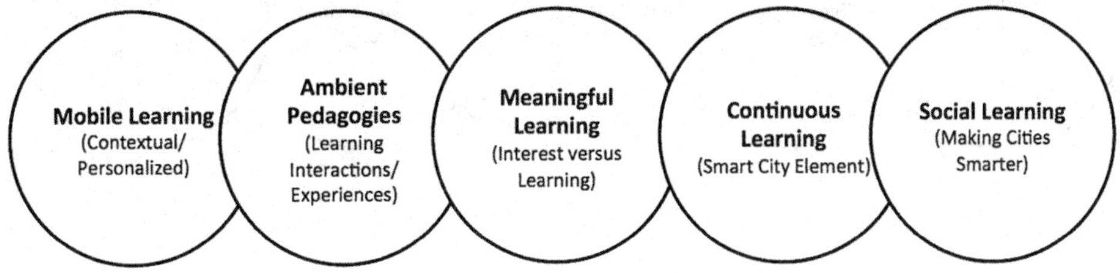

Additionally, Hjorth (2015) notes that ambient play "suggests a need for nuanced and dynamic readings of mobile media as it moves in and through place." Hjorth (2015) claims that ambience "conveys the way games infiltrate our social and emotional lives, afford particular sense perceptions and impact upon our movements through domestic and urban spaces." In exploring and re-conceptualizing "evolving understandings of jobs, work, and labour in the context of emerging requirements for learning, living, and creatively contributing in 21st century smart cities" McKenna (2017) noted that games emerged as opportunities for people to experience the city. Pink, Hjorth, Horst, Nettheim, and Bell (2018) describe ambient play as referring to "the significant and yet often tacit, unofficial and incidental forms of creativity, play and communication that surround mobile gaming practices in situ." However, with the "convergence of mobile, social and location-based gaming" the potential for ambient play is expanded "across a variety of everyday context" such that Pink, Hjorth, Horst, Nettheim, and Bell (2018) use the concept "to understand the work/play/playbour entanglements" while arguing that "engagement in ambient play is part of the way that people may experience being in the world." Pink, Hjorth, Horst, Nettheim, and Bell (2018) address ambient play in relation to the concept of atmospheres of home and call for an expanding of definitions for "play, plabour, and labour in and around digital media engagement to accommodate the emergent everyday mobile media uses of a growing middle class."

In summary, Figure 3 provides an overview of key issues, controversies, and challenges for ambient play highlighting ambience and how games affect spaces; experiences in relation to games and the city; mobile gaming and the nuanced and dynamic; entanglements as multiple; and atmospheres of home and the everyday as emergent.

Figure 3. Overview of key issues, controversies, and challenges for ambient play

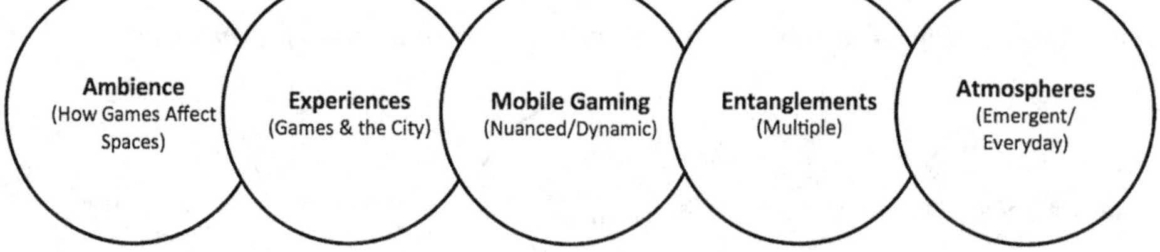

3.4 Inclusion in Smart Cities

Ravenscroft et al. (2010) address the implications of ambient pedagogies, meaningful learning, and social software for future trends when designing with inclusion in mind. Nam and Pardo (2011) point to digital inclusion as one of several factors of success for a smart city. Digital city, according to Nam and Pardo (2011) involves every function of the city such as work, housing, movement, recreation, and environment. Schmitt (2015) points to the importance of inclusion as a factor guaranteeing "the longevity, sustainability, and resilience of urban systems and cities." Schmitt (2015) claims that, "urban systems and countries built on inclusion and equality have consistently shown a higher quality of life, income, and resilience" noting the examples of "Swiss cities, Vienna, Munich, Vancouver, or Copenhagen" where "a high level of inclusiveness in making decisions" is present. Citing the work of Acemoglu and Robinson (2013), Schmitt (2015) indicates that while "growth can occur both in inclusion and in extractive systems" the latter "will not be sustainable growth." For Hjorth (2015) it is a combination of elements that "work to diversify our experience of being with others." McKenna advanced an ambient inclusion framework for smart cities (McKenna, 2018b) "accommodating ICT-enabled spaces, designs, and services that involve an interactive dynamic of people, technologies, and cities" where ICT refers to information and communication technologies. An active illustration of the framework (McKenna, 2018b) shows the movement from social interaction to the dynamic of smart cities to urban experiences to examples of ambient inclusion resulting in benefits related to meaningful engagement, learning, and participation. Findings showed how "the learning city can become an enabler of ambient inclusion" based on the combining of more aware people with aware technologies (McKenna, 2018b).

Figure 4. Overview of key issues, controversies, and challenges for ambient inclusion

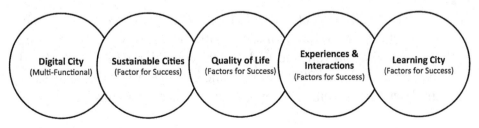

In summary, Figure 4 provides an overview of key issues, controversies, and challenges for ambient inclusion highlighting the digital city, sustainable cities, quality of life, experiences and interactions, and the learning city.

3.5 Issues, Controversies, Problems

Key issues, controversies, and problems emerging in the review of the research literature explored in this chapter are highlighted below. Coverage of issues, controversies, and problems is not intended to be exhaustive or comprehensive but rather, as illustrative of the nature, variety, and range.

Issues

Pink, Lanzeni, and Horst (2018) point to issues of trust and anxieties related to data in the everyday messiness of digital data and associated uncertainties. This work advances the need for evolving digital literacies in mitigating such issues of trust, anxieties, and uncertainties.

Controversies

Merchant (2010) confronts the "risky business" of "disturbing the fragile ecology" of education environments in addressing "new ways of communicating and collaborating that constitute digital literacy." Williamson (2015) introduces a debate articulating the interpretation of students and citizens as "data objects" and "computational operatives" in smart cities as an emerging understanding of "computational urbanism." This work seeks to move beyond dystopian and utopian perspectives in leveraging the combined potentials of more aware people interacting with each other and with aware technologies in arriving at emergent digital literacies in support of novel understandings of ambient learning, play, and inclusion.

Problems

Ravenscroft et al. (2010) identify problems associated with the "misalignment of social practices motivated by interest with those motivated by learning" in the use of social software and Web 2.0 for education while Pink, Hjorth, Horst, Nettheim, and Bell (2018) point to uncertainties associated with safety and digital data. In response, this work advances emergent digital literacies involving more ambient modes of learning, play, and inclusion through more direct and meaningful involvement of people in the design of educational and learning spaces as part of the design of smart cities and urbanities.

In summary, Table 1 provides an overview of issues, controversies, and problems for digital literacies.

Organized by by author(s) and year, emergent digital literacies for the ambient in smart cities are highlighted, in relation to learning, play, and inclusion. For learning, key elements highlighted are ambient learning, ambient pedagogies, learning cities, continuous learning, social learning, emergent learning, frictionless learning, people as computational operatives, and data relationships. In relation to play, key elements highlighted include games for learning; the notion of ambience for play and the nature of entanglements for play; play as urban experience; ambient play; atmospheres for play; and mobile gaming media. In relation to inclusion, key elements highlighted are games for inclusion; inclusion as a key factor in the success of smart cities; ambient inclusion; and digital inclusion.

Table 1. Perspectives on issues, controversies, and problems for digital literacies in smart cities

Emergent Digital Literacies for the Ambient in Smart Cities				
Author(s)	**Year**	**Learning**	**Play**	**Inclusion**
Kölmel & Kicin	2005	Ambient		
Ravenscroft et al.	2010	Ambient Pedagogies	Games for learning	Games for
Nam & Pardo	2011	Cities; Continuous; Social		
Signet; McKenna & Chauncey	2014	Emergent		
McKenna & Chauncey	2014	Frictionless		
Hjorth	2015		Ambience; Entanglements	
Williamson	2015	Computational operatives		
Schmitt	2015			As SC factor
McKenna	2017		As Urban Experience	
Pink, Hjorth, et al.	2018		Ambient; Atmospheres; Mobile gaming	
Pink, Lanzeni & Horst	2018	Data Relationships		
McKenna	2018b			Ambient
Mersand et al.	2019			Digital

By way of solutions and recommendations, issues, controversies, and problems identified in this section are re-conceptualized as challenges and opportunities to be addressed through operationalization of the conceptual framework for ambient learning, play, and inclusion in smart cities developed and presented in Section 4.

4. EMERGENT DIGITAL LITERACIES IN SMART CITIES

Based on the perspectives emerging from the review of the research literature in this chapter, understandings of emergent digital literacies encompassing ambient learning, ambient play, and ambient inclusion are advanced through formulation of a conceptual framework for smart cities as described in Section 4.1.

4.1 Ambient Learning–Play–Inclusion Framework: Solutions and Recommendations

Using the construct of learning in relation to aware people and aware technologies, a conceptual framework for ambient learning, play, and inclusion as meaningful in the context of smart cities is advanced, as depicted in Figure 5. The framework articulates the ambient in relation to digital data, education, and computational urbanism in digitally-enabled urban areas and regions where opportunities for increased literacies are enabling evolving perspectives on trust, fragile ecologies, and uncertainties.

Figure 5. Conceptual framework for ambient learning, play, and inclusion

Emergent Digital Literacies in Smart Cities

Aware People – Aware Technologies

AMBIENT Learning – Play – Inclusion
as *meaningful*

Digital Data – Education – Computational Urbanism
Trust – Fragile Ecologies – Uncertainties

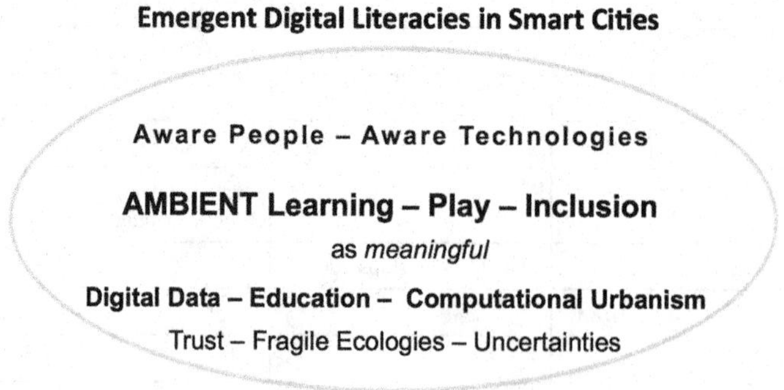

In exploring emergent digital literacies, this chapter focuses on aware people and aware technologies in smart cities in responding to the research question posed and restated as a proposition under exploration in this chapter, as follows:

P: *Learning* matters for urbanity in relation to emergent digital literacies in smart cities because of the highly dynamic and ever-changing ecologies and requirements.

As such, this work explores emergent digital literacies and ambient learning, play, and inclusion in smart cities in developing solutions and recommendations to issues, controversies, and problems summarized in Section 3.5.

4.2 Emergent Digital Literacies: An Exploration

How learning informs urbanity is explored in this chapter using a survey instrument and protocol-guided interviews with a diverse range of individuals in addition to discussions with groups and individuals across multiple sectors. The focus of the multiple methods used for data collection centered on emerging mechanisms and spaces for learning, play, and inclusion as ambient. Ambient is understood to refer to environments and elements that are more dynamic, in-the-moment, and adaptive, enabling new potentials for learning to occur at all stages, anywhere, anytime and in any type of environment, whether formal, informal, mobile and so on. Learning is explored as ambient; play is explored as ambient; and inclusion is explored as ambient and all three are then discussed in relation to emerging digital literacies in formulation of a framework for ambient literacies in smart city urbanities in contributing to solutions and recommendations for issues, controversies, and problems.

4.2.1. Learning as Ambient

Learning emerges as ambient for a community member based on the use of technologies "to experience the city in a different way" in terms of "the environment or the history." This individual suggested "there is a whole other layer that could be added in order to make the city more usable for everybody." An educator noted the "videoing and sharing of very traditional things constantly in social media" and the notion of "concurrent awareness" enabling "seamless behavior" also evident in the "seamless interrelationship of" the "local and global." In relation to data, city IT staff commented on "that hurdle of just really starting to educate" about "what could be done" and "educating ourselves." The additional hurdle was noted that, "we haven't had any kind of funding to do these things." A student suggested that, "learning becomes a subsumed subtext of what you are doing everyday, all the time" in support of continuous forms of learning that could be "formal, informal, fun, serious."

4.2.2. Play as Ambient

Play emerges as ambient through imagining ways in which urbanizing occurs in smart cities. For example, a community member suggested the potential to "create different games or opportunities for people" and to "make cities more friendly for our kids." A community member articulated "ways to animate a space" using the example of a city parkade embedded with sensor technology that "plays different sounds as you go up based on where you are in the stairwell" noting also that the "lighting changes." Supported by the city, this cross-sector urban collaboration involving people in technology, arts, and culture was described as "art in public places" where public artwork is described as being "about people interacting with each other" to "compose and create." The notion of play emerged in relation to budgeting where city IT described "a tool for the public to engage and play" enabling people to get "a sense of where the cost pressure points" are "around decision making" by turning the dial up or down on various services. A community member referred to the "game aspect" of the city in terms of "so many different choices" in relation to mobility and ways to move around and interact in urban spaces, "depending on the weather, the traffic, who you are with."

4.2.3. Inclusion as Ambient

Inclusion emerges as ambient through urban elements in smart cities such as multi-modality, multi-purpose, mixed-use, and identity. In terms of multi-modality, an e-TownHall was described by a city councilor as "an interactive experience that makes the city more real" enabling meaningful involvement and learning. Through social media, "documented engagement" was said to occur enabling feedback from people in the community to be considered and acted upon. Regarding mixed-use initiatives, an educator referred to the "conscious things" by governments, organizations, and communities to attract people to urban spaces and services such as housing, coffee shops, and so on and "because we've blended it all together, its exciting." A city councilor observed that through social media "the city has a personality on the Internet" where through "10s of 1000s of Twitter followers, it makes it all more accessible." An educator described a "mobile cloud-based app to capture and share insights, feedback, and knowledge" as a "simple, cost efficient" mechanism for "instant awareness" intended for a wide range of uses including "business, design, infrastructure, learning, safety, sport, and tourism."

Summarized in Figure 6, a glimpse of patterns, flows, relationships, and possibilities begin to emerge for digital literacies through learning, play, inclusion, and involvement in smart cities. Learning is described in relation to content that is co-created, with an emphasis on context and continuous, involving digital data in everyday environments in support of interactions and experiences that are social and meaningful. Play is articulated in terms of atmospheres and entanglements in support of improvisations benefitting from mobile media. Inclusion is described in relation to ambient pedagogy pertaining to experiences involving the digital, enabled through communication and interconnection. And finally, involvement emerges in relation to data as digital along with associated concerns enabling new forms of collaboration that are personalized providing openings for people to learn about and think about data issues to mitigate concerns with trust and uncertainty in aware environments that feature the Internet of Things (IoT), the Internet of People (IoP) and the Internet of Experience (IoE). Although neatly categorized across learning, play, inclusion, and involvement it is important to note that there is considerable overlap in that personalized is associated with learning for example as well as with involvement in the context of the complexities of emergent digital literacies. Also, the categories are necessarily incomplete and intended as an initial and summary overview.

4.2.4. Discussion of Ambient Learning, Play, and Inclusion as Emerging Digital Literacies

Based on findings in this chapter, emerging digital literacies are discussed in relation to ambient learning, play, and inclusion contributing to formulation of a framework for ambient literacies in smart city urbanities described in Figure 7.

Figure 6. Emerging digital literacies and smart cities through learning, play, inclusion and involvement

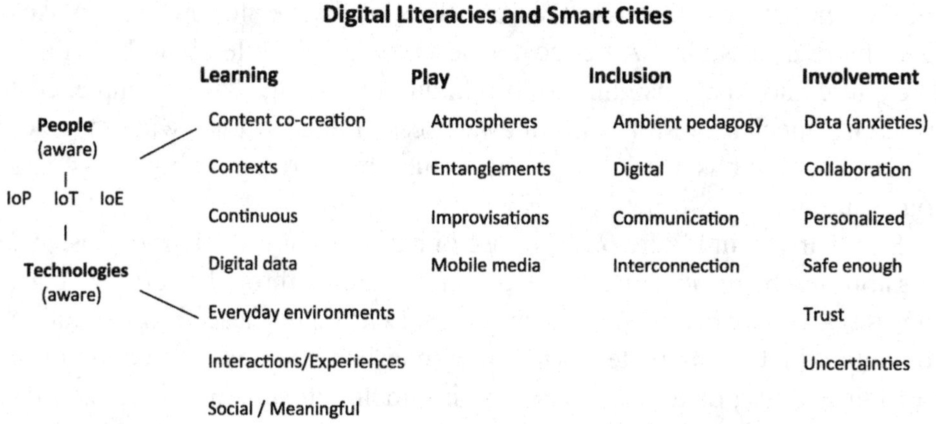

Digital Literacies and Smart Cities

	Learning	Play	Inclusion	Involvement
People (aware)	Content co-creation	Atmospheres	Ambient pedagogy	Data (anxieties)
	Contexts	Entanglements	Digital	Collaboration
IoP IoT IoE	Continuous	Improvisations	Communication	Personalized
	Digital data	Mobile media	Interconnection	Safe enough
Technologies (aware)	Everyday environments			Trust
	Interactions/Experiences			Uncertainties
	Social / Meaningful			

Ambient Learning and Emerging Digital Literacies

Attentive to concerns by Merchant (2010) with "disturbing the fragile ecology" of education environments, the ambient learning approach in this work fosters and supports increased awareness and spaces for the meaningful involvement of people in emerging digital literacies. The notion of ambient learning emerges in this work as the urbanizing of aware technologies where learning is said to become "a subsumed subtext" of everyday activities as continuous learning that may be "formal, informal, fun, serious." Community members, students, and educators acknowledged the value of technologies whether "to experience the city in a different way" to "learn about the environment or history" or to experience "concurrent awareness" through sharing in social media. The importance of "educating ourselves" and "starting to educate" was acknowledged by city IT staff in relation to the potential uses and value of urban data, along with the importance of funding as necessary to support such learning initiatives.

Ambient Play and Emerging Digital Literacies

The adaptive nature of ambient play responds and adapts to the "everyday messiness of data" that was described in terms of the anxieties and uncertainties articulated by Pink, Lanzeni, and Horst (2018) in the context of emerging digital literacies. For example, community members activated the notion of urbanizing aware technologies (McKenna, 2018a) in suggesting ways to "create different games" for people to "make cities more friendly for our kids" and "ways to animate a space." In a collaborative effort characteristic of smart cities, an art in public places initiative was described that was supported by the city and involved people from businesses working with sensor and light technologies, as well as with arts and culture while highlighting safety, engagement, and playfulness in creating welcoming community spaces, in this instance, an urban parking environment that is used on a daily basis.

Ambient Inclusion and Emerging Digital Literacies

In responding to concerns by Williamson (2015) with computational urbanism rendering people as "data objects" and "computational operatives", the ambient inclusion approach in this work fosters and supports increased awareness and spaces for meaningful involvement of people in emerging digital literacies. As if to illustrate the notion of urbanizing aware technologies (McKenna, 2018a), a city councilor pointed to an instance of community involvement and decision-making through the use of social media and other technology tools to enable and support an eTownHall meeting that was said to provide "an interactive experience that makes the city more real" resulting in "documented engagement" that can be acted upon by everyone involved, not just the city. Additionally, the "conscious things" enacted by collaborative efforts in cities to bring together the physical and digital were said to enable multi-modal, multi-use, and multi-purpose spaces for more vibrant, inclusive, and livable communities.

Findings in this chapter advance the concepts of ambient learning along with ambient play and ambient inclusion in coming to evolving understandings of emergent digital literacies for smart cities. Indeed, findings in this chapter give rise to the potential for emerging understanding of literacies as ambient, as depicted in Figure 7.

The framework for ambient literacies in smart city urbanities is organized around aware people and aware technologies encompassing the physical and digital in relation to experiences of ambient learning, ambient play, and ambient inclusion contributing further to the ambient turn in support of smart and responsive cities and urbanities. The combination of more aware people with more aware technologies in support of enhanced awareness, involvement, and collaborations in everyday, in-the-moment, continuous information streams fosters new spaces for formal, informal, and blended learning, play, and inclusion in urban environments. In the context of the ambient turn, challenges and opportunities have the potential to become ambient in terms of their dynamic, adaptive, and responsive possibilities.

Figure 7. Framework for ambient literacies in smart city urbanities

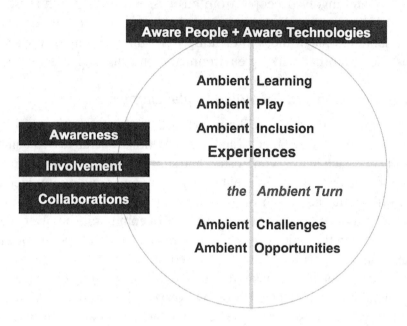

Ambient Literacies

Aware People + Aware Technologies

Awareness

Involvement

Collaborations

Ambient Learning

Ambient Play

Ambient Inclusion

Experiences

the **Ambient Turn**

Ambient Challenges

Ambient Opportunities

Dependent Variable (DV)

The dependent variable (DV) surfaced in this chapter is *learning and experiences* in relation to awareness, involvement, and collaboration. Associated independent variables include: make the city more usable for everybody, implying formal, informal, fun, serious; make cities more friendly, implying safe and welcoming; ways to animate a public space, implying the potential for the use of art and technology; and designing for interactive experiences, implying more meaningful involvement.

In summary, this chapter focuses on finding spaces, mechanisms, variables, and approaches for enabling ambient literacies in support of more adaptive and dynamic forms of learning, play, and inclusion, as in, ambient for smarter, more responsive cities and urbanities.

5. FUTURE RESEARCH DIRECTIONS

Future and emerging trends are identified in this chapter in sections 5.1 and 5.2 for practice and research.

5.1 Practice

This chapter opens up new understandings of learning, play, and inclusion in the context of emergent digital literacies in support of the work of city practitioners in evolving urban spaces for testing and practice. The notion of ambient literacies emerges from this chapter along with learning-related variables.

Ambient Literacies

This chapter provides exposure to the notion of ambient literacies in the form of ambient learning, ambient play, and ambient inclusion and invites participation by city and community practitioners and businesses in the development of initiatives for learning, play, and inclusion as ambient, as in, more dynamic, adaptive and responsive. Such initiatives would be designed to respond to contemporary urban challenges and opportunities, in the context of new and evolving understandings of learning cities, responsive cities, and more livable cities and urbanities. Through the ambient, spaces for real-time, dynamic, and adaptive contributions open up in relation to new approaches to issues of data trust, anxieties, and uncertainties and possibly novel purposes and uses of data in support of new forms of education and funding for emergent digital literacies and competencies.

Variables and Indicators

Learning is said to be a key dimension of smart cities (Nam and Pardo, 2011) and this chapter advances the potential for new forms of value related to emergent digital literacies on a practical level for the *learning and experiences* dependent variable and the independent variables associated with use, friendliness, animation, and designing for interactivity in urban spaces.

5.2 Research

From the perspective of emergent digital literacies, this chapter navigates a pathway for future research opportunities, challenges, debates, and theorizing related to the proposed concept of ambient literacies and the conceptual framework for ambient learning, play, and inclusion in smart cities.

Ambient Literacies

The concept of ambient literacies is advanced in this chapter as an example of a more adaptive, dynamic, connected, and continuous understanding of learning, play, and inclusion in and across urban spaces in support of creativity, innovation, more informed decision making, and novel services and responses.

Framework for Ambient Learning, Play, and Inclusion

The viability of the conceptual framework for ambient learning, play, and inclusion in smart cities (Figure 5), operationalized for use in this chapter, demonstrates early-stage potentials with opportunities and challenges for further testing and validation going forward. Potential areas for exploration include:

1. *Ambient learning* based on greater awareness and more flexible designs and uses in urban spaces
2. *Ambient Play* that provides spaces and atmospheres for broader involvement in urban environments
3. *Ambient Inclusion* that enables spaces for more meaningful involvement in urban planning and design with potentials for smarter governance

Framework for Ambient Literacies in Smart City Urbanities

Going forward, a framework for ambient literacies in smart city urbanities is proposed in advancing new understandings of the multiple and dynamic types of literacies needed for smart cities and ambient urbanities.

6. CONCLUSION

This chapter provides an exploration of learning, play, and inclusion in smart cities from the perspective of evolving understandings of emerging digital literacies and the ambient turn. Building on the importance of the issues identified in the literature review in this chapter related to data trust, anxieties, and safe enough solutions; controversies associated with the fragile ecology of education; and problems of uncertainties associated with the digital and data, what this chapter offers is an interpretation of learning, play, and inclusion as ambient, enabling emerging understandings of ambient literacies. The primary contributions of this chapter include: a) provision of a review of the research literature for learning, play, inclusion, and the ambient; b) formulation and operationalization of a conceptual framework for ambient learning, play, and inclusion for smart cities; c) development of a framework for ambient literacies in smart city urbanities; and d) extending of the existing research literature on urban theory by building out additional discourse, debate, and practice spaces for emerging smart city perspectives to include ambient learning, ambient play, ambient inclusion, and ambient literacies more generally, in further contributing to the ambient turn and ambient challenges and opportunities.

This chapter continues to give form, detail, and definition to the broader Ambient Urbanities Framework presented in Chapter 1 (Figure 4) through exploration of the learning construct in relation to play, inclusion, and literacies more generally. The analysis of findings in this chapter identifies variables associated with *learning and experiences* relevant to the study, practice, and management of emergent digital literacies in smart cities.

Insights of particular interest to the reader include the following:

1. The potential for meaningful learning-play-inclusion opportunities to inform emergent digital literacies
2. The interconnectedness of learning-play-inclusion as ambient literacies informing ambient urbanities
3. The surfacing of variables associated with *learning and experiences* in emergent digital urban spaces

Ideas highlighted in this chapter pertain to the following:

1. The importance of people becoming more aware of learning-play-inclusion as key digital literacies
2. The potential for people to be supported (funded) for learning and digital literacies in urban spaces
3. Ambient literacies as a novel approach contributing to smarter cities and to ambient urbanities

Lessons for the reader in this chapter are associated with the following:

1. The potential for meaningful learning-play-inclusion to influence/be influenced by aware technologies

2. The potential for aware technologies to enhance learning-play-inclusion potentials in urban spaces
3. The intractable issues, controversies, and problems for learning, play, inclusion, and digital literacies

This work will be of interest to a broad audience including, but not limited to, students, educators, researchers, urban practitioners, community members, business, artists, designers, and anyone concerned with more dynamic notions of learning, play, inclusion, and literacies as ambient in relation to the complex urban challenges of smart cities, learning cities, and responsive cities and urbanities.

REFERENCES

Acemoglu, D., & Robinson, J. (2013). *Why nations fail: The origins of power, prosperity, and poverty*. New York: Random.

Adams Becker, S., Cummins, M., Davis, A., Freeman, A., Hall Giesinger, C., & Ananthanarayanan, V. (2017). *NMC Horizon Report: 2017 Higher Education Edition*. Austin, TX: The New Media Consortium.

Bick, M., Kummer, T., Pawlowski, J. M., & Veith, P. (2007). Standards for ambient learning environments. In B. Konig-Ries, F. Lehner, R. Malaka, C. Turker (Eds.), *MMS 2007: Mobilität und mobile Informationssysteme; Proceedings of the 2nd Conference of GI-Fachgruppe MMS* (pp. 103–114). Bonn, Germany: Academic Press.

Hjorth, L. (2015). Narratives of ambient play: Camera phone practices in urban cartographies. In *Citizen's Right to the Digital City*. Singapore: Springer. doi:10.1007/978-981-287-919-6_2

Kölmel, B., & Kicin, S. (2005). Ambient learning: The experience of ambient technologies in eLearning. In J. P. Courtiat, C. Davarakis, & T. Villemur (Eds.), *Technology Enhanced Learning. IFIP International Federation for Information Processing* (Vol. 171). Boston, MA: Springer.

Leorke, D., Wyatt, D., & McQuire, S. (2018). *More than just a library: Public libraries in the smart city*. City, Culture and Society. doi:10.1016/j. ccs.2018.05.002

Li, X., Feng, L., Zhou, L., & Shi, Y. (2009). Learning in an ambient intelligent world: Enabling technologies and practices. *Knowledge and Data Engineering, 21*(6), 910–924. doi:10.1109/TKDE.2008.143

McKenna, H. P. (2016a). Innovating relationships for learning in 21st century smart cities. *Proceedings of the 9th Annual International Conference of Education, Research and Innovation (iCERi2016)*, 4695-4704. 10.21125/iceri.2016.2115

McKenna, H. P. (2016b). ReThinking learning in the smart city: Innovating through involvement, inclusivity, and interactivities with emerging technologies. In J. R. Gil-Garcia, T. A. Pardo, & T. Nam (Eds.), *Smarter as the new urban agenda: A comprehensive view of the 21st century city* (Vol. 11, pp. 87–107). Springer. doi:10.1007/978-3-319-17620-8_5

McKenna, H. P. (2018a). Creativity and ambient urbanizing at the intersection of the Internet of Things and People in smart cities. In M. Antona & C. Stephanidis (Eds.), *UAHCI 2018, LNCS 10908* (pp. 295–307). Springer. doi:10.1007/978-3-319-92052-8_23

McKenna, H. P. (2018b). Re-conceptualizing social inclusion in the context of 21st century smart cities. In J. Choudrie, S. Kurnia, & P. Tsatsou (Eds.), *Social inclusion and usability of ICT-enabled services. Routledge Studies in Technology, Work and Organizations*. Routledge.

McKenna, H. P., Arnone, M. P., Kaarst-Brown, M. L., McKnight, L. W., & Chauncey, S. A. (2013). Ambient and emergent learning with wireless grid technologies. *Proceedings of the 5th International Conference on Education and New Learning Technologies (EduLearn13)*, 4046-4053.

McKenna, H. P., & Chauncey, S. A. (2014). Frictionless learning environments for 21st century education and learning cities: A response to digital inequalities. *Proceedings of the 7th International Conference of Education, Research and Innovation (iCERi2014)*, 2505-2515.

McKenna, H. P., Chauncey, S. A., Arnone, M. P., Kaarst-Brown, M. L., & McKnight, L. W. (2014). Emergent learning through playful interactions and serious games when combining ambient intelligence with wireless grids. *Proceedings of the 8th International Technology, Education and Development (INTED 2014) Conference*, 5080-5090.

Merchant, G. (2010). Learning for the future: Emerging technologies and social participation. In S. Dasgupta (Ed.), *Social computing: Concepts, methodologies, tools, and applications* (pp. 2239–2251). Hershey, PA: IGI Global. doi:10.4018/978-1-60566-984-7.ch146

Mersand, S., Gasco-Hernandez, M., Udoh, E., & Gil-Garcia, J. R. (2019). Public libraries as anchor institutions in smart communities: Current practices and future development. *Proceedings of the 52nd Hawaii International Conference on System Sciences (HICSS)*, 3305-3314.

Nam, T., & Pardo, T. A. (2011). Conceptualizing smart city with dimensions of technology, people, and institutions. In *Proceedings of the 12th Annual International Conference on Digital Government Research* (pp. 282-291). ACM. 10.1145/2037556.2037602

Pendleton-Jullian, A., & Brown, J. S. (2016). *The pragmatic imagination*. Design Unbound.

Pink, S., Hjorth, L., Horst, H., Nettheim, J., & Bell, G. (2018). Digital work and play: Mobile technologies and new ways of feeling at home. *European Journal of Cultural Studies*, *21*(1), 26–38. doi:10.1177/1367549417705602

Pink, S., Lanzeni, D., & Horst, H. (2018, January). Data anxieties: Finding trust in everyday digital mess. *Big Data & Society*, 1-14.

Pink, S., Ruckenstein, M., Willim, R., & Duque, M. (2018, January). Broken data: Conceptualizing data in an emerging world. *Big Data & Society*, 1-13.

Ravenscroft, A., Sagar, M., Baur, E., & Oriogun, P. (2010). Ambient pedagogies, meaningful learning and social software. In S. Dasgupta (Ed.), *Social computing: Concepts, methodologies, tools, and applications* (pp. 472–489). Hershey, PA: IGI Global. doi:10.4018/978-1-60566-984-7.ch032

Schmitt, G. (2015). *Information Cities*. Retrieved from https://itunes.apple.com/us/book/information-cities/id970529491?mt=11

Shafriri, Y., & Levy, D. (2017). What are the unique characteristics of integrating mobile applications in learning? In J. Dron & S. Mishra (Eds.), *Proceedings of E-Learn: World Conference on E-Learning in Corporate, Government, Healthcare, and Higher Education* (pp. 1666-1680). Vancouver, British Columbia, Canada: Association for the Advancement of Computing in Education (AACE). Retrieved January 13, 2019 from https://www.learntechlib.org/primary/p/181325/

Signet. (2014). *What is emergent learning?* Signet Research and Consulting. Retrieved 13 April 2018 from http://www.signetconsulting.com/concepts/ emergent_learning.php

UNESCO. (2016). *Inclusion Through Access to Public Space*. Paris, France: United Nations Educational, Scientific, and Cultural Organization. Retrieved 12 April 2018 from www.unesco.org/new/en/social-and-human-sciences/ themes/ urban-development/migrants-inclusion-in-cities/good-practices/ inclusion-through-access-to-public-space

Williamson, B. (2015, July). Educating the smart city: Schooling smart citizens through computational urbanism. *Big Data & Society*, 1-13.

Zygiaris, S. (2013). Smart city reference model: Assisting planners to conceptualize the building of smart city innovation ecosystems. *J. Knowl. Econ.*, *4*(2), 217–231. doi:10.100713132-012-0089-4

ADDITIONAL READING

Descant, S. (2018). Digital literacy is at the heart of a thriving city. *Government Technology*. Retrieved 13 June 2018 from http://www.govtech.com/ applications/Digital-Literacy-Is-at-the-Heart-of-a-Thriving-Smart-City.html

Gil-Garcia, J. R., Pardo, T. A., & Nam, T. (2016). A comprehensive view of the 21st century city: Smartness as technologies and innovation in urban contexts. In J. R. Gil-Garcia, T. A. Pardo, & T. Nam (Eds.), *Smarter as the new urban agenda: A comprehensive view of the 21st century city. Public Administration and Information Technology Series* (Vol. 11, pp. 1–19). NY: Springer. doi:10.1007/978-3-319-17620-8_1

McKenna, H. P. (2016). Learning in the city: Leveraging urban spaces as real world environments for interactive solution-making. In *Proceedings of the 10th International Technology, Education & Development Conference (INTED2016)* (pp. 4367-4375). Valencia, Spain, 7-9 March. 10.21125/ inted.2016.2081

Morrison, J. (2018). With the growth of smart cities, how do we build smart citizens to match? *Calvium Blog*. Retrieved 13 June 2018 from https://calvium. com/growth-smart-cities-build-smart-citizens-match/

Neumann, M. M., Finger, G., & Neumann, D. L. (2017). A conceptual framework for emergent digital literacy. *Early Childhood Education Journal*, *45*(4), 471–479. doi:10.100710643-016-0792-z

Robinson, H. M. (2014). *Emergent digital literacy and mobile technology: Preparing technologically literate preservice teachers through a multisensory approach.* Hershey, PA: IGI Global. doi:10.4018/978-1-4666-4797-8.ch012

Sakamoto, M., Nakajima, T., & Akioka, S. (2014). A methodology for gamifying smart cities: Navigating human behavior and attitude. In N. Streitz & P. Markopoulos (Eds.), Lecture Notes in Computer Science: Vol. 8530. *Distributed, Ambient, and Pervasive Interactions. DAPI 2014* (pp. 593–604). Cham: Springer. doi:10.1007/978-3-319-07788-8_55

Wilberg, C. (2018). Game-inspired architecture and architecture-inspired games. *Interaction*, *25*(2), 68–70. doi:10.1145/3177814

KEY TERMS AND DEFINITIONS

Ambient Challenges: Challenges characterized as adaptive, dynamic, uncertain, and fluid in relation to highly unpredictable issues, events, circumstances, situations or the like.

Ambient Inclusion: Adaptive, fluid, and evolving contexts that accommodate ICT-enabled spaces, designs, and services involving an interactive dynamic of people, technologies, and cities featuring emerging forms (interactions, relationships, urbanizing) and attributes (awareness, choice, improvisation).

Ambient Learning: Adaptive, fluid, and evolving understandings of learning in formal and informal environments.

Ambient Literacies: Adaptive, fluid, evolving, and responsive understandings of digital and physical environments enabling and supporting ease, creativity, and interactivities in 21st century smart environments.

Ambient Opportunities: Opportunities characterized as adaptive, dynamic, uncertain, and fluid elements in relation to highly unpredictable issues, events, circumstances, situation, spaces, or the like.

Ambient Play: Adaptive, fluid, evolving, and responsive understandings of games and play for 21st century smart environments that may be fun or serious or anywhere in between.

Learning Relationships: Cross-sector based relationships in support of interactions that are adaptive, dynamic, evolving, emergent, and mutually beneficial with the intent to learn.

Chapter 6
Smart Information Architectures:
Ambient Data and Smarter Governance

ABSTRACT

The purpose of this chapter is to explore smartness in cities in relation to smart information architectures, with an approach that takes people into consideration, in understanding big and small data. This work seeks to shed light on the importance of data in urban environments and the purposeful leveraging of real-time analytics for interactions in the city in support of smarter governance. The research literature for information architectures, smart governance, and ambient data is explored in this chapter in the context of smart and responsive cities, enabling identification of issues, controversies, and problems. Using an exploratory case study approach, solutions and recommendations are advanced. This chapter makes a contribution to the research literature for ambient data, smart information architectures, and smarter governance; the evolving of urban theory for 21st century cities; and smart city urbanities through formulation of a framework for smart information architectures as an adaptive data management framework.

DOI: 10.4018/978-1-5225-7882-6.ch006

1. INTRODUCTION

The purpose of this chapter is to explore smartness in cities in relation to smart information architectures, advancing an approach that takes people into consideration in coming to understandings of big data (Batty, 2013) and small data (Estrin, 2014). As such, this work seeks to shed light on the importance of data in urban environments and the purposeful leveraging of real-time analytics for interactions in the city in support of smarter governance (Gil-Garcia, Zhang, and Puron-Cid, 2016). The research literature for information architectures (Schmitt, 2015), smart governance (Gil-Garcia, Zhang, and Puron-Cid, 2016; Eglé, Jurgita, and Jolanta, 2015), and ambient data (McKenna, 2017a) is explored in this chapter in the context of smart and responsive cities, enabling identification of issues, controversies, and problems. Using an exploratory case study approach, solutions and recommendations are advanced. This chapter makes a contribution to: a) the research literature for ambient data, smart information architectures, and smarter governance; b) the evolving of urban theory for 21st century cities; and c) smart city urbanities through formulation of a conceptual framework for smart information architectures as an adaptive data management framework.

Objectives: The objective of this chapter is to advance smart information architectures as an adaptive data management and governance framework for smart cities. As such the key research question posed is – How does smartness contribute to urbanity in contemporary urban environments?

2. BACKGROUND AND OVERVIEW

An approach to understanding urban data (Batty et al., 2012), big data (Batty, 2013; Kitchin, 2014; Hashem et al., 2016) and small data (Estrin, 2014) that takes people into consideration is explored in this chapter in becoming more aware of the purposes and value of real-time data about interactions in the city. The Internet of Data (IoD) (Fan, Chen, Ziong, and Chen, 2012), the Internet of Things (IoT) (Khatoun and Zeadally, 2016; Coletta and Kitchin, 2017; Memos et al., 2018), along with other emergent forms of sharing and collaboration are highlighted, in discussing the challenges and opportunities of data relationships in smart cities. This chapter builds upon the notion of adaptive governance by Janssen and van der Voort (2016) and Ben Letaifa's (2015) SMART model for the strategizing of smart cities. Gil-Garcia, Zhang, and Puron-Cid (2016) claim that to move beyond government 2.0 requires a re-thinking of "the role of governments, citizens, and other social actors" contributing to "possibilities of forging new processes, relationships, structures, and even a new governance model." Indeed, "in an era of wicked social problems", Gil-Garcia, Zhang, and Puron-Cid (2016), referring to the work of Gil-Garcia and Sayogo (2016), point to the need for "a smarter, more responsive, more efficient governance structure" in order to "take advantage of the enormous capability of the public to congregate, interact, and collaborate" as a mechanism for "finding solutions to intricate sociotechnical challenges."

Models and frameworks are identified and described by Caird, Hudson, and Kortuem (2016) for smart cities infrastructure management. This chapter argues for a re-thinking and extending of existing models and frameworks, proposing smarter information architectures in response to the wicked challenges and complexities posed by 21st century urban environments (Gil-Garcia, Pardo, and Nam, 2016) in moving toward smarter, responsive cities. Understanding smartness through the emerging purposes and value of urban data from the perspective of aware people using and interacting with aware technologies is advanced in this work as critical to the development of smarter city urbanities. Ambient data (McKenna, 2017a) is elucidated further, enabled by social media, information and communication technologies (ICTs), and open data initiatives in smart cities, extending to the public realm. Paskaleva, Cooper, and Concilo (2018) address the challenges of providing smart city services, highlighting the importance of skills and capacity related to governance. Theoretically, this work is situated at the intersection of adaptive governance, smarter organizational design, and ambient data.

2.1 Definitions

For the purposes of this work, definitions for key terms used in this chapter are presented here based on the research literature.

- **Ambient Data:** McKenna (2017a) argues that ambient data emerges from what Schmitt (2016) describes as "the constant flow of data" produced by "the inhabitants of the city."
- **Information Architecture:** Schmitt (2015) defines information architecture as "the necessary framework to understand architecture, urban systems and territories in the knowledge society."

- **Smart Governance:** In defining smart public governance, Eglé, Jurgita, and Jolanta (2015) highlight elements such as open and participatory; delivery of public value while being responsive to public demands with high quality services; and responsibility and creativity.
- **Smartness:** In defining smartness in government, Gil-Garcia, Zhang, and Puron-Cid (2016) suggest that the concept could encompass "more than technology" and that "each project makes a government smarter in some ways or in certain dimensions."

2.2 Overview

This chapter provides a range of perspectives in Section 3 on evolving understandings of information architecture, smarter governance, and ambient data in the context of smart cities, followed by a selection of associated issues, controversies, and problems. Based on the review of the research literature, Section 4 provides a conceptual framework for smart information architectures, operationalized for use in the exploration conducted in this chapter. In identifying the potential for solutions and recommendations to the issues, controversies, and problems identified in Section 3, a framework for ambient information architectures and governance in smart city urbanities is advanced in Section 4. Section 5 identifies future directions for research and practice and the surfacing of variables for *smartness and capacities*. Section 6 concludes with chapter coverage highlights, the major contributions, and the key insights, ideas, and lessons.

The primary audiences for this chapter include students, educators, researchers, policy makers, data and knowledge managers, and practitioners concerned with smart information architectures incorporating ambient data and smarter governance for more responsive urbanities.

3. SMART INFORMATION ARCHITECTURES

This chapter provides a review of the research literature for smart information architectures in relation to smart cities; smarter governance in smart cities; and an ambient data perspective for smarter, more responsive cities. Included in this review are perspectives on emerging frameworks and models for managing data in smart cities, drawing on the research literature for adaptive information architecture (EuroIA, 2017), organizational enterprise architecture, and frameworks and models (Khatoun and Zeadally, 2016) for managing the infrastructural complexities of smart cities (Finger, 2016).

3.1 Information Architecture in Smart Cities

Roeleven (2010) addressed the problem of why a significant proportion of EA (Enterprise Architecture) projects fail – citing problems associated with "the lack of EA awareness" and expectations related to the time involved as in, "longer than expected to set up an architecture" as well as compliance issues. The European Union (EU, 2011) employs "the enterprise architecture approach" to demonstrate "how architectures and the processes followed to produce them can help the development and improvement of e-government." Architecture for building is likened to ICT (information and communication technologies) architecture for "an e-service or an e-process" that "consists of a set of formal descriptions" such as "blueprints, models and samples" descriptive "of an information system's structural and behavioural properties" along with descriptive details pertaining to "how it may evolve or be adapted in the future." Espinosa, Boh, and DeLone (2011) identify the gap in "concrete metrics or evidence about the bottom line impact that EA has on the organization" while proposing "a framework for empirical research." Da Silva, Alvaro, Tomas, Afonso, Dias, and Garcia (2013) discuss a range of architectures for smart cities with varied purposes in developing a set of requirements for implementation. Mulligan and Olsson (2013) address the architectural implications of smart city business models, recommending an evolutionary process.

Schmitt (2015) articulates the concept of information architecture in the context of smart and responsive cities as descriptive of "metaphors and principles of physical architecture applied to digital data and information, to create an architecture of information, with the use of information as raw material." Schmitt (2015) claims that "in the realm of the built environment, information architecture visualizes the information inherent in a building" and in this way "makes the invisible visible" such that, "digital information" is "extracted from and applied to physical architecture." For Schmitt (2015), information architecture "serves as a metaphor to structure the vast amounts of data produced in modern society." McGinley and Nakata (2015) propose a community architecture framework (CAF) for smart cities, emphasizing a participatory approach, in order to include the interests of citizens and diverse stakeholders. McGinley and Nakata (2015) claim that the CAF "offers opportunities for innovation" that "would be challenging in a more rigid model" of EA. Pourzolfaghar, Bezbradica, and Helfert (2016) explore types of IT architectures in smart cities from an enterprise architecture perspective, identifying the need for a comprehensive business layer with associated architecture requirements (e.g., goals, objectives, services, processes, and responsibilities and roles). In a business white paper, of note is the SmartDframe project by Caird, Hudson, and Kortuem (2016) concerned with the evaluation and measurement of the city impact and outcomes of complex smart initiatives.

The EA^3 Cube (Bernard and Gøtze, 2016) originally developed in 2004 and updated in 2016 as the EA^{3-6} Cube, highlights the complexity of organizations through six sides or views – function, structure, risk, people, products, and value. Sobczak (2017) points to "an emphasis on the management of complexities and organizational changes" as confirmation of "the legitimacy of the use of the Enterprise Architecture concept when planning and conducting complex transformational projects" as in, "constructing a smart city." Sobczak (2017) advances an enterprise architecture-based model for the management of smart cities, referring to the work of Bernard (2004) where EA offers "both a transformation management program and a documentation method" for "a coherent view on strategic objectives, business processes, flow of information, and use of assets." Sobczak (2017) suggests this type of EA to be particularly appropriate in the management of complexities for smart cities.

Dang and Pekkola (2017) highlight enterprise architecture (EA) use in the public sector, contributing to increased efficiency and the use of information and communication technologies (ICT). Dang and Pekkola (2017) conducted a systematic review of the research literature focusing on the development, implementation, and adaptation of enterprise architecture in the public sector revealing the need for increased research on adaptation EA implementation in relation to interoperability and integration, alignment and strategy, and pragmatic challenges. In view of the challenges posed by smart city implementations, Bastidas, Bezbradica, and Helfert (2017) explore the notion of cities as enterprises, identify the "essential requirements of enterprise architecture in smart cities" and use the requirements "to review and compare current smart city frameworks." Laurini (2017) advances smart urban planning through "geographic knowledge infrastructure" as a potential "basis for a new generation of tools for urban planning." It is worth noting that the theme of the European Information Architecture (EuroIA, 2017) summit focused on information architecture (IA) and user experience (UX), described as "adaptation and designing for change." Additionally, EuroIA 2017 called for contributions on "the relationship between physical architecture and information architecture" and "sustainability in design" and "extension into organizational change by design." EuroIA 2018 (EuroIA, 2018) places a focus on humanogy as a space to "discuss the symbiosis between humans and technology" in learning how "to make a real difference in the world." EuroIA 2019 (EuroIA, 2019) places a focus on impact and "the ethical discourse around the role of designers and IA practitioners" in the context of "machine learning and artificial intelligence."

In summary, Figure 1 provides an overview of issues, controversies and problems associated with information architectures in smart cities. While enterprise architecture is used in the context of organizations and eGovernment, smart architectures are advanced with understandings of cities as enterprises. With information advanced as the new raw material of cities, the architecture of information is advanced and information visualization is said to have the potential to make the invisible visible. Knowledge infrastructures based on geographic information are advanced for the purposes of smart urban planning.

3.2 Smarter Governance in Smart Cities

In terms of the responsiveness of governance infrastructures, Johnston (2010) pointed to the importance of smart practices for the design of smart governance in anticipation of the interactivities of technologies and society in support of capabilities, enthusiasm, and participation. Kyriazopoulou (2015) provides a review of the literature for architectures and requirements for the development of smart cities, highlighting sectors identified by Giffinger et al. (2007) such as smart economy, people, governance, mobility, environment, and living as the focus for improvement. Kyriazopoulou (2015) claims that "offering citizens a great experience" is a primary goal of smart cities. Rodríquez Bolívar (2015) identifies the need for "new and innovative forms of governance" to meet the

Figure 1. Overview of issues, controversies, and problems for information architectures in smart cities

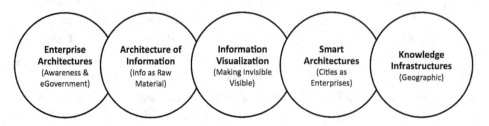

complexities of smart city challenges. Rodríquez Bolívar (2015) raised many questions for debate such as, the role of governments and the involvement of citizens. Eglé et al. (2015) explore the dimensions, characteristics, and criteria of smart public governance in advancing an assessment approach and methodology. Marsal-Llacuna (2015) defines smartness in terms of "the three pillars of sustainability (environmental, economic and social)" claiming that smartness in the smart city occurs when the three pillars "are safeguarded" and when "urban resilience is being improved by making use of technologies of information." Pointing to the "inherently unobservable nature of governance," Eglé et al. (2015) note that, "any empirical measures may be an imperfect proxy for the dimensions of smart public governance that they reflect."

Visnjic, Neely, Cennamo, and Visnjic (2016) refer to the concept of "extended enterprises" in the context of city governance. When understood as the "ecosystem of ecosystems", Visnjic et al. (2016) argue that "successful city governance requires an orchestration approach where leaders choose the appropriate structure and manage the ecosystem dynamically in a constantly changing environment." Janssen and van der Voort (2016) introduce the concept of adaptive governance in digital environments as a 'balancing act' to maintain stability while developing adaptive capabilities in responding to uncertainties and complexities. Scholl (2016) refers to a type of smartness emerging that goes beyond "traditional computers and communications devices connected via the Internet" to an Internet of Things that "powerfully complements" the former with "even smarter, more effective, and more efficient infrastructures" extending and encompassing "all areas of human activity and transactions" with implications for governance, smart government and smart cities. Scholl and AlAwadhi (2016) found that in the case of Munich, "sweepingly changing the governance over citywide information and communication technologies (ICTs)" turned out to be "at the core of creating an environment conducive to smart operations and smart services and smart city government." In relation to the co-production of smart city services, Paskaleva, Cooper, and Concilo (2018) caution that "no 'one-size-fits-all'" while highlighting "the importance of context-specific governance issues."

In summary, Figure 2 provides an overview of issues, controversies, and problems for smart governance in smart cities. Smart practices focus on design for interactivities; innovative governance on urban complexities; and governance is said to be unobservable by nature. Extended enterprises focus on dynamic management in dynamic environments and adaptive governance focuses on urban complexities and uncertainties.

Figure 2. Overview of issues, controversies, and problems for smart governance in smart cities

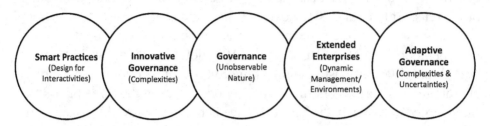

3.3 An Ambient Data Perspective for Smarter, Responsive Cities

Fan et al. (2012) articulated the Internet of Data (IoD) concept, indicating that "data standing alone has little or no meaning" but when made to interoperate, it is "the information of the relations between data" that "become more significant and useful." Big data is articulated by Batty (2013) from a human geography perspective as urban data "tagged to space and time" with implications for planning in smart cities. The importance of data traces is articulated by Estrin (2014), who argues that, "we as individuals should have access to our digital traces" to "mine them for our own purposes." According to Estrin (2014), we generate data as "most of us mediate, or at least accompany, our lives with mobile technologies" such that "we leave a continuously updated 'trail of data breadcrumbs' behind us" that "together make up our digital traces" based on day-to-day activities. As such, Estrin (2014) argues for the value of digital traces for "personalized data-driven insights." Schmitt (2015) describes big data as "an expression of the first decade of the 21st century" where "data generated by millions of people and billions of sensors" is such that "the amount of data available for urban planners, city governments, and the general public is exploding" shifting the challenge from "producing data to organizing and extracting" the data "in meaningful ways." Mulder (2015) describes the opening up of public sector data along with policy-making enabled by collaborative partnerships, experiences, and the making of meaningful applications as promising "in transforming towards a more transparent and sociable smart city." Lea (2015) articulates "the problems around exposing data, sharing data and using the data" in the two areas of "infrastructure data" and "citizen data."

Almirall, Wareham, Ratti, Conesa, Bria, Gaviria, and Edmondson (2016) highlight a series of things for governments to address. For example, Ratti (Almirall et al., 2016) encourages "governments to get people excited about creating apps and using data themselves" so that "if we can develop the right platforms, people can be the ones to address urban issues." Conesa (Almirall et al., 2016), focusing on the need for a legal framework and new business models, encourages governments "to require big enterprises to share the data they collect from users" including "better data protection for individuals." Edmondson (Almirall et al., 2016) points to the importance of collaboration across sector boundaries in support of diverse capabilities, noting that "access to and control over data has become a strategic asset for cities." As such, issues are identified with the platform economy including fragmentation, non-interoperable vertical solutions, and data silos. This gives rise to an opportunity for cities "to disrupt this data accumulation" in order to "make data available across vertical silos experimenting with decentralized data infrastructures and distributed ledgers" with proposals for "new frameworks and business models" to "incentivize openness, enabling data discovery, transactions, and secure data sharing." Also proposed for cities to undertake is to "design new legal, economic, and governance schemes to foster collaborative behaviors by individuals to contribute to data commons" with "the goal to foster open and socially beneficial behaviors." Ratti (Almirall et al., 2016) explores long-term potential, highlighting the notion of mobilizing not just people but also data. Ahlgren, Hidell, and Ngai, E. C.-H (2016) point to the importance of data interoperability in relation to the Internet of Things (IoT) and open data. Khatoun and Zeadally (2016) advance a smart city model consisting of the Internet of Things (IoT), the Internet of Services (IoS), the Internet of Data (IoD), and the Internet of People (IoP) where smart governance is featured as part of the IoD component. Thakuriah, Tilahun, and Zellner (2017) explore urban informatics and the potential for "leveraging novel sources of data" identifying four areas of potential pertaining to "strategies for dynamic urban resource management"; "knowledge discovery of urban patterns and processes"; "strategies for urban engagement and civic participation"; and "urban management, planning, and policy analysis." Hsieh, Alquaddoomi, Okeke, Pollak, Gunasekara, and Estrin (2018) propose applications architecture for a small data ecosystem addressing "the converse of the big data problem" as in, "draw insights about the individual across their own small data for personal growth and understanding." Others (Hu-manity.co, 2018) are proposing that access to data be the 31st human right.

In summary, Figure 3 provides an overview of issues, controversies, and problems for ambient data in smart cities.

Data relationships are highlighted and the value of data interoperability; spatial and temporal urban data; data traces in urban environments for personalized insights; making big data meaningful through an emphasis on organizing and extracting; and the small data ecosystems for insights, contributing to personal growth.

Summarized in Figure 4, a glimpse of patterns, flows, relationships, and possibilities begin to emerge for smarter information through architectures, data, governance, and collaboration in smart cities. Architectures are described in relation to adaptation and compliance along with behavioral changes in support of eGovernment in relation to visible and invisible information models and structures. For data, challenges and opportunities associated with the exposing, sharing, and using of data are articulated along with fragmented aspects and the importance of the meaningful and personalized while highlighting protection and relationships whether in terms of small or big data and data traces.

Governance is described as adaptive in relation to citizen experiences, complexities, dimensions, and the dynamic, supportive of innovative and smart practices in the midst of recognized tensions. And finally, collaboration emerges as critical in aware environments, featuring the Internet of Things (IoT), the Internet of People (IoP), the Internet of Experience (IoE), and the Internet of Data (IoD), highlighting the importance of developing capabilities that have cross-sector reach. Although neatly categorized across architectures, data, governance, and collaboration, it is important to note that there is considerable overlap in that adaptation is associated with architectures for example as well as with governance in the context of the complexities of smarter information environments. Also, the categories are necessarily incomplete and intended only as a summary overview.

Figure 3. Overview of issues, controversies, and problems for ambient data in smart cities

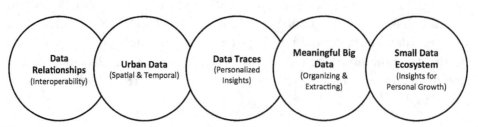

Figure 4. Smarter information in smart cities through architectures, data, governance & collaboration

Smarter Information in Smart Cities

	Architectures	Data	Governance	Collaboration
People (aware)	Adaptation	Exposing/Sharing/Using	Adaptive	Behaviors
	Behavioral	Fragmented	Citizen experiences	Capabilities
IoP IoT IoE IoD	Compliance	Meaningful	Complexities	Cross-sector
	eGovernment	Personalized	Dimensions	
Technologies (aware)	In/Visible	Protection	Dynamic	
	Models	Relations	Innovative	
	Structural	Small	Smart practices	
		Traces	Tensions	

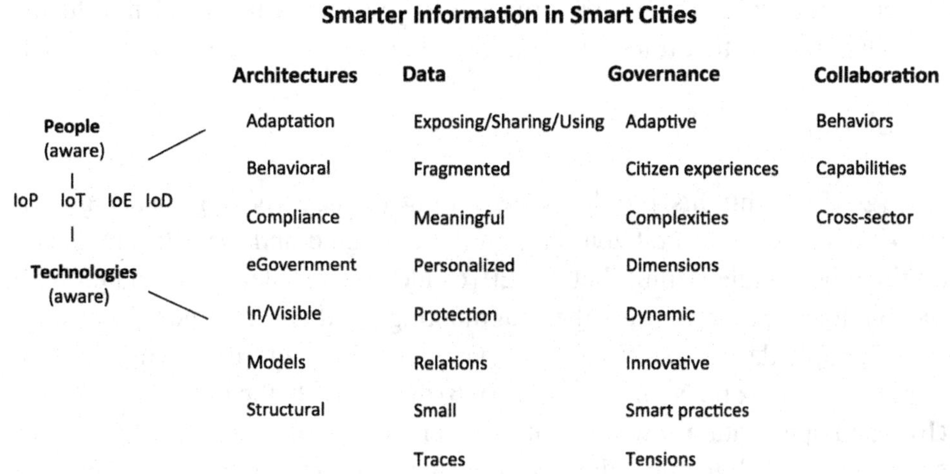

3.4 Issues, Controversies, Problems

Key issues, controversies, and problems emerging in the review of the research literature explored in this chapter are highlighted below. Coverage of issues, controversies, and problems is not intended to be exhaustive or comprehensive but rather, as illustrative of the nature, variety, and range.

Issues

Almirall et al. (2016) highlight a series of issues requiring attention by governments such as collaboration, data sharing, and privacy. Focusing on three types of data – embedded sensor technology data; existing data collected by cities; and citizen-generated data – from a law and policy perspective, Scassa (2017 identifies issues for governments related to ownership, privacy, control, and the re-use of data in smart cities. As such, this chapter proposes more aware and informed approaches to data in the form of a rethinking of data as ambient.

Controversies

Rodríquez Bolívar (2015) raises a range of controversies for debate pertaining to the role of governments and citizens in governance while Almirall et al.

(2016) speak in terms of tensions related to the form of governance, growth and innovation, and the sharing economy and modes of production. In response, this chapter proposes smarter approaches to governance involving new forms of collaborations that transcend traditional boundaries and silo-like spaces.

Problems

Lea (2015) highlights problems pertaining to the exposing, sharing, and use of data, related to citizen data on the one hand and infrastructure data on the other, while Almirall et al. (2016) identify problems associated with the platform economy and the fragmenting of data. The need for more interoperable data is identified by Fan et al. (2012) and further advanced by Ahlgren, Hidell, and Ngai, E. C.-H (2016) in relation to the Internet of Things (IoT) and open data. By way of solutions and recommendations, this chapter advances more dynamic, adaptive, informed, collaborative, and innovative notions of information architectures, governance, and approaches to data as ambient in smart city urbanities.

In summary, as depicted in Table 1, an overview of issues, controversies, and problems associated with smart information architecture, smarter governance, and ambient data by author and year, in the context of smart cities, is provided for the time period spanning 2010 to 2018.

The research literature for information architectures focuses on the failures of enterprise architecture (EA) related to gaps in awareness, compliance, and expectations; EA for e-government; metrics gaps related to the impact of EA; architectures focusing on implementation; information as raw building material in cities; a community architecture framework (CAF); the EA[3-6] Cube for organizational transformation and complexities; EA implementation and adaptation; cities as enterprises in support of EA for smart cities; the potential for geographic knowledge infrastructures; and the value of EA for smart city complexities. For smarter governance, the research literature covers smart practices; assessment and methodology; the importance of creating great experiences for citizens; sustainability in terms of supporting three key pillars (environmental, economic, social); new and innovative approaches to governance; conceptualizing smartness in government; adaptive governance; extended enterprises as dynamic, constantly changing environments; addressing issues associated with data ownership, privacy and control; and skills and capacity for co-production of smart city services.

Table 1. Issues, controversies & problems for smart information architecture, governance and data

Smart Information Architectures, Smarter Governance, and Ambient Data				
Author(s)	**Year**	**Information Architectures**	**Smarter Governance**	**Ambient Data**
Roeleven	2010	EA failures – Awareness, Compliance, Expectations		
Johnston	2010		Smart practices	
EU	2011	EA for e-Government		
Espinosa et al.	2011	Metrics gap for EA impact		
Fan et al.	2012			Data relations
Da Silva et al.	2013	Architectures for implementation		
Estrin	2014			Data traces
Eglé et al.	2015		Assessment/methodology	
Kyriazopoulou	2015		Great experiences	
Lea	2015			Exposing data
Marsal-Llacuna	2015		Sustainability – 3 pillars	
Mulder	2015			Open data
Rodríquez Bolívar	2015		New and innovative	
Schmitt	2015	Information as raw material		
McGinley & Nakata	2015	Community Architecture Framework		
Almirall et al.	2016			Data sharing
Bernard & Gøtze	2016	EA$^{3-6}$ Cube & complexities		
Gil-Garcia et al.	2016		Smartness in government	
Janssen & van der Voort	2016		Adaptive governance	
Visnjic et al.	2016		Extended enterprises	
Dank & Pekkola	2017	EA implementation & adaptation		
Helfert	2017	Cities as enterprises/EA & smart cities		
Laurini	2017	Geographic knowledge infrastructure		
Scassa	2017		Data ownership & control	
Sobczak	2017	EA for complexities in smart cities		
Thakuriah et al.	2017			Data sources
Hu-manity.co	2018			Data rights
Memos et al.	2018			IoT security
Paskaleva et al.	2018		Skills and capacity	

The notion of ambient data is captured in the research literature in terms of data relationships; data traces; exposing, sharing, and using data; open data; data sharing across boundaries; data sources; data rights; and IoT security. It is worth noting that adaptation emerges in relation to two or more of the columns of the columns in Table 1.

By way of solutions and recommendations, the issues, controversies, and problems identified in this section are re-conceptualized as challenges and opportunities to be addressed through operationalization of the conceptual framework for smart information architectures in smart cities developed and presented in Section 4.

4. SMART INFORMATION ARCHITECTURES

Based on the theoretical perspective developed in this chapter, this work advances the notion of smart information architectures for smart governance, and ambient data, enabled by more aware people and aware technologies in the context of smart cities. Formulation of a conceptual framework for smart information architectures in smart cities is depicted in Figure 5.

4.1 Framework for Smart Architectures: Solutions and Recommendations

Using the construct of smartness in relation to aware people and aware technologies, a conceptual framework for smart information architectures in the context of smart cities is advanced enabling evolving understandings of information architectures (IA), governance and ambient data, in digitally-enabled urban areas and regions where evolving perspectives on the Internet of Data, People, Experiences, and Things contribute to and are influenced by big and little data, and social approaches, as depicted in Figure 5.

Where enterprise architectures (EAs) such as that advanced by Bernard (2004) place an emphasis on the "baked in", this work seeks more adaptive solutions, keeping in mind Townsend's concerns with the brittleness (Townsend, 2013) of systems, making them prone to breakdowns. In support of more flexible systems and environments for urbanizing (McKenna, 2017b), this work explores smarter information architecture and governance along with ambient data in smart cities in providing solutions and recommendations to issues, controversies, and problems (Table 1).

Figure 5. Conceptual framework for smart information architectures in smart cities

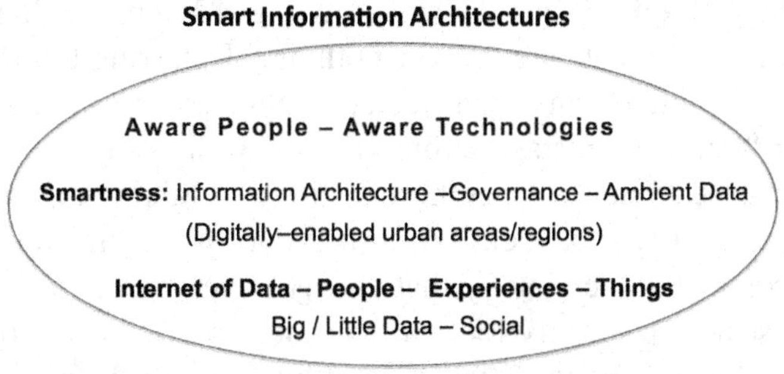

Smart Information Architectures

Aware People – Aware Technologies

Smartness: Information Architecture –Governance – Ambient Data
(Digitally–enabled urban areas/regions)

Internet of Data – People – Experiences – Things
Big / Little Data – Social

4.2 Smart Information Architectures, Governance, and Data: An Exploration

Through emerging understandings of smart information architectures, this chapter focuses on aware people and aware technologies in smart cities in responding to the research question posed in the Introduction of this chapter and restated as a proposition under exploration, as follows:

P: *Smartness* contributes to urbanity in contemporary urban environments through evolving understandings of information architectures in support of more adaptive approaches to data and governance.

How smartness informs urbanity is explored in this chapter in relation to emerging mechanisms and spaces for information architectures, governance, and ambient data in smart cities. Ambient data and smarter governance are then discussed in the context of smart information architectures as solutions and recommendations, contributing to formulation of a framework for ambient information architectures and governance in smart city urbanities.

4.2.1. Smartness and Information Architectures

Smartness emerges in relation to the community engagement part of IT (information technology) communications, said to be a core element of EA (enterprise architecture) in a higher education context. Higher education IT staff commented that the critical element is access in terms of "getting at that data and using it in constructive ways" so as to enable "benefit to the society and the citizens." In other words, "you can have all the connectivity you like but if there is no access to data in a meaningful manner" along with "no interpretation of that data leading to good public policy decisions then" smart environments are "all for nothing." Referring to urban bicycle infrastructure initiatives, an urban educator suggested the need to "build the capacity" or "build the infrastructure and just walk away and watch what happens" because "when you get these institutions talking together you just can't imagine what will happen." An urban educator commented that "the meeting becomes the technology that changes everything" as in, a kind of human infrastructure for city-focused learning programs "as robust social infrastructure towards better cities, around livability, and sustainability and engagement."

4.2.2. Smartness and Governance in Smart Cities

Smartness emerges in relation to governance when a city councilor commented on the value of the urban example of BikeMaps.org where "through your phone you are able to track accidents, find the place where accidents are happening and with the app create a map." The councilor added that, "with that information" as "a real life thing" together with "a phone, through an app, that information is being given back to the city so we can now go and create engineering fixes for those intersections and those high crash places." In the words of the councilor "its all connected and the tool of technology is augmenting the information" in support of decision making with a collaboration that "allows us to have a safer more vibrant city." An IT consultant observed there are "a lot of moving pieces to make a smart city" noting the complexity and the many levels. Regarding the complexities of governance, a city councilor noted "there are different types of engagement" including "engagement on decision-making, voting, and at the core of all of these things is creating a sense of ownership over the city." Focusing on engagement for example, the councilor added "we need a youth engagement strategy that will 1) meet skate boarders at the skate board park and 2) have online tools that will be designed for youth to create" and also "to bring them into some sort of online public, where they can find out about opportunities that speak to them" in order to "engage with them on the issues of the city that are most relevant."

4.2.3. Smartness and Ambient Data in Smart Cities

Smartness emerges in relation to ambient data when a student commented that "if people are making all this data, essentially in social media" then "all this data that can be searched and re-made and re-presented" is giving rise to "notions of smart delivery." Additionally, the student expressed concern with "queries and how you control this volume of information" in order to "give people what they're looking for" in addition to "where they need to plug in and the right community to be speaking with" in support of "how you might find purpose for the data that you are making." Instead of dashboards of data it was suggested that "you can take these bits of data and rather than just present numbers you can make beautiful artistic visualizations" and "project this on the walls" of buildings and other urban spaces to "make beautiful pictures, patterns, all kinds of beautiful things." For example, "from a cultural point of view" it was suggested that "you could take the data and make it do entirely different things than it would initially be thought of for the purpose" and "an illustration of what can be done with data to engage people, populations in an informal, playful way rather just in a very serious dry way that maybe alienates most people." As such, it was suggested that, "technical infrastructure can be made to constantly reciprocate the data flows that are happening between people – formal and informal." IT staff in higher education highlighted the question of occupancy data in building systems on campus asking "how do you leverage and expose some of the information in a way that you know is safe and make it available for other things" using the example of room booking information in combination with "the devices of people in rooms" as presence information in figuring out whether there are "people in the building and if there is a response" in the case of an emergency situation and "how we exchange that data."

In summary, this exploration surfaces insights for smartness in relation to architectures, governance, and data in smart cities, as depicted in Figure 6. In the context of a cities-technologies-people dynamic, ambient data emerges in relation to the notion of smart delivery enabled through the remaking and representing and sharing of data. The importance of building capacity is articulated in relation to urban infrastructures including those of a human and social nature. Data access is highlighted as key to the enabling of constructive uses of data. And mobile apps are discussed as an example of in-the-moment sharing of information by people while using city services such as bike paths to enable and inform collaborative decision making and the rapid and responsive enacting of improvements by the city staff.

Figure 6. Smartness and architectures, governance, and data in smart cities

Smartness: Architectures – Governance – Data

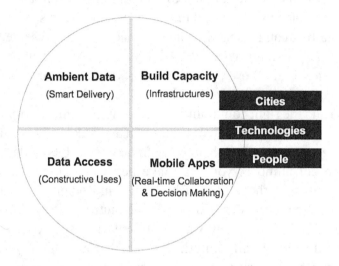

4.2.4. Discussion of Smart Information Architectures, Ambient Data, and Smarter Governance

How smartness informs information architectures and urbanity, enabled by aware people and aware technologies, is explored in this chapter through protocol-guided interviews, open-ended survey questions with voices emerging from small to medium to large sized cities, mostly in Canada but also extending to other cities (e.g., Tel Aviv) in other countries. Workshops and discussions were also conducted with groups and individuals across several Canadian cities.

Ambient Data and Smart Information Architectures

As if to acknowledge more ambient approaches to data, an urban-focused educator questioned "all the emphasis we're putting on archiving" suggesting instead that "data management is maybe not the direction" because "based on what we hear from young people" it seems that "they're not really interested in the archive, the data management, they're not interested in holding on to things in some ways."

Smarter Governance and Smart Information Architectures

Acknowledging the value and potential, a community member in St. John's referred to smart cities as "a great concept, a great idea" in that "its theoretical and practical" and as such, supportive of frameworks and models as well as architectures for everyday information practices and data analytics.

Findings in this chapter advance the construct of smartness in relation to information architecture, governance, and ambient data in coming to evolving understandings of the smart information architectures framework. Indeed, findings in this chapter give rise to the potential for emerging understanding of information architectures, governance, and data as ambient in smart city urbanities, as depicted in Figure 7. The combination of more aware people with more aware technologies in support of enhanced access, involvement, and collaborations in everyday, in-the-moment, continuous information streams fosters new spaces for formal and informal interactivities in urban environments. In the context of the ambient turn, capacities become ambient in terms of the potential for more dynamic, adaptive, and responsive infrastructures for interactions.

As such, this chapter focuses on finding spaces, mechanisms, and approaches for enabling smartness and innovation in information architectures, governance, and data as part of ambient urban information infrastructures, processes and urbanities.

Figure 7. Framework for ambient information architectures, governance, & data in smart city urbanities

Ambient Information Architectures & Governance

Aware People + Aware Technologies

Ambient Architectures (information)

Ambient Governance

Ambient Data

the Ambient Turn

Ambient Capacities

Access

Involvement

Collaborations

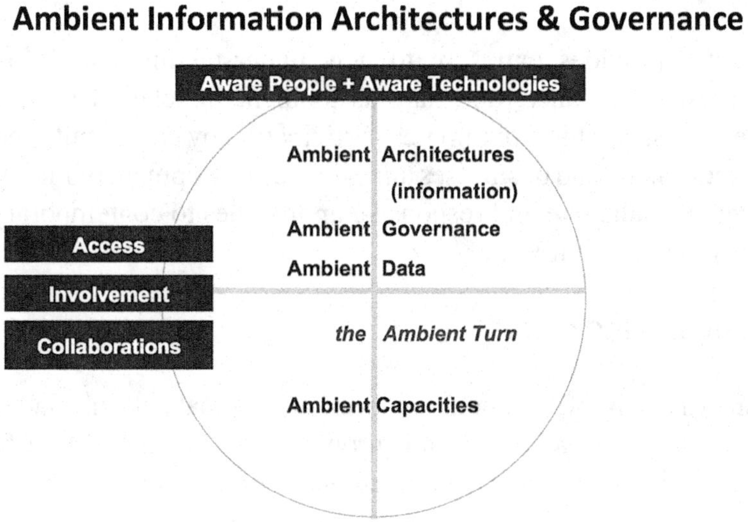

Dependent Variable (DV)

This chapter advances the potential for value to emerge through the dependent variable (DV) surfaced in this chapter as *smartness and capacities* in relation to information architectures, governance, and data. Associated independent variables (IV) include: using data in constructive ways, implying the potential for greater access; smart delivery of data, implying the potential for improved capacity building; interpretation of data, implying the potential for improved analytics; and availability of in-the-moment data for practical decision making, implying the potential for improved involvement and collaborations.

5. FUTURE RESEARCH DIRECTIONS

Future and emerging potentials are identified in this chapter for practice and research in Sections 5.1 and 5.2, pertaining to ambient information architectures, governance, and data.

5.1 Practice

Practically speaking, this chapter contributes to spaces for the rethinking of information architectures, governance, and data as ambient and the surfacing of the smartness and capacities dependent variable and associated independent variables.

Ambient Information Architectures, Governance, and Data

This chapter provides exposure to new understandings of information architectures, governance, and data as ambient in relation to smart city urbanities. As such, this work invites participation by community members, urban practitioners, and businesses alike, in the development of initiatives for more dynamic, adaptive and responsive approaches to contemporary urban challenges as opportunities.

Variables and Indicators

While smartness in government has been conceptualized in relation to 14 dimensions (Gil-Garcia, Zhang, and Puron-Cid, 2016), this work surfaces the dependent variable of *smartness and capacities* and a series of independent variables associated with using data, data delivery, data analytics, and real-time availability of data.

5.2 Research

This chapter points the way to future research opportunities where smart information architectures, governance, and data are understood from an ambient perspective along with the potential for building ambient capacities in support of access, collaboration, and involvement.

Smart Information Architectures, Governance, and Data

The viability of the conceptual framework for smart information architectures in smart cities, operationalized for use in this chapter, demonstrates early-stage potentials while offering and opening up new understandings for evolving urban spaces for testing and practice.

Ambient Information Architectures, Governance, and Data

Conceptualization of spaces for real-time, dynamic, and adaptive types of information architectures, governance, and data emerge in this chapter opening the way for new approaches to issues of data fragmentation, sharing, and use and possibly novel roles for citizens and governments, in fostering greater collaboration and involvement in the context of evolving understandings of smart and responsive cities. Areas for exploration potential include:

1. *Access* fostered through data initiatives focusing on learning and dynamic visualizations
2. *Collaboration* fostered through more dynamic and cross-sector approaches to governance
3. *Involvement* fostered through understandings of information as a type of smarter architecture

Ambient Capacities

This work opens the way to future research opportunities and challenges related to the potential for movement toward the building of capacities for information architectures, governance, and data to become more ambient in support of smart city urbanities.

Further, this work directs attention to the potential for modification of existing enterprise architecture (EA) frameworks and models such as the EA[3-6] Cube to more adaptive frameworks for smart and responsive governance in the form possibly of a dynamic *SmartCitiesCube* as a data management framework and information architecture capable of responding to emergent requirements.

6. CONCLUSION

This chapter provides an exploration of smart information architectures, governance, and data in contemporary urban environments from the perspective of evolving understandings of smartness and the ambient turn. Access, involvement, and collaboration emerge as key elements for smarter information architectures, governance, and data. These elements will be enabled through the building of infrastructural and learning capacities in support of more aware people and aware technologies. The primary contributions of this chapter include: a) formulation and operationalization of a conceptual framework for smart information architectures, governance, and data for smart cities taking people into consideration; b) development of a framework for ambient information architectures, governance, and data in smart city urbanities; c) extending of the research literature on urban theory by building out additional discourse, debate, and practice spaces for emerging smart city perspectives to include ambient information architectures, governance, data, and capacities; and d) re-thinking of existing models and frameworks for enterprise architectures as extensible to urban environments in the form of smart information architectures. As such, this chapter highlights the importance of smart cities infrastructure management involving more adaptive and dynamic approaches to information architectures, governance and data in meeting the wicked challenges and complexities posed by the evolving requirements of smarter and more responsive cities.

This chapter continues to give form, detail, and definition to the broader Ambient Urbanities Framework presented in Chapter 1 (Figure 4) through exploration of the smartness construct in relation to information architectures, governance, and data. The analysis of findings in this chapter identifies variables associated with *smartness and capacities* relevant to the study, practice, and management of smart information architectures, governance, and data in smart cities.

Insights of particular interest to the reader include the following:

1. The potential for meaningful access, involvement, and collaboration opportunities to inform evolving urban understandings
2. The interrelatedness of information architectures, infrastructures, governance, and data informing ambient urbanities
3. The surfacing of variables associated with *smartness and capacities* in evolving urban spaces

Ideas highlighted in this chapter pertain to the following:

1. The importance of people becoming more aware of the notion of ambient capacities for smarter cities
2. The potential for people to be recognized as capacity builders in relation to access, involvement, and collaboration in digital/physical urban spaces
3. Ambient information as a novel approach contributing to smarter cities and to ambient urbanities

Lessons for the reader in this chapter are associated with the following:

1. The potential for smarter access, involvement, and collaboration to influence and be influenced by aware technologies
2. The potential for aware technologies to enhance smartness possibilities for people in urban spaces
3. The intractable issues, controversies, and problems for information architectures, governance, and data in the context of the ambient turn and ambient capacity building

This work will be of interest to a broad audience including but not limited to students, educators, researchers, urban practitioners, community members, enterprise and information architects, data managers and analysts, and anyone concerned with more dynamic notions of information architectures, governance, and data as ambient in relation to the complex urban challenges of smart and responsive cities.

REFERENCES

Ahlgren, B., Hidell, M., & Ngai, E. C.-H. (2016). Internet of Things for smart cities: Interoperability and open data. *IEEE Internet Computing*, *20*(6), 52–56. doi:10.1109/MIC.2016.124

Almirall, E., Wareham, J., Ratti, C., Conesa, P., Bria, F., Gaviria, A., & Edmondson, A. (2016). Smart cities at the crossroads: New tensions in city transformation. Special Issue on City Innovation. *California Management Review*, *59*(1), 141–152. doi:10.1177/0008125616683949

Bastidas, V., Bezbradica, M., & Helfert, M. (2017). Cities as enterprises: A comparison of smart city frameworks based on enterprise architecture requirements. In *Smart-CT: International Conference on Smart Cities* (vol. 10268, pp. 20-28). Springer. 10.1007/978-3-319-59513-9_3

Batty, M. (2013). Big data, smart cities and city planning. *Dialogues in Human Geography*, *3*(3), 274–279. doi:10.1177/2043820613513390 PMID:29472982

Batty, M., Axhausen, K. W., Giannotti, F., Pozdnoukhov, A., Bazzani, A., Wachowicz, M., ... Portugali, Y. (2012). Smart cities of the future. *The European Physical Journal. Special Topics*, *214*(1), 481–518. doi:10.1140/epjst/e2012-01703-3

Ben Letaifa, S. (2015). How to strategize smart cities: Revealing the SMART model. *Journal of Business Research*, *68*(7), 1414–1419. doi:10.1016/j.jbusres.2015.01.024

Bernard, S., & Gøtze, J. (2016). *The EA cube framework*. International Enterprise Architecture Institute. Retrieved 17 December 2016 from http://internationaleainstitute.org/ea-approaches/ea-cube-framework/

Bernard, S. A. (2004). *An introduction to enterprise architecture* (3rd ed.). Bloomington, IN: AuthorHouse.

Caird, S., Hudson, L., & Kortuem, G. (2016). *A tale of evaluation and reporting in UK smart cities*. Milton Keynes, UK: The Open University. Retrieved 18 December 2016 from http://www.mksmart.org/wp-content/uploads/2016/04/Tales_Smart_Cities_Final_2016.pdf

Coletta, C., & Kitchin, R. (2017, July). Algorhythmic governance: Regulating the 'heartbeat' of a city using the Internet of Things. *Big Data & Society*, 1-16.

Da Silva, W., Alvaro, A., Tomas, G. H. R. P., Afonso, R. A., Dias, K. L., & Garcia, V. C. (2013). Smart cities software architectures: A survey. In *Proceedings of the 28th Annual ACM Symposium on Applied Computing (SAC'13)* (pp. 1722-1727). New York, NY: ACM. 10.1145/2480362.2480688

Dang, D., & Pekkola, S. (2017). Systematic literature review on enterprise architecture in the public sector. *The Electronic. Journal of E-Government*, *5*(2), 132–154.

Eglé, G., Jurgita, Š., & Jolanta, S. (2015). *Smart public governance: Dimensions, characteristics, criteria. International Research Society for Public Management (IRSPM)* Conference.

Espinosa, J. A., Boh, W. F., & DeLone, W. (2011). The organizational impact of enterprise architecture: A research framework. *Proceedings of the 44th Hawaii International Conference on System Sciences (HICSS)*. 10.1109/HICSS.2011.425

Estrin, D. (2014). small data, where n = me. *Communications of the ACM*, *57*(4), 32–34. doi:10.1145/2580944

EU. (2011). *Creating municipal ICT architectures: A reference guide from Smart Cities*. Smart Cities Project. European Union. Retrieved 19 August 2017 from http://www.smartcities.info/files/Creating%20Municipal%20ICT%20Architectures%20-%20Smart%20Cities.pdf

Euro, I. A. (2017). *Adaptation and design for change*. EuroIA Summit, Information Architecture and User Experience Conference. Retrieved 13 February 2019 from http://2017.euroia.org

Euro, I. A. (2018). *Humanogy*. EuroIA Summit, Information Architecture and User Experience Conference. Retrieved 13 February 2019 from http://2018.euroia.org

Euro, I. A. (2019). *Impact*. EuroIA Summit, Information Architecture and User Experience Conference. Retrieved 13 February 2019 from https://euroia.org

Fan, W., Chen, Z., Xiong, Z., & Chen, H. (2012). The Internet of Data: A new idea to extend the IoT in the digital world. *Frontiers of Computer Science*, *6*(6), 660–667.

Finger, M. (2016). Managing urban infrastructures. Lausanne, Switzerland: MOOC, Fall.

Giffinger, R., Fertner, C., Kramar, H., Kalasek, R., Pichler-Milanovic, N., & Meijers, E. (2007). *Smart Cities: Ranking of European medium-sized cities*. Vienna, Austria: University of Technology.

Gil-Garcia, J. R., Pardo, T. A., & Nam, T. (2016). A comprehensive view of the 21st century city: Smartness as technologies and innovation in urban contexts. In J. R. Gil-Garcia, T. A. Pardo, & T. Nam (Eds.), *Smarter as the new urban agenda: A comprehensive view of the 21st century city* (Vol. 11, pp. 1–19). Springer. doi:10.1007/978-3-319-17620-8_1

Gil-Garcia, J. R., & Sayogo, D. S. (2016). Government inter-organizational information sharing initiatives: Understanding the main determinants of success. *Government Information Quarterly*, 22(3), 572–582. doi:10.1016/j.giq.2016.01.006

Gil-Garcia, J. R., Zhang, J., & Puron-Cid, G. (2016). Conceptualizing smartness in government: An integrative and multi-dimensional view. *Government Information Quarterly*, 33(3), 524–534. doi:10.1016/j.giq.2016.03.002

Hashem, I. A. T., Chang, V., Anuar, N. B., Adewole, K., Yaqoob, I., Gani, A., ... Chiroma, H. (2016). The role of big data in smart city. *International Journal of Information Management*, 36(5), 748–758. doi:10.1016/j.ijinfomgt.2016.05.002

Hsieh, C. K., Alquaddoomi, F., Okeke, F., Pollak, J. P., Gunasekara, L., & Estrin, D. (2018). Small data: Applications and architecture. *Proceedings of the Fourth International Conference on Big Data, Small Data, Linked Data and Open Data*.

Hu-manity.co. (2018). *The problem*. Retrieved 13 February 2019 from https://hu-manity.co

Janssen, M., & van der Voort, H. (2016). Adaptive governance: Towards a stable, accountable and responsive government. *Government Information Quarterly*, 33(1), 1–5. doi:10.1016/j.giq.2016.02.003

Johnston, E. (2010). Governance infrastructures in 2020. Special Issue Part I: 2020: The good, the bad, and the ugly. *Public Administration Review*, 70, S122–S128. doi:10.1111/j.1540-6210.2010.02254.x

Khatoun, R., & Zeadally, S. (2016). Smart cities: Concepts, architectures, research opportunities. *Communications of the ACM*, 59(8), 46–57. doi:10.1145/2858789

Kitchin, R. (2014). The real-time city? Big data and smart urbanism. *GeoJournal*, *79*(1), 1–14. doi:10.100710708-013-9516-8

Kyriazopoulou, C. (2015). Architectures and requirements for the development of smart cities: A literature study. In Smartgreens 2015 and Vehits 2015 (CCIS 579, pp. 75-103). Springer. doi:10.1007/978-3-319-27753-0_5

Laurini, R. (2017). Towards smart urban planning through knowledge infrastructure. *GEOProcessing 2017: The Ninth International Conference on Advanced Geographic Information Systems, Applications, and Services*, 75-80.

Lea, R. (2015). Smart cities: Technology challenges for the IoT. *SenseTecnic Blog*. Retrieved 17 April 2018 from http://sensetecnic.com/technology-challenges-for-the-iot/

Marsal-Llacuna, M. L. (2015). Measuring the standardized definition of "smart city": A proposal on global metrics to set the terms of reference for urban "smartness". In Lecture Notes in Computer Science: Vol. 9156. *Computational science and its applications -- ICCSA 2015*. Cham: Springer. doi:10.1007/978-3-319-21407-8_42

McGinley, T., & Nakata, K. (2015). A community architecture framework for smart cities. In *Citizen's right to the digital city* (pp. 231–252). Singapore: Springer. doi:10.1007/978-981-287-919-6_13

McKenna, H. P. (2017a). Civic tech and ambient data in the public realm: Exploring challenges and opportunities for learning and smart cities. In N. Streitz & P. Markopoulos (Eds.), Lecture Notes in Computer Science: Vol. 10291. *Distributed, ambient and pervasive interactions (DAPI)*. Cham: Springer. doi:10.1007/978-3-319-58697-7_23

McKenna, H. P. (2017b). Urbanizing the ambient: Why people matter so much in smart cities. In S. Konomi & G. Roussos (Eds.), *Enriching urban spaces with ambient computing, the Internet of Things, and smart city design* (pp. 209–231). Hershey, PA: IGI Global. doi:10.4018/978-1-5225-0827-4.ch011

Memos, V. A., Psannis, K. E., Ishibashi, Y., Kim, B. G., & Gupta, B. B. (2018). An efficient algorithm for media-based surveillance system (EAMSuS) in IoT smart city framework. *Future Generation Computer Systems*, *83*, 619–628. doi:10.1016/j.future.2017.04.039

Mulder, I. (2015). Opening up: Towards a sociable smart city. In *Citizen's right to the digital city* (pp. 161–173). Singapore: Springer. doi:10.1007/978-981-287-919-6_9

Mulligan, C. E. A., & Olsson, M. (2013). Architectural implications of smart city business models: An evolutionary perspective. *IEEE Communications Magazine, 51*(6), 80–85. doi:10.1109/MCOM.2013.6525599

Paskaleva, K., Cooper, I., & Concilo, G. (2018). Co-producing Smart City Services: Does One Size Fit All? In Smart Technologies for Smart Governments (pp. 123-158). Springer.

Pourzolfaghar, Z., Bezbradica, M., & Helfert, M. (2016). Types of IT architectures in smart cities – A review from a business model and enterprise architecture perspective: Position paper. In *Pre-ICIS Workshop on IoT and Smart City Challenges and Applications*. International Conference on Information Systems (ICIS).

Rodríquez Bolívar, M. P. (2015). Smart cities: Big cities, complex governance? In M. P. Rodríquez Bolívar (Ed.), *Transforming city governments for successful smart cities*. Springer. doi:10.1007/978-3-319-03167-5_1

Roeleven, S. (2010). *Why two thirds of enterprise architecture projects fail: An explanation for the limited success of architecture projects*. Business White Paper. Software AG.

Scassa, T. (2017). *Smart cities: Data ownership and privacy issues*. Retrieved 4 October 2018 from http://www.teresascassa.ca/index.php?option=com_k2&view=item&id=241:smart-cities-data-ownership-and-privacy-issues&Itemid=81#

Schmitt, G. (2015). *Information Cities*. Retrieved from https://itunes.apple.com/us/book/information-cities/id970529491?mt=11

Schmitt, G. (2016). *Smart cities. Massive Open Online Course (MOOC), edX*. Zurich, Switzerland: ETH Zurich.

Scholl, H. J. (2016). Special issue on smartness in governance, government, urban environments, and the Internet of Things: An editorial introduction. *Information Polity, 21*(1), 1–3. doi:10.3233/IP-150377

Scholl, H. J., & AlAwadhi, S. (2016). Creating smart governance: The key to radical ICT over-haul at the City of Munich. *Information Polity, 21*(1), 21–42. doi:10.3233/IP-150369

Sobczak, A. (2017). Enterprise architecture-based model of management for smart cities. In A. Brdulak & H. Brdulak (Eds.), *Happy city – How to plan and create the best livable area for the people.* Cham, Switzerland: Springer International Publishing AG. doi:10.1007/978-3-319-49899-7_3

Thakuriah, P., Tilahun, N. Y., & Zellner, M. (2017). Big data and urban informatics: Innovations and challenges to urban planning and knowledge discovery. In P. Thakuriah, N. Tilahun, & M. Zellner (Eds.), *Seeing Cities Through Big Data. Springer Geography.* Cham: Springer. doi:10.1007/978-3-319-40902-3_2

Townsend, A. M. (2013). *Smart cities: Big data, civic hackers and the quest for a new utopia.* W. W. Norton & Company.

Visnjic, I., Neely, A., Cennamo, C., & Visnjic, N. (2016). Governing the city: Unleashing value from the business ecosystem. Special Issue on City Innovation. *California Management Review, 59*(1), 109–140. doi:10.1177/0008125616683955

ADDITIONAL READING

Javed, B., Khan, Z., & McClatchey, R. (2018). An adaptable system to support provenance management for the public policy-making process in smart cities. *Informatics, 5*(3), 1–26.

Jensen, A. Ø. (2010). *Government enterprise architecture adoption: A systemic-discursive critique and reconceptualization* (Master's thesis). Copenhagen, Denmark: Copenhagen Business School.

Lara, A. P., Da Costa, E. M., Furlani, T. Z., & Yigitcanlar, T. (2016). Smartness that matters: Towards a comprehensive and human-centered characterization of smart cities. *Journal of Open Innovation: Technology, Market, and Complexity, 2*(1), 8. doi:10.118640852-016-0034-z

McKenna, H. P. (2016). Innovating relationships for learning in 21st century smart cities. *Proceedings of the 9th Annual International Conference of Education, Research and Innovation (iCERi2016)* (pp. 4695-4704), 14-16 November, Seville, Spain. 10.21125/iceri.2016.2115

Wiberg, M. (2011). Making the case for "architectural informatics": A new research horizon for ambient computing? *International Journal of Ambient Computing and Intelligence, 3*(3), 1–7. doi:10.4018/jaci.2011070101

KEY TERMS AND DEFINITIONS

Ambient Architectures: Ambient architectures refer to more dynamic, adaptive, and open physical and digital structures.

Ambient Governance: Ambient governance refers to more dynamic, adaptive, and open modes of governance.

Ambient Information Architectures: Ambient information architectures refer to more dynamic, adaptive, and open information architectures.

Awareness: Awareness refers to the concept or quality of being aware as it applies to people on the one hand, to technologies on the other, and to a combination of aware people and aware technologies.

Responsive Cities: Responsive cities refer to more dynamic, adaptive, and open urban formations that are attentive, in-the-moment, to people and the broader ecosystem.

Smart Cities: Smart cities are urban areas, regions, territories, and beyond that are characterized by aware and engaged people, in combination with and aided by, the use of awareness enhancing technologies for mobility, livability, and sustainability.

Smartness: Smartness refers to more aware, adaptive, and responsive infrastructures (technical, human, and social), and services taking people into consideration and the broader ecosystem.

Section 3
Theories, Methods, Openness, and Metrics

Chapter 7

Visibilities and Invisibilities:
Methodologies and Theoretical
Spaces for Ambient Urbanities

ABSTRACT

The purpose of this chapter is to explore urban visibilities and invisibilities in terms of the physical and digital, giving rise to the need for new methodologies and theoretical spaces in understanding ambient urbanities. This chapter seeks to shed light on the importance of elements in urban environments informing theory and methodology for smart, responsive, and future cities. The research literature for urban theory, urban methodologies, and urban visibilities and invisibilities is explored in this chapter in the context of smart and responsive cities, enabling the identification of issues, controversies, and problems. Using an exploratory case study approach, solutions and recommendations are advanced. This chapter makes a contribution to the research literature for urban theoretical spaces and methodologies for smart and responsive cities, the evolving of urban theory and methods for 21st century cities and urbanities, and formulation of a conceptual framework for ambient methodologies and theoretical spaces.

DOI: 10.4018/978-1-5225-7882-6.ch007

1. INTRODUCTION

The purpose of this chapter is to explore urban visibilities and invisibilities in terms of the physical and digital, giving rise to the need for new methodologies and theoretical spaces in understanding ambient urbanities. As such, this chapter seeks to shed light on the importance of elements such as atmospheres (Abbas, 2018), ambiances (Thibaud, 2013), people (Morello and Piga, 2015), and experiences (Demers and Potvin, 2016) in urban environments, informing theory and methodology for urban design, urban representation, and augmentations in smart cities, responsive cities, and future cities. The research literature for urban theory (Roy, 2009), urban methodologies (Gavalas et al., 2017), and urban visibilities and invisibilities (Caprotti, 2017) is explored in this chapter in the context of smart and responsive cities (Schmitt, 2018), enabling identification of issues, controversies, and problems. Using an exploratory case study approach, solutions and recommendations are advanced. This chapter makes a contribution to: a) the research literature for urban theoretical spaces and methodologies for smart and responsive cities; b) the evolving of urban theory and methods for 21st century cities and urbanities; and c) formulation of a conceptual framework for ambient methodologies and theoretical spaces.

Objectives: The objective of this chapter is to explore and advance new theoretical spaces and methodologies in support of ambient urbanities. As such, the key research question posed is – Why are new theoretical and methodological approaches important for explorations of urbanity in relation to smart cities?

2. BACKGROUND AND OVERVIEW

In an introduction to the launch of the *Ambiances Review*, Thibaud (2013) points to "the far-reaching changes in the territories and habitats of contemporary life" that "demand new approaches" and "new models of intelligibility" and the "growing interest for the world of the senses." Brenner and Schmid (2015) proposed the concept of planetary urbanization to generate awareness of "new forms of urbanization" that go beyond traditional notions of "the urban as fixed, bounded and universally generalizable settlement." For Brenner and

Schmid (2015), realization of the "interconnections across places, territories and landscapes" is important in order for the urban to be "framed in a manner that attempts to overcome the compartmentalization and fragmentation" of spaces and struggles. Schmitt (2015) claims that, simulation is an important method in urban planning and design and "is needed to make the invisible visible" and to "test assumptions" as well as to "visualize the results of the design over time" in urban and territorial regions. From an architecture perspective, Morello and Piga (2015) claim there is "increasing interest in simulation by society and the profession" and point to questions of "how simulation technologies will enable us to pay more attention to the intangible values of the ambiance of spaces." Because "spatial design affects human well-being and health," Morello and Piga (2015) argue that, "this generates a serious return to people-centered design" along with "increased interest in transparency and participation in the process of decision making about urban spaces." Piga, Morello, and Salerno (2017) introduce a research perspective in urban design and urban representation, exploring urban simulation from interdisciplinary theoretical and practical perspectives. As such, the importance of more aware people is advanced in this chapter in coming to current and future understandings of the need for a rethinking of urban theory and methods for 21st century urban environments. Theoretically and methodologically, this chapter is situated at the intersection of urban ambiances, atmospheres, and awareness.

2.1 Definitions

For the purposes of this work, definitions for key terms used in this chapter are presented here based on the research literature.

- **Ambiances:** From an architectural perspective, Morello and Piga (2015) note that, "the concept of ambiance is related to the intangible aspects related to the use of spaces."
- **Atmospheres:** Friberg (2014) describes atmosphere "as an aspect of perception." Christiansen, Laursen, and Hvejsel (2017) refer to "the delicate notion of ambiance understood as a means for describing the atmosphere of a given space." Reviewing the work of Böhme, Bille (2018) refers to atmosphere "as that through which the world appears."
- **Simulation:** Schmitt (2015) defines simulation as "the imitation of the operation of a real-world process or system over time."

2.2 Overview

This chapter provides a range of perspectives in Section 3 on evolving understandings of visibilities and invisibilities, theoretical spaces, and new methodologies in the context of emerging smart, responsive, and future cities, followed by a selection of associated issues, controversies, and problems. Section 4 provides an overview of methodologies and theoretical spaces for smart cities; a conceptual framework for ambient methodologies and theoretical spaces; and operationalization of this framework for use in the exploration under investigation in this chapter. In identifying the potential for solutions and recommendations to issues, controversies, and problems identified in this chapter, a framework for ambient visibilities and invisibilities in smart city urbanities is advanced along with the surfacing of variables. Section 5 identifies future directions for research and practice and Section 6 concludes with chapter coverage highlights, the major contributions, and the key insights, ideas and lessons.

The primary audiences for this chapter include students, educators, researchers, policy makers, businesses, community members, urban planners and designers, and urban practitioners concerned with methods and theoretical spaces for working with visibilities and invisibilities associated with urban design, urban representation, and other challenges and opportunities in the context of smart cities, responsive cities, and future cities.

3. THEORETICAL SPACES AND NEW METHODOLOGIES FOR SMART CITIES

In the context of smart cities, this chapter provides a review of the research literature for visibilities and invisibilities; emerging theoretical spaces; and new methodologies in relation to the physical and digital and associated complexities pertaining to urban atmospheres, ambiences, people, and experiences.

3.1 Visibilities and Invisibilities

Harrison and Donnelly (2011) claim that the instrumentation of smart cities is "a key enabler for new theories of cities" that is "making the invisible visible" with "the ability to observe many individual behaviours in 'real time'." In other words, Harrison and Donnelly (2011) claim that the "Smart City approach" enables "access to real-time information at the level of individual citizen's choices and actions" as in, "making the invisible visible" while contributing to a rethinking of "the emerging roles of information and technology." Brenner and Schmid (2015) point to the problem of rendering invisible what is going on with non-urban landscapes by "equating the urban exclusively with large and/or dense population centers." Schmitt (2015) argues that "simulation is needed to make the invisible visible and to test and visualise future scenarios" in smart cities. Caprotti (2017) claims that, "the smart city is characterized by its invisibility" in that while "fibre networks are material" they are not visible because "they are laid on the bottom of canals, or exist underground." Caprotti (2017) adds that, "smart city projects are often computer-based and have little or no actual visible, tangible physical presence." Also noted by Caprotti (2017) is the realization that people are embedded in the smart city as in "were part of it" in combination with smartphones and the like. Chevalier (2018), in making "visible the invisible" through digital art, "reveals the essence of things in an ever-changing world." Through the use of "light, movement, energy," Chevalier (2018) illustrates the "new poetics of matter" along with "notions of flow and networks" employing "the virtual the elusive and translates the new forms of contemporary life and cities today" as in, "incessant renewal, speed, transformation" while "abandoning all chronological and linear memory" where the urban can be seen "between destruction and construction, growth and mutation."

Figure 1 provides an overview of key issues, controversies, and challenges posed by visibilities and invisibilities associated with smart cities. Instrumentation of cities is identified as a key enabler of new theories (Harrison and Donnelly, 2011) while making the invisible visible through the availability of in-the-moment, as in, real-time, observable behaviors. The Smart City approach (Harrison and Donnelly, 2011) is said to enable access to information pertaining to individual choices and actions. Caprotti (2017) claims that the smart city is characterized by invisibility due to the nature of technologies as embedded and the digital as intangible while non-urban landscapes (Brenner and Schmid, 2015) are rendered invisible by their lack of inclusion in the urban. Smart city projects tend to be digital and intangible and as such, invisible (Caprotti, 2017) and through digital art renderings by artists such as Chevalier (2018), the invisibility is being made visible.

Figure 1. Overview of key issues, controversies and problems for in/visibilities in smart cities

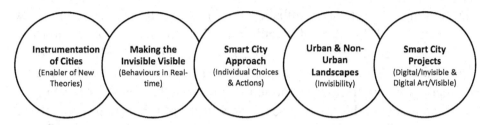

3.2 Theoretical Spaces

Theories of Cities

Augoyard (2002) identified deficiencies in the research literature for architectural and urban ambient environments pertaining to sound and everyday life, and through an interdisciplinary approach, advanced an integrative theory of architectural and urban ambience. The UN-Habitat (2006) articulated the emergence of the meta-city or hypercity as "massive sprawling conurbations of more than 20 million people" that "have changed the dynamics of urbanisation." Of note is the emergence of the Urban Theory Lab (UTL, 2018a) at Harvard University that focuses on critical urban theory and provides a space for the development of concepts, methods and cartographies. Harrison and Donnelly (2011) argue that while smart cities may be accomplishing great things, there is "little detailed understanding of why" and as such, the smart cities domain is described as "a field in want of a good theoretical base." Harrison and Donnelly (2011) identify steps toward the development of a theory of smart cities based on "a model that can unify the perspectives of the professions in the Urban Systems Collaborative" as an "inter-disciplinary collaboration." According to Harrison and Donnelly (2011), "smart cities provide a new form of instrumentation for observing in fine detail the way that people use the city" and this "may enable new approaches to theories of cities." As such, Harrison and Donnelly (2011) highlight the pervasiveness of information systems in urban environments enabling a "change" in terms of "opportunities to capture information" as in, real-time access at the individual level while acknowledging the need "to address serious issues of privacy and protection of Personal Information."

Ambiences

Highlighting the sensory, Thibaud (2013) points to the need for "new approaches" and "models of intelligibility" in the launch of the journal, *ambiances*. According to Schmitt (2015), "to better understand the city" there is a need for "theory, experiment, and simulation to work hand-in-hand." Brenner and Schmid (2015) explore the question of a new epistemology of the urban based on the emergence of "new forms of urbanization around the world that challenge inherited conceptions of the urban." Demers and Potvin (2016) describe the physical ambiences laboratory as an "adaptable structure in an outdoors environment" that "aims to connect the theory of ambiences with the actual complexity of experiencing on a site." From an architectural perspective, Abbas (2016) explores the cartography of ambiance as a spatial practice for wayfinding focusing on memory, data gathering, decoding, and encoding in urban environments. Exploring ambiance in relation to livability in contemporary cities, Christiansen et al. (2017) propose "to refine descriptions of ambiance as an integral part of the technical construction principles applied in the built environment" thus "considering it a continuous space, as suggested in theories of landscape urbanism" thereby "juxtaposing it with tectonic architectural theory" enabling tectonic perspectives for urban ambiance in urban design. Tectonics is considered to be "a contextual joining of aesthetics and technology at the architectural scale" providing a "challenge which crosses the architectural and urban domains." Christiansen et al. (2017) argue that to "live more densely" gives rise to "potentials for forming novel ambiances in the city" in support of "high quality urban environments" and "viable urban ambiances." As such, Christiansen et al. (2017) point to the importance of their work in addressing the task of "envisioning ambiance in the future city" and "linking it to an in-depth knowledge of the technologies that govern construction and planning practice."

Meta-Cities

Kostaropoulou (2017) explores the concept of meta-cities as conscious cities incorporating "an advanced form of urbanization processes" that "reflects the consciousness of decisions of the people who live within" these urban areas along with "their participation and contribution to the commons." Ramaprasad, Sánchez-Ortiz, and Syu (2017) provide a unified definition of a smart city from several domains along with a smart city ontology, enabling city officials to "assess the level of smartness of their cities from many perspectives at different levels of complexity." The ontology is said to also be an adaptable tool for use in a variety of ways and for a range of purposes including the identification of "gaps in the literature and practice." Urssi (2018) refers to the metacity concept in relation to data where "information accessed in real time" will "transform the city" to "the idea of a city updated by citizens" enabling "new forms of use and design."

Atmospheres

In reviewing a book on the work of Böhme, Bille (2018) refers to the value of the 'affective turn' for contributing to understandings of "affective and emotional aspects of human lives as they unfold through space." Bille (2018) notes how "atmospheres are active in shaping the world" in terms of how "the environment 'radiates' a quality of mood" on the one hand and how "the person participates in the mood with his/her own sensitivity" on the other. Abbas (2018) refers to atmospheres as "phenomena that enable us to bypass the classic dichotomy between real and virtual spaces" while emphasizing their dynamic, interactive, "fluid and connective character." As an interface for architecture, atmosphere is said to augment "sensible ambient human-computer interactions" (Abbas, 2018) using techniques such as staging, composing, and modeling. For Abbas (2018), potential exists for the use of atmospheres to guide the design of "meaningful ambient computing and electronic environments" through a combination of "narrating movement through space" and "scripting events and moments of connection" along with "testing sensory experience in real-time and space." Ibrahim, El-Zaart, and Adams (2018) provide a review of smart city roadmaps focusing on sustainability, identifying the gap of readiness for change. Using the theory of change (ToC) in relation to the smart sustainable cities (SSC) concept, together with a "theoretical logic model for transformation towards SSC", Ibrahim et al. (2018) advance "a coherent, systematic transformation roadmap that captures the cross-cutting readiness of a city along its infrastructures." Shutters (2018) argues for, "parallel advances in theory" in smart cities in order to "make sense of novel data streams" in relation to "the simulation and modeling of complex systems."

Figure 2 provides an overview of key issues, controversies, and challenges posed for theoretical spaces associated with smart cities.

Figure 2. Overview of key issues, controversies and problems for theoretical spaces in smart cities

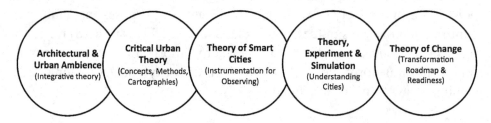

An integrative theory is advanced for architectural and urban ambience (Augoyard, 2002); critical urban theory is advanced by the Urban Theory Lab; a theory of smart cities is advanced (Harrison and Donnelly, 2011) enabled by instrumentation in support of real-time observation; theory, experiment, and simulation in combination is advanced (Schmitt, 2015) for understanding cities; and the theory of change (ToC) is used in developing a transformation roadmap for smart city implementation taking readiness into consideration (Ibrahim et al., 2018).

3.3 New Methodologies

Atmospheres

Augoyard (2002) pointed to deficiencies in the research literature for architectural and urban ambient environments and advanced an interdisciplinary and integrative approach to take into account sound on the one hand and the everyday on the other. As such, Augoyard (2002) explores "sonic research and everyday life" along with "the main dimensions of ordinary sounds." In the introduction of the *Ambiances Review* by Thibaud (2013) the need for new methods are emphasized in support of emerging understandings of urban spaces. For example, Griffero (2013) explores what constitutes an urban atmosphere using an atmospherological, as in, an aesthetical-phenomenological approach to investigate "what creates the overall impression (imageability) of a city" referring to the "atmospheric 'skin' of the city." Friberg (2014) combines the notion of atmosphere and aesthetic education to propose an approach to the exploration of performing everyday practices at the intersection of awareness of the sensorial and bodily in urban spaces. In exploring the urban, Brenner and Schmid (2015) inquire into what "categories, methods, and cartographies" are required in coming to contemporary understandings of urban life on the planet, proposing a "new epistemology of the urban in a series of seven theses" to advance debate on critical urban theory and practice. Edensor and Sumartojo (2015) highlight the "range of methods that are used to investigate atmospheres" with "an orientation towards the mundane" and everyday.

Experiment, Simulation, and the Experiential

Schaffers et al. (2011) describe the Living Lab concept, as "a methodology and a model for organizing innovation programmes and projects and conducting innovation experiments." Schmitt (2015) focuses on experiment as method, with the city as a living laboratory and considers simulation to be "an important method in addition to theory and experiment." Schmitt (2015) claims that simulation in architecture "is often used synonymously with visualization." Kolko (2015) described design thinking as an approach relevant to problem solving involving users' experiences and the use of prototypes in the context of increasing complexities associated with technology and business. In the introduction to a special issue on experiential simulation in architecture and urban space, Morello and Piga (2016) describe efforts to respond to challenges associated with how "it is difficult to communicate and test the anticipation of the ambiance of place" and "to assess how designers control the future ambiances in a scientific and sharable way." Demers and Potvin (2016) "developed, built, and inhabited" a physical ambiences laboratory "to compare existing and past ambiences" and "speculate on future ambiences." Claiming that such an endeavor "cannot be adequately approached with digital simulation," Demers and Potvin (2016) describe the lab as "a full-scale, adaptable structure that allows for the experience of architectural typologies, and enables spatial transformations through time." As such, Demers and Potvin (2016) define an ambience as involving "complexity because of the changing nature of the environmental conditions that generates it" including "light, wind, sun, and sound, creating varying distribution patterns of natural fluxes" and "people in the environment." According to Demers and Potvin (2016), this "research suggests that adaptive opportunities and reinterpretation of existing ambiences could ultimately translate into new spaces to experience environmental delight for responsive inhabitants." Gavalas et al. (2017) provide an overview of smart cities in terms of trends, methodologies, and applications from a technology perspective where the need is identified for "novel methods of management." Grieten et al. (2018)

provide an inquiry into appreciative inquiry (AI) as a methodology and an approach to "grounded and generative theory building from immersion in the field." From an evaluation perspective, according to Coghlan, Preskill, and Catsambas (2003), the focus of appreciative inquiry is on "the positive" while being "grounded in participants' actual experiences."

Wonder and Imagination

Patel (2017) describes three methods in the domain of architecture for working with the notion of wonder as – the frame, the spectacle, and the interruption. The frame features "an awe-inspiring moment at a distance" as in "a captivating view through a window" whereas the spectacle is concerned with wonder where, as with "a circus, everything is designed to capture your imagination" and the interruption is said to be "the most subtle" in that it "is happened-upon" as in "the strange hidden in the familiar." From a digital artistic perspective, Chevalier (2018) presents works that explore "the imagination of the city and its urban transformations" in an effort to "reinvent the city of tomorrow and imagine our future world" in response to "traffic flows" and "exchanges in real time" that give rise to a rethinking of the city. Using computer tools, Chevalier explores 'new digital cities' based on "fixed or moving worlds" creating cities "between reality and simulation, forming part of a transformable space-time." As if building on the vision of the Urban Theory Lab (UTL, 2018b) around the notion of planetary urbanization, Chevalier (2018) artistically renders "meta-cities" as "planetary cities, without location, without beginning or end, without centre and periphery" that consist of "wired buildings" and "generate themselves from software specially designed with the computer scientist Claude Michell" forming "an infinite virtual city." This "projected interactive virtual reality" installation enables exploration of "3 different urban universes" featuring "discovery via a touch interface in a dynamic chaos of unplanned flows." It is worth noting that a workshop featured at the Conference on Human Factors in Computing Systems (CHI, 2018) focuses on the methodology of the "living lab" encompassing smart homes and smart cities.

Sensing, Serendipity, and Contexts of Use

Konomi and Sasao (2018) describe the exploration of unconventional urban sensing approaches in the form of "techniques and tools for collecting detailed behavioral data in large public spaces" involving a number of researchers with technologies enabling them to "act according to mobile notifications." In this way, a novel approach is developed to "explore the challenges of human in the loop sensing" and the design of "a mobile behavior sampling tool based on smart notifications to address the challenges of in-situ sampling" for spatial analytics. Boonen and Lievens (2018) explore the potential for employing live prototypes as a proxy technology in developing a more effective methodology for the "complex context of use" characterizing smart cities where elements such as "serendipity" and "unforeseen types of use" can be accommodated. Farina, Kotsopoulos, and Casalegno (2018) point to the emergence of "new contexts of use and behavior" enabled by the "almost symbiotic bond" underlying the physical and digital, giving way to "hybrid connected spaces." Farina et al. (2018) identify the need for new design variables in support of the "integration of a digital, immaterial dimension" that include: spatial, cultural, social, and technological.

Figure 3 provides an overview of key issues, controversies, and challenges posed by methodologies associated with smart cities.

The need for new methodologies in smart cities gives rise to a range of challenges associated with atmospheres in everyday life (Augoyard, 2002); the use of experiment and simulation (Schmitt, 2015) in living laboratories; the experiential, using design thinking (Kolko, 2015) and the exploration of future ambiences (Demers and Potvin, 2016); wonder and imagination (Patel, 2017) in the exploration of spaces between reality and simulation (Chevalier, 2018); and sensing (Konomi and Sasao, 2018), serendipity and the complexity of contexts of use (Boonen and Lievens, 2018) calling for new approaches to urban design and the creation of new design variables (Farina et al., 2018).

Figure 3. Overview of key issues, controversies and problems for methodologies in smart cities

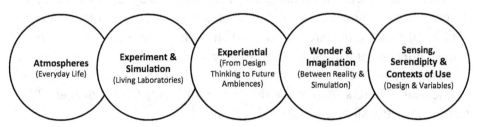

3.4 Issues, Controversies, Problems

Key issues, controversies, and problems emerging in the review of the research literature explored in this chapter are highlighted below. While coverage of issues, controversies, and problems is not intended to be exhaustive or comprehensive, it is designed to provide an overview of the nature, variety, and range.

Issues

Smart cities, by their very nature, have been described as invisible in terms of the embedding of technologies and the largely unnoticed gathering of large amounts of data, according to Harrison and Donnelly (2011), giving rise to requirements for privacy and the protection of personal information in relation to the capture and use of real-time data. As if opening pathways to new theories and methodologies for this chapter and this book on ambient urbanities, Christiansen et al. (2017) identify the urban design issue of densification and what it means for new forms of ambiance as continuous space. Piga et al. (2017) point to the issues of urban design and urban representation in contemporary urban environments, addressed by Patel (2017) in terms of three methods in architecture as framing, spectacle, and interruption for exploring wonder and imagination.

Controversies

The UN-Habitat (2006) argued that the emergence of metacities gives rise to the "call for a reassessment of urban governance" while Brenner and Schmid (2015) highlight controversies associated with the very definition of the urban itself. Kostaropoulou (2017) explores metacities as conscious cities, very much connected to the thinking and decision-making of inhabitants while Urssi (2018) explores the metacity as "a city updated by citizens" in support of new designs and uses. In coming to new understandings of smart cities, theories of smart cities are proposed (Harrison & Donnelly, 2011); theory from architecture and urban ambiance (Augoyard, 2002) is considered as well as atmospheres (Abbas, 2018; Bille, 2018); the importance of complexity is highlighted (Shutters, 2018); and the theory of change (Ibraham et al., 2018) in support of transformational thinking.

Problems

Schmitt (2015) identifies problems associated with existing city models and the need for alternative models to accommodate future cities thinking while Brenner and Schmid (2015) highlight that which is rendered invisible by urban age discourse, constrained by focusing on the urban as density while cities, as if in defiance, cross traditional boundaries to include surrounding regions, conurbations, and territories of economic, cultural, and other activities. Cities by their nature are complex calling for cross-domain, interdisciplinary, and novel thinking and collaborations in the revising, renovating, and creation of methodologies for the study of smart cities and urbanities with added digital layers of complexity. As such, a range of methodologies and approaches are advanced including modeling, simulation, design thinking, experiential, live prototyping, and digital art, to name a few. Not surprisingly, Farina et al. (2018) call for new variables in support of the design for smart cities, and it is worth noting that Wise and Shaffer (2015) point to the importance of theory, claiming that theory assists in determining "what variables a researcher should attend to and how to interpret a multitude of micro-results and make them actionable."

Summarized in Figure 4, a glimpse of patterns, flows, relationships, and possibilities begin to emerge, influencing methodologies and theoretical spaces through ambiences, atmospheres, augmentations, and in/visibilities in smart cities. Ambiences are described as adaptable and architectural in relation to complexities, continuous space, and envisioning for livability, taking into consideration elements such as density for the physical and urban. Atmospheres are highlighted in relation to aesthetics, the affective, the emotional and the everyday and the importance of impression, mood, and sensitivity. Augmentations pertain to technology in relation to information and the potential for the generation of dynamic chaos, contributing to reinterpretations and the impact of wonder. And finally, in/visibilities emerge as critical to behaviors in aware environments featuring the Internet of Things (IoT), the Internet of People (IoP), and the Internet of Expeiences (IoE), highlighting the importance of digital art, evolving urban discourse, instrumentation, new forms of flows and networks, along with the use of living labs and simulations while cognizant of privacy and related protections.

Although neatly categorized across ambiences, atmospheres, augmentations, and in/visibilities, it is important to note that there is considerable overlap in that the everyday is associated with atmospheres for example as well as with

Figure 4. Methods & theory in smart cities: ambiences, atmospheres, augmentations & in/visibilities

Methodologies and Theoretical Spaces in Smart Cities

	Ambiences	Atmospheres	Augmentations	In/Visibilities
People (aware)	Adaptable	Aesthetics	Dynamic chaos	Behaviors
	Architectural	Affective	Information	Digital art
IoP IoT IoE	Complexities	Emotional	Reinterpretation	Discourse
	Continuous space	Everyday	Wonder	Instrumentation
Technologies (aware)	Envisioning	Impression		Flow & networks
	Livability	Mood		Living labs
	Physical	Sensitivity		Privacy
	Urban			Simulation

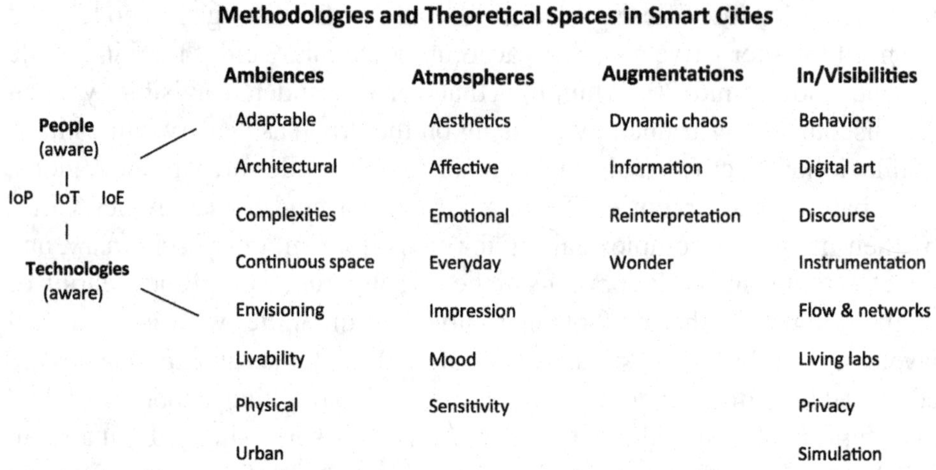

invisibilities in the context of living labs. Also, the categories are necessarily incomplete and intended only as a summary overview.

By author and year, Table 1 provides an overview of issues, controversies, and problems in the context of theory and methodologies for smart cities. A range of researchers address the invisibility issue of smart cities and regions from Brenner and Schmid (2015) to Schmitt (2015) on simulation as a technique to generate visibility, to Caprotti (2017) on the nature of smart city technologies and Chevalier (2018) on the use of digital art to render visibility. Integrative theory for the urban is proposed by Augoyard (2002), from an architectural and ambiance perspective, while Christiansen et al. (2017) explore ambiance and densification in the context of space as continuous. Harrison and Donnelly (2011) advance a theory of smart cities in relation to technologies and instrumentation while others advance the importance of metacities (Kostaropoulou, 2017; Urssi, 2018); atmospheres (Abbas, 2018; Bille, 2018); simulation, modeling, and complexity (Shutters, 2018); and the theory of change (Ibrahim et al., 2018) in relation to transformation.

Methodologies and approaches to the study of smart cities are many and varied including living labs (Schaffers et al., 2011); atmospheres (Griffero, 2013); ambiances (Thibaud, 2013); urban discourse (Brenner and Schmid, 2015), design thinking (Kolko, 2015); categories and cartographies (Schmitt, 2015); experiential (Demers and Potvin, 2016); wonder and imagination (Patel, 2017); live prototypes in accommodating serendipity and unforeseen

Table 1. Issues, controversies, and problems for theory and methodologies in smart cities

Theory and Methodologies for Smart Cities			
Author(s)	**Year**	**Theory**	**Methodologies**
Augoyard	2002	Architectural & Urban Ambiance	
Harrison & Donnelly Schaffers et al.	2011	Instrumentation & Theories of SC	Living Labs
Griffero	2013		Atmospheres
Thibaud	2013		Ambiances & Methods
Brenner & Schmid	2015	Non-urban as Invisible	Discourse & invisibility
Kolko	2015		Design Thinking
Schmitt	2015	Simulation & Invisible to Visible	Categories, Methods & Cartographies
Demers & Potvin	2016		Experiential
Caprotti	2017	Invisibility of SC Technologies	
Christiansen et al.	2017	Ambiance and Densification	
Kostaropoulou	2017	Metacities as Conscious Cities	
Patel	2017		Wonder & Imagination
Abbas; Bille	2018	Atmospheres	
Boonen & Lievens	2018		Live Prototypes, Serendipity & Unforeseen Uses
Chevalier	2018	Digital Art & Invisible to Visible	Digital Art
Farina et al.	2018		Contexts of Use and Behavior
Grieten et al.	2018		Appreciative Inquiry
Ibrahim et al.	2018	Theory of Change	
Konomi & Sasso	2018		Sensing & Humans in the Loop
Shutters	2018	Simulation-Modeling-Complexity	
Urssi	2018	Metacity & the Updatable City	

uses (Boonen and Lievens, 2018); digital art (Chevalier, 2018); contexts of use and behavior (Farian et al., 2018); appreciative inquiry (Grieten et al., 2018); and sensing and humans in the loop (Konomi and Sasso, 2018).

By way of solutions and recommendations, Section 4 develops, advances, and operationalizes a conceptual framework for ambient methodologies and theoretical spaces in smart cities for use in exploring the issues, controversies, and problems highlighted in Table 1.

4. METHODOLOGIES AND THEORETICAL SPACES FOR SMART CITIES

Based on the urban and smart city perspectives explored through the research literature in this chapter, methodological and theoretical spaces as ambient are advanced in this section as solutions and recommendations to what may seem to be intractable issues, controversies, and problems.

4.1 Ambient Methodologies/Theoretical Spaces: Solutions and Recommendations

Based on the review of the research literature presented in Section 3 of this chapter, a conceptual framework for ambient methodologies and theoretical spaces in the context of smart cities is advanced as depicted in Figure 5. Through the combining of the interactive dynamic of aware people and aware technologies, enabling evolving understandings of the nature of smart cities using the constructs of visibilities and invisibilities or more simply in/visibilities, dimensions of digitally-enabled urban areas and regions are explored through emerging perspectives on atmospheres and ambiances by people and their experiences in contributing to and being influenced by urban designs, simulations, and representations.

Through emerging understandings of the ambient, methodologies and theoretical spaces are explored in this chapter focusing on more aware people and aware technologies in smart cities in responding to the research question posed in the introduction of this chapter, and restated as a proposition under exploration in this chapter, as follows:

Figure 5. Conceptual framework for ambient methodologies and theoretical spaces

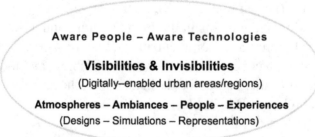

Ambient Methodologies & Theoretical Spaces

Aware People – Aware Technologies

Visibilities & Invisibilities
(Digitally–enabled urban areas/regions)

Atmospheres – Ambiances – People – Experiences
(Designs – Simulations – Representations)

P: New theoretical and methodological approaches are important for explorations of urbanity in smart cities in relation to emergent and evolving spaces for the invisible, visible, augmented, and other extensibilities.

How new methodologies and theoretical spaces inform urbanity is explored in this chapter in relation to in/visibilities (making the invisible visible), augmentations, and extensibilities. As such, under exploration are atmospheres, ambiances, and augmentations of, for example, the sensory, involving people and their experiences in coming to new understanding of the urban and urbanities as ambient. Ambient methodologies and theoretical spaces are understood to be more dynamic, in-the-moment, and adaptive, enabling new potentials for urbanizing and urbanities to emerge. As such, methodologies, theoretical spaces, and in/visibilities as ambient are discussed in relation to contemporary and future smart cities as solutions and recommendations for issues, controversies, and problems that are posing unprecedented challenges and opportunities.

4.2 Ambient Methodologies/Theoretical Spaces: An Exploration

In relation to smart cities, ambient methodologies are explored, ambient theoretical spaces, and ambient in/visibilities. Development of a framework for ambient in/visibilities is advanced along with the identification of associated variables.

4.2.1. Ambient Methodologies in Smart Cities

Ambient methodologies emerge in relation to an initiative developed to animate public spaces. Described by a city councilor, the musical railing is "designed to ensure that civic parkades are safe and welcoming" highlighting safety, engagement, and culture, among the many benefits (http://bit. ly/290HwIg). The musical rails initiative could be said to be a move toward the notion of the tectonic approach to urban design, situated as it is at the intersection of art, technology, and aesthetics in urban spaces. Based on the livestreaming of an eTownHall meeting, discussion content captured and shared in-the-moment through video and social media was described by city IT staff as an example of "documented engagement" enabled through people interacting in aware environments and contributing to the digitally generated data streams and traces. An educator designed a "mobile cloud-based app to capture and share insights, feedback, and knowledge" as a "simple, cost efficient" mechanism for "instant awareness" intended for a wide range of uses including "business, design, infrastructure, learning, safety, sport, and tourism." A design thinking approach was used by a community group to bring people together in a participatory fashion to generate and present ideas for reusing and recycling, as in upcycled urbanism, portions of an iconic, historic infrastructural urban element about to be decommissioned. Regarding the notion of urban atmospheres, an individual described their city as "almost like one giant museum" expanding the traditional, enclosed notion of the museum to open, everyday, emergent, and dynamic spaces.

4.2.2. Ambient Theoretical Spaces in Smart Cities

Ambient theoretical spaces emerged when a community leader described the collaborative example of the animation of a public space in the form of the musical railing parkade initiative, noting that, "there is a lot of theory around what makes vibrant spaces." Reference was made to the Downtown Business Association and their implementation of "a people counter" based on "a few cameras around downtown" that are "programmed so that they don't capture identity, like faces and so on" and using "infrared it records the blobs" as in, the "bodies going by." This information is captured "for business retailing purposes" in order to "say on certain streets" it is possible to "look at the data" such as "time of day, day of the week, season, that kind of thing and see how many hundreds of people are" moving in these areas. The community leader pointed to the importance of possibly using this example for application "with some of our public spaces, like plazas" and "smaller kind of plaza spaces" to capture "some of that anonymous kind of count" data to show that "at maximum this space anytime of the year would have 50 people on it and" what "the daily average" might be. A city councilor commented on the value of an eTownHall meeting where "we were talking about our strategic plan and we were able to get feedback from people who were watching the livestream video" of the event. According to the councilor, people were "watching, tweeting, sending direct messages that we could respond to" providing "an interactive experience that makes the city more real for those people." As such, the councilor came to realize in that moment the theoretical and practical value of combining aware people with aware technologies in-the-moment for urban planning and decision-making. Similarly, an academic described a mobile urban app designed to support collaborative decision-making in response to complex urban issues. A community member pointed to the importance of "the technology" component in cities in terms of "being smart on how we use it" adding that smart cities is "a great concept, a great idea because its both theoretical and practical."

4.2.3. Ambient In/Visibilities in Smart Cities

The notion of ambient visibilities and invisibilities emerged in discussion of an urban display to dynamically capture and display cycling data on a visual screen in-the-moment for a multi-use path. A community member pointed to the importance of what cities do to create "the visual sense of the city." A city councilor referred to BikeMaps.org as "a great example" where "through your phone you are able to track accidents" and "maybe find the hub, find the place where accidents are happening and with the app create a map, and with that information" as "a real life thing" via "a phone app, that information is being given back to the city so we can now go and create engineering fixes for those intersections and those high crash places." For the city councilor, this urban app provided an example of the coming together of place, people, information, experiences, such that "its all connected and the tool of technology is augmenting the information that we have and allows us to have a safer more vibrant city."

A city councilor spoke of the vibrancy of a city, the pulse of the city, using the examples of "Barcelona and Montreal, two cities pulsing with arts, culture and I think to me that is key" the people "not just people but people interacting with each other and with their surroundings." The councilor added, "I think that's when you get the pulse, whether its art on the walls, art on the side of a building that people are looking at" and engaging with through "exchanging how they feel when they walk by" as well as "when people actually say hi to each other on a path by the beach", all of these instances provide examples of "creating a pulse and a vibrancy because its creating activity." Another type of visibility/invisibility issue was described by IT staff in higher education who highlighted the question of occupancy data in building systems on campus asking "how do you leverage and expose some of the information in a way that you know is safe and make it available for other things" such as presence information in figuring out whether there are "people in the building and if there is a response" in the case of an emergency situation. The eTownHall example provided by the city councilor in Section

4.2.2 also serves to highlight how technology enables people, as well as city hall meetings and processes, to become more visible through social media and other e-based approaches.

Findings in this chapter advance the concepts of ambient methodologies and ambient theoretical spaces in coming to evolving understandings of a framework for ambient visibilities and invisibilities in smart city urbanities. As such, this chapter gives rise to the potential for emerging understandings of methodologies and theoretical spaces as ambient, as depicted in Figure 6. The framework is organized around aware people and aware technologies, encompassing the physical and digital in relation to ambiences, atmospheres, and augmentations, contributing to insights associated with in/visibilities and making the invisible, visible.

This framework contributes further to the ambient turn in support of smart and responsive cities and urbanities. In the context of the ambient turn, potential emerges for approaches and inquiries to become ambient when characterized as dynamic, adaptive, in-the-moment, and responsive.

Figure 6. Framework for ambient in/visibilities in smart city urbanities

Ambient In/Visibilities

Aware People + Aware Technologies

Ambient Methodologies
Ambient Theoretical Spaces

Ambiences

In/Visibilities

Atmospheres

Augmentations

the Ambient Turn

Ambient Approaches
Ambient Inquiry

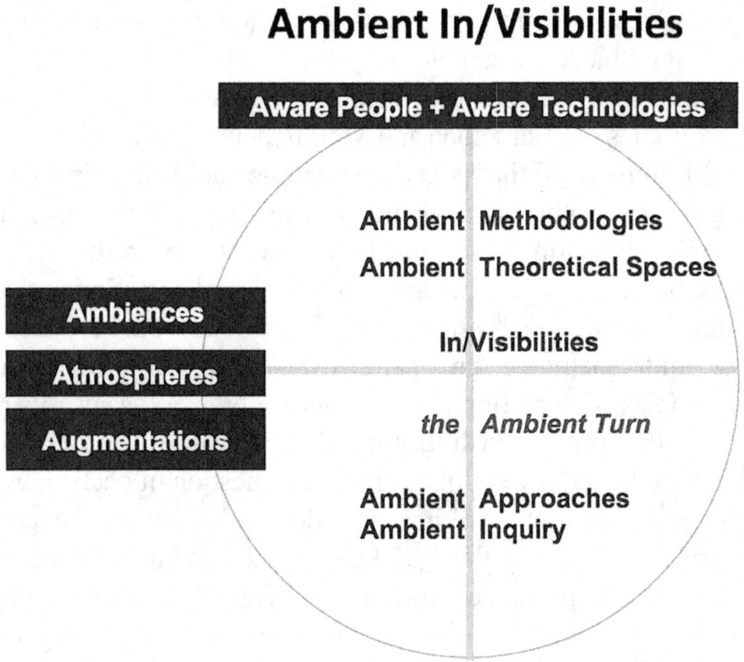

Dependent Variable (DV)

This chapter advances the potential for value of the dependent variable (DV) surfaced in this chapter as *in/visibilities and urban approaches* in relation to methodologies and theoretical spaces. Associated independent variables (IV) include: using a tectonic approach to urban design, implying the potential for the intersecting of art, technology, and aesthetics in urban spaces; animating public spaces, implying the potential for making the invisible, visible; the augmenting of meetings with technologies, implying the potential for improved and extended options for interactions; and the visual sense of the city, implying the potential for improved involvement and collaborations in making the invisible, visible.

Additionally, the *in/visibilities and urban approaches* variable has the potential to contribute further to the awareness-based ambient implementation explanatory model for smart cities (McKenna, 2019) in relation to one or more of the variable sets. Indeed, smart city visibilities and invisibilities, in terms of what is made visible and invisible, could be added as an independent variable to the *awareness and complexity* dependent variable (DV), in response to the call by Farina et al. (2018) for a design variable pertaining to the "digital, immaterial dimension." Further, the *awareness and complexity* dependent variable (DV) is associated with the independent variable of "sensing city-based feelings of comfort, safety, and other affective/emotive responses" as well as "the IoT as the instrumenting of things" and there are potentially key influencers for new methodologies and theoretical spaces in support of opportunities associated with ambiences, atmospheres, augmentations, and in/visibilities.

5. FUTURE RESEARCH DIRECTIONS

Future and emerging trends are identified in this chapter for practice and research in sections 5.1 and 5.2 respectively.

5.1 Practice

On a practical level, this chapter contributes to spaces for the rethinking of methods and approaches to addressing challenges associated with what is made visible or invisible in smart cities and to the surfacing of associated variables and indicators.

Ambient In/Visibilities

This chapter provides exposure to, and new understandings of, urban methodologies and theory in addressing smart city visibilities/invisibilities and as such, points to emerging potentials for the use of atmospheres, experiences, and augmentations as ambient in relation to urbanities. Crucially, this work invites participation by practitioners in the development of initiatives to shed light on methods and approaches to urban problem-solving that are more dynamic, adaptive and responsive to contemporary urban challenges and opportunities, and as such, more ambient, in the context of emergent smart, responsive, and future cities.

Variables and Indicators

This chapter surfaces the dependent variable of *in/visibilities and urban approaches* and a series of independent variables associated with urban design, animating public spaces, augmenting of meetings with technologies, and the visual sense of the city.

5.2 Research

This chapter advances the potential for future research opportunities and emerging discourse spaces for urban theoretical spaces and methodologies as ambient in the context of smart cities.

Ambient Methodologies and Theoretical Spaces

The viability of the conceptual framework for ambient methodologies and theoretical spaces operationalized for use in this chapter demonstrates early-stage potentials while offering and opening up new understandings for evolving urban spaces for testing and practice.

Ambient In/Visibilities

Conceptualization of spaces for real-time, dynamic, and adaptive types of approaches to making the invisible visible emerge in this chapter opening the way for new techniques and possibly novel roles and collaborations for citizens, businesses, researchers, and governments. As such, areas for exploration potential include:

1. *Ambiences* fostered through urban initiatives focusing on animating public spaces with dynamic and interactive visualizations
2. *Atmospheres* fostered through the making of more dynamic urban spaces with approaches designed to enhance vibrancy and the sense of the city
3. *Augmentations* fostered through understandings of extending meetings with technology-based options for interactions

Ambient Approaches

This chapter opens the way to future research opportunities and challenges related to the potential for movement toward the building of ambient approaches to urban research with implication for practice.

Ambient Inquiry

This chapter opens the way to future research opportunities and challenges related to the potential for movement toward the building of ambient inquiry as an urban research technique with implication for practice.

Additionally, this work directs attention to the potential for modification of existing methods and theory for urban research in making them more amenable to adaptive frameworks for smart, responsive, and future cities in the form possibly of more dynamic, interactive, and novel models and approaches responding to ever-emergent and complex requirements.

6. CONCLUSION

This chapter provides an overview of theoretical spaces and methodologies for smart cities in relation to what is rendered visible and invisible from a range of disciplinary perspectives, spanning urban planning to architecture. Ambiances, atmospheres, and augmentations emerge as key elements for making the invisible visible and for navigating new approaches and conceptualizations of methodologies and theoretical spaces for ambient urbanities. These elements will be enabled through fostering studies and inquiries in support of techniques featuring more aware people and aware technologies. The main contributions of this chapter include: a) articulation and operationalization of a conceptual framework for ambient methodologies and theoretical spaces in the context of smart cities; b) development of a framework for ambient visibilities and invisibilities in smart city urbanities; and c) arguing for a re-thinking of existing theoretical spaces and methodologies that take into consideration the intangible in relation to emerging technologies calling into play ambiances, atmospheres and augmentations in fostering smarter, more responsive, cities and urbanities.

Limitations of this chapter related to the abstract nature of visibilities, invisibilities, theoretical spaces, and ambient methodologies are mitigated by actual examples from the research literature and in-depth discussions with a range of individuals regarding everyday emergent practices. Further limitations related to literature review domain coverage are mitigated by the interdisciplinary potential to extend this review to other areas going forward.

This chapter continues to give form, detail, and definition to the broader Ambient Urbanities Framework presented in Chapter 1 (Figure 4) through exploration of the invisibilities and visibilities constructs in relation to ambiances, atmospheres, and augmentations. The analysis of findings in this chapter identifies variables associated with *in/visibilities and urban approaches* relevant to the study, practice, and management of methodologies and theoretical spaces for smart cities and ambient urbanities.

Insights of particular interest to the reader include the following:

1. The potential for opportunities to make the invisible visible in evolving understandings of smart cities
2. The interplay of ambiances, atmospheres, and augmentations in making visible the invisible
3. The surfacing of variables associated with *in/visibilities and urban approaches* informing theory and practice

Ideas highlighted in this chapter pertain to the following:

1. The importance of people becoming more aware of the invisible and intangible aspects of the smart cities phenomena
2. The potential for people to shed light on invisible spaces in digital/ physical urban spaces
3. Ambient inquiry as a novel approach to the study and practice of smarter cities and ambient urbanities

Lessons for the reader in this chapter are associated with the following:

1. The potential for approaches to making the invisible visible to be influenced by aware technologies
2. The potential for aware technologies to enhance possibilities for people in making the invisible visible in urban spaces
3. The intractable issues, controversies, and problems for methodologies and theoretical spaces as ambient in the study and practice of smart cities

This work will be of interest to a broad audience including students, educators, researchers, artists, urban planners, urban practitioners, community members, and anyone concerned with emerging theoretical spaces and methodologies that take into consideration the complex urban challenges and opportunities posed in renderings of the invisible as visible in smart, responsive, and future cities.

REFERENCES

Abbas, Y. (2016). The cartography of ambiance. In *Ambiances, tomorrow. Proceedings of 3rd International Congress on Ambiances* (*vol. 1*, pp. 253 – 258). Volos, Greece: International Network Ambiances, University of Thessaly.

Abbas, Y. (2018). Computing atmospheres. In N. Streitz & S. Konomi (Eds.), DAPI 2018 (LNCS 10922, pp. 267-277). Springer. doi:10.1007/978-3-319-91131-1_21

Augoyard, J.-F. (2002). *Deficiencies in the research about architectural and urban ambient environment and proposition of new tools: The sound example.* Architectural and Urban Ambient Environment: *First International Workshop*, Nantes, France.

Bille, M. (2018). Review: Gernot Böhme, 2017, The aesthetics of atmospheres, Edited by Jean-Paul Thibaud. London, Routledge. Ambiances: International Journal of Sensory Environment, Architecture and Space, 1065.

Boonen, M., & Lievens, B. (2018). The use of live-prototypes as proxy technology in smart city living lab pilots. In N. Streitz & S. Konomi (Eds.), DAPI 2018 (LNCS 10921, pp. 203-213). Springer. doi:10.1007/978-3-319-91125-0_17

Brenner, N., & Schmid, C. (2015). Towards a new epistemology of the urban? *City*, *19*(2-3), 151–182. doi:10.1080/13604813.2015.1014712

Caprotti, F. (2017). Research in the invisible city: Challenges for 'knowing' in the smart city. *UGEC Viewpoints: A Blog on Urbanization and Global Environmental Change*. Retrieved 17 June 2018 from https://ugecviewpoints. wordpress.com/2017/04/20/research-in-the-invisible-city-challenges-for-knowing-the-smart-city/

Chevalier, M. (2018). *Meta-Cities 7, Ubiquity 1 & 2*. Retrieved 22 April 2018 from https://www.mayorgallery.com/exhibitions/526/overview/

CHI. (2018). Living labs: Measuring human experiences in the built environment. *CHI 2018 Workshop*. Retrieved 13 February 2019 from https://sites.google.com/delosliving.com/chi2018

Christiansen, E. M., Laursen, L. H., & Hvejsel, M. F. (2017). Tectonic perspectives for urban ambiance? Towards a tectonic approach to urban design. *Ambiances: International Journal of Sensory Environment, Architecture and Space*, 886. Retrieved 21 April 2018 from https://journals.openedition.org/ambiances/886

Coghlan, A. T., Preskill, H., & Catsambas, T. T. (2003). *An overview of appreciative inquiry in evaluation. New Directions for Evaluation, no. 100*. Wiley Periodicals.

Demers, C., & Potvin, A. (2016). From history to architectural imagination: A physical ambiences laboratory to interpret past sensory experiences and speculate on future spaces. *Ambiances: International Journal of Sensory Environment, Architecture and Space*, 756.

Edensor, T., & Sumartojo, S. (2015). Designing atmospheres: Introduction to special issue. *Visual Communication*, *14*(3), 251–265. doi:10.1177/1470357215582305

Farina, C., Kotsopoulos, S. D., & Casalegno, F. (2018). Hybrid connected spaces: Mediating user activities in physical and digital spaces. In N. Streitz & S. Konomi (Eds.), DAPI 2018 (LNCS 10921, pp. 35-55). Springer.

Friberg, C. (2014). Performing everyday practices: Atmosphere and aesthetic education. *Ambiances: International Journal of Sensory Environment, Architecture and Space*, 464.

Gavalas, D., Nicopolitidis, P., Kameas, A., Goumopoulos, C., Bellavista, P., Lambrinos, L., & Buo, B. (2017). Smart cities: Recent trends, methodologies, and applications (Editorial). Wireless Communications and Mobile Computing.

Grieten, S., Lambrechts, F., Bouwen, R., Huybrechts, J., Fry, R., & Cooperrider, D. (2018). Inquiring into appreciative inquiry: A conversation with David Cooperrider and Ronald Fry. *Journal of Management Inquiry, 27*(1), 101–114. doi:10.1177/1056492616688087

Griffero, T. (2013). The atmospheric "skin" of the city. *Ambiances: International Journal of Sensory Environment, Architecture and Space*, 399.

Harrison, C., & Donnelly, I. A. (2011). A theory of smart cities. In *Proceedings of the 55th Annual Meeting of the International Society for the Systems Sciences.* University of Hull Business School.

Ibrahim, M., El-Zaart, A., & Adams, C. (2018). Smart sustainable cities roadmap: Readiness for transformation towards urban sustainability. *Sustainable Cities and Society, 37*, 530–540. doi:10.1016/j.scs.2017.10.008

Kolko, J. (2015). Design thinking comes of age. *Harvard Business Review*, (Sept): 66–71.

Konomi, S., & Sasao, T. (2018). Designing a mobile behavior sampling tool for spatial analytics. In N. Streitz & S. Konomi (Eds.), DAPI 2018 (LNCS 10922, pp. 92-100). Springer. doi:10.1007/978-3-319-91131-1_7

Kostaropoulou, M. (2017). Cities as meta-cities. *Conscious Cities*. Retrieved 23 April 2018 from https://www.ccities.org/cities-meta-cities/

McKenna, H. P. (In Press). Awareness and smart city implementations: Sensing, sensors, and the IoT in the public sector. In J. R. Gil-Garcia, T. A. Pardo, & M. Gascó (Eds.), *Beyond smart and connected governments: Sensors and the Internet of Things in the public sector.* Springer.

Morello, E., & Piga, B. E. A. (2016). Experiential simulation in architecture and urban space: Introduction to the special issue. *Ambiances: International Journal of Sensory Environment, Architecture and Space*, 671.

Patel, A. (2017). Wonder as an interruption. *Conscious Cities*. Retrieved 23 April 2018 from https://www.ccities.org/wonder-as-an-interruption/

Piga, B. E. A., Morello, E., & Salerno, R. (2017). Introducing a research perspective in urban design and representation. In B. E. A. Piga & R. Salerno (Eds.), *Urban design and representation: A multidisciplinary and multisensory approach.* Cham, Switzerland: Springer. doi:10.1007/978-3-319-51804-6_1

Ramaprasad, A., Sánchez-Ortiz, A., & Syu, T. (2017). A unified definition of a smart city. In EGOV2017 (LNCS 10428, pp. 13-24). Springer. doi:10.1007/978-3-319-64677-0_2

Roy, A. (2009). The 21st century metropolis: New geographies of theory. *Regional Studies*, *43*(6), 819–830. doi:10.1080/00343400701809665

Schaffers, H., Komninos, N., Pallot, M., Trousse, B., Nilsson, M., & Oliveira, A. (2011). Smart Cities and the Future Internet: Towards Cooperation Frameworks for Open Innovation. In The Future Internet. Berlin: Springer Berlin Heidelberg.

Schmitt, G. (2015). *Information Cities.* Retrieved from https://itunes.apple.com/us/book/information-cities/id970529491?mt=11

Schmitt, G. (2018). *Responsive cities.* Massive Open Online Course (MOOC). ETH Zurich. Retrieved 21 January 2019 from https://www.edx.org/course/responsive-cities

Shutters, S. T. (2018). Urban science: Putting the "smart" in smart cities. *Urban Science*, *2*(4), 94–97. doi:10.3390/urbansci2040094

Thibaud, J-P. (2013). Into the sensory world. *Ambiances: International Journal of Sensory Environment, Architecture and Space*, 188.

UN-Habitat. (2006). *Urbanization: Mega & meta cities, new city states?* Retrieved 23 April 2018 from http://mirror.unhabitat.org/documents/media_centre/sowcr2006/SOWCR%202.pdf

Urssi, N. J. (2018). Metacity: Design, data e urbanity. In A. Marcus & W. Wang (Eds.), DUXU 2018 (LNCS 10919, pp. 365-378). Springer.

UTL. (2018a). *Urban Theory Lab.* Harvard University. Retrieved 13 February 2019 from http://www.urbantheorylab.net/about/

UTL. (2018b). *Urban Theory Lab Vision.* Harvard University. Retrieved 13 February 2019 from http://www.urbantheorylab.net/vision/

Wise, A. F., & Shaffer, D. W. (2015). Why theory matters more than ever in the age of big data. *Journal of Learning Analytics, 2*(2), 5–13. doi:10.18608/jla.2015.22.2

ADDITIONAL READING

Bianchini, D., & Ávali, I. (2017). Smart cities and their smart decisions: Ethical considerations. *Technology and Society*, by ieee-ssit. Retrieved 17 June 2018 from http://technologyandsociety.org/smart-cities-and-their-smart-decisions-ethical-considerations/

de Wijs, L., Witte, P., & Geertman, S. (2016). How smart is smart? Theoretical and empirical considerations on implementing smart city objectives – a case study of Dutch railway station areas. *Innovation, 29*(4), 422–439.

Leenes, R., van Brakel, R., Gutwirth, S., & De Hert, P. (Eds.). (2017). *Data protection and privacy: (In)visibilities and infrastructures. Law, Governance, and Technology Series*. Cham, Switzerland: Springer.

Lemos, A. (2017). Smart cities, Internet of Things and performative sensibility: Brief analysis on Glasgow, Curitiba and Bristol's initiatives. *Artigo, 3*(2), 80–95.

Orbit. (2017). *Smart city transcendent: Understanding the smart city by transcending ontology*. UK: Observatory for Responsible Research and Innovation in ICT. Retrieved 17 June 2018 from https://www.orbit-rri.org/concepts/smart-city-transcendent/

Sadowski, J., & Pasquale, F. (2015). The spectrum of control: A social theory of the smart city. *First Monday, 20*(7). http://firstmonday.org/article/view/5903/4660 Retrieved17June2018. doi:10.5210/fm.v20i7.5903

Smart Cities. (2015). *Smart cities and the secret life of objects: (In)visibility at Glasgow, Curitiba, and Bristol's initiatives*. Maynooth University, National University of Ireland. Retrieved 17 June 2018 from https://www.maynoothuniversity.ie/news-events/smart-cities-and-secret-life-objects-invisibility-glasgow-curitiba-and-bristols-initiatives

Thompson, T. (2017). Understanding the contextual development of smart city initiatives: A pragmatist methodology. *Shi Ji: The Journal of Design, Economics, and Innovation, 3*(3), 210–228.

KEY TERMS AND DEFINITIONS

Ambient Methodologies: Ambient methodologies refer to more adaptive approaches to exploration of aware people and aware technologies encompassing the physical and digital in relation to ambiences, atmospheres, and augmentations contributing further to the ambient turn.

Ambient Theoretical Spaces: Ambient theoretical spaces refer to more adaptive conceptualizations in support of coming to new understandings of aware people and aware technologies encompassing the physical and digital in relation to ambiences, atmospheres, and augmentations contributing further to the ambient turn.

Ambient Visibilities/Invisibilities: Ambient visibilities/invisibilities refer to urban elements accommodating more aware people and aware technologies encompassing the physical and digital in relation to ambiences, atmospheres, and augmentations contributing further to the ambient turn.

Awareness: Awareness refers to the concept or quality of being aware as it applies to people on the one hand, to technologies on the other, and to a combination of aware people and aware technologies.

Invisibilities: Invisibilities refer to urban elements such as ambiances, atmospheres, and the unseen (e.g., embedded technologies) that present as intangibles.

Smart Cities: Smart cities are urban areas, regions, territories, and beyond that are characterized by aware and engaged people, in combination with and aided by, the use of awareness enhancing technologies for mobility, livability, and sustainability.

Visibilities: Visibilities refer to physical and other visible urban elements.

Chapter 8

Sharing–Collaboration– Openness:
Innovating Privacy for Smarter Urbanities

ABSTRACT

The purpose of this chapter is to explore sharing, collaboration, and openness in relation to smart cities in response to the state of the privacy construct that is said to be in disarray. A rethinking and innovating of the privacy construct is advanced in this chapter in evolving the ambient privacy framework in support of sharing, collaboration, and openness as critical dimensions of smart cities. The research literature for sharing, collaboration, and openness is explored in this chapter in the context of smart and responsive cities, enabling the identification of issues, controversies, and problems. Using an exploratory case study approach, solutions and recommendations are advanced. This chapter makes a contribution to 1) the research literature for urban sharing, collaboration, and openness in smart and responsive cities; 2) the innovating of privacy for 21st century cities; and 3) urban theory in formulating a conceptual framework for innovating privacy for smarter urbanities.

DOI: 10.4018/978-1-5225-7882-6.ch008

1. INTRODUCTION

The purpose of this chapter is to explore sharing, collaboration, and openness in relation to smart cities in response to the state of the privacy construct that is said to be in disarray (Solove, 2006). A rethinking and innovating of the privacy construct is advanced in this chapter in evolving and extending the ambient privacy framework (McKenna et al., 2013) in support of sharing, collaboration, and openness as critical dimensions of smart cities. The research literature for sharing, collaboration, and openness is explored in this chapter in the context of smart and responsive cities, enabling the identification of issues, controversies, and problems. Using an exploratory case study approach, solutions and recommendations are advanced. This chapter makes a contribution to: a) the research literature for urban sharing, collaboration, and openness in smart and responsive cities; b) the innovating of privacy for 21st century cities; and c) urban theory through formulation of a conceptual framework for innovating privacy for smarter urbanities.

Objectives: The objective of this chapter is to argue for a rethinking and innovating of the privacy construct in formulation of an ambient privacy framework in support of sharing, collaboration, and openness as critical dimensions of smart cities and by extension, ambient urbanities. As such, the key research question posed in this chapter is – Why is openness important for innovating privacy for urbanities in smart cities?

2. BACKGROUND AND OVERVIEW

This chapter explores the privacy construct (Solove, 2006) and describes the notion of ambient privacy (McKenna et al., 2013; McKenna, McKnight, and Chauncey, 2014) as a re-formulated understanding of privacy for smart cities. Judge and Powles (2015) pose a series of questions in the form of challenges, such as, "what if we could design objects that utilised the internet in truly smart, differentiated ways, while also communicating their own function?" Ambient privacy is articulated in this chapter in relation to people, infrastructures, and experience, taking into consideration emerging perspectives on privacy such as inverse privacy (Gurevich, Hudis, and Wing, 2016). Crabtree and Mortier (2016) urge that interdisciplinary action be taken in responding to the much-needed changes in privacy associated with emerging digital ecosystems and the Internet of Things (IoT). As such, this chapter calls for a re-thinking of the privacy construct and explores the ambient privacy construct in response to the wicked challenges and complexities posed by ambient data in technology-rich urban environments (McKenna, 2017).

2.1 Definitions

For the purposes of this work, definitions for key terms used in this chapter are presented here based on the research literature.

- **Ambient Privacy:** McKenna et al. (2014) claim that, "ambient privacy complements and extends privacy" adding that, "it accommodates an interweaving of elements, characteristic of complex interactions in the moment, contributing to the potential for smarter privacy." McKenna et al. (2014) provide a list of elements characterizing ambient privacy such as: "ad hoc, adaptive, analytics, collaborative, dynamic, fluid, learning, openness, participative, personalized, sharing, social, and trust."
- **Inverse Privacy:** Gurevich et al. (2016) suggest that you can "call an item of your personal information inversely private if some party has access to it but you do not."
- **Open City Innovation:** Mattsson and Sørensen (2015) claim that the open city innovation concept "suggests a new way of perceiving city renewal with its focus on the discovery and development of unpredictable solutions resulting from interactive, iterative, and reflexive processes" and because of "its complexity" can be thought of as "an extreme type of open innovation."

2.2 Overview

This chapter provides a range of perspectives in Section 3 on evolving understandings of sharing, collaboration, and openness in relation to innovating privacy in the context of smart, responsive, and future cities followed by a selection of associated issues, controversies, and problems. Section 4 provides an overview of innovating privacy for smarter urbanities by way of solutions and recommendations including the development of a conceptual framework for innovating privacy in smart cities and the surfacing of variables pertaining to openness. The framework is operationalized for use in exploring the proposition under investigation in this chapter. Section 5 identifies future directions for research and practice and Section 6 concludes with chapter coverage highlights, the major contributions, and the key insights, ideas and lessons.

The primary audiences for this chapter include students, educators, researchers, policy makers, businesses, community members, and urban practitioners concerned with sharing, collaboration, and openness in smarter, more responsive, privacy-aware cities, in addressing continually evolving complex urban challenges and opportunities.

3. COLLABORATION, OPENNESS, AND SHARING FOR INNOVATING PRIVACY

This chapter provides a review of the research literature for collaboration, openness, sharing, and privacy in smart cities while identifying key issues, controversies, and problems.

3.1 Collaboration, Openness, and Sharing in Smart Cities

Collaboration

Schaffers et al. (2011) describe models and frameworks such as the Living Labs concept where, in relation to smart cities, "it embodies open business models" intended to foster collaboration "between citizens, enterprises and local governments" along with "the willingness of all parties to engage actively in innovation." In moving toward the social smart city, Mulder (2015) points to the opening up of public sector data and policy-making enabled by collaborative partnerships, experiences, and the making of meaningful applications. Snow, Håkonsson, and Obel (2016) describe the smart city in relation to collaboration as a community encompassing citizens, business firms, knowledge institutions, and municipal agencies interacting with each other "to achieve systems integration and efficiency, citizen engagement, and a continually improving quality of life." Through an organizational framework for collaboration, as architecture for collaboration, encompassing the technological and social realms, Snow et al. (2016) describe infrastructures for actor-oriented organizational schemes as "systems that connect actors" and "enable large groups of collaborating actors to self-organize with only minimal use of hierarchical mechanisms." Gil-Garcia, Zhang, and Puron-Cid (2016) identify a series of dimensions of smartness in government with collaboration emerging in relation to a number of dimensions such as resiliency. Pereira, Cunha, Lampoltshammer, Parycek, and Testa (2017) address ICT-enabled participation and collaboration in smart city governance, focusing on "analyzing the phenomenon of smart collaboration."

Figure 1 provides an overview of key issues, controversies, and problems for collaboration in smart cities. The Living Labs concept (Schaffers et al., 2011) is highlighted in relation to collaboration and innovation; social smart cities (Mulder, 2015) point to collaborative partnerships and experiences; collaboration as community (Snow et al., 2016) provides an articulation of smart cities in terms of integration, efficiency, and engagement; architecture for collaboration (Snow et al., 2016) places an emphasis on technology and the social for self-organizing; and smart collaboration (Pereira et al., 2017) is explored for governance, based on ICT-enabled participation.

Openness

Schaffers et al. (2011) describe openness in relation to innovation where collaboration and user-driven figure strongly as well as open data, open infrastructures, open access, and open and federated platforms. As a form of open innovation, Egyedi, Mehos, and Vree (2012) introduce inverse infrastructures in the form of "unprecedented infrastructures emerging that are not owned by governments or large businesses" and are described as "user-driven, self-organizing, decentralized." Egyedi (2012) explores the policy implications of the disruptive nature and properties of inverse infrastructures, providing recommendations for bridging the gap with existing infrastructural arrangements. Mattsson and Sørensen (2015) extend the open innovation concept to open city innovation in "understanding complex development processes in society" in the form of "contemporary city renewal" involving

Figure 1. Overview of key issues, controversies and problems for collaboration

"public, private, and collective actors." Berrone, Ricart, and Carrasco (2016) present a general framework for open data initiatives in cities focusing on drivers, structure, and dynamics. Berrone et al. (2016) argue that "open data can enhance political and civic discussion" and if the framework is followed recursively, can contribute to transformational processes; support adjusting to the pace of change while minimizing risk; and enable the creation of real value in leveraging the power of open data. Gil-Garcia, Zhang, and Puron-Cid (2016) identify a series of dimensions for smartness in government including openness, claiming that, "when a government is open, it becomes more transparent and more accountable" making it "smarter government for its citizens, businesses, and other stakeholders" able to "use information in smarter ways." Bogers, Chesbrough, and Moedas (2018) explore the state of open innovation focusing on research, practices, and policies. Bogers et al. (2018) highlight major trends such as digital transformation contributing to the Three Opens (Open Innovation, Open Science, and Open to the World) and key challenges such as uncertainty.

Figure 2 provides an overview of key issues, controversies, and problems for openness in smart cities.

Inverse infrastructures (Egyedi et al., 2012) as open innovation are highlighted along with open city innovation (Mattsson and Sørensen, 2015) involving public, private, and collective actors; open data initiatives (Berrone et al. 2016) focusing on drivers, structures, and dynamics; open government (Gil-Garcia, Zhang, and Puron-Cid, 2016) as transparent, accountable, and smarter; and the three opens (Bogers et al., 2018) of innovation, science, and the world.

Sharing

For Schaffers et al. (2011), the sharing of resources, research, and facilities are important elements for innovation in addition to partnerships and

Figure 2. Overview of key issues, controversies and problems for openness

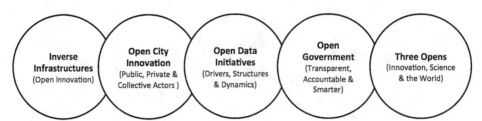

cooperation. McLaren and Agyeman (2015) articulate the notion of sharing cities, based on a "sharing paradigm", as smart and sustainable cities. Gil-Garcia, Zhang, and Puron-Cid (2016) identify a series of dimensions of smartness in government with sharing emerging in relation to a number of the dimensions such as effectiveness in terms of knowledge sharing and integration in terms of information sharing and interoperability. Findings by Pereira et al. (2017) point to the importance of the ICT (information and communication technologies) role in support of "information sharing and integration between government agencies and external stakeholders, including citizens" particularly with reference to developing countries.

Figure 3 provides an overview of key issues, controversies, and problems for sharing in smart cities highlighting sharing for innovation (Schaffers et al., 2011) focusing on resources, research, and facilities; sharing cities (McLaren and Agyeman, 2015) based on a sharing paradigm; and sharing in government (Garcia, Zhang, and Puron-Cid, 2016) of knowledge and information for interoperability.

3.2 Privacy in Smart Cities

Privacy by Design

Langheinrich (2001) provides an introduction to privacy issues in ubiquitous computing including privacy protection, legal status, and expected utility. Langheinrich (2001) advances six principles to guide design in relation to "a set of fair information practices" that was said to be "common in most privacy legislation in use" at the time. The principles include: notice, choice and consent, proximity and locality, anonymity and pseudonymity, security, and access and recourse. As such, Langheinrich (2001) advances the notion

Figure 3. Overview of key issues, controversies and problems for sharing, collaboration and openness

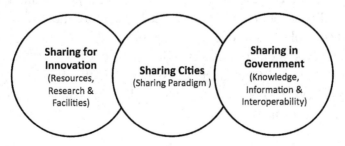

of privacy by design based on principles of privacy-aware ubiquitous systems, emphasizing the need for "guidelines for creating privacy-respecting infrastructures" in support of "new paradigms" making way for "new forms of human interactions" that "will evolve in society." Exploring why privacy matters in the context of ubiquitous computing, Langheinrich (2001) offers the four properties of ubiquity, invisibility, sensing, and memory amplification. Cavoukian and Popa (2016) advance a privacy by design (PbD) framework based on seven principles guiding the embedding or coding of privacy preferences into the technology, the Internet of Things, or other emerging technologies – proactive not reactive; privacy as the default setting; privacy embedded into design; full functionality for "optimized experiences"; end-to-end security; visibility and transparency; and respect for user privacy. Fedosov, Ojala, Olsson, Vaananen, and Langheinrich (2017) explore practices and privacy requirements for sharing emerging types of online content, focusing on "user needs, concerns and preferences." Privacy concerns associated with "novel online services and connected devices" that have "expanded the set of 'things' to share" were organized into four design themes based on study findings by Fedosov et al. (2017) for emerging content sharing, as follows: holistic access control, privacy and safety, quality of controls, and open sharing.

Differential Privacy

Dwork (2011) describes the concept of differential privacy as "providing accurate statistical information about a set of respondents while protecting the privacy of the individual" with applicability to "any private data set" where "it is desirable to release coarse-grained information while keeping private the details." In exploring privacy aware machine learning, Malle, Kieseberg, and Schrittwieser (2016) argue that "the goal of analyzing large amounts of data for information extraction collides with the privacy of individuals" and suggest that "to protect sensitive information, the effects of the right to be forgotten on machine learning algorithms need to be studied more extensively." In the context of emerging digital ecosystems and the Internet of Things (IoT), Crabtree and Mortier (2016) explore the "shifting locus of agency and control in the processing of personal data" focusing on a review of legal, policy, and industry initiatives designed to respond to "broad societal concerns over privacy." Controversies associated with differential privacy are revealed by Mervis (2019) in relation to explorations and discussions about uptake by the US Census Bureau.

Privacy Paradox

Judge and Powles (2015) argue that, "screens don't communicate anything about what they do" and that instead "they remove us from our surroundings" and "as we tap and swipe merrily past terms and conditions, our personal information is siphoned off to third parties so invisibly and incomprehensibly that we can easily ignore that it is happening." Judge and Powles (2015) pose the question, "what if we could understand this function intuitively, effortlessly?" And, wonder Judge and Powles (2015), "what if these objects actually showed us – through their design features, their data flows and their legally-binding background conditions – how our information is being used, who can access it, where it is going, and why?" Van Zoonen (2016) describes the city data landscape, highlighting the diversity of data in smart cities in relation to elements such as size, regularity, purpose, complexity, ownership, and visibility. A framework is then developed to explore the specific privacy concerns of people in smart cities (Van Zoonen, 2016). Van Zoonen (2016) speaks in terms of a "privacy paradox" where, on the one hand people have "clearly expressed concerns about their privacy" and on the other, people exhibit "a simultaneous lack of appropriate secure behavior." In an effort to make sense of this "disorder in the field", Van Zoonen (2016) identifies three factors "influencing people's concerns about privacy" as "the type of data, the purpose of data collection and usage, and the organization or persons collecting and using the data." A smart city privacy challenges framework is presented by Van Zoonen (2016) as a sensitizing instrument with data framed as personal or impersonal in relation to the purposes of service or surveillance, enabling "local governments to identify the absence, presence, or emergence of privacy concerns among their citizens."

Inverse Privacy

According to Gurevich et al. (2016), as people interact with organizations and businesses in everyday life "the provenance of your inversely private information can be totally legitimate" as your data is recorded by someone else and you do not have access to this data. However, "shared data decays into inversely private" and "more inversely private information is produced when institutions analyze your private data" and "whether collected or derived, allows institutions to serve you better." Yet Gurevich et al. (2016), as if in response to agency and control issues raised by Crabtree and Mortier (2016), suggest that "access to that information—especially if it were presented to you in a convenient form—would do you much good" enabling "you to correct possible errors in the data, to have a better idea of your health status and your credit rating, and to identify ways to improve your productivity and quality of life." Malle, Kieseberg, and Holzinger (2017) explore interactive anonymization issues related to privacy aware machine learning, particularly "the right to have data deleted" as "a serious impediment to research operations" and this is because "any anonymization results in a certain degree of reduced data utility." Grant (2017) describes research at the University of Waterloo to "make artificial intelligence more private and portable" using deep learning.

Landscape of Privacy

In relation to wireless grids, McKenna et al. (2013) provided an early stage conceptualization of ambient privacy for information spaces; proposed the notion of an ambient privacy interaction dynamic; advanced an ambient privacy research framework; and offered a research agenda for an ambient privacy society. In response to a request for information (RFI), McKenna et al. (2014) advanced the notion of ambient privacy and informational self-determination as components of a national privacy research strategy. Concerned with "usable privacy and security," Hong (2017) explores the landscape of privacy for pervasive computing, identifying seven dimensions as: awareness, depth of sensing, temporal scale, I/O (input/output capability), privacy software, third-party software, and manufacturer support. Hong (2017) organizes opportunities associated with privacy into three tiers of devices and the entities said to be involved with privacy such as users, developers, service providers and third parties. Arguing for "an ecosystem for privacy that can help shift the burden of privacy from being solely on users," Hong (2017) advances the potential for sharing of some of this burden more broadly to developers, service providers, governments, and third parties. Additionally, Hong (2017) highlights the importance of "addressing privacy issues and fostering trust by building systems that respect people as individuals" and that "offer tangible value" while providing "the right level of control and feedback, and that do what people expect them to do." It is also worth noting that Hong (2017) refers to concerns with the working definition of privacy used by policy makers in terms of "contextual integrity" (Nissenbaum, 2004) where the significant challenge in the case of pervasive computing is "in aligning often-rigid systems with fluid notions of context and norms" giving rise to the opportunity of figuring out if there are "scalable ways of using sensor and log data to help operationalize contextual integrity?" Gavalas, Nicopolitidis, Kameas, Goumopoulos, Bellavista, Lambrinos, and Buo (2017) describe SMARTIE, as an architecture for user privacy in smart cities, that is said to "support efficient and scalable security and user-centric privacy." Fietkiewicz and Henkel (2018) explore the state of data privacy protecting approaches in relation to fitness trackers in light of developments such as the General Data Protection Regulation (GDRP). Li, Niu, Kumari, Wu, and Choo (2018) address the challenge of security and privacy protection by proposing a robust biometric authentication scheme using the case of the GLObal MObility NETwork (GLOMONET) as "an important network infrastructure for smart city." Lindley, Coulton, and Cooper (2019) challenge two major design paradigms – that of Privacy by Design (PbD) and Human Centered Design (HCD) – arguing that, when unpacked of their levels of meaning, to describe "ships as unsinkable, systems as private, or designs as human centered—is irrational." However, Lindley et al. (2019) encourage instead that we "embrace those driving ideals" with a "healthy scepticism" while proposing the notion of "informed by design" and the use of "constellations of meaning" to "communicate and reveal the complexity" regarding "any relevant others' interests, activities, and agency."

Figure 4 provides an overview of key issues, controversies, and problems for innovating privacy in smart cities. Of note are discussions on privacy by design (Langheinrich, 2001; Cavoukian and Popa, 2016) in terms of privacy-aware systems; differential privacy (Dwork, 2011) and protecting confidentiality; the privacy paradox (Van Zoonen, 2016) and issues of invisibility and incomprehensibility (Judge and Powles, 2015); inverse privacy (Gurevich et al., 2016) and what it means for you and your data; and the landscape of privacy (Hong, 2017) from awareness (McKenna et al., 2013; McKenna et al., 2014) to contextual integrity (Nissenbaum, 2004) to informed by design (Lindley et al., 2019).

3.3 Issues, Controversies, Problems

Key issues, controversies, and problems emerging in the review of the research literature explored in this chapter are highlighted below. Coverage of issues, controversies, and problems is not intended to be exhaustive or comprehensive but rather, as illustrative of the nature, variety, and range.

Figure 4. Overview of key issues, controversies, and problems for innovating privacy in smart cities

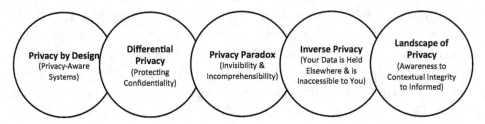

Issues

Langheinrich (2001) identifies the four properties of ubiquity, invisibility, sensing, and memory amplification as having social implications for ubiquitous computing, posing particular privacy challenges from legal, social, and ethical perspectives.

Controversies

Hong (2017) introduces the tension associated with "rich sensor and log data" pertaining to use for personal and societal benefit and the rapid introduction of many new privacy risks. Bogers et al. (2018) challenge the notion of open, by extending it to innovation, science, and the world. Attempts to innovate and address the privacy challenge contribute in some cases to controversy as illustrated by the proposed use of differential privacy with census data (Mervis, 2019) and a closer analysis of the privacy by design approach (Lindley et al., 2019).

Problems

Crabtree and Mortier (2016) point to the problem of "empowering users and giving them active control over the processing of personal data" while advancing and focusing on the emerging research area of *human-data interaction (HDI)*. A series of HDI challenges are identified by Crabtree and Mortier (2016), including the development of personal infrastructures enabling "users to manage the flow of data," dynamics, and collaboration in managing personal data, to name a few. Hong (2017) identifies the importance of fostering trust through the design of systems that take people into account in respectful ways, offer "tangible value" to people, and meet expectations of feedback and control. Hong (2017) also highlights problems with the working definition of privacy by policy makers, giving rise to opportunities for rethinking and innovation.

Summarized in Figure 5, a glimpse of patterns, flows, relationships, and possibilities begin to emerge influencing openness and smarter urbanities through sharing, collaboration, innovation, and privacy in smart cities. Sharing is described in relation to openness and open data, highlighting the importance of user concerns, needs, and preferences in online contexts with the suggestion that responsibilities or burdens associated with privacy be shared.

Sharing is also articulated as a dimension of smartness in public sectors spaces. Collaboration is described in terms of architecture, cross-sector interactions, flows of data, the social and technological and is associated with several dimensions of smartness in government. Innovation is described as open, is said to be one of several dimensions of smartness in government while the fostering of trust is highlighted as an important element. And finally, privacy emerges as critical to awareness in environments featuring the Internet of Things (IoT), the Internet of People (IoP), and the Internet of Experiences (IoE), highlighting the importance of the invisible and the visible; the paradox of privacy in terms of user choices; and the practices, preferences, protections, and risks associated with digital privacy. Although neatly categorized across sharing, collaboration, innovation, and privacy, it is important to note that there is considerable overlap in that smartness is associated with sharing for example as well as with collaboration and

Figure 5. Openness and smarter urbanities through sharing, collaboration, innovation and privacy

Openness for Smarter Urbanities

	Sharing	Collaboration	Innovation	Privacy
People (aware)	Concerns	Architecture	Open	Awareness
	Needs	Cross-sector	Smartness	In/visibility
IoP IoT IoE	Open	Flow of data	Trust	Paradox
Technologies (aware)	Preferences	Smart/ness		Practices
	Privacy burden	Social		Preferences
	Smartness	Technological		Protection
				Risks

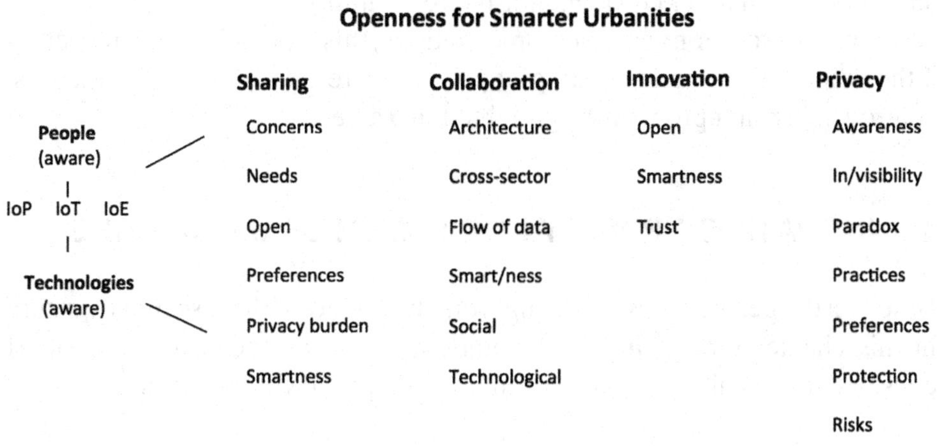

innovation. Also, the categories are necessarily incomplete and intended only as a summary overview.

By author and year, Table 1 provides an overview of issues, controversies, and problems associated with collaboration, openness, privacy, and sharing in smart cities.

Collaboration in smart cities is addressed in relation to the Living Labs concept (Schaffers et al., 2011); public sector data (Mulder, 2015); smartness in government (Gil-Garcia, Zhang, and Puron-Cid, 2016); an architecture for collaboration (Snow et al., 2016); and smart collaboration (Pereira et al., 2017). Openness in smart cities is addressed in relation to access, data, and infrastructures (Schaffers et al., 2011); inverse infrastructures (Egyedi et al., 2012); open city innovation (Mattsson & Sørensen, 2015); open data initiatives (Berrone et al., 2016); smartness in government (Gil-Garcia, Zhang, and Puron-Cid, 2016); and the state of open innovation (Bogers, et al., 2018). Privacy in smart cities is addressed in terms of privacy by design (Langheinrich, 2001; Cavoukian and Popa, 2016); differential privacy (Dwork, 2011; Mervis, 2019); ambient privacy (McKenna et al., 2013; McKenna et al., 2014); invisibilities and incomprehensibilities (Judge and Powles, 2015); personal data (Crabtree & Mortier, 2016); inverse privacy (Gurevich et al., 2016); aware machine learning (Malle et al., 2016; 2017); the privacy paradox (Van Zoonen, 2016); privacy practices (Fedosov et al., 2017); user-focused privacy (Gavalas et al., 2017); deep learning (Grant, 2017); a privacy ecosystem (Hong, 2017); data privacy protecting (Fietkiewicz & Henkel, 2018); and privacy "informed by design" (Lindley et al., 2019). Sharing in smart cities is addressed in relation to resources, research, and facilities (Schaffers et al., 2011); sharing cities based on a sharing paradigm (McLaren and Agyeman, 2015); smartness in government (Gil-Garcia, Zhang, and Puron-Cid, 2016); and information and knowledge for interoperability.

By way of solutions and recommendations, this work advances in Section 4 the potential for the innovating of privacy in response to complex issues, controversies, and problems highlighted in Table 1.

4. INNOVATING PRIVACY FOR SMARTER URBANITIES

Based on the perspectives emerging from the review of the research literature in this chapter for sharing, collaboration, openness and privacy in smart cites, a conceptual framework for innovating privacy for smarter urbanities

Table 1. Issues, controversies, and problems for collaboration, openness, privacy, and sharing in smart cities

Collaboration, Openness, Privacy, and Sharing for Smart Cities					
Author(s)	**Year**	**Collaboration**	**Openness**	**Privacy**	**Sharing**
Langheinrich	2001			By Design	
Dwork	2011			Differential	
Schaffers et al.	2011	Living Labs concept	Access, data, infrastructures		Resources, etc.
Egyedi et al.	2012		Inverse infrastructures		
McKenna et al.	2014			Ambient	
Judge & Powles	2015			Invisibilities	
Mattsson & Sørensen	2015		Open city innovation		
McLaren & Agyeman	2015				Cities, Paradigm
Mulder	2015	Public sector data			
Berrone et al.	2016		Open data initiatives		
Cavoukian & Popa	2016			By Design	
Crabtree & Mortier	2016			Personal data	
Gil-Garcia et al.	2016	Smartness in gov't	Smartness in gov't		Smartness/gov't
Gurevich et al.	2016			Inverse	
Malle et al.	2016			Aware ML	
Snow et al.	2016	Architecture			
Van Zoonen	2016			Paradox	
Fedosov et al.	2017			Practices	
Gavalas et al.	2017			User focused	
Grant	2017			Deep learning	
Hong	2017			Ecosystem	
Pereira et al.	2017	Smart (ICT-enabled)			Information
Fietkiewicz & Henkel	2018			Protecting	
Bogers et al.	2018		State of open innovation		
Lindley et al.	2019			Informed	
Mervis	2019			Differential	

is developed and operationalized in Section 4.1 for use in the exploration conducted into the innovating of privacy in Section 4.2.

4.1 Innovating Privacy in Smart Cities: Solutions and Recommendations

Formulation of a conceptual framework for innovating privacy for smarter urbanities is depicted in Figure 6, enabled by more aware people and aware technologies in the context of smart cities. Using the construct of openness and the sub-constructs of sharing and collaboration in digitally-enabled urban areas and regions, evolving understandings of ecosystems, people, interactions, and public spaces contributes to the realization of ambient privacy.

Through emerging understandings of innovating privacy for smarter urbanities, this chapter focuses on aware people and aware technologies in relation to openness in smart cities in responding to the question posed in the Introduction of this chapter, restated as a proposition under exploration in this chapter, as follows:

P: *Openness* is important for innovating privacy for urbanities in smart cities because it enables innovations in other related spaces associated with sharing, collaboration, and other creative interactions.

How innovating privacy informs urbanity is explored in this chapter using a survey instrument and protocol-guided interviews with a diverse range of individuals in addition to discussions across multiple sectors with groups and individuals. Innovating privacy is understood in this chapter to be a

Figure 6. Conceptual framework for innovating privacy for smarter urbanities

movement toward more dynamic, in-the-moment, informed, and adaptive forms of interactions, taking the privacy needs of people into consideration.

4.2 Innovating Privacy: An Exploration

The focus of the exploration in this chapter is centered on privacy and sharing, collaboration, and openness as ambient in smart cities. A discussion of findings is then provided enabling formulation of a framework for ambient privacy in smart city urbanities.

4.2.1. Privacy and Sharing, Collaboration, and Openness as Ambient in Smart Cities

Information Sharing: Amplifications

A community member in Greater Victoria identified the issue of "not being able to find out really what's going on in the city" while an educator in St. John's suggested the need to "provide user friendly and not too dense information on what's happening at a particular point" in the city "so that you can access information and know what's going on in real time almost." On an urban street level, a student described the pervasive sharing of "very traditional things" and events in daily lives such that people are "videoing them, sharing them constantly in social media" as "a seamless behavior" that is contributing to a "seamless interrelationship" of the "local and global" enabling "concurrent awareness." A community member in Toronto noted that, "the number one requested dataset from the city by the public is zoning and development data," adding that this "is not currently available as open data to cities." By way of example, the individual stated, "imagine if there was an app that told you all the notifications on this corner" and because "people would be affected, they would pay attention and they would suddenly be engaged" since "their environment is being changed" and "right now, nobody knows what's happening." Using the example of urban parking, a community leader speculated about whether technology could help with getting more clarity, at any moment in time, on the oversupply or undersupply situation of parking in terms of "people's perception" versus actual data.

Openness: Informed

Discussing civic data, city IT staff commented that, "fundamentally there is a desire to be very, very open with public data" while adhering to "privacy regulations" and being cognizant of "the public's preferences." More broadly, IT staff added that "we are interested in putting physical infrastructure in place" and "how we interpret using it is still open" enabling the potential for discussion and input. An educator suggested that civic apps "could be used from ideation to real life experimentations" establishing "proof of concept" and the "next stages of open innovation" as well as "capturing the evidence of the impact." City IT observed that open, diverse datasets enable "data analysis that you've not thought of" in support of the potential for "serendipitous or accidental usage" or "unintended usage" contributing to possibly unforeseen value. An example from business was provided where such usage revealed, "a win that wasn't even in our mindset" where staff began using data that was made available in the moment "as a predictive piece to inform their daily operations."

Collaboration: Practices

Referring to a mobile app for urban spaces, an educator pointed to the capability and potential for collaboration in terms of being "able to open this kind of feedback" to anyone in the city as a way "to transform contributions both in terms of unique ideas and the design of some urban space or buildings" enabling city officials "to understand what people want." A community leader described the need to figure out how to become more collaborative and "move away from sector driven strategies to ones that" feature "clusters" so as to "bring industries and sectors together rather than that sort of silo" mindset. A Vancouver-based IT professional at a higher education institution identified the issue of learning to work across systems and infrastructures of data involving buildings and room bookings, using an on-campus emergency situation as an example, and "how we exchange that data in a way that is safe" in order to generate "real occupancy information" in conjunction with the "devices of people to verify that someone is actually in the room." Highlighting the adaptive and complex nature of urban infrastructures, city IT staff observed that, "almost any technology now has the ability to be more than just a single service."

Privacy: Ecosystems

A student pointed to the need for addressing the wicked challenges associated with personal data privacy in order to "devise ways whereby you can create some kind of security to anonymize data and thereby make the data itself open and shared in some way that would still provide some kind of smart delivery too" so as to "actually make use of the data." Other wicked challenges identified included that of "control" as in "who owns the data, how is it housed, and the infrastructure by which it is shared." The example of accidental or serendipitous usage serves to challenge fixed and static notions associated with privacy and known, intended uses and purposes in increasingly fluid and dynamic environments. As if to capture the dynamic and adaptive nature of contemporary urban environments, an IT developer providing services to municipal governments and postsecondary institutions in Greater Victoria and Vancouver observed that there are "a lot of moving pieces to make a smart city." Challenged by social media and openness, a student questioned the veracity of information provided to online platforms, highlighting the frequent contributing of "made up" details as a mechanism on the part of the individual to maintain some degree of privacy in the absence of viable choices and options.

4.2.2. A Framework for Ambient Privacy in Smart City Urbanities

Findings in this chapter assist in advancing the notion of innovating privacy enabling the extending and reformulation of the framework for ambient privacy (McKenna et al., 2013) to accommodate smart city urbanities as depicted in Figure 7.

The potential for the understanding of privacy as ambient in urban spaces emerges, organized around aware people and aware technologies, encompassing the physical and digital in terms of evolving forms of collaboration, openness, and sharing as ambient in relation to the ever-emergent properties of amplifications for information sharing and informed openness in technology-pervasive urban environments in support of innovating.

In contributing to the ambient turn, ambient privacy provides challenges and opportunities for the development of ambient ecosystems and ambient practices in support of smart and responsive cities and urbanities. A key element underlying the significance of the framework is the dynamic and adaptive nature of all elements moving beyond the static and the fixed where privacy enters a space of more continuous choices and actions based on an awareness of the contextual and situational.

Figure 7. Framework for ambient privacy in smart city urbanities

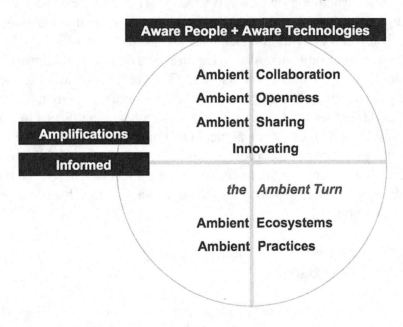

Dependent Variable (DV)

The dependent variable (DV) surfaced in this chapter is *openness and urban practices* in relation to sharing, collaboration, and privacy in smart cities. Associated independent variables (IV) include: what's going on in the city, implying a real-time awareness and in-the-moment responsiveness; concurrent awareness, implying connectivity and interoperability; understand what people want, implying collaborative practices; and make use of data, implying a range of requirements.

5. FUTURE RESEARCH DIRECTIONS

Future and emerging trends are identified in sections 5.1 and 5.2 in this chapter for practice and research, respectively.

5.1 Practice

For practitioners, this chapter invites opportunities for innovating privacy in smart city contexts; provides exposure to the ambient privacy concept in urban spaces; and sheds light on emerging potentials for understanding collaboration, sharing, and openness as ambient in smart cities.

Ambient Privacy

This chapter provides further exposure to, and new understandings of, ambient privacy as involving spaces for more continuous choices and actions based on an awareness of context and situations in addressing innovations afforded by smart cities. As such, this chapter invites involvement by practitioners in the development of initiatives to shed light on approaches to sharing, collaboration, and openness that are more dynamic, adaptive and responsive to contemporary urban challenges and opportunities. In this way, spaces for real-time, in-the-moment types of practices emerge contributing to the potential for new mechanisms for innovating privacy and associated challenges along with possibly novel roles for citizens, businesses, and governments in fostering greater involvement and support.

Variables and Indicators

This chapter advances the potential for value to emerge through surfacing of the dependent variable of *openness and urban practices* and a series of independent variables associated with what is going on in the city, concurrent awareness, understanding people and their needs, and making use of data.

5.2 Research

This chapter further develops and advances the ambient privacy construct in the context of the emerging research literature for smart cities, urban digital initiatives, and evolving understandings of innovating privacy.

Innovating Privacy for Smarter Urbanities

The viability of the conceptual framework for innovating privacy for smarter urbanities operationalized for use in this chapter demonstrates early-stage potentials while offering and opening up new and evolving urban spaces for testing and practice.

Ambient Privacy

Conceptualization of spaces for real-time, dynamic, and adaptive types of approaches to addressing privacy, as in ambient privacy, emerge in this chapter opening the way for new techniques and possibly novel roles and collaborations for citizens, businesses, researchers, and governments. As such, areas for exploration potential include:

1. *Amplifications* of information sharing in urban spaces associated with more aware people interacting with each other and with aware technologies
2. *Informed* openness fostered through the making of more dynamic urban spaces for dialogue, learning, experimentation, and data gathering and assessment

Ambient Ecosystems

This chapter opens the way to future research opportunities and challenges related to the potential for movement toward the building of ambient ecosystems in support of collaboration, privacy, and sharing that is also ambient, as in, highly dynamic, fluid, and adaptive with implications for urban research and theory and also for practice.

Ambient Practices

This chapter opens the way to future research opportunities and challenges related to the potential for movement toward the building of ambient practices as an urban research technique with implications for urban practitioners.

6. CONCLUSION

This chapter provides an exploration of innovating privacy for smart cities in relation to a range of disciplinary perspectives focusing on the construct of openness and the sub-constructs of collaboration and sharing. Amplifications of information sharing in urban spaces and more informed openness enabled through aware technologies emerge as key elements for fostering the innovating of privacy. This work makes several contributions in that it: a) provides emerging and evolving perspectives from the research literature on collaboration, openness, privacy, and sharing in smart cities; b) articulates and operationalizes a conceptual framework for innovating privacy for smarter urbanities; and c) develops a framework for ambient privacy in smart city urbanities. As such, this chapter argues for a re-thinking of the privacy construct in relation to collaboration, openness, and sharing involving more aware people and aware technologies in response to emerging requirements for smarter, more responsive, cities.

This chapter continues to give form, detail, and definition to the broader Ambient Urbanities Framework presented in Chapter 1 (Figure 4) through exploration of the openness construct in relation to collaboration, privacy, and sharing. The analysis of findings in this chapter identifies variables associated with *openness and urban practices* relevant to what is happening in the city, concurrent awareness, understanding people and their needs, and making use of data.

Insights of particular interest to the reader include the following:

1. The potential for meaningful openness opportunities to inform evolving urban understandings
2. The interconnectedness of collaboration, openness, privacy, and sharing as ambient, informing ambient urbanities
3. The surfacing of variables associated with *openness and urban practices* in evolving urban spaces

Ideas highlighted in this chapter pertain to the following:

1. The importance of people becoming more aware of the notion of ambient practices
2. The importance of people becoming more aware of the potential for ambient ecosystems in support of collaboration, openness, privacy, and sharing in urban spaces
3. Ambient practices as a novel approach contributing to smarter cities and to ambient urbanities

Lessons for the reader in this chapter are associated with the following:

1. The potential for ambient privacy to influence and be influenced by aware technologies in the design of spaces that afford more continuous choices and actions based on an awareness of context and situations
2. The potential for aware technologies to enhance openness possibilities for people in urban spaces
3. The intractable issues, controversies, and problems for collaboration, openness, privacy, and sharing in smart environments, as part of the ambient turn

This work will be of interest to a broad audience including students, educators, business, researchers, urban planners, information technology developers, community members, and urban practitioners and anyone concerned with innovating sharing, collaboration, openness, and privacy in support of aware people and aware technologies in meeting the complex urban challenges and opportunities of smarter, more responsive, urbanities.

REFERENCES

Berrone, P., Ricart, J. E., & Carrasco, C. (2016). The open kimono: Toward a general framework for open data initiatives in cities. *California Management Review*, 59(1), 39–70. doi:10.1177/0008125616683703

Bogers, M., Chesbrough, H., & Moedas, C. (2018). Open innovation: Research, practices, and policies. *California Management Review*, 60(2), 5–16. doi:10.1177/0008125617745086

Cavoukian, A., & Popa, C. (2016). *Embedding privacy into what's next: Privacy by design for the Internet of Things*. Ryerson University, Privacy & Big Data Institute. Retrieved 29 April 2018 from https://www.ryerson.ca/content/dam/pbdce/papers/Privacy-by-Design-for-the-Internet-of-Things.pdf

Crabtree, A., & Mortier, R. (2016). *Personal data, privacy and the Internet of Things: The shifting locus of agency and control. SSRN Scholarly Paper*. Rochester, NY: Social Science Research Network.

Dwork, C. (2011). Differential privacy. In C. A. Henk & S. J. van Tilborg (Eds.), *Encyclopedia of Cryptography and Security*. Boston, MA: Springer.

Egyedi, T. M. (2012). Disruptive inverse infrastructures: Conclusions and policy recommendations. In T. M. Egyedi & D. C. Mehos (Eds.), *Inverse infrastructures: Disrupting networks from below*. Cheltenham, UK: Edward Elgar Pub. doi:10.4337/9781781952290.00023

Egyedi, T. M., Mehos, D. C., & Vree, W. G. (2012). Introducing inverse infrastructures. In T. M. Egyedi & D. C. Mehos (Eds.), *Inverse infrastructures: Disrupting networks from below*. Cheltenham, UK: Edward Elgar Pub. doi:10.4337/9781781952290.00007

Fedosov, A., Ojala, J., Olsson, T., Vaananen, K., & Langheinrich, M. (2017). From travel plans to magic wands: A cross-domain study of practices and privacy requirements for sharing emerging types of online content. *Proceedings of 15th European Conference on Computer- Supported Cooperative Work - Exploratory Papers*. Reports of the European Society for Socially Embedded Technologies. Doi:10.18420/ecscw2017-2

Fietkiewicz, K. J., & Henkel, M. (2018). Privacy protecting fitness trackers: An oxymoron or soon to be reality? In G. Meiselwitz (Ed.), SCSM 2018 (LNCS 10913, pp. 431-444). Springer.

Gavalas, D., Nicopolitidis, P., Kameas, A., Goumopoulos, C., Bellavista, P., Lambrinos, L., & Buo, B. (2017). Smart cities: Recent trends, methodologies, and applications (Editorial). Wireless Communications and Mobile Computing.

Gil-Garcia, J. R., Zhang, J., & Puron-Cid, G. (2016). Conceptualizing smartness in government: An integrative and multi-dimensional view. *Government Information Quarterly*, *33*(3), 524–534. doi:10.1016/j.giq.2016.03.002

Grant, M. (2017). New technology makes artificial intelligence more private and portable. *Waterloo News*. University of Waterloo. Retrieved 20 November 2017 from https://uwaterloo.ca/news/news/new-technology-makes-artificial-intelligence-more-private

Gurevich, Y., Hudis, E., & Wing, J. M. (2016). Inverse privacy. *Communications of the ACM*, *59*(7), 38–42. doi:10.1145/2838730

Hong, J. (2017). The privacy landscape of pervasive computing. *IEEE Pervasive Computing*, *16*(3), 40–48. doi:10.1109/MPRV.2017.2940957

Judge, J., & Powles, J. (2015). Forget the internet of things – we need an internet of people. *The Guardian*. Retrieved 21 December 2017 from https://www.theguardian.com/technology/2015/may/25/forget-internet-of-things-people

Langheinrich, M. (2001). Privacy by design – Principles of privacy-aware ubiquitous systems. In G. D. Abowd, B. Brumitt, & S. Shafer (Eds.), Lecture Notes in Computer Science: Vol. 2201. *Ubicomp 2001: Ubiquitous computing*. Berlin: Springer. doi:10.1007/3-540-45427-6_23

Li, X., Niu, J., Kumari, S., Wu, F., & Choo, K. K. R. (2018). A robust biometrics based three-factor authentication scheme for global mobility networks in smart city. *Future Generation Computer Systems*, *83*, 607–618. doi:10.1016/j.future.2017.04.012

Lindley, J., Coulton, P., & Cooper, R. (2019). The IoT and unpacking the Heffalump's Trunk. In *Proceedings of the Future Technologies Conference (FTC) 2018* (pp. 134-151). Springer. 10.1007/978-3-030-02686-8_11

Malle, B., Kieseberg, P., & Holzinger, A. (2017). Interactive anonymization for privacy aware learning. In G. Krempl, V. Lemaire, R. Polikar, B. Sick, D. Kottke, & A. Calma (Eds.), IAL @ ECML PKSS 2017 Workshop and Tutorial on Interactive Adaptive Learning. Skopje: Academic Press.

Malle, B., Kieseberg, P., & Schrittwieser, S. (2016). Privacy aware machine learning and the "right to be forgotten." Special theme: machine learning. *ERCIM News*, 107. Retrieved 26 April 2018 from https://ercim-news.ercim.eu/en107/special/privacy-aware-machine-learning-and-the-right-to-be-forgotten

Mattsson, J., & Sørensen, F. (2015). City renewal as open innovation. *Journal of Innovation Economics & Management*, *1*(16), 195–215. doi:10.3917/jie.016.0195

McKenna, H. P. (2017). Civic tech and ambient data in the public realm: Exploring challenges and opportunities for learning cities and smart cities. In N. Streitz & P. Markopoulos (Eds.), Lecture Notes in Computer Science: Vol. 10291. *Distributed, Ambient and Pervasive Interactions (DAPI)* (pp. 312–331). Cham: Springer. doi:10.1007/978-3-319-58697-7_23

McKenna, H. P., Arnone, M. P., Kaarst-Brown, M. L., McKnight, L. W., & Chauncey, S. A. (2013). Ambient privacy with wireless grids: Forging new concepts of relationship in 21st century information society. *International Journal for Information Security Research*, *3*(1-2), 408–417.

McKenna, H. P., McKnight, L. W., & Chauncey, S. A. (2014). *Advancing ambient privacy and informational self-determination as key components of a national privacy research strategy*. Submission in Response to a Request for Information (RFI) - National Privacy Research Strategy, US, NITRD, 17 Oct. Outcomes are highlighted on the Computing Community Consortium (CCC) blog, 11 May 2015 - CCC community report for a national privacy research strategy. Our contribution is noted among a host of 'Community Contributors' to the document: Towards a privacy research roadmap for the computing community.

McLaren, D., & Agyeman, J. (2015). *Sharing cities: A case for truly smart and sustainable cities*. Cambridge, MA: MIT Press.

Mervis, J. (2019). *Can a set of equations keep U.S. census data private?* Science and Policy; doi:10.1126cience.aaw5470

Mulder, I. (2015). Opening up: Towards a sociable smart city. In *Citizen's right to the digital city* (pp. 161–173). Singapore: Springer. doi:10.1007/978-981-287-919-6_9

Nissenbaum, H. (2004). Privacy as contextual integrity. *Washington Law Review (Seattle, Wash.)*, *79*(1), 119–158.

Pereira, G. V., Cunha, M. A., Lampoltshammer, T. J., Parycek, P., & Testa, M. G. (2017). Increasing collaboration and participation in smart city governance: A cross-case analysis of smart city initiatives. *Information Technology for Development*, *23*(3), 526–553. doi:10.1080/02681102.2017.1353946

Schaffers, H., Komninos, N., Pallot, M., Trousse, B., Nilsson, M., & Oliveira, A. (2011). Smart Cities and the Future Internet: Towards Cooperation Frameworks for Open Innovation. In The Future Internet. Berlin: Springer Berlin Heidelberg.

Snow, C. C., Håkonsson, D. D., & Obel, B. (2016). A smart city is a collaborative community: Lessons from smart Aarus. *California Management Review*, *59*(1), 92–108. doi:10.1177/0008125616683954

Solove, D. J. (2006). A taxonomy of privacy. *University of Pennsylvania Law Review*, *154*(3), 477–560. doi:10.2307/40041279

Van Zoonen, L. (2016). Privacy concerns in smart cities. *Government Information Quarterly*, *33*(3), 472–480. doi:10.1016/j.giq.2016.06.004

ADDITIONAL READING

Dourish, P., & Anderson, K. (2006). Collective information practice: Exploring privacy and security as social and cultural phenomena. *Human-Computer Interaction*, *21*(3), 319–342. doi:10.120715327051hci2103_2

Dovey, K., Pafka, E., & Ristic, M. (Eds.). (2018). *Mapping urbanities: Morphologies, flows, possibilities*. New York, NY: Routledge.

Goffman, E. (1959). *The presentation of self in everyday life*. New York: Doubleday Anchor.

Karat, C. M., Brodie, C., & Karat, J. (2006). Usable privacy and security for personal information management. *Communications of the ACM*, *49*(1), 56–57. doi:10.1145/1107458.1107491

Palen, L., & Dourish, P. (2003). Unpacking 'privacy' for a networked world. *Proceedings of the SIGCHI Conference on Human Factors in Computing Systems (CHI2013)* (pp. 129-136). New York: ACM.

Smith, H. J., Dinev, T., & Xu, H. (2011). Information privacy research: An interdisciplinary review. *Management Information Systems Quarterly*, *35*(4), 989–1015. doi:10.2307/41409970

Solove, D. J. (2007). 'I've got nothing to hide' and other misunderstandings of privacy. *San Diego Law Review,* 44, 745-772. GWU Law School Public Law Research Paper No. 289. Retrieved 30 April 2018 from https://ssrn.com/abstract=998565

Weiser, M. (1999). The computer for the 21st century. *Mobile Computing and Communications Review*, *3*(3), 3–11. doi:10.1145/329124.329126

KEY TERMS AND DEFINITIONS

Ambient: The increasing presence of aware technologies in and around human activity affecting the nature and experience of awareness, information, economies, literacies, and everything.

Ambient Challenges: Adaptive, dynamic, uncertain, and fluid issues, events, circumstances, situations or the like.

Ambient Collaboration: Ambient collaboration refers to more adaptive, dynamic, cross-sector, and in the moment forms of working together.

Ambient Openness: Ambient openness refers to more adaptive, dynamic, cross-sector, and in the moment practices and approaches.

Ambient Opportunities: Opportunities characterized by adaptive, dynamic, uncertain, and fluid elements or the like.

Ambient Sharing: Ambient sharing refers to more adaptive, dynamic, cross-sector, and in the moment interactivities.

Innovating Privacy: Privacy characterized by the exploration and use of aware technologies in combination with more aware people in adaptive, dynamic, uncertain, and fluid ways.

Privacy-Awareness: Privacy enabled by more aware technologies in combination with more aware people in more adaptive, dynamic, uncertain, and fluid environments based on the design of spaces for more continuous choices and actions, in support of an awareness of the contextual and situational.

Chapter 9
Measuring Ambient Urbanities:
Metrics, Standards, and Indices

ABSTRACT

The purpose of this chapter is to explore mechanisms and potentials for measuring ambient urbanities. This work advances the ambient metrics concept as a way of shedding light on the evolving nature of measures, standards, and indices required by more dynamic, adaptive, and aware environments, characteristic of smart and responsive cities. In the form of ambient metrics, measures are sought that support more informed city experiences, increased engagement and participation, and improved quality of urban life. The research literature for smart city metrics, standards, and indices is explored in this chapter enabling identification of issues, controversies, and problems. Using an exploratory case study approach, solutions and recommendations are advanced. This chapter makes a contribution to the research literature for smart city metrics, standards, and indices; the evolving of urban theory for 21st century cities; and urban theory in formulating a conceptual framework for rethinking measures for smarter urbanities.

1. INTRODUCTION

The purpose of this chapter is to explore mechanisms and potentials for measuring ambient urbanities. This work advances the ambient metrics concept as a way of shedding light on the evolving nature of measures, standards, and indices (ISO, 2018; ISO, 2017; ISO, 2016; ISO, 2014; BSI, 2014d) required

DOI: 10.4018/978-1-5225-7882-6.ch009

by more dynamic, adaptive, and aware environments, characteristic of smart and responsive cities. In the form of ambient metrics, measures are sought that support more informed city experiences, increased engagement and participation, and improved quality of urban life. The research literature for smart city metrics (Cohen, 2014; BSI, 2014d), standards (Lea, 2016a; 2016b), and indices (PSD, 2016) is explored in this chapter enabling identification of issues, controversies, and problems. Using an exploratory case study approach, solutions and recommendations are advanced. This chapter makes a contribution to: a) the research literature for smart city metrics, standards, and indices; b) the evolving of urban theory for 21st century cities; and c) urban theory in formulating a conceptual framework for rethinking measures for smarter urbanities.

Objectives: The objective of this chapter is to explore metrics, standards, indices, and indicators in smart cities in the context of emerging aware technologies and more aware people for improved livability, more informed urban experiences, and more meaningful engagement and participation. As such, the key research question posed is – How and why are metrics important for ambient urbanities in smart cities?

2. BACKGROUND AND OVERVIEW

Marsal-Llacuna (2015) advanced the need for "measuring the standardized definition of smart city" while arguing for "global metrics" in relation to "urban smartness." In view of the emergent and continually evolving nature of smart city development, Lea (2016a) identifies the need for "making sense" of the landscape for standardization while describing the range and interrelationships of standards developed to date. For example, this chapter draws on the research literature for smart city standards (ISO, 2018; ISO, 2017; ISO, 2016; ISO, 2014; BSI, 2014a-d), metrics (Lea, 2016a-b), indices (PSD, 2016), data (WCCD, 2014), indicators (GCI, 2011), and other emerging measures (Díaz-Díaz, Muñoz, and Pérez-González, 2017) for understanding the smartness of cities in terms of sustainability and a wide range of other elements. Challenges (Cohen, 2014; BSId, 2014) and opportunities (Lea, 2016a; 2016b) for smart city metrics are discussed and approaches are explored to generating more dynamic and adaptive measures of smartness and associated analytics in the context of the complexities of 21st century cities. The Open University's course on smart cities (Open University, 2018) points to the importance of measurement as "a basis to track progress, make decisions and compare cities." This chapter argues for a rethinking of the metrics concept in formulation of a framework for measuring ambient urbanities in support of adaptive, dynamic, contextual, and responsive elements, advanced as a critical dimension of smart cities and communities.

2.1 Definitions

For the purposes of this work, definitions for key terms used in this chapter are presented here based on the research literature.

- **Indices:** City indexes of multiple types, referred to here as indices that use a series of indicators in support of measurement (IESE, 2017).
- **Indicators:** Focusing on key performance indicators (KPI), the Open University's course on smart cities (2018) describes a KPI as "a quantifiable measure that an organisation uses to assess performance on objectives." Bosch, Jongeneel, Rovers, Neumann, Airaksinen, and Huovila (2017) refer to indicators as "progress measures."
- **Metrics:** The Open University's course on smart cities (2018) claims "measurements that are based on a standardised method are called metrics."
- **Standards:** According to the International Standards Organization (ISO), "standards represent the international consensus on best practices in a wide range of areas that contribute to making a city function better and fulfill the United Nations Sustainable Development Goals to end poverty, protect the planet and ensure prosperity for all" (ISO, 2017).

2.2 Overview

This chapter provides a range of perspectives in Section 3 on efforts to develop metrics, standards, and indices and indicators for smart cities in relation to emerging and evolving understandings, followed by an overview of associated issues, controversies, and problems. Section 4 provides a rethinking of measures for smarter urbanities, including a conceptual framework that is operationalized for use in the exploration under investigation in this chapter. In exploring the potential for solutions and recommendations to the issues, controversies, and problems, a framework for measuring ambient urbanities in smart cities and communities is advanced. Section 5 identifies future directions for research and practice and Section 6 concludes with chapter coverage highlights, the major contributions, and the key insights, ideas, and lessons.

The primary audiences for this chapter include students, educators, researchers, policy makers, urban practitioners, and community members concerned with urban metrics, indicators, and standards as meaningful measures in relation to more aware people and aware technologies in the context of ambient urbanities in smart cities and regions, in the face of increasingly complex urban challenges and opportunities.

3. METRICS, STANDARDS, AND INDICES FOR SMART CITIES

This chapter provides a review of the research and practice literature for smart cities focusing on metrics, standards, and indices and indicators.

3.1 Metrics and Smart Cities

Anthopoulos and Vakali (2012) seek to measure the interrelationship of the smart city and urban planning, identifying "the meeting points between them." Goldsmith and Crawford (2014) address metrics for responsive cities in relation to data and civic engagement. From a human geography perspective, Lévy (2014) refers to topographical metrics in relation to territories "based on continuity and contiguity." Additionally, topological metrics are described by Lévy (2014) as networks and borders "based on discontinuity" including unfilled spaces. In terms of assessing smart city initiatives, Albino, Berardi, and Dangelico (2015) highlight the types of emerging metrics, referring to the work of Zygiaris (2013), who developed a measurement system based on six layers of a smart city. The layers include: *city layer* focusing on context; *the green city layer* focusing on environmental sustainability; the *interconnection layer* for the diffusion of green economies; the *instrumentation layer* in support of real-time smart meters and infrastructure sensors; the *open integration layer* with apps to communicate and share data, content, services, and information; the *application layer* enabling real-time responsive operation; and the *innovation layer* to foster new business opportunities. In view of "proclamations of being a smart and sustainable city" based on "synthetic quantitative indicators," Marsal-Llacuna (2015) points to the need for "global metrics to set the terms of references for urban smartness." Meanwhile, Al-Nasrawi, Adams, and El-Zaart (2015) highlight "the need for an accurate metric of comparison that considers the city's context." Caprotti, Cowley, Datta, Brot, Gao, Georgeson, Herrick, Odeandaal, and Joss (2017) point to key opportunities and challenges for policy and practices with metrics and measurements as part of the new urban agenda. Concerned with placing a stronger emphasis on people, Caprotti et al. (2017) identify the challenges of "a lack of data" and "difficulties in measuring urban realities" emphasizing that "measurement becomes entangled with people's lives and priorities" at the level of the urban. Among points identified for debate on the new urban agenda, two pertain to metrics, highlighting concerns with "how to ensure appropriate measurement and data for metrics" and whether "the focus on data and metrics lead away from a focus on urban development" (Caprotti et al., 2017).

Bosch et al. (2017) describe quantifiable metrics as "values that can be measured." Based on the need to understand the complexity of urban form, urban fabric metrics are analyzed "to measure the overall features and subtle features" of an urban block in order to build smart cities (Li, Cheng, Lv, Song, Jia, and Lu, 2018). Li et al (2018) use a combination of statistical methods, computational techniques, and machine learning to support optimal urban construction and conclude that improvements can be achieved with the use of three dimensional features and that additional "social and economic factors would be involved as complementary support to interpret the formation process of urban fabric." Bell, Banetti, Edwards, Laney, Morse, Picollo, and Zanetti (2018) describe smart city as "a concept that captures the way urban spaces are re-made by the incursion of new technology." Bell et al. (2018) describe the "making metrics meaningful (MMM) project" using 'Imagine' as a rapid participatory method "to gain insights from the general public" about their "concerns, needs, and ideas for novel information systems" that are also innovative. In the context of big data in smart cities, McKenna (2019) advances the need for an innovating of metrics for smarter, more responsive cities. McKenna provides an overview of theory and methodologies for innovating metrics in relation to data and smart cities; an innovation framework for emergent and evolving ambient metrics; and based on an urban level exploration for the innovating of metrics, identifies a series of variables relevant to the innovating of urban metrics pertaining to awareness, learning, openness, and engagement.

Figure 1. Overview of key issues, controversies and problems for metrics

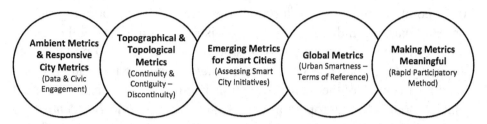

Figure 1 provides an overview of key issues, controversies, and problems for metrics and smart cities.

Highlights include ambient metrics (McKenna, 2019) and responsive city metrics focusing on data and civic engagement (Goldsmith and Crawford, 2014); topographical and topological metrics, concerned with continuity and contiguity and discontinuity respectively (Lévy, 2014); emerging metrics for smart cities in assessing initiatives (Zygiaris, 2013); global metrics for urban smartness in the form of terms of reference (Marsal-Llacuna, 2015); and making metrics meaningful as a rapid participatory method (Bell et al., 2018).

3.2 Standards and Smart Cities

As a leading country in the development of smart city standards (BSI, 2014d), the United Kingdom (UK) developed a vocabulary for smart cities (PAS 180) and a smart city framework (PAS 181) to guide strategy development for cities and communities. The World Council on City Data (WCCD, 2017) was launched in 2014 as well as the development of ISO 37120:2018 (ISO, 2018), an international standard for *Sustainable development of communities: Indicators for city services and quality of life.* The standard is based on the framework of the Global City Indicators Facility (GCI, 2014), consists of 100 indicators (46 of which are core) categorized into 17 themes, and is designed to measure the social, economic, and environmental performance of a city. Marsal-Llacuna (2015) provides an "analysis of covered and uncovered aspects" of smart city standards identifying the need for "wider standardization coverage" where "the citizen must be at the core of any city strategy (including smart city strategies)" and "intangible aspects of social sustainability need to be considered." According to Marsal-Llacuna (2015), "standards supporting the corresponding social policies need to be created." Indicating that research is still in the early stages, Marsal-Llacuna (2015) points to upcoming efforts "in the direction of elaborating one or more summarizing indices" in order "to visualize in a more synthetic way the performance of cities in terms of smartness." Lea (2016) points to the complexity of the smart city standardization landscape providing an overview and noting the work of the British Standards Institution (BSI) in development of data standards for interoperability and data sharing – *PAS 182, Smart city concept model: Guide to establishing a model for data* (2014b). Finger (2016) highlights the importance of standards in relation to infrastructure in smart cities, focusing on network data and city interoperability. Caird, Hudson, and Kortuem (2016) highlight the range of initiatives underway "to address challenges associated with smart city development and evaluation" pertaining to "standards relevant to smart city development, by the International Standards Organization (ISO), European Committee for Standardization (CEN) and the British Standards Institution (BSI)." Also of note, according to Caird et al. (2016), are several "city measurement indicator frameworks specially designed to support city approaches to smart city evaluation" such as, the European Smart Cities Ranking Model (Giffinger et al., 2007); the Smart City Reference Model developed by Zygiaris (2013); the Smart City Index Master Indicators developed through the Smart Cities Council provided by Cohen (SCC, 2014); and the Smart City Maturity Model developed by the International Data Corporation (CivSource, 2013).

According to the ISO (2017), standards include "overarching frameworks that city leaders and planners can use to define their objectives and priorities for making their cities more sustainable" along with "specific guidelines for things like energy management systems, road safety, intelligent transport, responsible water consumption, health and well-being, cyber security, connectivity and more." Simply put, "ISO standards provide cities with an overall framework for defining what 'being smart' means for them and how they can get there" (ISO, 2017). ISO 37101 is said to provide a "starting point for cities" and "is supported by different standards" for "terminology and key indicators for measuring the performance of city services" and this is important because they "offer specific guidance for developing strategies and implementing them" (ISO, 2017). Six points for debate on the new urban agenda were identified by Caprotti et al. (2017), one of which pertains to standards – "how to standardize the (sustainable) city." Indeed, examples of dynamic, adaptive standards as ambient are presented in relation to air quality and weather by government (DEP, 2019).

Figure 2. Overview of key issues, controversies and problems for standards

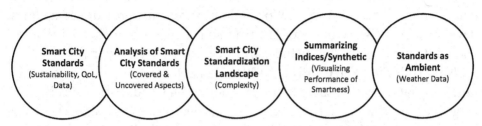

Figure 2 provides an overview of key issues, controversies, and problems for standards and smart cities.

Highlights include smart city standards pertaining to sustainability, quality of life, and data (ISO, 2018; WCCD, 2017); the analysis of smart city standards in terms of aspects that are covered and uncovered (Marsal-Llacuna, 2015); the smart city standardization landscape and the complexity involved (Lea, 2016); the movement toward summarizing indices of a synthetic nature for visualizing the performance of smartness in cities (Marsal-Llacuna, 2015); and standards as ambient in relation to weather data (DEP, 2019).

3.3. Indices and Indicators for Smart Cities

Lombardi, Giordano, Farouh, and Yousef (2012) explore the modeling of smart city performance using the triple helix model, designed as "a reference framework for the analysis of knowledge-based innovation systems" whereby "the three main agencies in the process of knowledge creation and capitalization" said to be the "university, industry and government" are investigated to learn about "multiple and reciprocal relationships." Lombardi et al. (2012) identify a list of indicators for use in application of the triple helix model to smart cities to inform policy-making. Schmitt (2015) draws attention to four indices for smart cities in terms of livability – Monocle's Most Livable Cities Index, The EIU's Liveability Ranking and Overview, Mercer Quality of Living Survey, and The Global Liveable Cities Index. In assessing the performance of smart sustainable cities (SSC), Al-Nasrawi et al. (2015) point to the need for a multidimensional model based on an exploration of existing measurement models internationally. Models selected for the exploration by Al-Nasrawi et al. (2015) include – Global Competitiveness Index, Network Readiness Index, ICT Development Index, Global Innovation Index, E-Government Development Index, Digital Economy Ranking, Change Readiness Index, Green City Index, and Better Life Index. Caird et al. (2016)

point to "general city indexes" as "a major source of indicators, measures and data to inform smart city evaluation and measurement" providing examples developed in 2014 that include, The Ericsson Networked Society City Index and The Cities of Opportunity Index by PricewaterhouseCoopers/Partnership for New York City. Yet, Caird et al. (2016) lament that, "surprisingly few city indexes (that have published their methodology) have identified specifically smart city indicators and metrics." Definitional issues are also identified by Caird et al. (2016) related to "so-called smart cities" since many "are at different stages of becoming smart future cities."

It is worth noting that examples of dynamic, adaptive indicators as ambient are presented in relation to air quality and governments (ECCC, 2018). The CityKeys Project (Eurocities, 2015) provides a "set of indicators for assessing the success of projects" based on a common performance measurement framework. Bosch et al. (2017) report on the indicators for smart city projects with a focus on people (social sustainability), planet (environmental sustainability), prosperity (economic sustainability), governance, and propagation (diffusion potential) and at the smart cities level with a focus on people, prosperity, and governance. Drawing on work by the UNICEF Monitoring and Evaluation Training Resources, CityKeys outlines a typology of indicators according to "stage in the process" that includes several types of indicators – input, process, output, outcome, and impact. The Cities in Motion Index (CIMI) is described as a "synthetic index" and this is because "it is a function of the partial indicators available" (IESE, 2017). CIMI aims "to create awareness and generate innovative tools to achieve smarter governments" while "constructing a 'breakthrough' indicator" highlighting "completeness and comparability" among other features. A smart sustainable cities (SSC) assessment model is introduced by Al-Nasrawi, Adams, and El-Zaart (2017) said to ensure, in design, "the integral sustainability of the systems of the city" while "including the human system."

Patel (2017) claims there is a need to "be designing to make individuals aware of the in-between" while raising questions pertaining to "how do we attempt to reach the unmeasurable?" Hunter (2018) articulates the "ambient contextuality" concept, suggesting that, "there is information hidden all around us that helps clarify our intent in any given conversation." For Hunter (2018), something is occurring "between people, processes and things that fuels usability" enabled by the Internet of Things (IoT). Abdel-Basset and Mohamed (2018) address vagueness and other issues with data in smart cities through use of the theory of neutrosophic rough sets based on measures "for dealing with incompleteness" and "indeterminate and inconsistent data" and proposing a "general framework for dealing with imperfect and incomplete information." Garau and Pavan (2018) formulate and apply "a methodology to measure the quality of urban life based on investigative checklists" along with "objective and subjective indicators" that are "aggregated to develop an index to evaluate a city's level of smart urban quality." Mollá-Sirvent, Mora, Gilart-Iglesias, Pérez-delHoyo and Andújar-Montoya (2018) advance an accessibility index for smart cities to determine "how accessible a city is and its progression" over time.

Figure 3 provides an overview of key issues, controversies, and problems for indices and indicators in smart cities.

Highlights include indicators for policy makers using the triple helix model (Lombardi et al., 2012); indices for liveability from rankings to quality of life (Schmitt, 2015); models for assessing the performance of smart sustainable cities (Al-Nasrawi et al., 2015); CityKeys and key performance indicators for smart cities and smart city projects (Bosch et al., 2017); and the unmeasurable and ambient contextuality (Hunter, 2018).

3.4 Issues, Controversies, and Problems

Key issues, controversies, and problems emerging in the review of the research literature explored in this chapter are highlighted below. Coverage of issues, controversies, and problems is not intended to be exhaustive or comprehensive but rather, as illustrative of the nature, variety, and range.

Issues

Concerns with "lack of data" and how to measure "urban realities" (Caprotti et al. (2017), together with the need articulated by Bell et al. (2018) to make "metrics meaningful" when presented with the "unmeasurable" (Patel, 2017) and "hidden information all around us" contributing to what Hunter refers to

Figure 3. Overview of key issues, controversies and problems for indices and indicators

as "ambient contextuality" provide important and fundamental motivations for this chapter related to measuring ambient urbanities. Additionally, Bell et al. (2018) identify issues related to the "uncertainty of information in various forms" while highlighting the themes of risk, predictability, and reliability in the context of smart city transportation systems.

Controversies

Caprotti at al. (2017) identify the controversial issue of "the role of experts in defining people's lives" suggesting instead that "scientists, technicians and experts should not be given the responsibility of arbitrating political debates" and instead that citizens "should be invited to join them as recognized participants." Standards as ambient (DEP, 2019) and indicators as ambient (ECCC, 2018) in relation to weather data assume a particular significance for smart cities when considered in relation to the interdisciplinary work of Jeremijenko (2016) who makes visible the invisible through art installations and projects such as Amphibious Architecture enabling "audiences to visualize river health and water quality in real time with a tangible, visual representation of what is happening in their river."

Problems

Al-Nasrawi et al. (2015) point to the importance of multidimensionality in the assessment of smart cities and to understandings of smartness in the context of the particular city or country being assessed, identifying these factors as gaps or problem with existing models. Al-Nasrawi et al. (2015) point to the issue of synthetic quantitative indicators and the problem of the "partial indicators available" where data may be incomplete. On the other hand, Basset and Mohamed (2018) make a case for use of the theory of neutrosophic rough sets in proposing a framework to address the presence of "imperfect and incomplete information" for application in smart cities.

Summarized in Figure 4, a glimpse of patterns, flows, relationships, and possibilities begin to emerge influencing measures for smarter urbanities through indices, indicators, metrics, and standards in smart cities. Indices are described in terms of multidimensional models in relation to livability, performance, and sustainability while highlighting the synthetic and the un-measurable. Indicators are highlighted in relation to assessment, breakthrough, the dynamic and the adaptive and the importance of evaluating progress;

learning and monitoring, performance; the four Ps of sustainability (people, planet, prosperity, and propagation); and the development of trust. Metrics pertain to accurate comparisons; the importance of context and the global; dynamic and adaptive aspects; challenges associated with the lack of data, policy and practices, the quantifiable; and perspectives on the urban fabric and urban realities. And finally, standards highlight the importance of complexity; covered and uncovered elements; data; the dynamic and adaptive, their use for evaluation and performance; and more people-centered approaches. Although neatly categorized across indices, indicators, metrics, and standards, it is important to note that there is considerable overlap in that performance is associated with indices for example as well as with indicators and standards. Also, the categories are necessarily incomplete and intended only as a summary overview.

By author and year, Table 1 provides an overview of issues, controversies, and problems associated with metrics, standards, and indicators/indices in smart cities. Of note are metrics for responsive cities (Goldsmith & Crawford, 2014); topographic and topological metrics (Lévy, 2014); emergent metrics for smart cities (Albino et al., 2015); the need for metrics focusing on comparison and context; global metrics for urban smartness; quantifiable metrics; metrics to guide policy and practices; the need for making metrics meaningful; consideration of metrics for the unmeasurable; metrics for urban

Figure 4. Measures for smarter urbanities through indices, indicators, metrics, and standards

Measures for Smarter Urbanities

	Indices	Indicators	Metrics	Standards
People (aware)	Multidimensional models	Assessment	Accurate comparisons	Complexity
	Livability	Breakthrough	Context / Global	Covered/Uncovered
IoP IoT IoE	Performance	Dynamic / Adaptive	Dynamic / Adaptive	Data
Technologies (aware)	Sustainability	Evaluate progress	Lack of data	Dynamic / Adaptive
	Synthetic	Learn / Monitor	Policy & Practices	Evaluation
	Unmeasurable	Performance	Quantifiable	People-centered
		Sustainability (4Ps)	Urban fabric	Performance
		Trust	Urban realities	

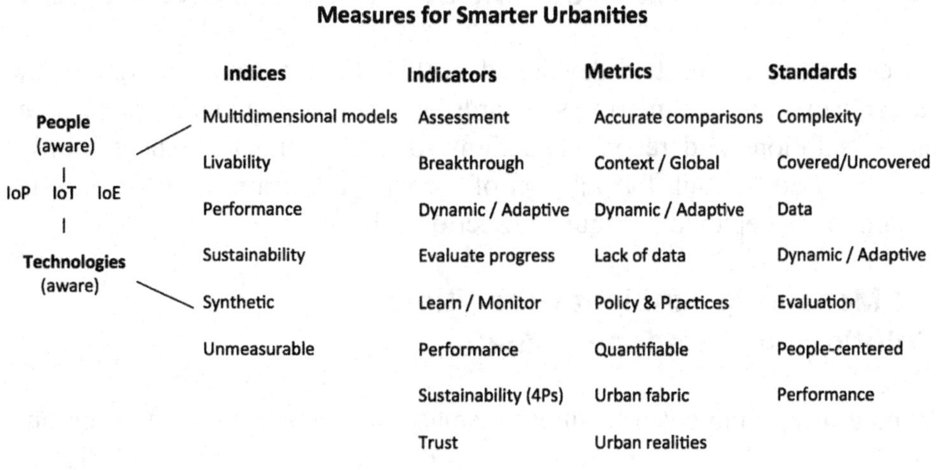

fabric; and ambient metrics and the innovating of metrics in the context of big data and smart cities.

Standards are advanced for smart cities (BSI, 2014d); the covered and uncovered aspects of standards (Marsal-Llacuna, 2015); the need for evaluating smart city standards is identified (Caird et al, 2016); the need for infrastructure standards is identified (Finger, 2016); the complexity of the standards landscape is discussed (Lea, 2016); standards for sustainable smart cities are emphasized; city data standards are advanced (WCCD, 2017); as well as standards for city services and quality of life (QoL) (ISO, 2018); and standards as ambient for air quality (DEP, 2019).

For indicators and indices, emphasis is placed on policy making (Lombardi et al., 2012); the global city (GCI, 2014); the use of models (Al-Nasrawi et al., 2015); performance (Eurocities, 2015); livability (Schmitt, 2015); key performance indicators/KPIs (Bosch et al., 2017); the synthetic (IESE); addressing the synthetic challenge of incomplete data (Basset and Mohamed, 2018); the unmeasurable (Patel, 2017); the ambient (ECCC, 2018); smart urban quality (Garau & Pavan, 2018); and accessibility (Mollá-Sirvent et al., 2018).

By way of solutions and recommendations, the issues, controversies, and problems presented in Table 1 are re-conceptualized as challenges and opportunities to be addressed in this chapter through operationalization of the conceptual framework for rethinking measures for smarter urbanities, developed and presented in Section 4.

4. RETHINKING MEASURES FOR SMARTER URBANITIES

Based on the perspective developed in this chapter from a review of the research literature for metrics, standards, and indicators and indices for smart cities, solutions and recommendations for measuring ambient urbanities are advanced through formulation of a conceptual framework for smarter urbanities as depicted in Figure 1, Section 4.1.

4.1 Measuring Ambient Urbanities: Solutions and Recommendations

In measuring ambient urbanities in smart city environments and regions, this work builds upon and extends recent work on innovating metrics for

Table 1. Issues, controversies, and problems for metrics, standards, and indicators/ indices in smart cities

Metrics, Standards, and Indicators/Indices for Smart Cities				
Author(s)	**Year**	**Metrics**	**Standards**	**Indicators/Indices**
Lombardi et al.	2012			Policy making
Zygiaris	2013			
BSI	2014d		Smart Cities	
GCI	2014			Global City
Goldsmith & Crawford	2014	Responsive City		
Lévy	2014	Topographic; Topological		
Albino et al.	2015	Emergent		
Al-Nasrawi et al.	2015	Comparison & Context		Models
Eurocities	2015			Performance
Marsal-Llacuna	2015	Global – urban smartness	Un/Covered aspects	
Schmitt	2015			Livability
Caird et al.	2016		Evaluation	
Finger	2016		Infrastructure	
Lea	2016		Complexity of Landscape	
Bosch et al.	2017	Quantifiable		CityKeys / KPIs
Caprotti et al.	2017	Policy & Practices	Sustainability	
IESE	2017			Synthetic / CIMI
Patel	2017			Unmeasurable
WCCD	2017		City Data	
Basset & Mohamed	2018			Synthetic challenge
Bell et al.	2018	Making Metrics Meaningful		
ECCC	2018			Ambient
Garau & Pavan	2018			Smart urban quality
Hunter	2018	Unmeasurable		
ISO	2018		City Services & QoL	
Li et al.	2018	Urban fabric		
Mollá-Sirvent et al.	2018			Accessibility
DEP	2019		Ambient	
McKenna	2019	Ambient; Innovating		

smarter, responsive cities in the context of big data challenges and more specifically, the innovation framework for emergent and evolving ambient metrics (McKenna, 2019). This chapter shifts the focus more subtly to smarter urbanities, again characterized by aware people and aware technologies, in formulation of a conceptual framework for rethinking measures that take into consideration experiences, engagement, and participation, as depicted in Figure 5, using the construct of metrics in relation to standards, indices, and indicators enabling evolving understandings of real-time adaptive elements involving multidimensionality, people, and uncertainty contributing to and enriching the notion of ambient metrics.

Through emerging understandings of rethinking measures for more adaptive, dynamic, and responsive urban environments, this chapter responds to the research question posed and restated as a proposition under exploration, as follows:

P: *Metrics* are important for ambient urbanities in smart cities through more adaptive standards, indices, and other dynamic indicators because of the emergent, continuous, and evolving nature of the people-technologies-cities ecosystem.

How the rethinking of measures informs urbanities is explored in this chapter in terms of metrics including standards, indices, indicators and other creative interactions, involving people and their experiences in coming to new understandings of the urban and urbanities as ambient. Rethinking measures

Figure 5. Conceptual framework for rethinking measures for smarter urbanities

Rethinking Measures for Smarter Urbanities

Aware People – Aware Technologies

(Experiences – Engagement – Participation)

Metrics: Standards – Indices – Indicators

Multidimensionality – People – Uncertainty

Ambient Metrics

as more dynamic, in-the-moment, and adaptive, enables new potentials for urbanizing and measuring ambient urbanities to emerge.

4.2 Measuring Ambient Urbanities: An Exploration

In exploring the measuring of ambient urbanities, the rethinking of metrics, standards, and indicators and indices in smart cities is undertaken in the sections that follow. Based on findings in this exploration, together with the review of the research literature, a framework for measuring ambient urbanities in smart cities and communities is advanced in support of contemporary and future urban challenges and opportunities.

4.2.1. Rethinking Metrics in Smart Cities

From a business perspective, an individual wondered about the "metrics you use if we're in an adjudication process to compare or to determine whether some place crosses the threshold to be a smart designation zone." In other words, "what are the metrics that cities use?" and is there "a set of metrics that are really broadly adopted?" Another individual in the business sector wondered if it would "make sense to think that all cities have the same objectives and the same metrics" highlighting the importance of being "very specific about what their objectives are" and "how they will measure their performance against those objectives." City IT staff emphasized the issues of education and funding related to the use of urban data, referring to "that hurdle of starting to educate what could be done while acknowledging that "I don't think we are really taking full advantage of the data that we currently have", indicating that "we are starting to look at the tools to help us mine the data that we already have an interest in", as if echoing data reporting issues highlighted by the work of Caird et al. (2016).

4.2.2. Rethinking Standards in Smart Cities

From a non profit perspective, interest in ISO standards was expressed in terms of being able to "benchmark and look at progress over time" for "figuring out the key ones to tell the story." From a business perspective, reference was made to building standards as "a codified standardized process" for "use across the landscape so that everybody speaks a single common language" giving rise to the question of whether this exists for smart cities. Frameworks for smart cities such as that by ESRI (2019) were identified, focusing on well run, liveable, healthy, prosperous and safe and sustainable with "human driven framing." It is worth noting that the ESRI framework contains many elements common to the CityKeys framework (Bosch et al. (2017). Interest was expressed in learning more from youth populations about "what does smart mean to them" and "what does the future look like." An individual in the sustainable technology industry questioned the smart city designation for Victoria "with a highway going through part of the city" making "walking downtown very stressful" while suggesting that the city is "really good for things like community involvement, community gardening."

4.2.3. Rethinking Indices and Indicators in Smart Cities

IT staff in a higher education institution commented on the "interesting performance indicators" in the context of innovative smart city initiatives involving education based on collaborative work with the city in addressing and solving everyday urban issues. From a business perspective, the question was raised as to whether individuals "have their own set of indices" while another person in the business sector wondered if indexes for smart cities "actually favor certain cities who have picked the metrics they are measuring." From the perspective of civic engagement, a community leader identified the importance of "that anonymous kind of count" detail to learn more about the use of public spaces enhanced by information from interactive sharing platforms where, based on "observations of any given space" by people, it becomes possible to "analyze what's working and what isn't and what could improve it." An urban application developer and educator advanced a tool to support real-time feedback from people in their city and the sharing of "unique ideas" that could contribute to "the design of some urban space or buildings or some city smart infrastructure." The hope is that city officials would "listen and understand what people want" based on information from the app as a "form of evidence."

4.2.4. A Framework for Measuring Ambient Urbanities in Smart City Urbanities

Findings in this chapter highlight the interest in urban metrics across a variety of sectors from business to non profits. Support also emerges for a rethinking of measures in coming to evolving understandings of a framework for ambient urbanities in smart cities and communities. Indeed, findings in this chapter give rise to the potential for measuring ambient urbanities, as depicted in Figure 6, organized around aware people and aware technologies encompassing metrics, standards, indices and indicators in the physical and digital realms in relation to the ever-emergent and evolving properties of adaptive, dynamic, contextual, and responsive elements in urban environments, in support of motion and movement, in the context of the ambient turn, opening the way for performance and progress to potentially become ambient. This chapter proposes the more meaningful and direct involvement of people with metrics for smart city urbanities as a way of addressing concerns with synthetic indicators and the prevalence of incomplete data. This framework enables exploration of the potential for contributing further to existing work on smart city variables, conditions, determinants, factors and other parameters (McKenna, In Press) and the innovating of metrics in smart cities in relation to big data (McKenna, 2019) by extending this thinking to the measuring of ambient urbanities in relation to the issues, problems, and controversies that emerged through the literature review and highlighted in Table 1 in this chapter.

Figure 6. Framework for measuring ambient urbanities in smart cities

Measuring Ambient Urbanities

Aware People + Aware Technologies

Ambient Metrics

Ambient Standards

Ambient Indices/Indicators

Adaptive

Motion / Movement

Dynamic

Contextual

the Ambient Turn

Responsive

Ambient Performance
Ambient Progress

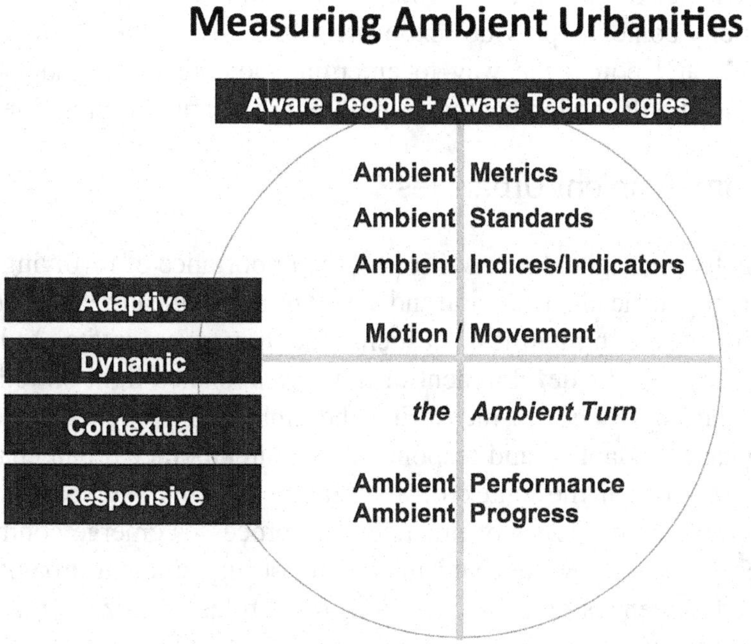

Dependent Variable (DV)

The dependent variable (DV) surfaced in this chapter is *metrics and motion/movement* in relation to standards, indicators, and indices. Associated independent variables (IV) include: smartness thresholds, implying movement on a spectrum; objectives aligned with metrics, implying the notion of performance; benchmarking over time, implying the notion of progress as a story; and activities in urban spaces, implying real-time, interactive movement and motion.

5. FUTURE DIRECTIONS

This chapter advances the measuring of ambient urbanities in the context of the emerging research literature on standards, indices, and measures for smart and responsive cities and future directions and potentials for both practice and research are identified in Sections 5.1 and 5.2 respectively.

5.1 Practice

Practically speaking, this chapter invites opportunities for rethinking metrics in smart city contexts; provides exposure to the idea of measuring ambient urbanities; and points the way to emerging potentials for understanding metrics, standards, and indicators as ambient in relation to urbanities.

Measuring Ambient Urbanities

This chapter highlights for practitioners the importance of involving people more directly in the identification and development of meaningful metrics for smart cities and communities. As such, practitioners are invited to become more involved in the development of initiatives to shed light on rethinking metrics and approaches to measuring the ambient in urban spaces, as in, more dynamic, adaptive and responsive to contemporary urban challenges and opportunities, in the context of smarter cities. In this way, spaces for real-time, in-the-moment types of practices and processes emerge contributing to the potential for new mechanisms for measuring ambient urbanities and associated challenges, along with possibly novel roles for citizens, businesses, and governments in fostering greater involvement and support.

Variables and Indicators

This chapter surfaces the dependent variable of *metrics and motion/movement* and a series of independent variables associated with a smartness threshold; objectives and performance; benchmarking and progress; and the unfolding of activities in urban spaces.

5.2 Research

This chapter serves to guide the way to further advancing and developing the ambient metrics concept in the context of the emerging research literature for standards, indicators, and indices for smart cities and a rethinking of what and how to measure in ambient environments.

Framework for Rethinking Measures for Smarter Urbanities

The viability of the conceptual framework for rethinking measures for smarter urbanities that is operationalized for use in the exploration in this chapter demonstrates early-stage potentials while offering and opening up new understandings for evolving urban spaces for testing and practice. As such, this chapter has implications for urban theorizing in aware environments and for theorizing the measuring of ambient urbanities by developing and advancing the value, importance, and potentials for metrics as smarter and more dynamic and adaptive, as part of the 'ambient turn'. Areas with exploration potential include:

1. *Adaptive* dimensions through which to consider metrics and measuring the ambient
2. *Dynamic* interactions in urban spaces configured for the generation of meaningful metrics
3. *Contextual* activities and how they can be leveraged to enrich urban metrics
4. *Responsive* ways to use urban apps to inform the making of meaningful metrics

Measuring Ambient Urbanities

This chapter navigates the way to future research opportunities and challenges related to the potential for movement toward approaches for measuring more dynamic forms of metrics in the context of ambient urbanities.

Ambient Performance

Future research opportunities and challenges emerge in this chapter related to the potential for movement toward the assessing of metrics and indicators for performance as ambient, with implication for urban practitioners.

Ambient Progress

Future research opportunities and challenges emerge in this chapter related to the potential for movement toward the assessing of metrics and indicators of smartness on a dynamic continuum, where progress is viewed as ambient, with implication for urban practitioners.

6. CONCLUSION

This chapter explores metrics, standards, indices, and indicators for smart cities through a review of the research and practice literature from an interdisciplinary perspective and then in contemporary urban environments. Adaptive, dynamic, contextual, and responsive emerge as key elements for the rethinking of metrics, standards, indicators, and indices in smart cities. These elements will also be important for the measuring of ambient urbanities. This chapter makes several contributions in that it: a) provides emerging and evolving perspectives from the research literature on metrics in smart cities; b) articulates and operationalizes a conceptual framework for rethinking measures for smarter urbanities; and c) develops a framework for measuring ambient urbanities in smart cities and communities. As such, this chapter argues for a re-thinking of the metrics concept for aware people and aware technologies in response to the requirements for measuring ambient urbanities in smart cities and regions.

This chapter continues to give form, detail, and definition to the broader Ambient Urbanities Framework presented in Chapter 1 (Figure 4) through exploration of the metrics construct in relation to standards, indicators, and indices for smart cities. The analysis of findings in this chapter identifies variables associated with *metrics and motion/movement* relevant to the study and practice of the smartness threshold; objectives and performance; benchmarking and progress; and the unfolding of activities in urban spaces for smart cities.

Insights of particular interest to the reader include the following:

1. The potential for meaningful metrics to provide opportunities to inform evolving understandings of ambient urbanities
2. The interconnectedness of metrics, standards, indicators, and indices informing ambient urbanities
3. The surfacing of variables associated with *metrics and motion/movement* in evolving the measuring of ambient urbanities

Ideas highlighted in this chapter pertain to the following:

1. The importance of people becoming more aware of ambient metrics and the ambient turn
2. The potential for people to be rewarded (valued) for their participation in developing and contributing to ambient metrics in urban spaces and measuring ambient urbanities
3. Ambient metrics as a novel approach contributing to smarter cities and to ambient urbanities

Lessons for the reader in this chapter are associated with the following:

1. The potential for measuring ambient urbanities to influence and be influenced by aware technologies
2. The potential for aware technologies to enhance participation possibilities for people in becoming more directly involved in the design and development of measuring ambient urbanities
3. The intractable issues, controversies, and problems for metrics, standards, indicators, and indices in measuring the ambient and the ambient turn

This work will be of interest to a broad audience including students, educators, researchers, urban planners, information technology developers, and urban practitioners and anyone concerned with rethinking and evolving metrics in support of involving more aware people and aware technologies in meeting the complex urban challenges and opportunities of measuring ambient urbanities.

REFERENCES

Abdel-Basset, M., & Mohamed, M. (2018). The role of single valued neutrosophic sets and rough sets in smart city: Imperfect and incomplete information systems. *Measurement*, *124*, 47–55. doi:10.1016/j.measurement.2018.04.001

Al-Nasrawi, S., Adams, C., & El-Zaart, A. (2015). A conceptual multidimensional model for assessing smart sustainable cities. *Journal of Information Systems and Technology Management*, *12*(3), 541–558.

Al-Nasrawi, S., Adams, C., & El-Zaart, A. (2017). The anatomy of smartness of smart sustainable cities: An inclusive approach. *Proceedings of the International Conference on Computer and Applications*, 348-353. 10.1109/COMAPP.2017.8079774

Albino, V., Berardi, U., & Dangelico, R. M. (2015). Smart cities: Definitions, dimensions, performance, and initiatives. *Journal of Urban Technology*, *22*(1), 3–21. doi:10.1080/10630732.2014.942092

Anthopoulos, L. G., & Vakali, A. (2012). *Urban planning and smart cities: Interrelations and reciprocities. In The Future Internet Assembly*. Berlin: Springer.

Bell, S., Banetti, F., Edwards, N. R., Laney, R., Morse, D. R., Picollo, L., & Zanetti, O. (2018). Smart cities and M^3: Rapid research, meaningful metrics and co-design. *Systemic Practice and Action Research*, *31*(1), 27–53. doi:10.100711213-017-9415-x

Bosch, P., Jongeneel, S., Rovers, V., Neumann, H.-M., Airaksinen, M., & Huovila, A. (2017). *CITYkeys indicators for smart city projects and smart cities.* European Commission and H2020 Programme. Retrieved 1 May 2018 from http://nws.eurocities.eu/MediaShell/media/ CITYkeysD14Indicatorsforsmartcityprojectsandsmartcities.pdf

BSI. (2014a). *Mapping smart city standards: Based on a data flow model.* Retrieved 17 May 2018 from https://www.bsigroup.com/LocalFiles/en-GB/smart-cities/resources/BSI-smart-cities-report-Mapping-Smart-City-Standards-UK-EN.pdf

BSI. (2014b). *PAS 182 smart city concept model: Guide to establishing a model for data interoperability.* British Standards Institute. Retrieved 11 January 2017 from https://www.bsigroup.com/en-GB/smart-cities/Smart-Cities-Standards-and-Publication/PAS-182-smart-cities-data-concept-model/

BSI. (2014c). *The role of standards in smart cities.* BSI Group.

BSI. (2014d). *UK takes the lead as first country to develop smart city standards.* Retrieved 17 May 2018 from https://www.bsigroup.com/en-GB/ about-bsi/media-centre/press-releases/2014/February/UK-takes-the-lead-as-first-country-to-develop-Smart-Cities-standards-/

Caird, S., Hudson, L., & Kortuem, G. (2016). *A tale of evaluation and reporting in UK smart cities.* Milton Keyes, UK: The Open University. Retrieved 20 May 2018 from http://oro.open.ac.uk/46008/7/__userdata_documents4_ ctb44_Desktop_Tales_Smart_Cities_Final_2016.pdf

Caprotti, F., Cowley, R., Datta, A., Brot, V. C., Gao, E., Georgeson, L., ... Joss, S. (2017). The new urban agenda: Key opportunities and challenges for policy and practice. *Urban Research & Practice, 10*(3), 367–378. doi:1 0.1080/17535069.2016.1275618

CivSource. (2013). IDC releases first smart city maturity model. *CivSource.* Retrieved 14 February 2019 from https://civsourceonline.com/2013/04/15/ idc-releases-first-smart-city-maturity-model/?utm_source=feedburner&utm_ medium=feed&utm_campaign=Feed%3A+Civsource+%28CivSource%29

Cohen, B. (2014). The smartest cities in the world 2015: Methodology. *FastCoExist.* Retrieved 19 December 2016 from https://www.fastcoexist. com/3038818/the-smartest-cities-in-the-world-2015-methodology

DEP. (2019). *Ambient standards – National ambient air quality standards.* Pennsylvania, Department of Environmental Protection (DEP). Retrieved 31 January 2019 from http://www.dep.pa.gov/Business/Air/BAQ/ PollutantTopics/Pages/Ambient-Standards.aspx

Díaz-Díaz, R., Muñoz, L., & Pérez-González, D. (2017). The business model evaluation tool for smart cities: Application to SmartSantander use cases. *Energies, 10*(3), 262. doi:10.3390/en10030262

ECCC. (2018). *Canadian environmental sustainability indicators: Air quality.* Environment and Climate Change Canada (ECCC). Retrieved 1 February 2019 from https://www.canada.ca/content/dam/eccc/documents/pdf/cesindicators/ air-quality/air-quality-en.pdf

ESRI. (2019). *Smart communities: Every community aspires to be a smart community.* Retrieved 2 February 2019 from http://www.esri.com/smart-communities

Eurocities. (2015). *CityKeys smart city index.* Retrieved 1 February 2019 from http://www.citykeys-project.eu/citykeys/cities_and_regions/Smart-city-index

Finger, M. (2016). Managing urban infrastructures. Lausanne, Switzerland: Massive Open Online Course (MOOC).

Garau, C., & Pavan, V. M. (2018). Evaluating urban quality: Indicators and assessment tools for smart sustainable cities. *Sustainability, 10*(3), 575. doi:10.3390u10030575

GCI. (2014). *Global City Indicators Facility.* Toronto: Global Cities Institute, University of Toronto. Retrieved 18 May 2018 from http://www. globalcitiesinstitute.org

Giffinger, R., Fertner, C., Kramar, H., Kalasek, R., Pichler-Milanović, N., & Meijers, E. (2007). *Smart cities ranking of European medium-sized cities, final report.* Vienna, Austria: Centre of Regional Science, Vienna University of Technology; Department of Geography, University of Ljubljana; and Research Institute for Housing, Urban and Mobility Studies, Delft University of Technology, October. Retrieved 20 May 2018 from http://www.smart-cities. eu/download/smart_cities_final_report.pdf

Goldsmith, S., & Crawford, S. (2014). *The responsive city: Engaging communities through data-smart governance.* San Francisco, CA: John Wiley & Sons Inc.

Hunter, J. (2018). IoT 'conversation' and ambient contextuality. *TechCrunch.* Retrieved 23 May 2018 from https://techcrunch.com/2018/04/24/tell-me-something-good-iot-conversation-and-ambient-contextuality/

IESE. (2017). *Cities in motion index (ST-442-E).* IESE Business School, University of Navarra. Retrieved 22 May 2018 from https://www.mos.ru/upload/documents/files/9743/IESECitiesinMotionIndexIESECitiesinMotionIndex.pdf

ISO. (2014). *How does your city compare to others? New ISO standard to measure up.* Geneva, Switzerland: International Standards Organization.

ISO. (2016). *ISO 37101:2016.* Geneva, Switzerland: International Standards Organization.

ISO. (2017). *ISO and smart cities: Great things happen when the world agrees.* Geneva, Switzerland: International Standards Organization. Retrieved 21 May 2018 from https://www.iso.org/files/live/sites/isoorg/files/store/en/PUB100423.pdf

ISO. (2018). *ISO 37120: 2018(en) Sustainable cites and communities – Indicators for city services and quality of life.* Geneva, Switzerland: International Standards Organization. Retrieved 4 January 2019 from https://www.iso.org/obp/ui/#iso:std:iso:37120:ed-2:v1:en

Jeremijenko, N. (2016). *Natalie Jeremijenko.* GASP. Retrieved 1 February 2019 from http://gasp.org.au/2015/12/natalie-jeremijenko/

Lea, R. (2016). Making sense of the smart city standardization landscape. *IEEE E-Magazine*, 6(4). Retrieved from http://www.standardsuniversity.org/e-magazine/november-2016-volume-6-issue-4-smart-city-standards/making-sense-smart-city-standardization-landscape/

Lea, R. (2016b). Smart city standards: An overview. *UrbanOpus blog.* Retrieved from http://urbanopus.net/smart-city-standards-an-overview/

Lévy, J. (2014). Inhabiting. In R. Lee, N. Castree, R. Kitchin, V. Lawson, A. Paasi, C. Philo, ... C. W. J. Withers (Eds.), *The Sage handbook of human geography, Part I* (pp. 45–68). Thousand Oaks, CA: Sage. doi:10.4135/9781446247617.n4

Li, X., Cheng, S., Lv, Z., Song, H., Jia, T., & Lu, N. (2018). Data analytics of urban fabric metrics for smart cities. *Future Generation Computing Systems.*

Lombardi, P., Giordano, S., Farouh, H., & Yousef, W. (2012). Modelling the smart city performance. *Innovation (Abingdon)*, *25*(2), 137–149. doi:10.10 80/13511610.2012.660325

Marsal-Llacuna, M. L. (2015). Measuring the standardized definition of "smart city": A proposal on global metrics to set the terms of reference for urban "smartness". In Lecture Notes in Computer Science: Vol. 9156. *Computational science and its applications -- ICCSA 2015*. Cham: Springer. doi:10.1007/978-3-319-21407-8_42

McKenna, H. P. (2019). *Innovating metrics for smarter, responsive cities. Data*. Special Issue – Big Data Challenges in Smart Cities.

McKenna, H. P. (In Press). Awareness and smart cities implementation: Sensing, sensors, and the IoT in the public sector. In J. R. Gil-Garcia, T. A. Pardo, & M. Gasco (Eds.), *Beyond Smart and Connected Governments: Sensors and the Internet of Things in the Public Sector*. Springer.

Mollá-Sirvent, R. A., Mora, H., Gilart-Iglesias, V., Pérez-delHoyo, R., & Andújar-Montoya, M. D. (2018). Accessibility index for smart cities. *Proceedings*, *2*(19), 1219. doi:10.3390/proceedings2191219

Open University. (2018). *Smart city measurement: Metrics and indicators*. Smart Cities online course – Week 8. Retrieved 20 May 2018 from http://www. open.edu/openlearn/ocw/mod/oucontent/view.php?id=67889&section=1

Patel, A. (2017). Wonder as an interruption. *Conscious Cities*. Retrieved 23 April 2018 from https://www.ccities.org/wonder-as-an-interruption/

PSD. (2016). *2016 open cities index – top 20 results*. London, Canada: Public Sector Digest. Retrieved 19 December 2016 from https://publicsectordigest. com/2016-open-cities-index-top-20-results

Schmitt, G. (2015). *Information cities*. Retrieved from https://itunes.apple. com/us/book/information-cities/id970529491?mt=11

SMC. (2014). *Smart city index master indicators survey*. Reston, VA: Smart Cities Council. Retrieved 14 February 2019 from https://smartcitiescouncil. com/resources/smart-city-index-master-indicators-survey

WCCD. (2014). *The WCCD and ISO 37120: Created by cities, for cities – World Council on City Data: ISO 37120 the first international standard on city indicators.* Retrieved 19 December 2016 from http://www.cityindicators. org/Deliverables/WCCD%20Brochure_9-16-2014-178620.pdf

WCCD. (2017). *WCCD ISO 37120: Created by cities, for cities.* Toronto: Data for Cities, World Council on City Data. Retrieved 18 May 2018 from http://www.dataforcities.org/wccd/

Zygiaris, S. (2013). Smart city reference model: Assisting planners to conceptualize the building of smart city innovation ecosystems. *Journal of the Knowledge Economy, 4*(2), 217–231. doi:10.100713132-012-0089-4

ADDITIONAL READING

Beck, A. (2017). *Happiness as a (smart) city metric.* Smart City Council. Retrieved 22 June 2018 from https://anz.smartcitiescouncil.com/article/ happiness-smart-city-metric

Bennati, S., Dusparic, I., Shinde, R., & Jonker, C. M. (2018). *Volunteers in the smart city: Comparison of contribution strategies on human-centered measures.* Retrieved 22 June 2018 from https://arxiv.org/pdf/1805.09090.pdf

BSI. (2018). *Smart city standards and publications.* UK: BSI. Retrieved 22 June 2018 from https://www.bsigroup.com/en-GB/smart-cities/Smart-Cities-Standards-and-Publication/

CITI.IO. (2015). *A 21st century smart metrics guide for smart cities.* Retrieved 22 June 2018 from https://www.citi.io/2015/10/09/a-21st-century-smart-metrics-guide-for-smart-cities/

Dotti, G. (2016). How to measure the quality of life in smart cities? *Technology / Energy & Green Tech.* Retrieved 26 June 2018 from https://phys.org/ news/2016-04-quality-life-smart-cities.html

Hara, M., Nagao, T., Hannoe, S., & Nakamura, J. (2016). New key performance indicators for a smart sustainable city. *Sustainability, 8*(3), 206. doi:10.3390u8030206

UNECE. (2017). *United 4 smart sustainable cities: Collection methodology for key performance indicators for smart sustainable cities*. Retrieved 22 June 2018 from https://www.unece.org/fileadmin/DAM/hlm/documents/Publications/U4SSC-CollectionMethodologyforKPIfoSSC-2017.pdf

Zuccardi Merli, M., & Bonollo, E. (2014). Performance Measurement in the Smart Cities. In R. Dameri & C. Rosenthal-Sabroux (Eds.), *Smart City. Progress in IS*. Cham: Springer. doi:10.1007/978-3-319-06160-3_7

KEY TERMS AND DEFINITIONS

Ambient Indicators: Ambient indicators refer to more adaptive, dynamic, contextual, and responsive understandings of indicators in urban spaces, environments, and regions.

Ambient Indices: Ambient indices refer to more adaptive, dynamic, contextual, and responsive understandings of indices in urban spaces, environments, and regions.

Ambient Measures: Ambient measures refer to more adaptive, dynamic, contextual, and responsive understandings of measures in urban spaces, environments, and regions.

Ambient Metrics: Ambient metrics refer to more adaptive, dynamic, contextual, and responsive understandings of metrics in urban spaces, environments, and regions.

Ambient Standards: Ambient standards refer to more adaptive, dynamic, contextual, and responsive understandings of standards in urban spaces, environments, and regions.

Synthetic Indicators: Synthetic indicators refer to the use of inferential data for indicators in the absence of complete datasets.

Synthetic Indices: Synthetic indices refer to the use of inferential data for indices in the absence of complete datasets.

Section 4
A Synthesis and Future Directions

Chapter 10
Ambient Urbanities:
A Synthesis

ABSTRACT

The purpose of this chapter is to provide a synthesis in terms of the key elements emerging throughout this book related to the range of constructs and dimensions identified in Chapter 1 and explored chapter by chapter that contribute to and constitute ambient urbanities. The conceptual framework for ambient urbanities is revisited and revised to reflect additional elements, dimensions, and constructs that became salient during the study. The synthesis provides an overview of the fuller picture developed in each chapter, enabling a graphic depiction of the interrelated elements – constructs, ambient dimensions, aspects and components, and research and practice directions. Tabular views enable a comparative look at a range of elements in relation to dimensions and constructs, such as issues, controversies, and problems; dependent and independent variables; insights; ideas; lessons; and the value advanced. The modularity of the ambient urbanities framework is described for flexible and adaptive use going forward.

DOI: 10.4018/978-1-5225-7882-6.ch010

1. INTRODUCTION

The purpose of this chapter is to provide a synthesis of the key elements emerging throughout this book related to the range of constructs and dimensions identified in Chapter 1 and explored chapter by chapter, that contribute to and constitute ambient urbanities. The conceptual framework for ambient urbanities is revisited and revised to reflect additional elements, dimensions, and constructs that became salient during the study. The synthesis provides an overview of the fuller picture developed in each chapter, enabling a graphic depiction of the interrelated elements – constructs; ambient dimensions; aspects and components; and research and practice directions. Tabular views enable a comparative look at a range of elements in relation to dimensions and constructs, such as: issues, controversies, and problems; dependent and independent variables; insights; ideas; lessons; and the value advanced. The modularity of the ambient urbanities framework is described for flexible and adaptive use going forward.

Further, this chapter provides a summary of the book with commentary on the conceptual framework for ambient urbanities going forward. Openings are suggested for new paths of inquiry, along with evolving methodologies, approaches, and practices for understanding, complementing, and extending Internet infrastructures. As such, this chapter points to the potential for ambient urbanities to open new spaces for a rethinking of many aspects of urban life while introducing novel perspectives and frames of reference from culture, to sharing and collaboration, to metrics for the analysis of 21st century cities, to information management, to learning, to name a few. The conceptual framework for ambient urbanities is revisited and revised in providing guidance on future direction for practitioners at the urban level and for researchers.

Objectives: The objective of this chapter is to provide a summary of the book in terms of: an overview of the key constructs and dimensions contributing to and constituting ambient urbanities; a synthesis of issues, problems, and controversies; the value of the ambient urbanities perspective marking the emergence of the ambient turn involving aware people and aware technologies; and directions for practice and research.

1.1 Background

Highlighting the interdisciplinary nature of ambient urbanities, this chapter provides a synthesis of the research literature presented throughout the book on smart cities (Gil-Garcia, Pardo, and Nam, 2016) in combination with that on the ambient (McKenna, 2017; McCullough, 2013); human geography (Lévy, 2015), urbanization (Brenner, 2017), and urbanism (Lévy, 2015); and pervasive and aware technologies contributing to smartness in government (Gil-Carcia, Zhang, and Puron-Cid, 2016). Schmitt (2017) argues for a movement from smart cities to responsive cities, cognizant of people in support of the notion of ambient urbanities developed throughout this work.

1.2 Overview

This chapter provides a synthesis of ambient urbanities in Section 2, highlighting frameworks and sub-frameworks developed; issues, controversies, and problems; variables surfaced; and insights, ideas, lessons, and value. Section 3 provides an overview of future directions for practice and research going forward and Section 4 highlights key limitations and provides concluding comments.

The primary audiences for this chapter include students, educators, researchers, policy makers, urban practitioners, city managers, architects, businesses, and community members concerned with urban future potentials in support of more aware people and aware technologies in the context of smarter, more responsive cities in the face of increasingly complex urban challenges and opportunities.

2. AMBIENT URBANITIES

The synthesis provided in this chapter will begin with a revisiting of the ambient urbanities framework from Chapter 1 (Figure 4), highlighting the dimensions and constructs; key issues, controversies, and problems; frameworks developed and operationalized; conceptual frameworks advanced from the chapter by chapter urban level explorations; variables and indicators surfaced; key insights, ideas, and lessons; and the value to be gleaned from each chapter.

2.1 Ambient Urbanities Framework Revisited

This chapter revisits the conceptual framework for ambient urbanities developed in chapter one, as depicted in Figure 1, with a view to revising, based on the chapter by chapter dimensions and the array of constructs explored in relation to people, technologies, and cities through an interplay of the Internet of Things (IoT), the Internet of People (IoP), and the Internet of Experiences (IoE) featuring aware people and aware technologies. Implementation as ambient is added to the framework as an additional dimension, based on emerging work by McKenna (In Press). Other elements added to the framework are: inclusion of the Internet of Data (IoD) as part of the IoT-IoP-IoE dynamic; further development of the culture and economies dimension to include personalization; and expanding of the constructs to include InVisibilities. Throughout this book, sub-frameworks derived from the main framework in Figure 1, in combination with reviews of the research literature, are developed to guide the various ambient dimensions explored, including: sensing cities and getting smarter with the IoT, IoP, and IoE; emerging urban layers and spaces in smart cities; the ambient turn and smart cities; ambient learning, play, and inclusion; smart information architectures in smart cities; ambient methodologies and theoretical spaces; innovating privacy for smarter urbanities; and rethinking measures for smarter urbanities.

Figure 1. Conceptual framework for ambient urbanities revisited

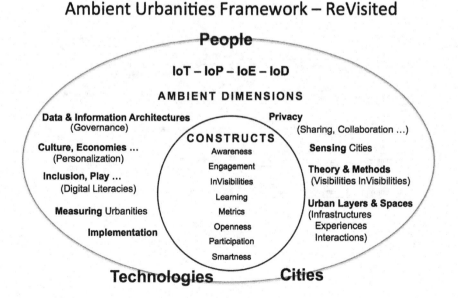

Additionally, explorations in each chapter result in the development of frameworks for future testing and validation including: ambient sensing in smart city urbanities; ambient engagement in smart city urbanities; ambient participation in smart city urbanities; ambient literacies in smart city urbanities; ambient information architectures, governance, and data in smart city urbanities; ambient in/visibilities in smart city urbanities; ambient privacy in smart city urbanities; and measuring ambient urbanities in smart cities. Depicted graphically, frameworks developed to guide exploration in this work, contributing to the development of frameworks intended to guide future research and practice, are presented in Figure 2.

Figure 3 presents an overview of the constructs, ambient dimensions, aspects and components, and research and practice directions on a chapter by chapter basis from Chapter 2 to Chapter 9.

This graphic enables a view of how the ambient urbanities framework functions using the constructs to explore a given dimension. The literature reviews reveal the aspects and components that emerge while the explorations conducted at the urban level in each chapter further enrich the literature in revealing research and practice directions.

Figure 2. Exploration frameworks leading to frameworks for use in research/practice

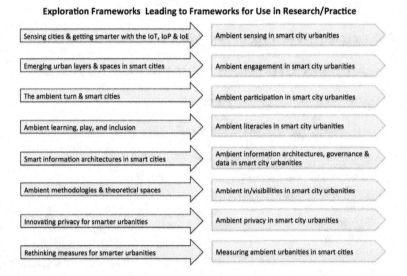

Figure 3. Chapter by chapter reveal of the ambient urbanities framework

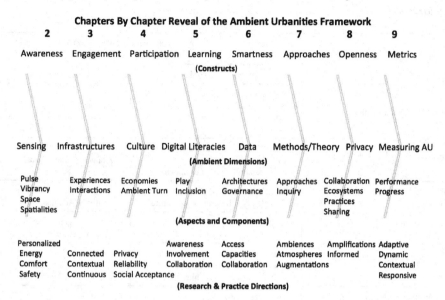

2.2 Synthesis of Issues, Controversies and Problems by Dimension and Construct

This work identified issues, controversies, and problems from a review of the research literature for each of the dimensions explored in relation to the construct guiding each exploration. Looking broadly and generally, a chapter by chapter comparative view of issues, controversies, and problems is presented in Table 1.

Issues and problems for urbanities and smart cities focus on complexities, digital traces, urban representations, and understandings of urbanity while controversies highlight tensions associated with vibrancy, liveliness, and density. Using the construct of awareness, issues and problems associated with sensing and the IoT, IoP, and IoE pertain to data reliability and trust as well as interoperability of the IoT and the social while controversies pertain to data generation and sensing. Using the construct of engagement, issues and problems associated with layers and infrastructures pertain to financing and competencies as well as to complexity, human infrastructures, and the seamful while controversies revolve around messiness, creativity, and adaptability. Using the construct of participation, issues and problems associated with cultures and economies pertain to co-creative partnerships and improvisatory activities while controversies emerge around awareness gaps and personal

Table 1. Issues, controversies, and problems for dimensions of ambient urbanities in smart cities

Dimensions and Constructs	Ambient Urbanities and Smart Cities: Issues, Controversies and Problems	
	Issues and Problems	Controversies
Urbanities & Smart Cities	• Complexities • Digital traces • Urban representations • Urbanity	• Tensions -vibrancy-liveliness & density
Sensing & the IoT, IoP, IoE Awareness	• Data reliability & trust (machine / human) • Interoperability of IoT & Social	• Data generation & sensing
Layers - Infrastructures Engagement	• Financing & Competencies • Complexity Infrastructures Seamful	• Messiness • Creativity/Adaptability
Culture, Economies Participation	• Co-creative partnerships • Improvisatory activities	• Awareness gap • Personal privacy
Digital Literacies, Play Learning	• Data trust / anxieties / safe enough • Uncertainties (digital data) • Social practices & learning	• Fragile ecology • Education / urbanism • Computational operatives
Data & Information Architectures Smartness	• Smart practices • Exposing, sharing, using data	• Data ownership & Control • Data relations, traces, rights
Methodologies & Theoretical Spaces In/Visibilities	• Ambiance & Densification • Urban models: discourse & invisibility	• Definition of urban • Sensing & Humans in the loop
Innovating Privacy Openness	• In/visible information & awareness • Privacy-Reliable-Social • Empowering users (agency & control) • Ubiquity Sensing Memory	• Creative city • Uncertainty & Change • Benefits-Risks-Openness • Privacy paradox
Measuring Ambient Urbanities Metrics	• Context & Multidimensionality • Synthetic indicators & Uncertainty	• Role of experts/people issues • The unmeasurable

privacy. Using the construct of learning, issues and problems associated with digital literacies and play pertain to data trust, anxieties, and uncertainties as well as to social practices and learning while controversies point to the fragile ecology, education and urbanism, and the notion of computational operatives. Using the construct of smartness, issues and problems associated with data and information architectures pertain to smart practices and exposing, sharing and using data while controversies center around data ownership and control and data relationships, traces, and rights. Using the construct of in/visibilities, issues and problems associated with methodologies and theoretical spaces pertain to urban models of discourse and invisibility and understandings of ambiance and densification while controversies focus on the definition of urban and the matter of sensing and enabling humans to be in the loop. Using the construct of openness, issues and problems associated with innovating privacy pertain to the in/visibilities of information and awareness, the notion of privacy-reliable-social, empowering users with agency and control, and notions of ubiquity-sensing-memory while controversies pertain to creative city, uncertainty and change, benefits-risk-openness, and the privacy paradox. Using the construct of metrics, issues and problems associated with measuring ambient urbanities pertain to context and multidimensionality along with synthetic indicators and data uncertainties while controversies center around the role of experts and ordinary citizens as well as the unmeasurable.

This tabular summary reveals a rich array of emerging and recurring themes pertaining to complexities, context, data, density, invisibility, uncertainty, along with many other people-centered concerns and tensions. As such, this initial comparative glimpse is suggestive of emergent openings in many areas requiring future research along with challenges and opportunities for practice.

Summarized in Figure 4, a glimpse of patterns, flows, relationships, and possibilities begin to emerge, contributing to a synthesis for ambient urbanities through complexities, contextuality, trust, and uncertainty, depicted on a spectrum in smart cities.

Complexities are highlighted in relation to architectures, collaboration and sharing, innovation, in/visibilities, and representations. Contextuality points to the digital, collaboration and sharing, interoperability, in/visibilities,

Figure 4. Ambient urbanities: A synthesis

Ambient Urbanities: A Synthesis

	Complexities	Contextuality	Trust	Uncertainty

People (aware)

|

IoP IoT IoE IoD

|

Technologies (aware)

-------------Architectures--------Digital-------Data----------Infrastructures-----

---------Collaboration & Sharing--

------------------------------Interoperability----------------------------------

--Innovation--

----------------In/Visibilities---

--Measures--------------------------------

---Privacy--------------

-------Representations ---

---Tensions-------------

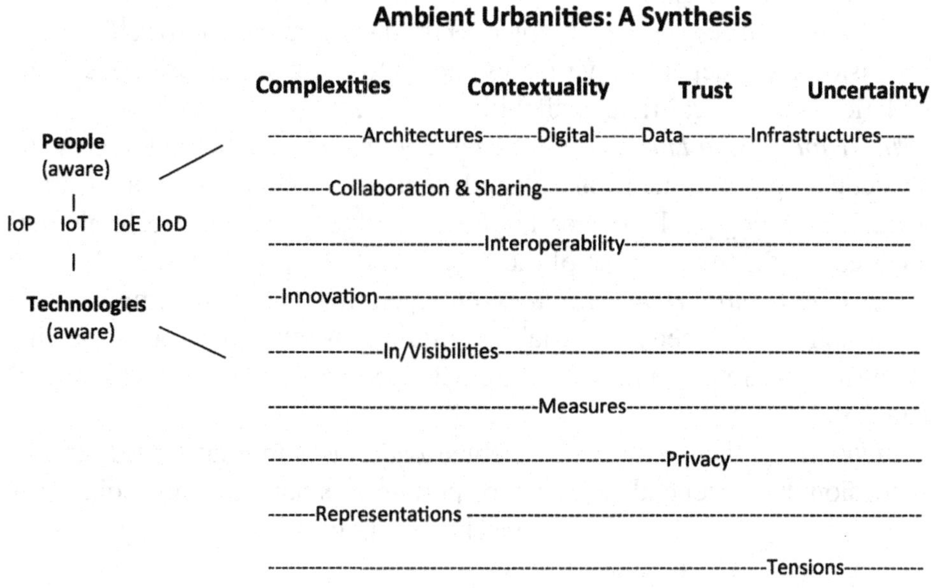

measures, and representations. Trust emerges in relation to data and privacy while uncertainty appears in relation to infrastructures, privacy, and tensions. The spectrum for each category is necessarily incomplete and intended only as a summary overview.

2.3 Synthesis of Variables for Ambient Urbanities

Table 2 provides an overview of dependent variables surfaced for each dimension of the ambient urbanities framework along with associated independent variables.

For the sensing and the IoT, IoP, and IoE dimension, *awareness and affect* emerged as the dependent variable and the associated independent variables pertain to the body insight scale (BIS) used and feelings of comfort, safety, and tension in the city.

Engagement and personalization emerged for the layers and infrastructures dimension and independent variables pertain to connection, social capital, and continuous informed awareness.

Participation and personalization emerged for the culture and economies dimension and independent variables pertain to the creative impulse, smart city thought processes, rewarding participation, and improvisations for privacy in social media spaces.

Learning and experiences emerged for the digital literacies, play, and inclusion dimension and independent variables pertain to use, friendliness, animation, and designing for interactivity in urban spaces.

Smartness and capacities emerged for the data & information architectures dimension and independent variables pertain to using data, data delivery and analytics, and the real-time availability of data.

In/Visibilities and urban approaches emerged for the methodologies and theoretical spaces dimension and independent variables pertain to urban design, animating public spaces, augmenting of meetings with technologies, and creating the visual sense of the city.

Openness and urban practices emerged for the innovating privacy dimension and independent variables pertain to what's going on in the city, concurrent awareness, understanding what people want, and making use of data.

Metrics and motion/movement emerged for the measuring ambient urbanities dimension and independent variables pertain to smartness thresholds, city objectives aligned with metrics, benchmarking of smart city progress over time, and activities in urban spaces.

Table 2. Synthesis of variables by dimension for ambient urbanities in smart cities

Dependent and Independent Variables	
Dimensions and Dependent Variables	**Independent Variables**
Sensing & the IoT, IoP, IoE *Awareness & Affect*	• Feelings of comfort and urban elements • Feelings of safety and sense of the city • Feelings of tension and urban experience
Layers - Infrastructures *Engagement and Personalization*	• Connecting all the pieces • Spaces for the generation of social capital • Spaces for continuous informed awareness
Culture, Economies *Participation and Personalization*	• Support for the creative impulse • Smart city thought process • Rewarding participation • Veracity of social media data as a privacy workaround
Digital Literacies, Play *Learning and Experiences*	• Use • Friendliness • Animation • Designing for interactivity in urban spaces
Data & Information Architectures *Smartness and Capacities*	• Using data • Data delivery • Data analytics • Real-time availability of data
Methodologies & Theoretical Spaces *In/Visibilities and Urban Approaches*	• Urban design • Animating public spaces • Augmenting of meetings with technologies • Visual sense of the city
Innovating Privacy *Openness and Urban Practices*	• What's going on in the city • Concurrent awareness • Understanding what people what • Make use of data
Measuring Ambient Urbanities *Metrics and Motion/Movement*	• Smartness thresholds • Objectives aligned with metrics • Benchmarking over time • Activities in urban spaces

2.4 Synthesis of Insights, Ideas, Lessons, and Value

A synthesis of insights emerging from this work, organized by dimensions and constructs, is presented in Table 3. This is followed by a synthesis for ideas in Table 4, a synthesis for lessons in Table 5, and a synthesis for value contributed by this work in Table 6.

For urbanities and smart cities, insights pertain to the rich history of research associated with urbanity, the importance of extending urbanity to accommodate technology-rich spaces, and ambient urbanities as an approach and framework for fostering more aware and informed people. For the sensing and the IoT, IoP, and IoE dimension, insights pertain to multi-sensory capabilities to

Table 3. Synthesis of insights for ambient urbanities in smart cities

Insights for Ambient Urbanities in Smart Cities	
Dimensions and Constructs	**Insights**
Urbanities & Smart Cities	• The rich history of research associated with urbanity • Extend understandings of urbanity to accommodate technology-rich spaces • Ambient urbanities as approach/framework to foster aware/informed people
Sensing & the IoT, IoP, IoE *Awareness*	• Multi-sensory capabilities to inform urban designs, experiences & smartness • The interconnectedness & interrelationships of the IoT, IoP & IoE • Variables associated with *awareness and affect* for sensing in smart cities
Layers - Infrastructures *Engagement*	• Meaningful engagement opportunities to inform urban layers & spaces • The interconnectedness of infrastructures, experiences, and interactions • Variables associated with *engagement & personalization* for urban layers
Culture, Economies *Participation*	• Meaningful participation opportunities to inform urban understandings • Interconnectedness of culture, economies & everything as ambient • Variables associated with *participation & personalization* in urban spaces
Digital Literacies, Play *Learning*	• Meaningful learning-play-inclusion opportunities to inform digital literacies • Interconnectedness of learning-play-inclusion as ambient literacies • Variables associated with *learning & experiences* in digital urban spaces
Data & Information Architectures *Smartness*	• Meaningful access, involvement & collaboration to inform urban awareness • Interrelatedness of info architectures, infrastructures, governance & data • Variables associated with *smartness & capacities* in evolving urban spaces
Methodologies & Theoretical Spaces *In/Visibilities*	• Opportunities to make the invisible visible in understandings of smart cities • Ambiances, atmospheres & augmentations interplay to make invisible visible • Variables for *in/visibilities & urban approaches* informing theory & practice
Innovating Privacy *Openness*	• Meaningful openness opportunities to inform evolving urban understandings • Interconnectedness of collaboration, openness, privacy & sharing as ambient • Variables associated with *openness & urban practices* in urban spaces
Measuring Ambient Urbanities *Metrics*	• Meaningful metrics providing opportunities to inform ambient urbanities • Interconnectedness of metrics, standards, indicators & indices as ambient • Variables for *metrics & motion/movement* in measuring ambient urbanities

inform urban designs, experiences, and smartness; the interconnectedness and interrelationships of the IoT, IoP, and IoE; and variables associated with awareness and affect for sensing in smart cities. For the layers and infrastructures dimension, insights pertain to meaningful engagement opportunities; the interconnectedness of infrastructures, experiences, and interactions; and variables associated with engagement and personalization. For culture and economies, insights pertain to meaningful participation opportunities; the interconnectedness of culture, economies and everything as ambient; and variables associated with participation and personalization. For the digital literacies, play and inclusion dimension, insights pertain to meaningful learning-play-inclusion; the interconnectedness of learning-play-inclusion as ambient literacies; and variables associated with learning and experiences. For the data and information architectures dimension, insights pertain to meaningful access, involvement, and collaboration; the interrelatedness of information architectures, infrastructures, governance, and data; and variables associated with smartness and capacities. For the methodologies and theoretical spaces dimension, insights pertain to opportunities for making the invisible visible; the interplay of ambiances, atmospheres, and augmentations for making the invisible visible; and variables associated with in/visibilities and urban approaches. For the innovating privacy dimension, insights pertain to meaningful openness opportunities; the interconnectedness of collaboration, openness, privacy, and sharing; and variables associated with openness and urban practices. For the measuring ambient urbanities dimension, insights pertain to meaningful metrics; the interconnectedness of metrics, standards, indicators, and indices as ambient; and variables associated with metrics and motion/movement.

A synthesis of ideas emerging from this work, organized by dimensions and constructs, is presented in Table 4.

For urbanities and smart cities, ideas pertain to more aware people as a fundamental element of ambient urbanities; people interacting with each other and through aware technologies; and the ambient concept for aiding understandings of smart spaces and interactions. For the sensing and IoT-IoP-IoE dimension, ideas pertain to multi-sensory capabilities in urban spaces; aware technologies benefiting from aware people; and ambient sensing as an integrating element for aware people and technologies. For the layers and infrastructures dimension, ideas pertain to people as more aware of infrastructure elements; the value of experiences and interactions in digital spaces; and ambient engagement as an integrative approach on an ambient spectrum. For culture and economies, ideas pertain to the importance of people becoming more aware of the ambient turn and the smart city phenomena; the importance of people being rewarded (valued) for participating in digital/physical urban spaces; and ambient participation as a novel approach. For the digital literacies, play and inclusion dimension, ideas pertain to the awareness of learning-play-inclusion as key digital literacies; the importance of support and funding for learning and digital literacies in urban spaces; and ambient literacies as a novel approach. For the data and information architectures dimension, ideas pertain to building ambient capacities; people as capacity builders; and ambient information as a novel approach. For the methodologies and theoretical spaces dimension, ideas pertain to awareness of the invisible and intangible; people shedding light on invisible spaces; and ambient inquires as a novel approach to the study and practice of urbanities. For the innovating privacy dimension, ideas pertain to ambient practices; ambient ecosystems for collaboration, privacy and sharing; and ambient practices as a novel approach. For the measuring ambient urbanities dimension, ideas pertain to ambient metrics; people rewarded/valued for participation, contributing to ambient metrics; and ambient metrics as a novel approach.

A synthesis of lessons emerging from this work, organized by dimensions and constructs, is presented in Table 5.

For urbanities and smart cities, lessons pertain to the transformative potential; the use of constructs to guide and explore; and adaptive and cross-domain mindsets. For the sensing and IoT-IoP-IoE dimension, lessons pertain to sensing by aware people to augment aware systems; and aware systems to enhance multi-sensorial capabilities. For the layers and infrastructures dimension, lessons pertain to meaningful engagement experiences to influence and augment aware technologies; and aware technologies to enhance engagement.

Table 4. Synthesis of ideas for ambient urbanities in smart cities

Ideas for Ambient Urbanities in Smart Cities	
Dimensions and Constructs	**Ideas**
Urbanities & Smart Cities	• More aware people as a fundamental element of ambient urbanities • Value of people interacting with each other & through aware technologies • Ambient concept for aiding understandings of smart spaces & interactions
Sensing & the IoT, IoP, IoE *Awareness*	• People becoming more aware of multi-sensorial capabilities in urban spaces • Urban spaces infused with aware technologies benefiting from aware people • Ambient sensing as an integrating element for aware people & technologies
Layers - Infrastructures *Engagement*	• People as more aware of infrastructure elements in urban layers & spaces • People benefit from the value of experiences & interactions in digital spaces • Ambient engagement as an integrative approach on an ambient spectrum
Culture, Economies *Participation*	• People becoming aware of the ambient turn & the smart cities phenomena • People rewarded (valued) for participating in digital/physical urban spaces • Ambient participation as a novel approach to smarter cities & urbanities
Digital Literacies, Play *Learning*	• People becoming aware of learning-play-inclusion as key digital literacies • People supported (funded) for learning & digital literacies in urban spaces • Ambient literacies as a novel approach to smarter cities & ambient urbanities
Data & Information Architectures *Smartness*	• People becoming aware of the notion of ambient capacities for smarter cities • People recognized as capacity builders in digital/physical urban spaces • Ambient information as a novel approach to smarter cities & urbanities
Methodologies & Theoretical Spaces *In/Visibilities*	• People becoming aware of the invisible & intangible aspects of smart cities • People as shedding light on invisible spaces in digital/physical urban spaces • Ambient inquiries as a novel approach to the study & practice of urbanities
Innovating Privacy *Openness*	• People becoming more aware of the notion of ambient practices • People as aware of ambient ecosystems for collaboration, privacy & sharing • Ambient practices as a novel approach to smarter cities & ambient urbanities
Measuring Ambient Urbanities *Metrics*	• People becoming more aware of ambient metrics & the ambient turn • People rewarded (valued) for participation, contributing to ambient metrics • Ambient literacies as a novel approach to smarter cities & ambient urbanities

Table 5. Synthesis of lessons for ambient urbanities in smart cities

Lessons for Ambient Urbanities in Smart Cities	
Dimensions and Constructs	**Lessons**
Urbanities & Smart Cities	• Transformative potential of the ambient urbanities conceptualization • Constructs to guide, explore & understand dimensions of ambient urbanities • Adaptive & cross-domain mindsets for people acting in smart environments
Sensing & the IoT, IoP, IoE *Awareness*	• Sensing by people in urban environments to augment aware systems • Aware systems to enhance the multi-sensorial capabilities of people • The vast array of issues, controversies & problems for the IoT, IoP & IoE
Layers - Infrastructures *Engagement*	• Meaningful engagement experiences to influence & augment aware tech • Aware technologies to enhance engagement for people in urban spaces • Myriad issues, controversies & problems for infrastructures & experiences
Culture, Economies *Participation*	• Meaningful participation to influence & be influenced by aware technologies • Aware tech to enhance participation possibilities & ambient creativity • Issues, controversies & problems for culture, economies & the ambient turn
Digital Literacies, Play *Learning*	• Meaningful learning-play-inclusion to influence/be influenced by aware tech • Aware tech to enhance learning-play-inclusion potentials in urban spaces • Issues, controversies & problems for play, inclusion & digital literacies
Data & Information Architectures *Smartness*	• Smarter access, involvement & collaboration influencing aware technologies • Aware tech enhancing smartness possibilities for people in urban spaces • Issues, controversies & problems for info architectures, governance & data
Methodologies & Theoretical Spaces *In/Visibilities*	• Approaches to making the invisible visible influencing aware technologies • Aware tech to enhance possibilities for people in making the invisible visible • Issues, controversies & problems for methodologies & theory as ambient
Innovating Privacy *Openness*	• Ambient privacy influencing aware tech & design of spaces: choices & actions • Aware tech to enhance openness possibilities for people in urban spaces • Issues, controversies & problems: privacy & sharing in smart spaces
Measuring Ambient Urbanities *Metrics*	• Measuring ambient urbanities to influence & be influenced by aware tech • Aware tech enhancing participation for people as more directly involved in the design and development of measuring ambient urbanities • Issues, controversies & problems for measuring the ambient

For culture and economies, lessons pertain to meaningful participation to influence and be influenced by aware technologies; and the importance of aware technologies to enhance participation possibilities and ambient creativity. For the digital literacies, play and inclusion dimension, lessons pertain to meaningful learning-play-inclusion to influence and be influenced by aware technologies; and the importance of aware technologies to enhance learning-play-inclusion potentials. For the data and information architectures dimension, lessons pertain to smarter access, involvement, and collaboration; and aware technologies enhancing smartness possibilities for people. For the methodologies and theoretical spaces dimension, lessons pertain to approaches to making the invisible visible; and the potential for aware technologies to enhance possibilities for people in making the invisible visible.

For the innovating privacy dimension, lessons pertain to the potential for the ambient privacy notion to influence aware technologies and the design of urban spaces affording choices and actions; and the potential for aware technologies to enhance openness possibilities. For the measuring ambient urbanities dimension, lessons pertain to the potential for influencing aware technologies; and for enhancing participation to more directly involve people in the design and development. With all dimensions, a key lesson is the vast array of issues, problems, and controversies.

A synthesis of value emerging from this work, organized by dimensions and constructs, is presented in Table 6.

For urbanities and smart cities, value in this work pertains to development of the ambient urbanities concept; the novelty of the operationalization of the framework for smart cities; and use of the framework as a guide to involving people more meaningfully and directly in smart cities. For the sensing and IoT-IoP-IoE dimension, value pertains to use of the body insight scale (BIS) as a method for data generation and the comparing of experiences in the city for comfort, safety, and tension. For the layers and infrastructures dimension, value pertains to new forms of value associated with infrastructures,

Table 6. Synthesis of value for ambient urbanities in smart cities

Value for Ambient Urbanities in Smart Cities	
Dimensions and Constructs	**Value**
Urbanities & Smart Cities	• Development of the ambient urbanities concept • Novelty of operationalization of the framework for smart cities • Use of framework as guide to involve people more meaningfully & directly
Sensing & the IoT, IoP, IoE *Awareness*	• BIS for data & comparing experiences of the city comfort, safety, tension
Layers - Infrastructures *Engagement*	• New forms of value associated with infrastructures, experiences, interactions
Culture, Economies *Participation*	• Variables for intangible & invisible elements of ambient urbanities
Digital Literacies, Play *Learning*	• Variables for urban use, friendliness, animation & designing for interactivity
Data & Information Architectures *Smartness*	• Variable of *smartness & capacities* for info architectures, governance & data
Methodologies & Theory Spaces *In/Visibilities*	• Variable of *in/visibilities & urban approaches* for methodologies & theory
Innovating Privacy *Openness*	• Variable of *openness & urban practices* & city related variables
Measuring Ambient Urbanities *Metrics*	• Urban theorizing in aware environments & for measuring ambient urbanities

experiences, and interactions. For culture and economies, value pertains to variables for intangible and invisible elements of ambient urbanities. For the digital literacies, play and inclusion dimension, value pertains to variables for use, friendliness, animation, and designing for interactivity. For the data and information architectures dimension, value pertains to the variable of smartness and capacities for information architectures, governance, and data. For the methodologies and theoretical spaces dimension, value pertains to the variable of in/visibilities and urban approaches. For the innovating privacy dimension, value pertains to the variable of openness and urban practices and city related variables. For the measuring ambient urbanities dimension, value pertains to urban theorizing in aware environments and approaches for measuring ambient urbanities.

2.5 The Ambient Urbanities Framework and Associated Frameworks

The ambient urbanities framework serves as a guide for explorations of all aspects of ambient urbanities and affords the development of associated frameworks for the multiple dimensions. As such, the ambient urbanities framework affords modularity and flexibility while adaptive reuse is encouraged. Looking to the future, the framework accommodates application to future directions for practice and research summarized in Section 3.

3. FUTURE DIRECTIONS

Future directions for practice and research emerging from this work are presented in Table 7 in the form of a synthesis of elements. Directions common to both practice and research include: use of the body insight scale (BIS); ambient engagement; ambient participation; ambient challenges and opportunities; ambient literacies; ambient information architecture, governance, and data; ambient in/visibilities; ambient privacy; and measuring ambient urbanities.

Future directions for research include: ambient sensing; intuitive inquiry; the ambient turn; smart information architectures, governance, and data; ambient capacities; ambient methodologies and theoretical spaces; ambient approaches; ambient inquiry; innovating privacy for smarter urbanities; ambient ecosystems; ambient practices; rethinking measures for smarter urbanities; ambient performance; and ambient progress.

Table 7. Synthesis of future directions for practice and research

Future Directions for Practice and Research	
Practice	**Research**
Body Insight Scale (BIS)	• Ambient Sensing • Body Insight Scale (BIS) • Intuitive Inquiry
Ambient Engagement	• Ambient Engagement
Ambient Participation Ambient Challenges & Opportunities	• Ambient Participation • Ambient Turn • Ambient Challenges & Smart Cities • Ambient Opportunities & Smart Cities
Ambient Literacies	• Ambient Literacies - Ambient Learning; Ambient Play; Ambient Inclusion
Ambient Info Architectures, Governance & Data	• Smart Information Architectures, Governance & Data • Ambient Information Architectures, Governance & Data - Access, Collaboration & Involvement • Ambient Capacities
Ambient In/Visibilities	• Ambient Methodologies & Theoretical Spaces • Ambient In/Visibilities - Ambiences, Atmospheres & Augmentations • Ambient Approaches • Ambient Inquiry
Ambient Privacy	• Innovating Privacy for Smarter Urbanities • Ambient Privacy – Amplifications, Informed • Ambient Ecosystems • Ambient Practices
Measuring Ambient Urbanities	• Rethinking Measures for Smarter Urbanities - Adaptive, Dynamic, Contextual & Responsive • Measuring Ambient Urbanities • Ambient Performance • Ambient Progress

Additionally, future research directions associated with ambient literacies include: ambient learning, ambient play, and ambient inclusion. Future research directions associated with ambient information architectures include: access, collaboration and involvement. Future research directions associated with ambient in/visibilities include: ambiences, atmospheres and augmentations. Future research directions associated with rethinking measures for smarter urbanities include: adaptive, dynamic, contextual and responsive.

Because the ambient urbanities framework is highly integrated with the Internet in terms of the IoT, IoP, IoE, and IoD and existing computing approaches and platforms, it is conceivable that requirements exist to support other emerging paradigms such as quantum computing and other forms of energy grids. As such, Chapter 11 offers a glimpse of ambient urbanities and beyond with the framework able to operate in parallel and complementary fashion with other frameworks.

4. CONCLUSION

This chapter provides an overview and synthesis of evolving understandings of ambient urbanities for smart cities emerging from the previous nine chapters. This chapter makes several contributions in that it: a) provides a synthesis of the ambient urbanities framework and associated frameworks developed chapter by chapter in this work; b) shows how exploration frameworks lead to the development of frameworks for research and practice; and c) presents a chapter by chapter reveal of the ambient urbanities framework including constructs, dimensions, aspects and components, and research and practice directions while providing a synthesis of emergent elements in the form of variables, insights, ideas, lessons, and value. From the synthesis of issues, problems, and controversies emerging from the reviews of the research literature across the nine chapters and the insights, ideas, and lessons based on the urban level study conducted, a synthesis of future directions for practice and research is provided.

Limitations of this work related to the abstract nature of ambient urbanities and smart cities in relation to the invisible and the intangible are mitigated by actual examples from the research literature and in-depth discussions with a range of individuals regarding everyday emergent practices. Limitations of this work related to literature review domain coverage are mitigated by the interdisciplinary potential to extend this work to other areas going forward. Similarly, while the individuals contributing to underlying survey, interviews, and discussions for this work are limited to small to medium to large sized cities mostly in Canada and extending also to other countries, the potential exists for undertaking further work in additional countries; megacities and regions exceeding populations of ten million people; and metacities (UN-Habitat, 2006; Kostaropoulou, 2017) with populations exceeding twenty million people. The challenge of studying emergent, dynamic, and evolving constructs and concepts such as ambient urbanities and as yet fully defined concepts such as smart cities are mitigated by opportunities to explore the making of openings and spaces for innovative potentials going forward.

What Is Missing?

This first edition of ambient urbanities is by no means complete and gaps are already evident. For example, areas to be explored going forward include robotics, the smart home, and the blurring of private and public spaces. As indicated in Section 3 of this chapter, a glimpse beyond ambient urbanities and current integrations with the Internet will be addressed in the concluding chapter, Chapter 11, where the ambient urbanities framework accommodates use in parallel and complementary fashion with other emerging frameworks.

A key take-away from this chapter is the importance of the ambient turn as a critical moment in history for people, technologies, and cities/urban spaces and regions, at the juncture of aware people and aware technologies in smart cities.

This work will be of interest to a broad audience including city managers, students, educators, researchers, urban planners, information technology developers, practitioners and anyone concerned with evolving and innovating understandings of urbanities in support of more aware people and aware technologies in meeting the complex urban challenges and opportunities of smarter, more responsive urbanities.

REFERENCES

Brenner, N. (2017). *Critique of urbanization: Selected essays.* Basel, Switzerland: Birkhauser.

Gil-Garcia, J. R., Pardo, T. A., & Nam, T. (2016). A comprehensive view of the 21st century city: Smartness as technologies and innovation in urban contexts. In J. R. Gil-Garcia, T. A. Pardo, & T. Nam (Eds.), *Smarter as the new urban agenda: A comprehensive view of the 21st century city* (Vol. 11, pp. 1–19). Springer. doi:10.1007/978-3-319-17620-8_1

Gil-Garcia, J. R., Zhang, J., & Puron-Cid, G. (2016). Conceptualizing smartness in government: An integrative and multi-dimensional view. *Government Information Quarterly.*

Kostaropoulou, M. (2017). Cities as meta-cities. *Conscious Cities.* Retrieved 23 April 2018 from https://www.ccities.org/cities-meta-cities/

Lévy, J. (2015). Urbanisation and urbanism. In EPFLx: SpaceX Exploring Humans' Space: An Introduction to Geographicity. Massive Open Online Course (MOOC), edX, Fall.

McCullough, M. (2013). *Ambient commons: Attention in the age of embodied information.* Cambridge, MA: The MIT Press. doi:10.7551/mitpress/8947.001.0001

McKenna, H. P. (2017). Urbanizing the ambient: Why people matter so much in smart cities. In S. Konomi & G. Roussos (Eds.), *Enriching urban spaces with ambient computing, the Internet of Things, and smart city design* (pp. 209–231). Hershey, PA: IGI Global. doi:10.4018/978-1-5225-0827-4.ch011

McKenna, H. P. (In Press). Awareness and smart cities implementation: Sensing, sensors, and the IoT in the public sector. In J. R. Gil-Garcia, T. A. Pardo, & M. Gasco (Eds.), *Beyond Smart and Connected Governments: Sensors and the Internet of Things in the Public Sector*. Springer.

Schmitt, G. (2017). *Future Cities*. MOOC (Massive Open Online Course). Zurich, Switzerland: ETHzurich. Retrieved 11 December 2017 from https://www.edx.org/course/future-cities-ethx-fc-01x

UN-Habitat. (2006). *Urbanization: Mega & meta cities, new city states?* Retrieved 23 April 2018 from http://mirror.unhabitat.org/documents/media_centre/sowcr2006/SOWCR%202.pdf

KEY TERMS AND DEFINITIONS

Ambient Spectrum: The ambient spectrum acknowledges the dynamic and adaptive movement and progress of people and cities in relation to aware technologies and ecosystems.

Chapter 11
Ambient Urbanities and Beyond:
Perspectives Going Forward

ABSTRACT

The purpose of this chapter is to provide a review of the research literature for works that are pushing the boundaries of smart cities in providing a glimpse of perspectives going forward. This chapter focuses on ambient explorations, microgrids and smartgrids, wise cities, and the quantum concept in shedding light on the evolving nature of the people-technologies-cities dynamic for more adaptive urban environments, characteristic of smart and responsive cities. Using an exploratory case study approach, solutions and recommendations are advanced. An analysis is provided of issues, controversies, and problems along with a discussion of the solutions and recommendations offered. Perspectives emerge for looking beyond and into the future of ambient urbanities in identifying potential directions for practitioners and researchers. This chapter makes a contribution to 1) the research literature for smart cities and future cities and 2) perspectives beyond ambient urbanities that encompass parallel and complementary potentials for smarter urbanities.

DOI: 10.4018/978-1-5225-7882-6.ch011

1. INTRODUCTION

The purpose of this chapter is to provide a review of the research literature for works that are pushing the boundaries of smart cities in providing a glimpse of perspectives going forward. This chapter focuses on ambient explorations, microgrids and smartgrids, wise cities, and the quantum concept in shedding light on the evolving nature of the people-technologies-cities dynamic for more adaptive urban environments, characteristic of smart and responsive cities. Using an exploratory case study approach, solutions and recommendations are advanced. An analysis is provided of issues, controversies, and problems along with a discussion of the solutions and recommendations offered. Perspectives emerge for looking beyond and into the future of ambient urbanities in identifying potential directions for practitioners and researchers. This chapter makes a contribution to: a) the research literature for smart cities and future cities; and b) perspectives beyond ambient urbanities that encompass parallel and complementary potentials for smarter urbanities.

Further, this chapter suggests new paths of inquiry, along with evolving methodologies, approaches, and practices for understanding, complementing, extending, and moving beyond Internet infrastructures (e.g., through smartgrids/microgrids, etc.). As such, ambient urbanities open new spaces, perspectives, and frames of reference for a rethinking of many aspects of urban life from culture, to sharing and collaboration, to metrics for the analysis of 21st century cities, to information management, to learning, and so on. Additionally, the conceptual framework for ambient urbanities is further enriched, providing guidance on future direction for both practitioners and researchers.

Objectives: The objective of this chapter is to provide a look beyond and into the future of ambient urbanities. As such, the key research question posed is – How and why are ambient and quantum elements important for ambient urbanities in smart cities and beyond?

2. BACKGROUND AND OVERVIEW

Highlighting the interdisciplinary nature of ambient urbanities, this chapter provides a look to the future, beyond structures such as the Internet to microgrids/smartgrids (McCullough, 2015a; McCullough, 2015b). Baude (2016), for example, focuses on the ends of the Internet while Schmitt (2017) argues for a movement from smart cities to responsive cities, cognizant of people. Williams (2017) argues for a movement from smart cities to wise cities to incorporate a more human-centered perspective. Hunter (2018) predicts that ambient contextuality will be "the next big game changer in technology interface" as in "enabling a reliable conversational interaction with technology in order to overcome the friction humans experience when we use our modern tools" from "apps, phones, cars or semi-autonomous coffee makers." Evolving directions for the ambient are highlighted in an experiment on "emergent forms of literature" described by Schwab (2018) and referred to as ambient literature, designed to "make use of novel technologies and social practices to create more robust and evocative experiences for readers."

2.1 Definitions

For the purposes of this work, definitions for key terms used in this chapter are presented here based on the research literature.

- **Ambient Contextuality:** Hunter (2018) claims that ambient contextuality is connected to the notion that "there is information hidden all around us that helps clarify our intent in any given conversation."
- **Ambient Literature:** In describing ambient literature, Dovey (2016) speaks of "a situated literary experience that begins in our general sense of and immersion in the ambience of a situation, which may then be subtly manipulated to produce modes of attention that become immersive through the way they make cultural experiences from ambient materials."
- **Microgrids:** McCullough (2015a) describes the microgrid as "clean, local, physically integrated and highly adaptable" where "today's re-electrification is mainly a revolution of use."
- **Quantum City:** Schmitt (2015) explains that, "the definition of the quantum city expression is not complete yet" and, citing the work of Arida (2002), indicates that it "explores the metaphorical relationship between quantum theory, urban design, and the concept of the city."

2.2 Overview

This chapter provides a range of perspectives in Section 3 on ambient explorations, microgrids and smartgrids, smart cities and wise cities, and quantum cities in the context of emerging and evolving understandings of smart, responsive, and future cities, followed by an overview of associated issues, controversies, and problems. Section 4 provides a conceptual framework for ambient urbanities and beyond; use of this framework is advanced as a mechanism for operationalization of the exploration in this chapter in identifying the potential for solutions and recommendations; and the advancing of a framework for ambient, grid, and quantum urbanities in smart, future city. Section 5 identifies future directions for research and practice and Section 6 concludes with chapter coverage highlights, the major contributions, and the key insights, ideas, and lessons.

The primary audiences for this chapter include students, educators, researchers, policy makers, futurists, urban practitioners, and community members concerned with urban potentials going forward in support of more aware people and aware technologies in the context of smarter, more responsive, and future cities in the face of contemporary urban challenges and opportunities.

3. AMBIENT URBANITIES

Pushing the edges of ambient urbanities, this chapter provides a review of the research literature for ambient explorations; microgrids and smartgrids; smart cities and wise cities; and quantum cities.

3.1 Ambient Explorations

The Institute For The Future (Jensen, 2016) explores technology horizons in relation to ambient resources where "workspaces will sense our presence and dynamically pull information to enhance the ways we collaborate." Jensen (2016) envisions a movement toward an Internet of Actions where "we will redefine our relationship with the physical world and the digital intelligence that powers it." Looking to future potentials, augmented by technologies, the IFTF (2017) suggests that, "our objects and spaces become as anticipatory and personalized as our communications streams" such that "the ways we interact with the physical world will only be limited by our imaginations" contributing to emerging understandings of "ambient communications." Harrison (2017a) claims to be searching for a theory of cities, believing that "since cities are becoming the platforms for almost all of human life" what is needed "will be a Theory of Everything." Additionally, Harrison (2017b) claims to be "strongly in favour of Augmented Intelligence or Intelligence Amplification (IA)" as "the collaboration between machine intelligence and human specialists" and is "confident that through Augmented Intelligence we will develop an overall theory of cities that will provide far deeper insights into how technology can help cities achieve their goals." Naunes, Sá Silva, and Boavida (2018) claim that, "it is likely that human-machine collaboration will play an important role in future technologies." Hunter (2018) argues that, "to achieve truly conversational interactions" the answers to "deeper questions like how and why" will "need to be captured" and "also learned and retained." As such, for Hunter (2018) "the challenge now is to make our machines 'speak' human – to imbue them with context and inference and informality so that conversation flows naturally" in "reducing interface friction" in support of "responsibly developed and useful conversations with our technological world."

The Ambient Literature project (AmbientLit, 2018) is described as work "focused on the study of emergent forms of literature that make use of novel technologies and social practices in order to create robust and evocative experiences for readers." The AmbientLit project (2018) is said to "allow researchers to study the processes of innovation and negotiation that become visible" through "new forms opened up by the idea of ambient literature." Described as "an interdisciplinary project focused on understanding how the situation of reading is changing through pervasive and ubiquitous computing", the project gives rise to questions such as "what happens when data aspires to literary form?" and "what does it mean when the place where you're reading becomes the stage for the story?" and "how might writing, reading and the idea of the book itself change when we use technology to design stories, rather than just present them?" When undertaking the ambient literature research project in 2016, Abba (2018) acknowledged that, "we don't know what ambient literature is" adding that, "we've started to map the territory, to define by identifying borders and by testing the edges." However, in articulating the ambient literature concept, Abba (2018) emphasized that "we don't want to reduce the idea to something tight and defined" and instead "our intention is to open it up" as in "show by doing, making and thinking." Now, at the end of the two-year project, Abba (2018) claims to have "made progress toward a set of rules and grammars for making work in this form" indicating that "ambient literature has been an extended conversation about storytelling, situation, audience, presence" that pertains to "the future of reading and writing." Describing the project, Schwab (2018) asks, "what if screens could bring another dimension to literature" as in "utilizing tech to create a new kind of experience where books respond to your presence as a reader, making the world around you part of the story?" Schwab (2018) explains that, based on the collaborative work of "writers, academics, and creative technologists", Ambient Lit stories "adapt to the reader's environment using GPS and weather data from their phone", utilizing "a world dominated by smartphone" for storytelling "to turn reading stories on a screen into a new kind of immersive experience." Noting that, "matching the form of the story to how technology brings it alive is a crucial tenet of Ambient Lit," Schwab (2018) cites Anna Gerber of Editions at Play who claims that "we never start with tech because we believe that the story needs to be the driver for the experience that we would like to share with readers."

Figure 1 provides an overview of key issues, controversies, and problems for ambient explorations ranging from ambient resources featuring smart workplaces (Jensen, 2016) to the Internet of Actions and evolving relationships with the physical and digital (Jensen, 2016) to ambient communications where objects and spaces become anticipatory and personalized (IFTF, 2017) to cities as platforms through machine + people collaborations (Naunes et al., 2018; Harrison, 2017b) to the notion of ambient literature enabled through novel technologies and social practices (AmbientLit, 2018).

3.2 Microgrids and SmartGrids

McCullough (2015a) speaks of the importance of an "awareness of context" highlighting locality in relation to design and microgrids as "intrinsically local instances of this larger smartgrid movement." As such, for McCullough

Figure 1. Overview of key issues, controversies and problems for ambient explorations

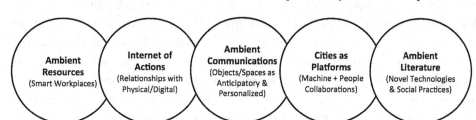

(2015a), the microgrid "invites more participatory neighborhood design and governance" while "experientially, it tends toward increased participation in surroundings" advancing the microgrid as well in terms of "a state of mind." Indeed, the importance and value of electricity for "almost any aspect of living" contributes to the need for "grid awareness" that, according to McCullough (2015a) "is no longer just for its planners and engineers" and instead "contextual awareness becomes an ever more vital sensibility for almost anyone." In terms of metrics, McCullough (2015a) points out that "comfort remains a pursuit, and cultural perception, not merely a measurable attribute of engineering performance, not reducible to uniformity." McCullough (2015b) advances the notion of inhabiting technology focusing on comfort, convenience, interactivity, and energy. In the context of "increasingly sensate operations," McCullough (2015b) argues that, "notions of comfort and convenience may involve new aspects of response but also repose." Highlighting the invisibility of electricity, McCullough (2015b) draws parallels with the invisible embedding of pervasive technologies giving rise to the need to "rethink many values, not only of technology but also of use." Focusing on the microgrid as "a local, self-contained energy system with a varying relation to the more massive public utility grid", McCullough (2015b) claims the "primary justification" to be "in resilience" as in, able to "run as independent" and as a "disconnected island in event of downtime or crisis." McCullough (2015b) argues that, "by sometimes giving, taking, or storing power from the utilities, a distribution of microgrids does better than a centralized monolithic system at accommodating the variability of intermittent sources such as sun and wind." While "advances in sensing, switching, and microtransactions among digital things make it go", McCullough (2015b) claims that "future horizons suggest energy materials that are themselves more micro" such that "a micogrid's main transformation is toward more active local governance, participation, variability, conservation, and systems integration." As such, McCullough (2015b) points the way to microgrids as "numerous and situated rather than centralized to one standard" so as to "introduce much greater diversity in the cultural expectations around these patterns of use", giving rise to "inquiry into technological possibility, appropriateness, and expectations." Taking a long view backward and forward, McCullough (2015b) notes that "notions of comfort and convenience do change" as in, "disturbing convenience" calling for a return to "wisdom" and "downtime on the microgrid" where repose is enabled by downtime such that "turning things off can be an optimistic act, and not a rejection of anything" (McCullough, 2015a). As if to illustrate the potential of microgrids, Grant (2017) describes emerging research from the

University of Waterloo involving "the use of stand-alone deep-learning AI" that "could lead to much lower data processing and transmission costs" as well as "greater privacy and use in areas where existing technology is impractical due to expense or other factors."

Figure 2 provides an overview of key issues, controversies, and problems for microgrids and smartgrids. McCullough (2015a; 2015b) describes microgrids as a local instance of the smartgrids movement; microgrids as supportive of participatory design and governance; electricity use as important for grid awareness; and contextual awareness and the importance for sensibilities related to notions of comfort and convenience. Grant (2017) describes stand-alone deep learning AI in terms of benefits associated with cost, privacy, and use.

3.3 Smart Cities and Wise Cities

The Wise Cities project directed by the Barcelona Centre for International Affairs (CIDOB, 2017) involved a global network of think tanks from 2015-2017 advancing a more human-centered model for cities. Williams (2017) highlights an urban sociology perspective, focusing on "the patterns of people's lives and behaviour" along with "how they interact with their environment and with each other." According to Williams (2017), "the development of culture and how complex all this can be" will "need to be embedded into an urban strategy that aims to be 'wise' and not just 'smart'." Williams argues that, "the attempt to systematize behaviour that is fundamentally unsystematic will be futile" while insisting that, "leaving space for some degree of disorder and unpredictability is crucial" noting that, "the capability of machines to act autonomously doesn't render our input obsolete." Williams claims that "it is imperative that humans are placed at the center of the conversation about the future of cities" and this is because "the culture, identity, and ethos of a city is determined not by designers but by citizens themselves." Williams (2017)

Figure 2. Overview of key issues, controversies and problems for microgrids and smartgrids

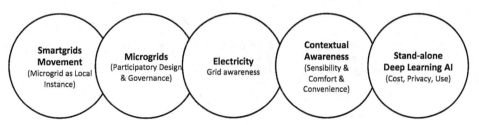

refers to the "deep characteristics that make cities attractive places to enrich our lives" such as "diversity, creativity, identity, history, and community." Highlighting "the extremely nuanced and often unpredictable variables that shape the development arc of a city" Williams (2017) stresses "the need to understand the city unit as a system of interrelated parts – an ecology wherein autonomous actors (both individual and collective) are connected to one another as well as to organisations, markets and places." Making a case for the wise city, Williams (2017) argues that a systemic view is needed in "recognising the linkages and causality between different elements of the complex city structure" and that "whilst the smart cities vision appeared to take this approach, joining up big data and digital devices through a vast web run through the 'internet of things'" there remains a "routine failure to acknowledge how humans fit into the picture." As such, according to Williams (2017) with little guidance on "what will make a city 'good' in the future" the potential for failure is high for "any city built on a limited view of how humans behave individually and collectively" and "their wants and needs."

Questioning who is responsible for future cities, a cross-disciplinary panel at Harvard (Nobel, 2017) engaged in a discussion "guided by a question of sovereignty" as in, "Who should be in charge of building, managing, and controlling the cities of the future? The government? The entrepreneurs? The citizens?" In response to the question of whether autonomous cities are the vision for future cities, Norman (2018) suggests instead that, in the interests of sustainability and addressing increasing urban complexities, the tendency will likely be toward "working together from the local to the global scale."

Figure 3 provides an overview of key issues, controversies, and problems for smart cities and wise cities with the movement from smart to wise (CIDOB, 2017; Williams, 2017), to cities of the future and the question of sovereignty (Nobel, 2017), to urban futures as autonomous or collective (Norman, 2018).

Figure 3. Overview of key issues, controversies and problems for smart cities and wise cities

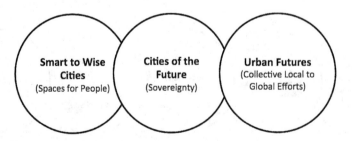

Smart to Wise Cities (Spaces for People)   Cities of the Future (Sovereignty)   Urban Futures (Collective Local to Global Efforts)

3.4 Quantum Cities

Schmitt (2015) speaks of "infinite data streams" in the context of the notion of a Quantum City as a possible alternative urban simulation model. According to Schmitt (2015), Quantum City, citing the work of Arida (2002), has the "very serious aim to radically change the way the urban realm is both experienced and designed." Arida (2002) introduces the construct of "diventity" that, as defined, "allows identity to continuously emerge from the density of diversity" and "is about being able to recognize similarity and difference simultaneously without the risk of one aspect obliterating the other" such that "a sense of individuality is constantly checked with a sense of community of others." It is worth noting that Arida (2002) associated diventity with awareness and sensitivity. According to Arida (2002), the Quantum City "is by no means a homogenization of cultures, but a continuous, dynamic dialogue and creation of new cultures" where "expressed architecturally" what emerges is "a true creative and mutual reinterpretation of form" with "the incorporation of *meaning* as a necessary and relevant ingredient" acknowledging contextuality. For Arida (2002), a quantum city is characterized by, "a highly vibrant potentiality field that allows a great diversity of choices of existence to its inhabitants and visitors" and "can be read as part of a quantum agglomeration, or city region." Arida (2002) claims that "in the quantum metaphor, no description or action of any constituent of the urban realm is possible without its co-ordinates in the society-space-time (SST) continuum" where the SST continuum is "an energy field of potential events." Perhaps in support of the quantum city, "quantum theory seemed to describe a world of complementary dualities, of both/and values, of uncertainty, of choices at all scales, of interactive relationships, emergent qualities and of sustainable vibrant ecologies" (Arida, 2002). Thom (2018) describes quantum computing as complementary to current pervasive computing systems with an emphasis on the adaptive.

Figure 4 provides an overview of key issues, controversies, and problems for quantum cities. Quantum city is advanced as: an urban simulation model (Schmitt, 2015); a quantum agglomeration with vibrant and diverse potentialities (Arida, 2002); and a metaphor (Arida, 2002) with constituent urban realm co-ordinates of society-space-time (SST). Quantum computing is described by Thom (2018) as complementary to existing computing approaches while the construct of diventity is advanced by Arida (2002) as a continuous dynamic for identify and culture, associated with awareness, sensitivity, and contextuality.

Figure 4. Overview of key issues, controversies and problems for quantum cities

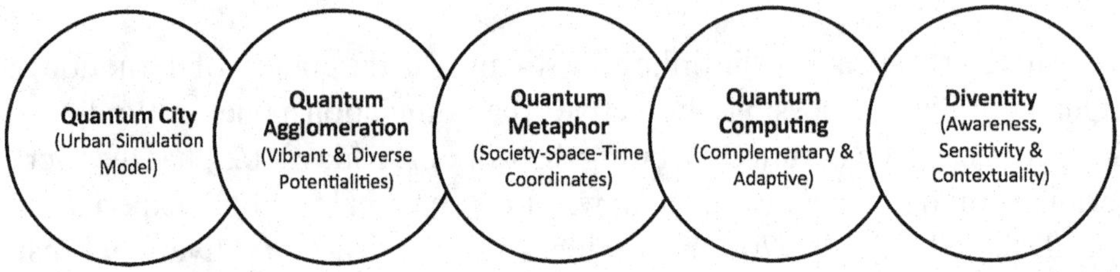

Quantum City
(Urban Simulation Model)

Quantum Agglomeration
(Vibrant & Diverse Potentialities)

Quantum Metaphor
(Society-Space-Time Coordinates)

Quantum Computing
(Complementary & Adaptive)

Diventity
(Awareness, Sensitivity & Contextuality)

3.5 Issues, Controversies, Problems

Key issues, controversies, and problems emerging in the review of the research literature explored in this chapter are highlighted below. Coverage of issues, controversies, and problems is not intended to be exhaustive or comprehensive but rather, as illustrative of the nascent and evolving nature, variety, and range.

Issues

Looking to the future, the IFTF (2018) identifies a key issue as that of trust, as in, "renegotiating organizational trust in a world of intelligent autonomous machines." Researchers are also busy addressing ethical issues with a special issue focusing on machine ethics (Trussell, 2018) and with the fourth industrial revolution (IEEE, 2019) focusing on cyber-physical systems and the need for education associated with the Internet of Things (IoT), robotics, autonomous vehicles, and artificial intelligence (AI). It is likely the ambient and the quantum would run in a complementary fashion, similar to how Thom (2018) believes contemporary and pervasive computing and quantum computing will run.

Controversies

McCullough (2015c) identifies the controversial matter of having the choice to turn devices "off" and "on" in a technology pervasive world. Pressing questions and dialogues associated with where the responsibility lies for "building, managing and controlling" future cities (Nobel, 2017) are well underway. In keeping with understandings of smart, responsive, and future cities and the associated complexities, this chapter argues for shared responsibility for future cities through a combination of government, entrepreneurs, and citizens, as well as educators, designers, community members, and others working in collaboration across sectors.

Problems

The AmbientLit Project (Dovey, 2016) identifies the notion of ambient tensions in relation to different understandings of the ambient concept. Regarding the problem of context, while ambient computing enables "the delivery of context specific content" where "we experience data flows in context, the city, the street, the bus", according to Dovey (2016), "these contexts cannot and should not be erased" because, citing McCullough (2015c), "surroundings provide sites, objects and physical resource interfaces for those electronic flows to be about."

Summarized in Figure 5, a glimpse of patterns, flows, relationships, and possibilities begin to emerge, contributing to a parallel and complementary view of ambient urbanities and other emerging infrastructures and technologies through explorations, micro/smartgrids, smart and wise cities, and quantum cities. This diagram shows the Internet-based and other aware technologies on the left with the IoP, IoT, IoE, and IoD alone and in parallel with and complemented by grid (microgrids and smartgrids) and quantum technologies and thinking on the right.

Figure 5. Ambient urbanities and other parallel and complementary potentials

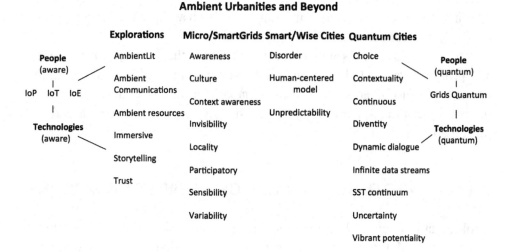

Ambient explorations include ambient literature, communications, and resources along with immersive experiences, storytelling and trust. Microgrids and smartgrids include the elements of awareness, culture, context awareness, invisibility, locality, participatory, sensibility, and variability. The movement from smart cities to wise cities encompasses disorder, the human-centered model, and unpredictability. The notion of quantum cities encompasses choice, contextuality, continuous, diventity, dynamic dialogue, infinite data streams, the SST (society-space-time) continuum, uncertainty, and vibrant potentiality.

By author and year, Table 1 provides an overview of issues, controversies, and problems associated with ambient explorations, microgrids, wise cities, and the quantum in smart cities. Ambient explorations highlight tensions associated with the ambient; ambient resources; the future of reading and writing; ambient literatures; and immersive experiences. Smartgrids, microgrids, wise cities, and smart cities highlight microgrids with off and on choice; a wise cities model; stand-alone deep learning AI; questions pertaining to who is responsible for the design, development, and ethics of future cities; wise + smart cities; the reducing of interface friction; trust in the context of intelligent autonomous machines; and machine + people collaborations. The quantum enables spaces for discussion, pertaining to quantum urban agglomerations and regions; quantum cities; the quantum metaphor; and quantum computing.

This tabular summary reveals a rich array of emerging and recurring themes pertaining to complexities, context, data and resources, invisibility, trust, uncertainty, along with many other people-centered elements and tensions. As such, this initial comparative glimpse is suggestive of evolving openings for many areas requiring future research along with challenges and opportunities for practice.

By way of solutions and recommendations, the issues, controversies, and problems presented in Table 1 are re-conceptualized as challenges and opportunities to be addressed in this chapter through operationalization of the conceptual framework for ambient urbanities and beyond, developed and presented in Section 4.

4. LOOKING TO THE FUTURE FOR AMBIENT URBANITIES

Looking at ambient urbanities in smart cities and beyond to smarter, more responsive and future cities, it is worth noting that elements identified

Table 1. Issues, controversies, and problems for ambient explorations, wise cities and quantum cities

Ambient Explorations, Wise Cities, and Quantum Cities				
Author(s)	**Year**	**Ambient Explorations**	**Grids, Wise/Smart Cities**	**Quantum**
Arida	2002			Agglomerations; Cities; Metaphor
McCullough	2015a-c		Microgrids – Off & On	
Schmitt	2015			Cities
Dovey	2016	Ambient Tensions		
CIDOB	2017		Wise Cities Model	
Grant	2017		Stand-alone Deep Learning AI	
Jensen	2016	Ambient Resources		
Harrison	2017a-b		Machines + People	
Nobel	2017		Responsibility	
Williams	2017		Wise + Smart	
Abba	2018	Reading/Writing Futures		
AmbientLit	2018	Ambient Literature		
Hunter	2018		Reducing Interface Friction	
IFTF	2018		Trust	
Naunes et al.	2018		Machine/People Collaborations	
Schwab	2018	Immersive Experiences		
Thom	2018			Computing

as characteristic of quantum cities pertain very much to smart cities and responsive cities, incorporating possibly more balanced approaches to the people-technologies-cities dynamic.

4.1 Ambient Urbanities and Beyond: Solutions and Recommendations

Based on findings in this exploration, together with the review of the research literature, this chapter advances the conceptual framework for ambient urbanities and beyond, as depicted in Figure 6. More flexible and adaptive potential emerges in this extended framework for parallel and complementary interactions and interoperabilities with other technologies and approaches such as grids (e.g., microgrids and smartgrids) and the quantum (e.g., quantum understandings, quantum computing, and the like).

The ambient urbanities and parallel frameworks for grids and the quantum depicted in Figure 6 are intended to support existing and future urban challenges and opportunities. Through emerging understandings of approaches that are more adaptive, dynamic, and responsive in urban environments, this chapter highlights the need for constantly evolving ambient urbanities in relation to other complementary technologies, perspectives, and mindsets.

Considering the issues, controversies, and problems emerging from multiple and diverse perspectives in this chapter, related to future cities and going beyond smart cities, the research question identified in the Introduction is restated as a proposition under exploration in this chapter, as follows:

P: *Ambient and other elements (e.g., quantum)* are important for ambient urbanities in smart cities and beyond because of the emergent, continuous, and evolving nature of the people-technologies-cities ecosystem looking to future cities.

How ambient explorations and other elements such as microgrids, wise cities, and the quantum inform urbanity is explored in this chapter in relation to ambient contextualities and quantum urbanities enabling formulation of a framework for ambient, grid, and quantum urbanities in smart and future cities in the context of the emergent, continuous, and evolving nature of the people-technologies-cities dynamic.

Figure 6. Conceptual Framework for Ambient Urbanities and Beyond

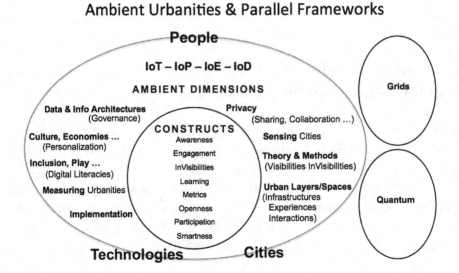

4.2 Ambient, Grid, and Quantum Urbanities: An Exploration

Ambient, grid, and quantum urbanities are explored in terms of ambient contextualities in smart cities and communities, and then in terms of quantum urbanities in quantum cities. Development of a framework for ambient, grid, and quantum urbanities in smart and future cities is advanced along with the identification of associated variables.

4.2.1. Ambient Contextualities in Smart Cities and Communities

An educator made the suggestion to "think about" 'Wise City' or more generally, 'Wise Place' as in, "friendly, comfortable" which "reflects human values and needs." Values were said to include "freedom and openness" along with a "sense of intimacy" wherein navigating a 'Wise Way' "is to find the way to include both" – wisdom "together" with smartness in order for "the IoT, Big Data, and other tech systems to make the city a better place." From a city IT (Information Technology) perspective, emergent and evolving processes were acknowledged in the statements, "I don't think we've really taken full advantage of the data that we currently have" that "has context" so "we're very much immature in that overall data sense." Using the example of "the context of educational institutions", an individual in IT spoke of the "greater communities where postsecondary institutions are situated" and "the interplay with those communities" in terms of "educating the public or those communities." Further, this individual indicated that in relation to "sustainable practices such as recycling, 3D printers, maker labs" as spaces for "studying", initiatives are underway for "looking at how to design all kinds of things" while inviting all to "come on in" where "we'll open our doors and we can have different age groups" in support of inclusion and an "interplay between communities and postsecondary institutions."

4.2.2. Quantum Urbanities in Quantum Cities

A range of individuals articulated characteristics of Arida's (2002) notion of the quantum city. For example, the values of freedom and openness and also of wisdom, together with smartness, identified by an educator are in keeping with the "complementary dualities, of both/and values" articulated by Arida

(2002). Further, it is worth noting that, characteristic of quantum cities, inclusiveness is discussed as well as uncertainty. For example, an education innovator highlighted the notion of an "uncertain future" that "needs all of us working on this together." According to the educator innovator, regarding the future, "we just don't know what that's going to be" indicating that "we think there is a lot of connection between education and business" while "still trying to find the link between education and technology" echoing many and varied levels of in/visiblilities. As for "vibrant ecologies" as characteristic of a quantum city, in the words of a city councilor, a vibrant city is "a place where you get to know your neighbors and you get to learn what you have in common with people and what is different" and "celebrate those differences and what you have in common." Additionally, the councilor referred to "people coming together from across sectors to work on things collaboratively, in hubs" that may "look like neighborhood village centers and sometimes they look like a coffee shop." Further, the councilor described vibrant cities as "pulsing with arts, culture" where the "key is people" and "people interacting with each other and with their surroundings" in "creating a pulse and a vibrancy because its creating activity." According to the councilor, incorporating the technology layer, using the example of bike apps, illustrates "a place where it is all connected and the tool of technology is augmenting the information that we have" and this "allows us to have a safer more vibrant city."

4.2.3. A Framework for Ambient, Grid, and Quantum Urbanities in Smart, Future Cities

Findings in this chapter advance the notion of ambient, grid, and quantum urbanities bringing together elements that characterize both ambient and quantum environments in coming to evolving understandings of a framework for smart, future city. Indeed, findings in this chapter give rise to the potential for emerging understanding of complementarity, overlap, and uncertainty as ambient, as depicted in Figure 7.

Organized around aware people and aware technologies encompassing the physical and digital in relation to the potential for more adaptability of urban experiences, there is a highlighting of contextuality, in/visibilities, and trust, contributing further to the ambient turn in support of choices and trust as ambient in future cities and urbanities.

Figure 7. Framework for ambient, grid, and quantum urbanities in smart, future cities

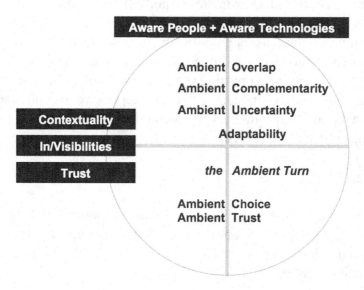

Dependent Variable (DV)

This chapter advances the potential for value of the dependent variable (DV) surfaced in this chapter as *complementarity and adaptability* in relation to ambient urbanities and beyond. Associated independent variables (IV) include: reflecting human values and needs, implying the potential for choice and trust in urban spaces; looking at how to design all kinds of things, implying the potential for an interplay between communities, institutions, and others for learning; and the need for all of us working on cities together, implying the potential to find the connections for interactions.

5. FUTURE DIRECTIONS

Future and emerging trends are identified in this chapter for both practice and research in Sections 5.1 and 5.2 pertaining to perspectives going forward and beyond for ambient urbanities and other complementary approaches.

5.1 Practice

In terms of practice, this chapter invites opportunities for thinking forward about urbanities while providing exposure to the notion of ambient, grid, and quantum urbanities potentials for practitioners in urban spaces. As such, this work invites participation by practitioners in the development of initiatives to shed light on approaches to innovating urbanities for problem-solving as in, initiatives that are more dynamic, adaptive and responsive to contemporary urban challenges and opportunities, in the context of new and evolving understandings of smart, future cities.

Variables and Indicators

This chapter surfaces the dependent variable of *complementarity and adaptability* and a series of independent variables associated with human values and needs; designing all kinds of things; and the need for everyone working on cities together.

5.2 Research

This chapter further advances and develops the ambient urbanities concept in the context of the emerging research literature for smart cities, grids, and evolving understandings of future cities as quantum. As such, this chapter has implications for urban theorizing by developing and advancing potentials for ever more dynamic and adaptive understandings, as part of the 'ambient turn' and possibly even the 'quantum turn' (Cooper, 2017).

Conceptual Framework for Ambient Urbanities and Beyond

From the perspective of more aware people enabled through more aware technologies, the focus of this chapter on ambient urbanities and beyond, as in quantum, contributes to the overall body of insights about the interdisciplinary, multidimensional, and ever evolving nature of ambient urbanities in the development and enriching of this book's theme. Going forward, areas for exploration potential include:

1. *Contextuality* fostered through urban initiatives focusing on the interplay between communities, institutions, and people
2. *In/visibilities* surmounted through the making and designing of all kinds of things, together
3. *Trust* fostered through understandings of human needs and values

Ambient, Grid, and Quantum Urbanities

This chapter provides early stage thinking toward parallel and complementary potentials for ambient, grid, and quantum urbanities.

Ambient Choice

Research opportunities and challenges emerge in this chapter related to the potential for choice as ambient, with implication for urban practitioners.

Ambient Trust

Research opportunities and challenges emerge in this chapter related to the potential for trust as ambient, with implication for urban practitioners.

7. CONCLUSION

This chapter provides an exploration of ambient urbanities and beyond for future cities in relation to a range of disciplinary perspectives focusing on the elements of microgrids, wise and smart cities, and quantum cities. Contextuality, in/visibilities, and trust emerge as key elements along with issues of overlap, complementarity, and uncertainty. This chapter makes several contributions in that it: a) provides emerging and evolving perspectives on ambient urbanities and complementary approaches going forward; b) articulates a conceptual framework for ambient urbanities and beyond; and c) advances a framework for ambient, grid, and quantum urbanities in smart, future cities. The analysis of findings in this chapter identifies the variable of *complementarity and adaptability* along with associated variables relevant to study and practice that takes into consideration human values and needs; how to design all kinds of things collaboratively across sectors; and the importance of working together on cities.

This chapter builds upon the research literature for smart cities across multiple, diverse sectors to imagine, extend, and evolve current understandings of urbanities to meet the emerging complexities, challenges, and opportunities of ambient urbanities in 21st century cities and beyond.

Insights of particular interest to the reader include the following:

1. The potential for the quantum to inform evolving urban understandings
2. The interconnectedness of microgrids, wise/smart cities and the quantum, informing ambient urbanities
3. The surfacing of variables associated with *complementarity and adaptability* in evolving urban spaces

Ideas highlighted in this chapter pertain to the following:

1. The importance of people becoming more aware of the potential for choice as ambient in smart cities
2. The importance of people becoming more aware of the potential for trust as ambient in smart cities
3. Ambient and quantum as a novel parallel and complementary approach to smarter cities and urbanities

Lessons for the reader in this chapter are associated with the following:

1. The potential for microgrid and quantum technologies to influence ambient and aware technologies
2. The potential for microgrid and quantum technologies to enhance and augment aware technologies
3. The issues, controversies, and problems for microgrids, wise/smart cities, and quantum cities

This chapter will be of interest to a broad audience including students, educators, researchers, urban planners, information technology developers, futurists, and practitioners and anyone concerned with evolving and innovating understandings of urbanity in support of aware people and aware technologies in meeting the complex urban challenges and opportunities of smart, responsive, future, and quantum cities and urbanities.

REFERENCES

Abba, T. (2018). Approaching the end. In *Ambient Literature*. Arts & Humanities Research Council; UWE Bristol; Bath Spa University; and University of Birmingham. Retrieved 25 May 2018 from https://ambientlit. com/index.php/2018/04/03/approaching-the-end/

AmbientLit. (2018). About. *The Ambient Literature Project*. Retrieved 26 May 2018 from https://ambientlit.com/index.php/about-the-project/

Arida, A. (2002). *Quantum City*. Oxford, UK: Architectural Press.

Baude, B. (2016b). The ends of the Internet. Amsterdam: Institute of Network Cultures.

CIDOB. (2017). *Wise cities: A global think tank network 2015-2017*. Barcelona Centre for International Affairs (CIDOB). Retrieved 5 February 2019 from https://www.cidob.org/en/projects/wise_cities

Cooper, B. (2017). The quantum turn in social science: Social humanism as the new metaphysics. *The Abs-Tract Organization*. Retrieved 9 February 2019 from https://medium.com/the-abs-tract-organization/the-quantum-turn-in-social-science-4dad9f92a6a5

Dovey, J. (2016). Ambient tensions. *The Ambient Literature Project*. Retrieved 1 June 2018 from https://ambientlit.com/index.php/2016/10/04/ambient-tensions/

Grant, M. (2017). New technology makes artificial intelligence more private and portable. *Waterloo News*. Retrieved 2 June 2018 from https://uwaterloo. ca/news/news/new-technology-makes-artificial-intelligence-more-private

Harrison, C. (2017a). The search for a theory of cities. *Meeting of the Minds blog*. Retrieved 4 February 2019 from http://meetingoftheminds.org/search-theory-cities-23642

Harrison, C. (2017b). The limits of data. *Meeting of the Minds blog*. Retrieved 4 February 2017 from http://meetingoftheminds.org/the-limits-of-data-22875

Hunter, J. (2018). IoT 'conversation' and ambient contextuality. *TechCrunch*. Retrieved 23 May 2018 from https://techcrunch.com/2018/04/24/tell-me-something-good-iot-conversation-and-ambient-contextuality/

IEEE. (2019). *What is the fourth industrial revolution*. Retrieved 6 February 2019 from https://innovate.ieee.org/innovation-spotlight-ieee-fueling-fourth-industrial-revolution/?LT=XPLHL_XPL_1.2019_LM_Innovation_Spotlight_4IR

IFTF. (2017). *From an Internet of information toward an Internet of actions – Technology horizons 2017*. Palo Alto, CA: The Institute For The Future. Retrieved 24 May 2018 from http://www.iftf.org/fileadmin/user_upload/downloads/th/2017_IFTF_TH_ResearchAgenda.pdf

IFTF. (2018). *Future 50: The details*. Palo Alto, CA: The Institute For The Future. Retrieved 24 May 2018 from http://www.iftf.org/iftf-you/future-50-details/

Jensen, M. (2016). *Technology horizons 2017 research: Toward an Internet of Actions*. Palo Alto, CA: Institute For The Future (IFTF). Retrieved 24 May 2018 from http://www.iftf.org/future-now/article-detail/searchable-matter-from-an-internet-of-information-to-an-internet-of-action/

McCullough, M. (2015a). *Activating the microgrid*. Retrieved 24 May 2018 from http://www-personal.umich.edu/~mmmc/WORK/ActivatingMicrogridAbstract.pdf

McCullough, M. (2015b). *Downtime on the microgrid*. Retrieved 24 May 2018 from http://www-personal.umich.edu/%7Emmmc/WORK/Preamble.pdf

McCullough, M. (2015c). Distraction reconsidered: On the cultural stakes of the ambient. In U. Ekman, J. D. Bolter, L. Diaz, M. Sondergaard, & M. Engberg (Eds.), *Ubiquitous Computing, Complexity and Culture* (pp. 205–213). New York: Routledge.

McKenna, H. P. (2017). Urbanizing the ambient: Why people matter so much in smart cities. In S. Konomi & G. Roussos (Eds.), *Enriching urban spaces with ambient computing, the Internet of Things, and smart city design* (pp. 209–231). Hershey, PA: IGI Global. doi:10.4018/978-1-5225-0827-4.ch011

Naunes, D., Sá Silva, J., & Boavida, F. (2018). *A practical guide to human-in-the-loop cyber-physical systems*. Hoboken, NJ: Wiley.

Nobel, C. (2017). *Who is responsible for the future of cities?* Research Event. Harvard Business School, Working Knowledge, Business Research for Business Leaders. Retrieved 2 June 2018 from https://hbswk.hbs.edu/item/who-is-responsible-for-the-future-of-cities

Norman, B. (2018). Are autonomous cities our urban future? *Nature Communications,9*(1),2111.doi:10.103841467-018-04505-0PMID:29844312

Schmitt, G. (2015). *Information Cities.* Retrieved from https://itunes.apple.com/us/book/information-cities/id970529491?mt=11

Schmitt, G. (2017). *Responsive cities.* MOOC. ETH Zurich, Future Cities Laboratory. Retrieved 21 October 2017 from https://www.edx.org/course/responsive-cities-ethx-fc-04x

Schwab, K. (2018). AmbientLit: The ambitious project to redesign fiction for phones. *Co-Design.* Retrieved 23 May 2018 from https://www.fastcodesign.com/90171896/ambient-lit-the-ambitious-project-to-redesign-fiction-for-phones

Thom, M. (2018). *Keynote presentation on quantum computing at D-Wave.* Vancouver, BC: Future Technology Conference.

Trussell, H. J. (2018). Why a special issue on machine ethics. *Proceedings of the IEEE, 106*(10), 1774–1776. doi:10.1109/JPROC.2018.2868336

Williams, P. (2017). From smart to wise: Cities of the future. *RSA (Royal Society for the Encouragement of Arts, Manufactures, and Commerce) 21st Century Enlightenment blog.* Retrieved 31 May 2018 from https://www.thersa.org/discover/publications-and-articles/rsa-blogs/2017/11/from-smart-to-wise-cities-of-the-future

ADDITIONAL READING

Arida, A. (2018). *Quantum city: Urbanism needs a conceptual revolution* (website). Retrieved 25 June 2018 from http://www.quantumcity.com/about/quantum-city-table-of-contents/

European Commission. (2006). *European SmartGrids technology platform: Vision and strategy for Europe's electricity networks of the future.* Brussels: European Commission, Directorate-General for Research. Retrieved 25 June 2018 from https://ec.europa.eu/research/energy/pdf/smartgrids_en.pdf

Hebner, R. (2017). Nanogrids, microgrids, and big data: The future of the power grid. *IEEE Spectrum*. Retrieved 25 June 2018 from https://spectrum. ieee.org/energy/renewables/nanogrids-microgrids-and-big-data-the-future-of-the-power-grid

Jäckle, D., Stoffel, F., Kwon, B. C., Sascha, D., Stoffel, A., & Keim, D. A. (2015). Ambient grids: Maintain context-awareness via aggregated off-screen visualization. Proceedings of Eurographics Conference on Visualization (EuroVis)-Short Papers.

Maize, K. (2017). Microgrids: An old concept could be new again. *Power Magazine* Retrieved 25 June 2018 from http://www.powermag.com/microgrids-an-old-concept-could-be-new-again/

Roberts, D., & Chang, A. (2017). Meet the microgrid, the technology poised to transform electricity. *Vox*. Updated 24 May 2018. Retrieved 25 June 2018 from https://www.vox.com/energy-and-environment/2017/12/15/16714146/greener-more-reliable-more-resilient-grid-microgrids

Swaminathan, R. (2017). Quantum urbanism, step two, let it roll counterintuitively. *GovernanceNow*. Retrieved 25 June 2018 from https://www.governancenow.com/views/columns/quantum-urbanism-step-two-let-it-roll-counterintuitively

US Department of Energy. *What is the smart grid?* Retrieved 25 June 2018 from https://www.smartgrid.gov/the_smart_grid/smart_grid.html

KEY TERMS AND DEFINITIONS

Ambient Complementarity: Ambient complementarity refers to the increasing presence of aware technologies in and around human activity affecting the nature, experience, and perception of interrelationships.

Ambient Explorations: Ambient explorations refer to explorations of the literature pertaining to initiatives involving aware people in combinations with aware technologies.

Ambient Overlap: Ambient overlap refers to the increasing presence of aware technologies in and around human activity affecting the nature and experience of interactivities.

Ambient Quantum Cities: Ambient quantum cities refer to urban areas, spaces, and extensions involving the interplay of the ambient with the quantum.

Ambient Quantum Urbanities: Ambient quantum urbanities refer to urban areas, spaces, and extensions involving people in the interplay of the ambient with the quantum.

Ambient Uncertainty: Ambient uncertainty refers to the increasing presence of aware technologies in and around human activity affecting the nature and experience of certainty.

Quantum Urbanities: Quantum urbanities refer to an extending of the urbanities concept into the realm of the quantum in urban areas, spaces, and extensions.

About the Author

H. Patricia McKenna is the founder and President of AmbientEase (Emergent Adaptive Solutions Everywhere) focused on smart cities and learning cities and is the founder of the UrbanitiesLab. Patricia works within and across diverse domains of scholarship and practice (interdisciplinary) and collaborates in team efforts to set up international, national, regional, and local information services, research projects, startups, and other creative and future-oriented initiatives. Author of approximately 40 publications, Patricia is a regular presenter of papers at international conferences. With a focus on smart cities and learning cities, Patricia engages with diverse sectors around use experience and unexpected possibilities for leveraging and generating new relevancies and vibrancies in 21st century information spaces. Patricia holds a BA from the University of New Brunswick, an MLS from McGill University and a Doctorate in information management from Syracuse University.

Index

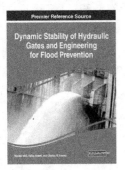

Ensure Quality Research is Introduced to the Academic Community

Become an IGI Global Reviewer for Authored Book Projects

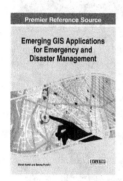
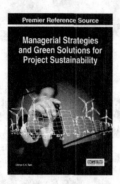

The overall success of an authored book project is dependent on quality and timely reviews.

In this competitive age of scholarly publishing, constructive and timely feedback significantly expedites the turnaround time of manuscripts from submission to acceptance, allowing the publication and discovery of forward-thinking research at a much more expeditious rate. Several IGI Global authored book projects are currently seeking highly qualified experts in the field to fill vacancies on their respective editorial review boards:

Applications may be sent to:
development@igi-global.com

Applicants must have a doctorate (or an equivalent degree) as well as publishing and reviewing experience. Reviewers are asked to write reviews in a timely, collegial, and constructive manner. All reviewers will begin their role on an ad-hoc basis for a period of one year, and upon successful completion of this term can be considered for full editorial review board status, with the potential for a subsequent promotion to Associate Editor.

If you have a colleague that may be interested in this opportunity, we encourage you to share this information with them.

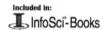